旅游让世界和生活更美好

BETTER TOURISM, BETTER LIFE, BETTER WORLD

2024世界旅游联盟
旅游助力乡村振兴案例
（中英文双语版）

**WTA BEST PRACTICES OF
RURAL REVITALIZATION THROUGH TOURISM 2024**

(CHINESE-ENGLISH BILINGUAL EDITION)

世界旅游联盟 ◎编著

中国·武汉

内容简介

2024年，世界旅游联盟携手中国国际减贫中心，依托世界旅游联盟会员单位及中国各省级文化和旅游部门等渠道，广泛搜集到一批优秀案例，根据可持续性、可复制性、可量化、创新性、材料的完整性和积极的社会影响等标准，经专家评选后，最终遴选出50个典型案例。这些案例展示了旅游业在推动案例所在地脱贫致富、促进创业就业、提升居民生活质量，以及促进地方经济发展方面的突出贡献。

Content Summary

In 2024, the World Tourism Alliance, in collaboration with the International Poverty Reduction Center in China, leveraged the channels of member organizations and provincial cultural and tourism departments across China to gather a range of outstanding cases. Based on criteria including sustainability, replicability, quantifiability, originality, material integrity, and positive social impact, these cases underwent rigorous evaluation by experts, ultimately resulting in the selection of 50 exemplary cases. These cases demonstrate the significant contributions of tourism in fostering poverty eradication and prosperity, promoting entrepreneurship and employment, enhancing residents' quality of life, and accelerating local economic development in their respective locations.

图书在版编目(CIP)数据

2024世界旅游联盟：旅游助力乡村振兴案例：汉英对照 / 世界旅游联盟编著. -- 武汉：华中科技大学出版社，2024. 10. -- ISBN 978-7-5772-1291-3

Ⅰ. F592.3

中国国家版本馆CIP数据核字第20247SY908号

2024世界旅游联盟：旅游助力乡村振兴案例（中英文双语版） 世界旅游联盟　编著

2024 Shijie Lüyou Lianmeng: Lüyou Zhuli Xiangcun Zhenxing Anli（Zhong-yingwen Shuangyu Ban）

策划编辑：	李　欢
执行编辑：	魏雨楠
责任编辑：	鲁梦璇　阮晓琼
封面设计：	普曦乐　廖亚萍
责任校对：	刘小雨
责任监印：	周治超
出版发行：	华中科技大学出版社（中国·武汉）　　电话：（027）81321913
地　　址：	武汉市东湖新技术开发区华工科技园　　邮编：430223
录　　排：	华中科技大学惠友文印中心
印　　刷：	湖北新华印务有限公司
开　　本：	787 mm×1092 mm　1/16
印　　张：	25.25
字　　数：	783千字
版　　次：	2024年10月第1版 第1次印刷
定　　价：	168.00元

投稿邮箱：283018479@qq.com
本书若有印装质量问题，请向出版社营销中心调换
全国免费服务热线：400-6679-118　　竭诚为您服务
版权所有　侵权必究

前言

　　中国在 2021 年就已经完成了消除绝对贫困的艰巨任务，成为世界上率先完成联合国千年发展目标中减贫目标的国家。旅游在消除绝对贫困中发挥了积极作用，从旅游促进减贫到旅游助力乡村振兴，有很多案例经验值得总结提炼，供大家学习参考。

　　世界旅游联盟作为旅游减贫事业的倡导者和推动者，一直将"旅游促进减贫"视为自身发展的重要使命之一。自 2018 年以来，世界旅游联盟联合世界银行、中国国际减贫中心等单位，连续发布了三期《世界旅游联盟旅游减贫案例》、三期《世界旅游联盟旅游助力乡村振兴案例》，累计收录了两百多个全球旅游减贫和旅游助力乡村振兴经典案例，为减贫和乡村振兴事业贡献了范例、传播了经验。同时，联盟以典型案例为蓝本，联合中央广播电视总台连续拍摄了四季微纪录片《旅游让世界和生活更美好》，以更加生动、立体的视角展示了乡村建设新成就、乡村旅游新面貌，在国内外获得了广泛关注和高度评价。

　　六年来，世界旅游联盟不仅为那些成功通过发展旅游业摆脱贫困的乡村感到高兴，也为联盟在旅游减贫、乡村振兴方面的工作能够影响到更多的乡村而感到欣慰。2024 年，中国继续奋力推进乡村由脱贫向振兴的有效转变。为继续发挥典型案例的示范效应，总结出更多可供借鉴的旅游助力乡村振兴发展路径，世界旅游联盟继续联合中国国际减贫中心，向中国各省级文化和旅游主管部门、联盟会员单位广泛征集相关案例，依据可持续性、可复制性、可量化、创新性、材料的完整性和积极的社会影响等标准，最终遴选出 50 个典型案例，汇编成《2024 世界旅游联盟：旅游助力乡村振兴案例（中英文双语版）》。

　　我们不忘初心，坚持做全球旅游减贫事业的倡导者和推动者；我们满怀信心，坚信旅游的力量将为更多的乡村带来振兴的希望。让我们并肩同行，共同创造"旅游让世界和生活更美好"的未来。

Foreword

In 2021, China has already accomplished the arduous task of eradicating absolute poverty and become the first country in the world to achieve the poverty reduction target of the United Nations Millennium Development Goals, in which tourism played an active role. From poverty alleviation through tourism to rural revitalization through tourism, many cases and practices in the country are worth studying for the reference of the rest of the world.

As an advocate and promoter of the role of tourism in poverty alleviation, the World Tourism Alliance (WTA) has always regarded "poverty alleviation through tourism" as one of its missions. Since 2018, together with the World Bank and the International Poverty Reduction Center in China (IPRCC), it has released three consecutive issues of *WTA Best Practices of Poverty Alleviation through Tourism* and another three of *WTA Best Practices of Rural Revitalization through Tourism*, including more than 200 global best practices of poverty alleviation and rural revitalization through tourism, to share models and experience in poverty alleviation and rural revitalization. Based on these practices, the WTA also co-produced with China Global Television Network (CGTN) a four-season mini-documentary series titled *Better Tourism, Better Life, Better World*, to present the latest rural developments and the new look of rural tourism in a more vivid and three-dimensional way, which has received wide attention and high praise at home and abroad.

The WTA is pleased to see so many villages emerge from poverty through tourism development and many more benefit from its hard work in poverty reduction and rural revitalization through tourism over the past six years. In 2024, China is striving to effectively shift the focus of its rural work from poverty alleviation to revitalization. To continue to leverage the demonstration effect of typical cases and find more paths toward rural revitalization and development through tourism that are worth learning, the WTA and the IPRCC again solicited relevant practices from provincial culture and tourism authorities and WTA members in China. Then as per the criteria of sustainability, replicability, quantifiability, originality, material integrity, and positive social impact, 50 of them were finally selected and formed this *WTA Best Practices of Rural Revitalization through Tourism 2024*.

Remaining true to our founding mission, the WTA has been a staunch advocate and promoter of global poverty alleviation through tourism. We are confident that a strong tourism industry will bring hope of revitalization to more villages. Let's work together to create a future of "Better Tourism, Better Life, Better World".

目录 / Contents

湖南省郴州市北湖区：以全域旅游助推乡村全域振兴 001
Beihu District, Chenzhou City, Hunan Province: Promoting Rural Revitalization through All-for-One Tourism 005

四川省成都市龙泉驿区桃源村：民宿产业高质量转型推进乡村全面振兴 011
Taoyuan Village, Longquanyi District, Chengdu City, Sichuan Province:
   High-quality Transformation of the Homestay Industry Promotes Comprehensive Rural Revitalization 015

上海市崇明区建设镇虹桥村：民宿旅游赋能乡村振兴 020
Hongqiao Village, Jianshe Town, Chongming District, Shanghai City:
   Homestay Tourism Empowers Rural Revitalization 023

安徽省合肥市庐江县百花村：茶乡旅游赋能乡村振兴 028
Baihua Village, Lujiang County, Hefei City, Anhui Province: Tea Country Tourism Empowers Rural Revitalization 032

海南省五指山市水满乡水满村（方诺寨）：茶文农旅融合蝶变美丽乡村 037
Shuiman Village (Fangnuozhai), Shuiman Township, Wuzhishan City, Hainan Province:
   The Integration of Tea Culture, Agriculture, and Tourism Transforms the Countryside 041

浙江旅游职业学院：共富学院助推山区海岛县乡村振兴 047
Tourism College of Zhejiang:
   The School for Common Prosperity Promotes Rural Revitalization in Mountainous Island Counties 050

山东省济宁市邹城市大洪沟村：激活沉睡文旅基因，探索乡村振兴新路 055
Dahonggou Village, Zoucheng City, Jining City, Shandong Province:
   Awake Dormant Cultural Tourism Genes and Explore New Paths for Rural Revitalization 058

河北省衡水市武强县周窝村：用音乐奏响乡村振兴新乐章 062
Zhouwo Village, Wuqiang County, Hengshui City, Hebei Province:
   Play a New Chapter of Rural Revitalization with Music 065

重庆市丰都县包鸾镇：整合资源，串点成线，旅游绘就乡村振兴新画卷 070
Baoluan Town, Fengdu County, Chongqing City:
   Integrating Resources and Tour Lines, Tourism Paints a New Picture of Rural Revitalization 073

福建省泉州市德化县佛岭村：推动农文旅融合 打造和美乡村 078
Foling Village, Dehua County, Quanzhou City, Fujian Province: Promoting the Integrated Development of
   Agriculture, Culture, and Tourism to Build a Harmonious and Beautiful Village 081

江苏省苏州市吴江区开弦弓村：农文旅融合书写中国·江村新篇章 085
Kaixiangong Village, Wujiang District, Suzhou City, Jiangsu Province:
   Promoting the Integrated Development of Agriculture, Culture, and Tourism to Write a New Chapter of Development 088

新疆维吾尔自治区阿克苏地区温宿县塔格拉克村：景村融合描绘乡村振兴美丽画卷 093
Tagelake Village, Wensu County, Aksu Prefecture, Xinjiang Uygur Autonomous Region:
   Promoting Rural Revitalization through Landscape-Village Integration 096

2024 世界旅游联盟：旅游助力乡村振兴案例（中英文双语版）
WTA Best Practices of Rural Revitalization through Tourism 2024（Chinese-English Bilingual Edition）

贵州省黔东南苗族侗族自治州榕江县："村超"文体旅融合发展助力乡村振兴 100
Rongjiang County, Qiandongnan Prefecture, Guizhou Province:
　The Village Super League Boosting Rural Revitalization through the Integration of Culture, Sports and Tourism 104

广西壮族自治区桂林市阳朔县：国际乡村旅居地特色之路 109
Yangshuo County, Guilin City, Guangxi Zhuang Autonomous Region:
　A Path towards the International Rural Living Destination with Distinctive Characteristics 113

中国国家铁路集团有限公司：铁路旅游赋能乡村振兴 118
China State Railway Group Co., Ltd.: Rail Tourism Empowers Rural Revitalization 122

山西省高平市河西镇苏庄村："喜"文化赋能古村活化 128
Suzhuang Village, Hexi Town, Gaoping City, Shanxi Province:
　An Ancient Village Given a New Life by the Reviving Wedding Traditions 131

山东省潍坊市青州市桐峪沟村：景村共建谱写乡村振兴新篇章 135
Tongyugou Village, Qingzhou City, Weifang City, Shandong Province: A New Chapter in Rural Revitalization through
Integrated Scenic and Village Development 138

湖北省恩施土家族苗族自治州咸丰县彭家沟村：湖北文旅集团助力"穷沟沟"变"金窝窝" 142
Pengjiagou Village, Xianfeng County, Enshi Tujia and Miao Autonomous Prefecture, Hubei Province:
　The Path to Prosperity with the Help of Hubei Cultural Tourism Group 145

安徽省黄山市休宁县齐云山镇：祥源·齐云山生态文化旅游度假区助力乡村振兴 149
Qiyunshan Town, Xiuning County, Huangshan City, Anhui Province:
　Promoting Rural Revitalization with Qiyunshan Eco-Cultural Resort 152

山西省大同市云州区：黄花新质生产力赋能区域高质量发展 156
Yunzhou District, Datong City, Shanxi Province:
　Empowering Regional High-Quality Development with the Daylily Industry 159

海南省东方市三家镇红草村：鳄珍科技助力乡村振兴 164
Hongcao Village, Sanjia Town, Dongfang City, Hainan Province:
　Hainan CR&TPB Crocodile Industry Technology Co., Ltd. Boosting Rural Revitalization 167

浙江省江山市廿八都镇：农文旅融合助千年古镇蝶变 171
Nianbadu Town, Jiangshan City, Zhejiang Province:
　Integration of Agriculture, Culture, and Tourism Transforms the Thousand-Year-Old Town 175

广东省清远市清新区三坑镇：三禾·稻里民宿项目助力乡村振兴 180
Sankeng Town, Qingxin District, Qingyuan City, Guangdong Province:
　Promoting Rural Revitalization with the Sanhe Daoli Homestay Project 183

宁夏回族自治区石嘴山市大武口区龙泉村：农文旅融合赋能乡村振兴 187
Longquan Village, Dawukou District Shizuishan City, Ningxia Hui Autonomous Region:
　Integration of Agriculture, Culture, and Tourism to Empower Rural Revitalization 190

重庆市酉阳土家族苗族自治县："酉女织梦"：绣出一片桃花源 194
Youyang Tujia and Miao Autonomous County, Chongqing City:
　"You Women Embroidering Dream": To Embroider a Land of Peach Blossoms 197

福建省南平市武夷山市五夫镇：农文旅融合发展赋能乡村振兴 202
Wufu Town, Wuyishan City, Nanping City, Fujian Province:
　　Empowering Rural Revitalization through the Integration of Agriculture, Culture, and Tourism 205

新疆维吾尔自治区伊犁哈萨克自治州特克斯县琼库什台村：打造国家级哈萨克族文化名村 209
Qiongkushitai Village, Tekes County, Ili Kazak Autonomous Prefecture, Xinjiang Uygur Autonomous Region:
　　Build a National Kazak Cultural Village 212

甘肃省甘南藏族自治州舟曲县土桥子村：庭院小葡萄助力乡村大振兴 216
Tuqiaozi Village, Zhouqu County, Gannan Tibetan Autonomous Prefecture, Gansu Province:
　　Small Vineyards Drive Great Rural Revitalization 219

国家电网辽宁省电力有限公司：助力中国万里海疆第一岛走出绿色产业致富路 223
State Grid Liaoning Electric Power Co., Ltd.: Assisting China's First Island along the Vast Coastline in
　　Blazing a Path to Prosperity through Green Industrial Development 226

湖北省咸宁市通城县内冲瑶族村：文旅融合助力乡村振兴 231
Neichong Yao Village, Tongcheng County, Xianning City, Hubei Province:
　　Promoting Rural Revitalization through Culture-Tourism Integration 234

黑龙江省齐齐哈尔市铁锋区查罕诺村：推进旅游高质量发展，构建宜居宜业美丽新乡村 238
Chahannuo Village, Tiefeng District, Qiqihar City, Heilongjiang Province:
　　Promoting High-Quality Tourism Development and Building a Beautiful, Attractive Village to Live and Work in 241

广东省广州市花都区塱头村：文化振兴助力古村蝶变 245
Langtou Village, Huadu District, Guangzhou City, Guangdong Province:
　　Transforming the Ancient Village through Cultural Revitalization 248

河南省信阳市光山县东岳村：文化产业特派员制度创新助力乡村振兴 253
Dongyue Village, Guangshan County, Xinyang City, Henan Province:
　　Promoting Rural Revitalization with the Cultural Industry Specialist System 256

陕西省汉中市留坝县：交旅深融合 乡村新画卷 260
Liuba County, Hanzhong City, Shaanxi Province:
　　Deep Integration of Transportation and Tourism for New Rural Landscape 263

四川省乐山市夹江县石堰村："中国纸艺第一村"的乡村振兴之路 268
Shiyan Village, Jiajiang County, Leshan City, Sichuan Province:
　　The Road to Rural Revitalization of "China's No. 1 Paper Art Village" 271

云南省德宏傣族景颇族自治州芒市出冬瓜村：弘扬乡土文化 助力乡村振兴 276
Chudonggua Village, Mang City, Dehong Dai and Jingpo Autonomous Prefecture, Yunnan Province:
　　Carrying forward Local Culture to Boost Rural Revitalization 279

飞猪旅行：五力模型助力乡村振兴 283
Fliggy Travel: The Five-Force Model Helps Rural Revitalization 286

宁夏回族自治区固原市原州区姚磨村："旅游＋冷凉蔬菜"助力乡村振兴 291
Yaomo Village, Yuanzhou District, Guyuan City, Ningxia Hui Autonomous Region:
　　"Tourism + Cool-Climate Vegetables" Boost Rural Revitalization 294

河北省邢台市内丘县杏峪村：精品民宿集群赋能乡村振兴 299
Xingyu Village, Neiqiu County, Xingtai City, Hebei Province:
　　Boutique Homestay Clusters Empower Rural Revitalization 302

广西壮族自治区来宾市金秀瑶族自治县：瑶医药产业赋能乡村振兴 306
Jinxiu Yao Autonomous County, Laibin City, Guangxi Zhuang Autonomous Region:
　　Empowering Rural Revitalization with the Yao Medicine Industry 310

江苏省盐城市大丰区恒北村：梨旅融合蹚出乡村振兴致富路 316
Hengbei Village, Dafeng District, Yancheng City, Jiangsu Province:
　　Integrating Pear Cultivation and Tourism to Blaze a Path to Rural Revitalization and Prosperity 319

贵州省遵义市正安县：吉他文化旅游赋能乡村振兴 324
Zheng'an County, Zunyi City, Guizhou Province:
　　Guitar Cultural Tourism Injects Impetus into Rural Revitalization 327

吉林省梅河口市小杨满族朝鲜族乡古城村：坚持以绿色发展走农旅融合之路 332
Gucheng Village, Xiaoyang Manchu and Korean Ethnic Township, Meihekou City, Jilin Province:
　　Pursue Green Development by Integrating Agriculture and Tourism 335

湖北省宜昌市长阳土家族自治县郑家榜村：农文旅融合催生山乡巨变 339
Zhengjiabang Village, Changyang Tujia Autonomous County, Yichang City, Hubei Province:
　　Agriculture, Culture and Tourism Integration Effecting Profound Changes in the Mountainous Village 342

黑龙江省牡丹江市穆棱市孤榆树村："抗联路"里走出的"致富路" 346
Guyushu Village, Muling City, Mudanjiang City, Heilongjiang Province:
　　Leveraging the Heritage of the Northeast Anti-Japanese United Army for Rural Prosperity 349

河南省洛阳市栾川县陶湾镇：伊源康养谷沟域旅游助力乡村振兴 353
Taowan Town, Luanchuan County, Luoyang City, Henan Province:
　　Promoting Rural Revitalization with All-Area-Advancing Tourism of Yiyuan Wellness Valley 356

山东省烟台市蓬莱区东方海岸果谷：海岸苹果品牌化助力乡村振兴 361
Oriental Coast Fruit Valley in Penglai District, Yantai City, Shandong Province:
　　Coastal Apple Branding Helps Rural Revitalization 364

陕西省榆林市佳县赤牛坬村：农文旅融合助力乡村振兴 369
Chiniuwa Village, Jia County, Yulin City, Shaanxi Province:
　　Integration of Agriculture, Culture and Tourism Promotes Rural Revitalization 372

云南省楚雄彝族自治州楚雄市紫溪彝村：农文康旅融合助力乡村振兴 376
Zixi Yi Village, Chuxiong City, Chuxiong Yi Autonomous Prefecture, Yunnan Province:
　　Integration of Agriculture, Culture, Health and Tourism Promotes Rural Revitalization 380

内蒙古自治区锡林郭勒盟多伦县温塘河村：挖掘滦河文化 谱写振兴篇章 385
Wentanghe Village, Duolun County, Xilin Gol League, Inner Mongolia Autonomous Region:
　　Uncovering Luan River Culture and Writing a Chapter of Revitalization 388

湖南省郴州市北湖区：
以全域旅游助推乡村全域振兴

摘　要

北湖区位于湖南省郴州市中部，是郴州的政治、经济、文化、商贸和物流中心。近年来，北湖区大力实施全域旅游助推乡村全域振兴战略，坚持以文塑旅、以旅彰文，以地方特色为"切入点"，以乡村风貌为"着力点"，以群众增收为"落脚点"，推进"文化+旅游+农业+商业"的深度融合发展，着力构建"吃住行游购娱"全产业链条。此举不仅推动了区域内多个亮点项目的涌现，还实现了沿线景观的连片成景，整体面貌焕然一新，走出了一条以全域旅游助推乡村全域振兴的新路径。

挑战与问题

北湖区有2200多年的建城史,被誉为"微晶石墨之都""中国有色金属之乡""中国温泉之乡"等。但因北湖区地处南岭山区,地势西南高、东北低,呈阶梯状倾斜,辖区多为山地,该区乡村村民收入主要以种植、养殖业为主。尽管北湖区拥有丰富的旅游资源和多样化的农副产品,但近年来面临着资源整合不充分、收入来源单一化以及劳动力外流等挑战,农民增收陷入停滞状态。当前,北湖区面临的主要问题是如何将生态资源优势和农副产品优势有效转化为特色旅游体验产品,最大限度地将旅游资源转化为旅游经济收益,显著提升农民的综合收入水平,这是一个亟待解决的重要课题。

措施

1. 以地方特色为"切入点"

一是利用龙头景区仰天湖的高山资源优势,创新实施"唤醒老屋"行动。以市场化手段盘活利用农村闲置房屋,成功地将一批原本荒废的老屋和闲置的宅院转型升级,转变为农产品展销馆、特色民宿、特色餐饮服务等业态。二是将当地笋干、蜂蜜等优质农副产品整合,并创新性地推出了全市首款融合"农业＋文化＋旅游"元素的文创产品——"郴心郴意",该产品凭借其独特性和创意性,在2021年荣获湖南省旅游商品大赛金奖。

2. 以乡村风貌为"着力点"

一是打造郴仰公路农旅融合示范带。通往仰天湖景区的郴仰公路经历了提质改造工程,同步完善了安防、绿化、旅游标志标线等附属设施,成为全国第一条"农旅体艺"融合带动乡村振兴的旅游标准示范公路。郴仰公路沿线的村庄巧妙地融合了传统民居、瑶族文化元素与现代审美,创作了丰富多彩的墙绘艺术,吸引了众多游客前往参观打卡。受此带动,周边村民充分利用地理优势,发展了民宿、农家乐及采摘园等产业,使得该地区成为休闲娱乐的好去处。二是打造西河乡村振兴示范带。该示范带充分利用沿线稻田、花海、果园、菜园等资源,推动田园观光、农耕体验、文化休闲、特色民宿、研学实践等新产业新业态快速发展。同时从诗词歌赋、历史典故中挖掘文化内涵,为西河沿线传统村落注入灵魂,精心打造了"醉美"吴山、好客招旅、瑶岭月峰等9个诗画乡村。此外,还成功举办了西河乡村旅游文化节,发布了多条乡村旅游精品线路,签约多项农业和文旅项目。三是立足小埠村天然的区位优势和古村魅力，高标准、大规模地建设入湘首站旅游接待服务中心，为游客提供旅游产品租售、旅游线路推介、车辆租赁、智能机器人服务等全方位一站式服务，打造了一个集古村、科教、研学、民宿于一体的小埠生态文旅城。

3. 以群众增收为"落脚点"

一是围绕全域旅游促乡村振兴，大力推进"一乡一品"培育行动，推广乡村旅游多元发展模式，鼓励村党组织领办旅游专业合作社，培育壮大村集体经济。二是在陂副村开展邓华将军故居红色乡村振兴示范村项目建设，该项目同步规划了国家3A级旅游景区建设，涵盖了邓华上将生平业绩陈列馆、游客接待中心、红色教育培训基地及停车场等基础设施。此外，还进行了村委会的改造升级、村庄环境综合整治及"五园"建设，使得陂副村发展成为省内外知名的红色教育基地和旅游景区。三是乡村旅游的全面发展带动了当地经济结构的转型，居民收入来源从传统的单一农业向多元化转变。旅游服务业的兴起，如民宿客栈经营、特色餐饮提供、手工艺品与特色产品的销售、景区景点解说服务以及务工和自主创业等，均成为村民增收的重要途径。

成效

发展全域旅游显著推动了北湖全区乡村的全面转型，乡村面貌焕然一新，乡村产业蓬勃发展，村民的收入水平持续提升，呈现出点上出彩、线上成景、面上开花的良好态势。2023年，北湖区接待国内外游客总人数1454.15万人次，同比增长47.19%，排名全市第一；旅游总收入146.9亿元，同比增长41.66%，位居全市第一。全区民宿发展至220余家7000间床位数，带动就业超5000人次，人均增收5000元。郴仰公路、西河沿线村组通过自建联营模式设立"宽洞之家"民宿连锁品牌，发展乡村民宿101家，增加客房数1154个，年营收额达5394万元。枝青乡村度假酒店率先探索集体化流转模式，采取"村集体＋企业＋农户"的方式，不仅解决就业200余人，更为每户农户增收2万元以上，实现村集体、村民和企业多方受益。"郴心郴意"系列产品常年吸收6家企业、560余户农户（其中原建档立卡贫困户370余户）提供的农副产品，累计销售9600余万元。

郴仰公路荣获了全国优质旅游示范路与全国自驾旅游标准化景观大道的称号；仰天湖景区被授予了省级旅游度假区、国家级5C级自驾车旅居车营地以及南方最美高山草原休闲露营地等多项荣誉；小埠古村亦获得了全国文明村与中国美丽休闲乡村等荣誉。此外，该地区还成功创建了9个省级美丽乡村示范村和保护了10个中国传统村落。

经验与启示

1. 全域旅游对资源整合的驱动作用

北湖区以全域旅游为引导，大力发展乡村旅游，一方面高效整合了闲置房屋、优质农产品、特色文化等资源，大力促进了乡村风貌提质、人才回流、产业发展。此举不仅发挥了乡村的资源优势，还促进了乡村第一、二、三产业的深度融合，实现了区域经济社会资源的全面优化与提升；另一方面，乡村居民的生态环境意识得到了显著增强，他们更加注重对古村古镇、自然资源、生态环境、文化遗址的保护，协力推进乡村环境的整治，致力于打造一个集自然美和人文美于一体的大美乡村，推动乡村生态文明建设。

2. 全域旅游对乡村产业的带动作用

北湖区充分发挥全域旅游对乡村产业发展的带动

作用，引导村民和村集体积极发展观光农业、游憩林业、休闲牧业、体验渔业、研学旅游、康养旅游等乡村产业，优化乡村产业结构，构建乡村全域旅游产业链。例如华塘镇发挥草莓优势，以家庭为单位、以现代农业为基础，打造以旅游研学为核心的家庭农场，形成"莓+稻""莓+市场经营主体""莓+文创""莓+衍生产品"的乡村产业链。

3. 全域旅游对促进投资的撬动作用

北湖区以全域旅游为抓手，吸引各方资金进入北湖，带动全产业链条蓬勃发展。例如在2023年，"唤醒老屋"行动计划发布会引进市场主体6家，引资1.2亿元；茅坪村发挥黑米种植传统优势，吸引农业龙头企业"黑米姐姐"投资450万元进驻老屋，打造黑米姐姐米粉铺、黑米姐姐酒铺等特色文旅餐饮体验馆；第二届湖南旅游发展大会期间，北湖区共推出了5个重点观摩项目，这些项目的总投资额达到了25.84亿元，其中社会资本投资额为21.06亿元，占据了总投资额的81.5%。

下一步计划

第一，加强顶层设计、谋划全局。进一步巩固拓展全域旅游助推乡村全域振兴制度成果，将全域旅游的发展有机融入全区乡村建设行动全过程。准确定位北湖区各乡村的发展方向和特色旅游发展主题，使各乡镇、村组的旅游资源得以一体发展、优化开发和整体效能。

第二，注重因地制宜、分类施策。针对全区各地特色和差异，科学制定分类发展策略，大力实施业态升级、招商引资、宣传推介、服务提升等专项行动。持续提质升级北湖不夜天"商圈游"、龙女温泉"休闲游"、仰天湖大草原"浪漫游"、小埠"研学游"，推动"文化+旅游+农业+商务+体育"深度融合发展。

第三，坚持文化引领、增势赋能。充分挖掘全区乡村田园风光、古建筑文化、地方风俗文化、特色美食文化等乡村文化资源，全面激活乡村历史文化基因，以文化引领乡村旅游发展。注重把文化融入村味、村品、村艺、村趣之中，用文化元素装点乡村旅游景点，提升乡村旅游的独特魅力和韵味。

Beihu District, Chenzhou City, Hunan Province:

Promoting Rural Revitalization through All-for-One Tourism

Abstract

Beihu District is located in the central part of Chenzhou City, Hunan Province. It is the political, economic, cultural, commercial and logistics center of Chenzhou City. In recent years, Beihu District has vigorously implemented the strategy of promoting the revitalization of rural areas through all-for-one tourism, adhering to shaping tourism with culture and promoting culture with tourism, and taking local characteristics as the "starting point", rural landscapes as the "focus", and increasing people's income as the "goal", so as to promote in-depth integration and development of "culture + tourism + agriculture + commerce", and make a point of building the full industrial chain covering catering, accommodation, transportation, travel, shopping and entertainment. The whole district presents a thriving picture of revitalization with highlights in multiple aspects, and has blazed a new path for promoting the revitalization of rural areas through all-for-one tourism.

Challenges and Problems

Beihu District has a history of more than 2,200 years and is known as the "Capital of Microcrystalline Graphite", "Source of China Nonferrous Metals", "Spot Blessed with Hot Springs", etc. However, due to Beihu District being located in the Nanling Mountains, the stepped terrain is high in the southwest and low in the northeast. Most of the area under jurisdiction is mountainous, and the income of rural villagers mainly comes from planting and breeding. Although Beihu District has rich tourism resources and diverse agricultural and sideline products, in recent years, due to the inadequate integration of resources, single source of income and labor outflow, villagers' way of earning income has been deadlocked. How to effectively transform the advantages of ecological resources and agricultural and sideline products into distinctive tourism experience products, maximize the conversion of tourism resources into tourism economic benefits and significantly increase farmers' comprehensive income has become a major issue that needs to be addressed in Beihu District.

Measures

1. Take local characteristics as the "starting point"

Firstly, we take advantage of the high mountain resources of Yangtian Lake in Longtou Scenic Area and innovatively implement the "revitalizing old houses" action. We use market-oriented means to revitalize and utilize idle rural houses, and a number of old houses have been transformed into agricultural product exhibition halls, distinctive homestays, characteristic restaurants and the like. Secondly, we integrate local high-quality agricultural and sideline products such as dried bamboo shoots and honey, and innovatively create the city's first "agriculture + culture + tourism" cultural and creative product *"Chenxin Chenyi"*, which won the gold medal of the Hunan Tourism Merchandise Competition in 2021.

2. Take rural landscape as the "focus"

Firstly, it is to build the Chenyang Highway agricultural tourism integration demonstration zone. We improve the Chenyang Highway leading to the Yangtian Lake Scenic Area, and simultaneously improve the security, greening, tourism signs and markings and other ancillary facilities, making it the first national tourism standard demonstration highway that integrates "agriculture, tourism, sports and art" to drive rural revitalization. The villages along the Chenyang Highway have painted colorful wall paintings through the integration of traditional dwellings, Yao culture and modern aesthetics, attracting a large number of tourists. The surrounding villagers have developed homestays, farmhouses and orchards based on local conditions, making the area a good destination for leisure and entertainment. Secondly, it is to build the Xihe rural revitalization demonstration zone. The demonstration zone makes full use of the resources along the route, such as rice fields, flower seas, orchards, and vegetable gardens, and promotes the rapid development of new industries and new formats such as rural tourism, farming experience, cultural leisure, distinctive homestays, and research study tours. Meanwhile, we dig into the cultural connotations from poems, songs and historical allusions, give souls to traditional villages along the Xihe River, and create nine poetic and picturesque villages such as "intoxicating" Wushan, hospitable Zhaolu, and Yaoling Yuefeng. The Xihe Rural Tourism Cultural Festival was held to release high-quality rural tourism routes and sign agreements on agricultural and cultural tourism projects. Thirdly, based on the natural location advantages and charm of the ancient village of Xiaobu, a high-standard and large-scale tourism reception service center has been built in the first stop in Hunan, which can provide tourists with one-stop services such as tourism product rental and sales, tourism route promotion, vehicle rental, and intelligent robot services; it has become a Xiaobu ecological cultural tourism city integrating ancient villages, science and education, study tours, and homestays.

3. Take the increase of people's income as the goal

Firstly, we will promote rural revitalization around all-for-one tourism, vigorously advance the "one village, one product" action, promote the diversified development model of rural tourism, encourage village party organizations to lead the development of tourism professional cooperatives, and cultivate and expand the village collective economy. Secondly, we will carry out the construction of the Red Rural Revitalization Demonstration Village Project of General Deng Hua's Former Residence in Pifu Village, and create a national 3A-level scenic spot by building a display hall of General Deng Hua's life and achievements, a tourist reception center, a red education and training base, and a parking lot. We have carried out the renovation and repair of the village committee, the comprehensive improvement of the village, and the construction of the "Five Parks". Pifu Village has become an important spot for red education in the province and the city, and a well-known red tourist attraction. Thirdly, through the development of a series of rural tourism combinations, the local people have bid farewell to the single source of agricultural income and earn income from multiple channels. Tourism service income, including income from homestays, distinctive restaurants, handicrafts, specialty products, scenic spot guides, etc., income from employment, and income from one's own managerial decisions has become important channels for villagers to enhance their wellbeing.

Results

The development of all-for-one tourism has significantly promoted the overall transformation

of the villages in Beihu District, rural industries have flourished, and villagers' income has continued to increase, showing a heartening look. In 2023, Beihu District received a total of 14.5415 million domestic and foreign tourists, a year-on-year increase of 47.19%, ranking first in the city; the total tourism revenue was 14.69 billion yuan, a year-on-year increase of 41.66%, ranking first in the city. The district has developed to have more than 220 homestays with 7,000 beds, creating more than 5,000 jobs and increasing per capita income by 5,000 yuan. The villages along Chenyang Highway and Xihe River established the "Kuandong Home" homestay chain brand through a self-built joint venture model, developed 101 rural homestays, increased the number of guest rooms by 1,154, and achieved an annual revenue of 53.94 million yuan. Zhiqing Township Resort Hotel took the lead in exploring the collective circulation model, and adopting the "village collective + enterprise + farmer" approach, which not only provided employment for more than 200 people, but also increased the income of each farmer by more than 20,000 yuan, thus benefiting the village collective, villagers and enterprises. The "*Chenxin Chenyi*" series of products buys in agricultural and sideline products provided by six enterprises and more than 560 farmers (including more than 370 registered poor households) all year round, with cumulative sales of more than 96 million yuan.

Chenyang Highway has been recognized as the National High-quality Tourism Demonstration Road and National Standard Scenic Avenue for Self-driving Tourism; Yangtian Lake Scenic Area has been awarded the titles of the Provincial Tourism Resort, the National 5C Self-driving RV Campground, the Most Beautiful Alpine Grassland Leisure Campground of South China, and other honors; Xiaobu Ancient Village has been awarded the titles of the National Exemplary Village and the Beautiful Leisure Village of China. In addition, the district has successfully created nine provincial-level beautiful rural demonstration villages and 10 Chinese traditional villages.

Experiences and Inspirations

1. The driving effect of all-for-one tourism on resource integration

Beihu District takes all-for-one tourism as its guide and vigorously develops rural tourism. On the one hand, it has efficiently integrated idle houses, high-quality agricultural products, characteristic culture and other resources, vigorously promoted the improvement of rural landscape, the return of talents, and industrial development, so that the countryside can give full play to its resource advantages, drive the deep integration and development of the primary, secondary and tertiary industries in the countryside, and achieve all-round improvement of economic and social resources in the region. On the other hand, it has further improved the ecological environment awareness of rural residents, and everyone pays more attention to the protection of ancient villages and towns, natural resources, ecological environment, and cultural relics, and works together to promote rural environmental improvement, so as to create a beautiful countryside that integrates natural beauty and cultural beauty, and promotes the construction of rural ecological civilization.

2. The driving effect of all-for-one tourism on rural industries

Beihu District gives full play to the driving effect of all-for-one tourism on the development of rural industries; guides villagers and village collectives to actively develop rural industries such as sightseeing agriculture, recreational forestry, leisure animal husbandry, experience-based fishery, study tour, health tourism, etc.; optimizes the rural industrial structure; and builds a rural all-for-one tourism industrial chain. For example, Huatang Town takes advantage of strawberries, takes families as units and modern agriculture as the basis, builds family farms with tourism and research at the core, so as to build a rural industry chain of "berry + rice" "berry + market operator" "berry + cultural and creative industries", and "berry + derivative products".

3. The contribution of all-for-one tourism to investment

Beihu District uses all-for-one tourism as a starting point to attract funds from all parties to the district, driving vigorous development of the entire industrial chain. For example, in 2023, the press conference for the "Revitalizing the Old Houses" action plan attracted six market entities and attracted 120 million yuan of investment; Maoping Village took advantage of its traditional black rice planting to attract the leading agricultural enterprise "Black Rice Sister" to invest 4.5 million yuan and settle in the old houses to create special cultural tourism and catering experience halls such as Black Rice Sister

Rice Noodle Shop and Black Rice Sister Wine Shop. During the Second Hunan Tourism Development Conference, the total investment in the five key demonstration projects in Beihu District was 2.584 billion yuan, and private capital investment was 2.106 billion yuan, accounting for 81.5% of the total investment.

Plans

Firstly, we will strengthen top-level design and plan the overall situation. We will further consolidate and expand the achievements of the system of promoting rural revitalization through all-for-one tourism, and organically integrate the development of all-for-one tourism into the entire process of rural construction in the district. We will accurately identify the development direction and the theme of characteristic tourism development of each village in Beihu District so that the tourism resources of each township and village group can be developed in an integrated manner, with overall efficiency enhanced.

Secondly, we should focus on taking measures according to local conditions and implementing policies in a classified manner. In view of the characteristics and differences of various parts in the region, we should appropriately formulate classified development strategies and vigorously implement special actions such as business form upgrading, investment attraction, publicity and promotion, and service improvement. We should continue to improve the quality of Beihu Never-Night "business district tour", Longnv Hot Spring "leisure tour", Yangtian Lake Prairie "romantic tour", and Xiaobu "study tour", and promote the in-depth integration and development of "culture + tourism + agriculture + business + sports".

Thirdly, we will adhere to cultural guidance and empowerment. We shall fully tap into the rural cultural resources of the region, such as rural pastoral scenery, ancient architectural culture, local customs and culture, and characteristic food culture; fully activate the historical and cultural genes of the countryside; and use culture to lead the development of rural tourism. We make a point of integrating culture into the village style, village products, village art, and village fun, and use cultural elements to beautify rural tourist attractions to enhance the unique charm and flavor of rural tourism.

四川省成都市龙泉驿区桃源村：
民宿产业高质量转型推进乡村全面振兴

摘 要

成都市龙泉驿区山泉镇桃源村统筹考虑环境承载能力和市场接受程度，坚持"审慎、保护、绿色、可持续"的原则和"规模化、特色化、品牌化"的发展方向，持续限增量、优存量、提质量，打造乡村工坊、农耕研学、康养度假、休闲运动、创意设计、文创开发等多类型、多主题、多场景的乡村民宿产品，形成具有美学震撼力、视觉冲击力、文化浸润力、长效生命力的"天府桃花源"民宿聚落，高质量推进民宿产业整体迭代升级，促进乡村全面振兴。

挑战与问题

桃源村自20世纪80年代起，凭借其作为成都龙泉驿桃花荟核心承载地的独特优势，积极推进以农家乐为主要形式的乡村旅游产业发展，奠定了坚实的产业基础。随着乡村旅游持续发展，市场对农家乐的风貌环境、产品供给、服务品质、体验深度等提出了更高要求。为抢占发展新赛道，桃源村从2018年开始，引导农家乐向乡村精品民宿整体转型。在转型过程中，基础设施配套不足导致承载能力弱、政策支撑不够引发民宿野蛮生长、资源管控利用不到位造成村民和村集体利益受损、业态同质竞争致使产业发展呈现"短命"现象等问题，以及产业发展与挤占生态空间、侵占耕地红线等矛盾极为突出，这些都成为桃源村面临的严峻挑战。

措施

1. 统筹规划布局，夯实产业基础

一是坚持规划引领，依托第三次全国国土调查、村规编制，将村集体闲置资产、资源和有意向、有条件发展民宿的农房合理布局，科学划分产业发展核心区、拓展区、留白区，确保产业持续发展。二是完善产业配套，出台《加快民宿产业发展专项行动方案（2021—2025）》，村集体投资完善要素保障、道路交通、水电供给、污水处理等七个方面配套，提升产业承载能力。三是引导资源转型，村集体对闲置资源统一掌握、建档立卡，根据产业发展规划设置准入门槛，在区农村产权交易所公开挂牌招商，让闲置资源在民宿产业发展中焕发新活力的同时避免民宿产业的野蛮生长。

2. 发掘在地文化，突出美学价值

一是制定《桃源村乡村民宿建设导引》，注重严守耕地、环保和安全红线等问题，同时将农居从文化艺术、园林建筑、生活美学的角度进行改造升级，形成"一幢一风景"，成功培育了五星级农家乐"水云涧"、成都市独具特色的主题旅游客栈"噶拉邦嘎音乐艺术空间"，以及荣获金熊猫天府创意设计奖的项目"城里的月光club"等优质旅游与文化业态。二是激活文化价值，农房改建与违建清理、农村人居环境提升同步进行，引导民宿主营造"微绿地""小景观"和网红打卡点；同时发展"民宿+非遗""民宿+农耕""民宿+禅修"等融合业态，支持民宿开展乡村诗歌大赛、国学讲坛、非遗体验等活动，同步构建民宿环境生态景观和文化生态圈。

3. 健全产业链条，做优宣传营销

一是通过引进主题民宿，拓展露营、骑行、登山、观鸟、研学等项目，创新营造休闲运动、生态康养、文化教育等多元场景，成功打造了近观城市全景、远眺西岭雪山、朝迎旭日初升、夜览万家灯火等四大特色场景，形成"餐饮住宿+商务接待+电商文创+物业服务"全产业链。二是引进创意设计机构、线上营销平台、知名网红博主，搭建公共宣传营销平台，全村产业形成营销的良好态势。

成效

一方面，桃源村通过推动民宿产业整体提档升级，促进了道路交通、污水管网、环境风貌有机更新。近年来，黑化亮化旅游道路4.2千米，改建生态停车场12500平方米，新建污水管网1.8千米，完成国家3A级旅游景区桃花故里整体提档升级。另一方面，桃源村成立村集体公司，搭建统一公共服务平台，为民宿提供用人用工、物业管理、宣传营销、技能培训、代驾租车等服务，此举措显著增强了村集体的自我发展能力与经济效益。

2023年，桃源村共接待游客236.5万人，实现旅游综合收入2.96亿元，村集体实现增收120万元。以一个典型的三口之家普通农户为例，该家庭每年通过出租房屋可获得约8万元的租金收入；同时，每位家庭成员在民宿或村集体公司工作，每年可各自赚取约5万元的薪资收入；此外，他们还利用民宿的便利条件，就近销售自家种植的水蜜桃，实现约8万元的额外收入。综合以上各项，该家庭年均总收入达到约31万元。

经验与启示

1. 加强规划引领是民宿产业发展的"牛鼻子"

发展民宿产业需要高位统筹规划引导，注重从本地实际出发，结合资源禀赋和产业特色，形成布局合理、规模适度、特色鲜明的民宿发展格局。龙泉驿区成立了民宿产业发展工作专班，高标准编制了民宿产业专项规划，出台支持民宿产业发展的意见或细则，统筹专项资金用于引导支持民宿产业发展，全方位加强对民宿产业发展支持。

2. 优化资源配置是民宿产业发展的"关键招"

资源市场化配置能够有效推动生产要素从低质低效领域向优质高效领域流动，将沉睡资产变成现实资本。桃源村通过村集体对闲置资源统一掌握、建档立卡，根据产业发展规划设置准入门槛，在区农村产权交易所公开挂牌招商，让闲置资源在民宿产业发展中焕发新活力。

3. 规范管理是民宿产业健康发展的"生命线"

一是实行民宿"选址预审＋方案预审＋开工预审＋业主承诺＋设计师承诺"审批"五步法",建立民宿项目"容缺容后"机制,为民宿产业快速高质量发展保驾护航。二是推动行业自治,成立龙泉山乡村民宿产业联盟,制定"桃源村乡村旅游环境品质提升红黑榜"等考核评价措施,形成"村委会＋行业联盟＋经营者＋社会公众"的监管模式,保障民宿产业健康发展。

下一步计划

为达成建设城市森林公园新门户、打造全域乡村旅游新高地,以及创建乡村振兴示范新样板的目标,桃源村以推进和美乡村建设为关键举措,采取了双管齐下的策略。一是对现有单体民宿进行了二次提档升级,成功建设了一批在形态上拥有优美景观风貌、强进入性的民宿,同时在业态上实现了产品供给的互补与优质体验感的提升,文态方面则凸显了独特的文化符号,增强了民宿的辨识度,使其成为精品爆款。二是桃源村遵循"村集体经济组织＋国有平台公司＋市场主体"的合作建设模式,通过实施宅基地自愿有偿腾退政策,成功引进了龙头文旅企业,对片区进行了整体开发,旨在高品质地打造城市会客厅,进一步提升乡村旅游的品质与吸引力。在此过程中,桃源村持续致力于促进产业的深度融合与发展,不断探索以民宿产业的高质量转型为引领、带动乡村全面振兴的"桃源路径",为实现乡村振兴的宏伟目标奠定了坚实基础。

Taoyuan Village, Longquanyi District, Chengdu City, Sichuan Province:

High-quality Transformation of the Homestay Industry Promotes Comprehensive Rural Revitalization

Abstract

Taoyuan Village, Shanquan Town, Longquanyi District, Chengdu City comprehensively considers the environmental carrying capacity and market acceptance, adheres to the principles of "prudence, protection, greenness, and sustainability" and the development direction of "large-scale, specialization, and branding", and continues to limit the increase, optimize the existing stock, and improve the quality. It launches rural workshops, agricultural research, health tourism space, leisure sports, creative design, cultural and creative development projects among others which come in diverse types, themes, and scenarios, forming a "Tianfu Peach Blossom Land" homestay cluster with aesthetic appeal, visual impact, cultural charm, and long-lasting vitality, pushing the overall iteration and upgrading of the homestay industry up to a high level, and promoting the comprehensive revitalization of rural areas.

Challenges and Problems

Since the 1980s, Taoyuan Village has relied on the core advantages of Chengdu Longquanyi Taohuahui to vigorously develop the rural tourism industry dominated by farmhouses, and has built a good foundation. With the continuous development of rural tourism, the market has put forward higher requirements upon the style and environment of farmhouses, product supply, service quality, and richness of experience. In order to seize the new development track, Taoyuan Village has guided the overall transformation of farmhouses into quality rural homestays since 2018. In the process of transformation, issues such as insufficient infrastructure leading to weak carrying capacity, insufficient policy support causing the barbaric growth of homestays, inadequate resource management and utilization causing damage to the interests of villagers and village collectives, homogeneous competition among businesses of the same kind leading to "short-lived" industrial development, as well as the contradiction between advancing industrial development and squeezing out ecological space and encroaching on the red line of cultivated land are extremely prominent, have all become severe challenges faced by Taoyuan Village.

Measures

1. Conduct overall planning of the layout to consolidate the industrial foundation

Firstly, it is to adhere to the guidance of planning, rely on the third national land survey and the compilation of village regulations to rationally arrange the idle assets and resources of the village collective and the farmhouses that are willing and have the conditions to develop homestays, and appropriately make out the core area, expansion area and blank area of industrial development to ensure the sustainable development of the industry. Secondly, it is to improve the supporting industries, and roll out the *Special Action Plan for Accelerating the Development of the Homestay Industry (2021-2025)*. The village collective has invested in improving the supporting facilities in seven aspects, such as road traffic, water and electricity supply and sewage treatment to enhance the carrying capacity of the industry. Thirdly, it is to guide the transformation of resources. The village collective manages and files the idle resources in a uniform way, sets up access thresholds according to the industrial development plan, and publicly attracts investment in them at the district rural property rights exchange so that idle resources can be revitalized in the development of the homestay industry while the barbaric growth of the homestay industry is avoided.

2. Explore local culture to highlight aesthetic value

Firstly, it is to formulate the *Guidelines for the Construction of Rural Homestays in Taoyuan Village*; while strictly guarding the red lines of cultivated land, environmental protection and safety, we have transformed and upgraded rural residences from the perspectives of culture, art, garden architecture, and life aesthetics, developing "one view for one building", and have developed high-quality business formats such as the five-star rural tourism resort "Shuiyunjian", the uniquely themed tourist inn in Chengdu "Galabangga Music Art Space", and the project "Moonlight in the City Club" which won the Golden Panda Tianfu Creative Design Award. Secondly, it is to bring out the cultural value of farmhouse reconstruction and illegal construction clearance, improve the rural living environment simultaneously, guide homestay owners to create "micro green space", "small landscape" and Internet famous spots; at the same time, we develop "homestay + intangible cultural heritage", "homestay + farming", "homestay + meditation" and other integrated businesses, support homestays to carry out rural poetry competitions, Chinese studies forums, intangible cultural heritage experiences and other activities, and simultaneously build homestay environmental ecological landscapes and cultural ecosystems.

3. Improve the industrial chain and optimize publicity and marketing

Firstly, by developing themed homestays, we endeavor to expand camping, cycling, mountaineering, bird watching, study tours, and innovatively create multiple scenarios for leisure sports, ecological healthcare, and education among others. We have successfully created four distinctive scenes: a close-up panoramic view of the city, a distant view of the Xiling Snowy Mountain, the rising sun in the morning, and the night scene of numerous lights, forming a full industrial chain of "catering and accommodation + business reception + e-commerce of cultural creations + property services". Secondly, we have brought in creative design agencies, online marketing platforms, and well-known Internet celebrities and bloggers to build a public publicity and marketing platform so that the whole village industry enjoys sound marketing momentum.

Results

On the one hand, Taoyuan Village has boosted the overall upgrading of the homestay industry, which has promoted the organic renewal of road traffic, sewage pipe network, and environmental landscape. Over recent years, 4.2 kilometers of tourism roads have been blackened and illuminated, 12,500 square meters of ecological parking lots have been rebuilt, and the 1.8-kilometer-long new sewage pipe network has been built so that the overall upgrading of the national 4A-level scenic spot Peach Blossom Hometown was done. On the other hand, Taoyuan Village has established a village collective company and built a unified public service platform to provide the homestays with employment, property management, publicity and marketing, skills training, and car rental services to strengthen their own capabilities in increasing income.

In 2023, Taoyuan Village received a total of

2.365 million tourists, and realized a comprehensive tourism income of 296 million yuan; and the village collective realized an increase of 1.2 million yuan in income. Taking a typical three-person family of ordinary farmers as an example, this family can earn an annual rental income of about 80,000 yuan by renting out their houses; at the same time, each family member works in a homestay or a village collective company that can earn a salary of about 50,000 yuan per year; in addition, they also use the convenience of the homestay to sell their own peaches nearby, obtaining an additional income of about 80,000 yuan. Taking all the above into consideration, the family's annual total income reaches about 310,000 yuan.

Experiences and Inspirations

1. Strengthening planning guidance is the key to the development of the homestay industry

The development of the homestay industry requires high-level planning and guidance, we focus on local realities, associate resource endowments with industrial characteristics, and build a homestay development pattern with a reasonable layout, appropriate scale, and distinctive characteristics. Longquanyi District has set up a special work group for the development of the homestay industry, compiled a special plan for the homestay industry up to high standards, issued opinions and rules to support the development of the homestay industry, and coordinated special funds to guide and support the development of the homestay industry, so as to support the development of the homestay industry in an all-round way.

2. Optimizing resource allocation is crucial to the development of the homestay industry

Market-oriented resource allocation can effectively promote the flow of production factors from low-quality and low-efficiency areas to high-quality and high-efficiency areas, turning dormant assets into real capital. The Taoyuan Village has unified the control and filing of idle resources through the village collective, set access thresholds according to the industrial development plan, and publicly

sought investment in the district rural property rights exchange so that idle resources can be revitalized in the development of the homestay industry.

3. Standardized management is the "lifeline" for the healthy development of the homestay industry

Firstly, it is to implement the "five-step method" for the approval of prospective homestays, including "site selection pre-examination + scheme pre-examination + construction pre-examination + owner's commitment + designer's commitment", and establish a "tolerance for the missing and later submission of documents" mechanism for homestay projects to safeguard the rapid and high-quality development of the homestay industry. Secondly, it is to promote industrial autonomy. We have established the Longquanshan Rural Homestay Industry Alliance, formulated assessment and evaluation measures such as the *Taoyuan Village Rural Tourism Environment Quality Improvement Red and Black Lists*, and put in place a "village committee + industry alliance + operators + the public" supervision model to ensure the healthy development of the homestay industry.

Plans

To achieve the goals of establishing a new portal of the urban forest park, building a new highland of rural all-in-one tourism in the whole region, and creating a new model of rural revitalization demonstration, Taoyuan Village aims to promote harmonious and beautiful rural construction through efforts as follows. Firstly, the village has undertaken a secondary upgrading of existing individual homestays, successfully building a number of homestays with beautiful landscapes and strong accessibility in terms of form. Simultaneously, in terms of business formats, it has achieved complementary product supply and enhanced the quality of the experience, while in terms of cultural expression, it has highlighted unique cultural symbols, enhancing the recognizability of the homestays and turning them into elite hits. Secondly, Taoyuan Village follows the cooperative construction model of "rural collective economic organization + state-owned platform company + market subject". By implementing a voluntary and compensated homestead relinquishment policy, it has successfully introduced leading cultural tourism enterprises to comprehensively develop the area, aiming to create a high-quality urban reception hall and further improve the quality and attractiveness of rural tourism. In this process, Taoyuan Village has continued to promote the deep integration and development of industries, and has continually explored the "Taoyuan Path" of driving comprehensive rural revitalization led by the high-quality transformation of the homestay industry, laying a solid foundation for realizing the grand goal of rural revitalization.

2024 世界旅游联盟：旅游助力乡村振兴案例（中英文双语版）
WTA Best Practices of Rural Revitalization through Tourism 2024 (Chinese-English Bilingual Edition)

上海市崇明区建设镇虹桥村：
民宿旅游赋能乡村振兴

摘 要

上海市崇明区建设镇虹桥村紧邻东平国家森林公园，依托上海市乡村振兴示范村建设计划，结合国家 3A 级旅游景区升级建设，坚持从生态、生产、生活"三生融合"入手，通过"农业+旅游"发展路径，依托"民宿+"支柱产业，以"一核两区"为重点，着力打造以中荷现代花卉田园综合体为核心区，以顾伯伯乡村民宿、也山西红花基地为两大特色组团片区的"一核两区"发展格局，建设惠及本地村民的精品旅游村。

挑战与问题

上海市崇明区建设镇虹桥村位于崇明区中部,村域总面积3.84平方千米,其中可耕地面积2平方千米,林地面积0.76平方千米。全村共有37个村民小组,农户1366户,户籍人口2948人。虹桥村虽然其地理位置优越,基础设施较为完善,但是乡村旅游设施落后,服务质量不高,难以吸引和留住游客。此外,自然环境和文化资源无法得到充分利用,这加剧了村庄经济发展的困境。

措施

1. 全方位提升村容村貌

一是虹桥村以"白墙青瓦坡屋顶,林水相依满庭芳"为主题,打造融合人文与生态的崇明特色乡村风貌。村委会特别设计了虹桥村主题Logo作为村庄的独特标识,农宅外立面色调统一,局部墙面增添了立体绿化景观和精致的墙体彩绘。二是虹桥村村委会向农户发放花卉和果树种苗,并在农户的自留田区域精心规划布局小菜园、小果园和小花园。三是虹桥村定期组织村庄清洁行动,确保村庄的整洁与美观。对重点区域的水泥路面进行了升级改造,同时实施了河道景观提升工程,在河道两岸设置了亲水平台,以满足村民和游客的观光休闲需求。

2. 全力打造旅游产业集群

一是打造民宿产业集群。虹桥村鼓励和支持村集体和农民,充分利用并盘活闲置宅基地资源,共同制定《建设镇虹桥村民宿业主自我管理办法》,明确统一标准,目前全村共有127家民宿,占据了整个崇明岛民宿总数的12%,拥有612间客房和1102个床位。顾洪斌和顾洪宇兄弟创立的顾伯伯农家乐逐步发展壮大,成功吸纳了周边村民的加入与合作,形成"顾伯伯"民宿品牌。目前,该品牌拥有192间客房、307个床位和530个餐位,集住宿、餐饮、采摘、垂钓以及农产品销售等多项功能于一体。二是引进上海自然卷卷牧野羊驼观光牧场。该牧场集羊驼特色养殖、观光旅游、亲子教育以及健康疗愈等多项功能于一体,现有各色羊驼60余头,为游客提供了独特的"牧旅融合型"都市康养体验。三是发展西红花基地建设。虹桥村自2009年起与上海药材公司合作,建立了一个集生产、销售、科研为一体的0.3平方千米西红花种植示范基地。基地配备了8000平方米的室内栽培房和加工设施,并打造了西红花文化展示厅,还定期举办崇明上药西红花采摘节等系列活动。虹桥村通过"示范基地+合作社+农户"的运作模式,持续扩大种植面积,丰富衍生产品。

成效

一是虹桥村近年来注重农村人居环境的优化与提升工作,已成功打造了超过900户的"小三园"项目,同时还拥有1146亩的林地,森林覆盖率高达38%,这一比例远超上海市的平均水平。二是严格落实河道管理责任制,成功消除了劣Ⅴ类水体,并实施生态河道治理项目。三是村庄道路已实现全面硬化,村主要道路和支路均采用白色混凝土铺设,总长达11.48千米。四是全村范围内实现了污水处理的全面覆盖,且处理后的水质达到了Ⅰ级A标准,确保了水资源的清洁与安全。同时,垃圾分类工作得到了有效推广与实施,分类率高达98%以上,减量率接近30%。

虹桥村依托农文旅产业的发展,实现了显著的经济增长。通过自主经营民宿,村民的平均收入增加了

10万元；通过房屋租赁，户均增加收入5万元；通过农产品销售，户均收入提高了6000元。全村人均收入达到了4.5万元。此外，虹桥村已有10家民宿荣获上海市星级民宿称号，35家民宿被评为崇明区星级民宿。2020年底，虹桥村成功创建了国家3A级旅游景区，并在2021年获得市级乡村振兴示范村称号。

经验与启示

1. 改善基础设施

虹桥村不断增加对民宿集中区域的旅游基础设施建设的投资，通过整合政府项目，如污水处理、垃圾分类、河道生态治理、绿化升级、道路拓宽及修复等，全面提升区域环境。此外，村委会还增设健身步道、市民公园、停车场、公共卫生间、游客服务中心等设施，并实现Wi-Fi全覆盖，以满足游客的多样化需求。在民宿集中区，积极引导乡村餐饮和购物经营者实现集中、规范经营。

2. 加强人才培养

一是依托区域旅游产业发展的人才库资源，构建高效的培训平台，邀请业内资深的导师和专家，对民宿从业人员进行系统化、分层次的培训，培育出一支精通旅游策划、营销和管理的专业团队。二是采取"走出去、引进来"的策略，组织旅游从业人员赴近郊及周边省市的民宿旅游发展典范地区进行深入学习和考察，汲取先进经验和创新理念。同时加大宣传，吸引

高学历、高素质的人才加入虹桥村的旅游管理团队和投身民宿经营，提升整个旅游民宿行业的人员素质和服务品质。

3. 推进产业融合

农业作为农村的核心组成部分，可与旅游民宿产业深度融合。虹桥村不断推动以健康为主题的农旅融合模式。在民宿周边开发一系列农旅体验产品，如花开观赏、农耕文化体验、现场种植采摘等，为实现"吸引游客、留住游客、让游客玩得开心、让游客还想再来"的旅游发展目标而不断前行。通过这些举措，农旅体验成为民宿产业中的重要支柱和示范亮点。

下一步计划

一是进一步吸引投资，并积极引进更多元化的文旅项目，打造"虹桥花乡"高质量景区，在提供丰富多彩的旅游产品与服务基础上，满足游客日益增长的多元化需求。二是推进民宿集群的标准化建设，着手制定并不断完善相关标准，提高民宿服务的质量和运营效率。虹桥村将继续通过旅游产业的蓬勃发展，绘制出一幅乡村振兴的壮美画卷。

Hongqiao Village, Jianshe Town, Chongming District, Shanghai City:

Homestay Tourism Empowers Rural Revitalization

Abstract

Hongqiao Village, Jianshe Town, Chongming District, Shanghai, is adjacent to Dongping National Forest Park. Relying on the construction of Shanghai Rural Revitalization Demonstration Village and seizing the opportunity of the upgrading and construction of the national 3A-level scenic spot, it adheres to starting from the "three-in-one integration" of ecology, production and life, and takes the "agriculture + tourism" development path. Relying on the pillar industry of "homestay +", it focuses on the "one core and two areas" to build a boutique tourist village that benefits local villagers, with the Sino-Dutch Modern Flower Rural Complex as the core area, and the two special groups of Uncle Gu's Rural Homestay and Yeshan Safflower Base as the two key areas.

groups. Although Hongqiao Village has a superior geographical location and relatively complete infrastructure, its rural tourism facilities are backward and the service quality is poor such that the village hardly attracts and retains tourists. In addition, the natural environment and cultural resources cannot be fully utilized, which aggravates the difficulties of the village in advancing its economic development.

Challenges and Problems

Hongqiao Village, Jianshe Town, Chongming District, Shanghai, is located in the central part of Chongming District. The total area of the village is 3.84 square kilometers, including 2 square kilometers of arable land and 0.76 square kilometers of forest land. The village has 1366 farming households with 2948 registered residents in 37 villager

Measures

1. Comprehensively improve the appearance of the village

Firstly, Hongqiao Village takes "white walls, black tiles, sloping roofs, forests and waters, and fragrant courtyards" as the theme to create a Chongming-style rural landscape that integrates culture and ecology. The village committee has specially designed the Hongqiao Village logo as the

village's unique mark. The facades of the farmhouses are put in a unified color, and some walls are added with three-dimensional green landscapes and exquisite wall paintings. Secondly, the Hongqiao Village Committee distributes flower and fruit tree seedlings to farmers, and carefully plans small vegetable plots, small orchards, and small gardens in the farmers' private field. Thirdly, Hongqiao Village regularly organizes village cleaning operations to ensure the cleanliness and beauty of the village. The cement roads in key areas have been upgraded and the river landscape improvement project has been implemented, with waterfront platforms set up on both sides of the river to meet the sightseeing and leisure needs of villagers and tourists.

2. Make every effort to build a tourism industry cluster

Firstly, it is to build a homestay industry cluster. Hongqiao Village encourages and supports the village collective and farmers to make full use of and revitalize idle homestead resources, jointly formulate the *Self-Management Measures for Homestay Owners in Hongqiao Village, Jianshe Town*, and clarify unified standards. At present, there are 127 homestays in the village, accounting for 12% of all the homestays on Chongming Island, with 1,102 beds in 612 rooms. The Uncle Gu Farmhouse, founded by the brothers Gu Hongbin and Gu Hongyu, has gradually grown and developed, and successfully absorbed the participation and cooperation of surrounding villagers to form the "Uncle Gu" homestay brand. It currently has 192 rooms with 307 beds and 530 dining seats, integrating accommodation, catering, picking, fishing and agricultural product sales. Secondly, it draws on the experience of Shanghai Naturally Curly Alpaca Sightseeing Ranch, which integrates alpaca breeding, sightseeing, parent-child education and healthcare. There are more than 60 alpacas of various colors, providing tourists with unique healthcare experience through pastoral tourism. Thirdly, it is to advance the saffron base construction. Since 2009, Hongqiao Village has cooperated with Shanghai Pharmaceutical Company to establish a 3.84-square-kilometers saffron planting demonstration base integrating production, sales and scientific research, with 8,000 square meters of indoor cultivation rooms and processing facilities, and a saffron cultural exhibition hall where a series of activities like the Chongming Shanghai Pharmaceutical Saffron Picking Festival have been regularly held. Hongqiao Village continues to expand the planting area and enrich derivative products through the "demonstration base + cooperative + farmers" operation model.

Results

Firstly, Hongqiao Village puts a premium on

improving the rural living environment. In recent years, it has successfully built a "Three Small Gardens" project covering more than 900 households. In addition, the forest area reaches 0.76 square kilometers, and the forest coverage rate is 38%, much higher than the average level of Shanghai. Secondly, the village strictly implements the river management responsibility system, eliminates Class V water bodies, and implements ecological river management projects. Thirdly, the village roads are fully hardened, and the main roads and branch roads in the village are all white concrete roads with a total length of 11.48 kilometers. Fourthly, the village is fully covered by sewage treatment, with water quality reaching Class Ⅰ - A standards, ensuring the cleanliness and safety of water resources. At the same time, the garbage classification is effectively promoted and implemented, with a classification rate of over 98% and a reduction rate close to 30%.

Based on the development of rural cultural and tourism industries, Hongqiao Village has achieved remarkable economic growth. Through the independent operation of homestays, the average income of villagers has increased by 100,000 yuan; through house rental, the average income per household has increased by 50,000 yuan; through the sales of agricultural products, the average income per household has increased by 6,000 yuan. The per capita income of the whole village has reached 45,000 yuan. In addition, 10 homestays in Hongqiao Village have been awarded the title of Shanghai Star-rated Homestay, and 35 homestays have been rated as Chongming District Star-rated Homestay. At the end of 2020, Hongqiao Village successfully established a national 3A scenic spot and was awarded the title of "Model Village for Municipal Rural Revitalization" in 2021.

Experiences and Inspirations

1. Improve infrastructure

Hongqiao Village has continuously increased investment in tourism infrastructure construction in the areas where homestays are concentrated. By integrating government projects such as sewage treatment, garbage classification, river ecological management, greenery upgrading, road widening and repair, the regional environment is improved all-roundly. In addition, the village committee has added fitness trails, citizen parks, parking lots, public toilets, tourist service centers and other facilities; and ensured full Wi-Fi coverage to meet the diverse needs of tourists. In the areas where homestays are

concentrated, efforts are made to guide those running rural catering and shopping centers to conduct centralized and standardized operations.

2. Strengthen talent cultivation

Firstly, relying on the talent pool resources for regional tourism industry development, we will build an efficient training platform, invite senior mentors and experts in the industry to conduct systematic and layered training for those engaging in the homestay industry, and cultivate a professional team that is proficient in tourism planning, marketing and management. Secondly, we will adopt the "going out and bringing in" strategy, and organize tourism practitioners to go to the suburbs and surrounding provinces and cities to conduct in-depth study and investigation in model areas of homestay tourism development, and to draw others' advanced experience and innovative ideas. At the same time, we will increase publicity to attract highly educated and high-caliber talents to join the tourism management team of Hongqiao Village and engage in homestay operations, so as to improve the personnel competence and service quality of the entire tourism homestay industry.

3. Promote industrial integration

Agriculture, as a core component of rural areas, can be deeply integrated with the tourism homestay industry. Hongqiao Village continues to promote the health-themed model integrating agriculture and tourism. A series of agricultural tourism experience products have been developed around homestays, such as flower viewing, farming culture experience, on-site planting and picking, etc., with a view of "attracting tourists, retaining tourists, enabling tourists to have fun, and making tourists willing to come again". Through these measures, agricultural tourism experience has become an important pillar and demonstration highlight in the homestay industry.

Plans

Firstly, it is to further attract investment and implement more diversified cultural and tourism projects to build the "Hongqiao Flower Village" high-quality scenic spot, and meet the growing diversified needs of tourists by offering rich and colorful tourism products and services. Secondly, it is to promote the standardization of homestay clusters. Hongqiao Village will start to formulate and continuously improve relevant standards to improve the quality and operational efficiency of homestay services, and will continue to draw a magnificent picture of rural revitalization through the vigorous development of the tourism industry.

安徽省合肥市庐江县百花村：
茶乡旅游赋能乡村振兴

摘　要

安徽省合肥市庐江县百花村秉持"融合发展"理念，利用本村风貌、风俗、风物、风情、风味，以农促旅，以旅兴农，发展花乡茶谷、精品民宿等项目，依托山区林业、茶业资源，有效整合汤池镇白马尖景区、金汤湖湿地公园、百花茶谷等周边文化和旅游资源，推出篝火、采摘、越野等体验项目，策划并推广科普研学、温泉康养、户外露营、美食之旅等多条线路，形成集旅游、餐饮、住宿、休闲于一体的乡村旅游模式，助力乡村振兴。

挑战与问题

百花村属山区村,坐落在大别山余脉之尾,群山环抱,自然环境优越。全村面积10.2平方千米,总人口4425人。百花村是物产丰富的原生态村落,素有茶乡、林乡、花乡、竹乡和菜乡的美誉。但在发展过程中,百花村一方面受地理区位、交通条件等方面的影响,旅游基础设施比较薄弱,交通、通信和公共服务设施等有待建设和完善;另一方面,百花村群众自主意识不强,旅游资源开发程度较低,村庄内生态旅游项目单一,得天独厚的生态资源没有被盘活,未能实现经济变现。

措施

1. 完善旅游配套设施

一是对基础设施、服务设施、人居环境进行升级改造,先后完成3个中心村建设,14个较大自然村庄整治,安全饮水、电网改造实现全覆盖,路面硬化率和道路亮化率达到100%。二是建成休闲驿站3所,游客停车场5处,并配套建造了农家乐、精品民宿以及儿童游乐园等设施。三是发展旅游餐饮,以农家生活为主题,加强特色菜、农家菜、山野菜等菜品开发,将乡村美食打造成具有特色的旅游吸引物。

2. 壮大特色民宿产业

百花村成立经济合作社,合作社与村民签订闲置农房租赁合同,随后合作社又与运营公司签订整体租赁合同,共同开发"少间·王圩里"精品民宿和家庭民宿。农房面积一般在100—150平方米,房况破旧且年代久远。为了使农房焕发新生,设计师在运用现代设计手法的同时,保留传统建筑的记忆和乡村气息,如将夯土墙作为装饰元素融入其中,在原址上进行拆除、翻新等工作。这些举措能将"农村记忆"呈现给不同人群,让人们在王圩里重寻童年的记忆与情怀。

3. 挖掘特色旅游资源

百花村充分挖掘地域特色,发挥资源优势,积极探索"乡村旅游+民宿+特色农产品产业"的经济发展模式。为此,该村精心打造了百花谷森动山野户外运动综合体、金汤湖森动水世界户外运动综合体等文旅项目,提升了白马岭、金汤湖湿地公园、王岭玻璃栈道、百花茶谷等景区的旅游品质,还设置了乡村篝火、野果采摘、溪畔寻鱼、山间越野等乡村旅游体验项目,旨在持续延伸和完善产业链,推动休闲民宿与乡村旅游互融共促新格局。

4. 发展特色农耕产业

百花村一方面根据自身的山区特色,积极将茶叶、山珍菜的栽培和改良作为挖掘保护优秀农耕文化的着重点。同时,该村还兴建村史馆,以此为平台保护和展示传统农业技艺,展现其优越的自然环境和传统的乡村特色,成功塑造了百花菜与茶叶的地域性特色品

牌。另一方面，依托茶文化主题积极开发少儿研学市场，百花村与专业的研学团队合作，开发个性化研学课程，讲好茶故事，举办茶文化旅游节，促进茶文旅融合发展。

得感和幸福感的双提升。

百花村先后荣获国家森林乡村、全国乡村旅游重点村、全国乡村治理示范村、安徽省首批特色旅游名村、安徽省乡村振兴示范村、安徽省美丽宜居村庄、安徽省"特色美食村"等荣誉称号。

成效

百花村累计发展和改造优质茶园 350 亩（一亩约等于 666.67 平方米），发展地方特色百花菜 700 多亩，培育百花苗约 20 亩，成立农业专业合作社 6 个，带动 120 多户贫困户脱贫。自乡村旅游运营开展以来，百花村已累计接待游客近 50 多万人次。2021 年村集体收入达到 60.77 万元，2022 年村集体收入达到 138.8 万元，2023 年村集体收入达到 517.86 万元。2024 年 1 月 13 日举办首届"汤池镇百花村股份经济合作社收益分红大会"，提取 12.38 万元给群众进行收益分红，让群众共享村集体经济发展红利，实现获

经验与启示

1. 因地制宜发挥优势

百花村充分利用村庄原有风貌，保持乡村特色，通过"民宿+总部经济"运营模式这把"发展密钥"，盘活村内闲置民房和宅基地，积极争取乡村振兴衔接资金，引进"少间·王圩里"品牌进行乡村运营。先后建成了王圩里一期、二期、三期民宿项目，并成功招租运营。将乡村资源优势、生态优势成功转化为经济优势、发展优势，演绎了一个小山村在乡村振兴路上的精彩蝶变。

2. 以点带面共同致富

"少间·王圩里"精品民宿一是为当地村民提供就业岗位，二是积极发动村民成为酒店的"供应商"，打造了以茶叶、百花菜、有机农产品为主的特色伴手礼产品；新鲜的苋菜、韭菜、百花菜、辣椒、茄子和土鸡、活鱼也成为酒店餐桌上纯正的山村美食。三是酒店管理公司运营团队结合本地农特产，将百花菜做成水饺，开办了合肥乡饺饺食品有限责

任公司，极大地促进村内农副产品销售，吸引更多年轻群体返乡创业。

3. 以旅促农融合发展

百花村以旅游业为发展核心，紧密联结农业和农民，使农民能够直接参与到旅游产品的生产及乡村旅游服务的提供中。除了租赁和收储农民民房进行改建、翻建，发展民宿，百花村还依托本地丰富的农特产，成功孵化了"百花人家"及"茶香谷茶叶合作社"等产业项目，实现了农业和旅游业的深度融合，共同推动了乡村经济的稳健增长。

下一步计划

百花村紧紧围绕农旅融合，成功构建了休闲农业、文化旅游、餐饮住宿等多产业协同发展的格局，把"和"的理念贯穿推进农村现代化的全过程、全方面，着力打造彰显徽风皖韵的宜居宜业和美乡村。一是加入创新元素，为满足乡村旅游多元化体验的需求，尤其是针对亲子乐园等公共设施安全性能的更高要求，百花村创新乡村旅游载体，避免乡村旅游成为一日游、一次游。二是积极构建茶特色旅游产品，打造茶文化特色旅游路线，推动茶文化的传承与创新，提升乡村旅游潜力。三是继续鼓励群众发展家庭民宿，为游客提供多类型、高性价比的特色乡村住宿体验。百花村将继续秉持"融合发展"的理念，利用绿色生态、建筑艺术、农业茶园等元素，推动乡村旅游由观光型向休闲度假、深度体验转型升级，持续赋能乡村振兴。

Baihua Village, Lujiang County, Hefei City, Anhui Province:

Tea Country Tourism Empowers Rural Revitalization

Abstract

Baihua Village, Lujiang County, Hefei City, Anhui Province, adheres to the concept of "integrated development" by utilizing its local scenery, customs, local products, local conditions and flavors. It promotes tourism through agriculture and vice versa; and develops projects such as Huaxiang Tea Valley and boutique homestays. Relying on the forestry and tea resources in the mountainous area, it effectively integrates the surrounding cultural and tourism resources such as Baimajian scenic area in Tangchi Town, Jintang Lake Wetland Park and Baihua Tea Valley; launches bonfire, picking, off-road driving and other experience projects; plans and promotes tours for science popularization, hot spring healthcare, outdoor camping, tasty food and other routes, developing a rural tourism model integrating tourism, catering, accommodation and leisure, to help rural revitalization.

Challenges and Problems

Baihua Village is located at the end of the Dabie Mountains is surrounded by mountains and blessed with a superior natural environment. The village covers an area of 10.2 square kilometers and has a total population of 4,425. Baihua Village is an original ecological village with rich resources, known as the place blessed with quality tea, forest, flowers, bamboo and vegetables. However, in the process of development, Baihua Village is affected by its geographical location and transportation conditions. Its tourism infrastructure is relatively weak, and its transportation, communication and public service facilities have yet to be built and improved. Moreover, the villagers in Baihua Village have a weak sense of autonomy, tourism resources are less than developed, the eco-tourism projects in the village are monotonous, and the unique ecological resources have not been fully utilized, failing to bring any economic benefit.

Measures

1. Improve supporting tourism facilities

Firstly, it is to upgrade and renovate infrastructure, service facilities, and living environment. We have completed the construction of three central villages, renovated 14 large natural villages, achieved full coverage of safe drinking water and power grid transformation, and had all the roads hardened and lighted. Secondly, we have built three leisure stations and five tourist parking lots, and also built supporting facilities such as farmhouses, boutique homestays, and children's amusement parks. Thirdly, it is to develop tourism and catering; take farm life as the theme to strengthen the development of special dishes, farm dishes, wild vegetables, and other dishes; and make rural food a distinctive tourist attraction.

2. Strengthen the characteristic homestay industry

Baihua Village established an economic cooperative, which signed lease contracts for idle farmhouses with villagers, and then signed an overall lease contract with the operating company to develop "Shaojian-Wangxuli" boutique homestays and household-based homestays. The farmhouses generally range from 100 to 150 square meters in floor space and are dilapidated and old. In order to rejuvenate the rural houses, the designers have retained the traditional architectural memory and rural atmosphere while using modern design techniques such as incorporating rammed earth walls as decorative elements and carrying out demolition and renovation work on the original site. These measures can present the "rural memories" to different groups of people, and enable them to rediscover their childhood memories and feelings in Wangxuli.

3. Tap into characteristic tourism resources

Baihua Village fully explores regional characteristics, gives full play to resource advantages, and actively explores the economic development model of "rural tourism + homestay + characteristic agricultural products industry". It has developed cultural tourism projects such as Baihua Valley Sendong Mountain Outdoor Sports Complex and Jintang Lake Sendong Water World Outdoor Sports Complex; upgraded scenic spots such as Baimaling, Jintang Lake Wetland Park, Wangling Glass Plank Road and Baihua Tea Valley; and set up rural tourism experience projects such as rural bonfires, wild fruit picking, creek fishing, trail running in the mountain, etc., so as to continue to extend and improve the industrial chain, and promote the integration of leisure homestays and rural tourism for the advancement of a new development pattern.

4. Develop characteristic farming industries

On the one hand, Baihua Village, based on the characteristics of the mountainous area, actively takes the cultivation and improvement of tea and wild vegetables as the focus of exploring and protecting excellent farming culture. Meanwhile, the village also builds a village history museum as a platform to protect and display traditional agricultural skills, shows its superior natural environment and traditional rural characteristics, and successfully creates the regional characteristic brands of Baihua vegetables and tea. On the other hand, tapping into the theme of tea culture, the village vigorously develops the children's study market, cooperates with professional

study teams to develop customized study courses, does a good job in telling tea stories, holds tea culture tourism festivals, and promotes integrated development of tea, culture and tourism.

Results

Baihua Village has developed and renovated 350 *mu* (one *mu* is approximately equal to 666.67 square meters) of high-quality tea gardens, developed more than 700 *mu* of local specialty Baihua vegetables, cultivated about 20 *mu* of Baihua seedlings, established six agricultural professional cooperatives, and helped more than 120 households which used to be poor shake off poverty. Since the launch of rural tourism, Baihua Village has registered nearly 500,000 tourist visits. The village's collective income reached 607,700 yuan in 2021, 1.388 million yuan in 2022, and 5.1786 million yuan in 2023. On January 13, 2024, the first "Shareholding Economic Cooperative Income Dividend Conference in Baihua Village, Tangchi Town" was held, and 123,800 yuan was earmarked to be distributed as dividends among the masses, allowing the masses to share the dividends of the village collective economic development and enabling them to feel a sense of gains and happiness.

Baihua Village has successively won the honorary titles of National Forest Village, National Key Village for Rural Tourism Development, National Rural Governance Demonstration Village, one of the first batch of characteristic tourism villages of Anhui Province, Anhui Province Rural Revitalization Demonstration Village, Anhui Province Beautiful and Livable Village, and Anhui Province's "Characteristic Food Village".

Experiences and Inspirations

1. Take advantage of local conditions

Baihua Village makes full use of the original style of the village, maintains the rural characteristics, leverages the "homestay + headquarters economy" operation model as the "key to development" to revitalize idle houses and homesteads in the village, endeavors to win rural revitalization connection funds, and adopts the "Shaojian-Wangxuli" brand for rural operations. The first, second, and third phases of Wangxuli homestay projects have been completed and successfully leased and operated. The rural resource advantages and ecological advantages have been successfully transformed into economic advantages and development advantages, which empowers the wonderful "butterfly change" of a small mountain village on the road to rural revitalization.

2. Promote common prosperity

The boutique homestay "Shaojian-Wangxuli" provides jobs for local villagers and actively mobilizes villagers to become "suppliers" of the hotel, offering special souvenir products such as tea, cauliflower, and organic agricultural products; fresh amaranth, leeks, Baihua Vegetables, pepper, eggplant, free range chicken, and live fish have also become authentic mountain village delicacies on the hotel table. Besides, the hotel management company's operating team leverages local agricultural specialties, makes Baihua Vegetable into dumplings, and runs Hefei Xiangjiao Dumpling Food Co., Ltd., which greatly promotes the sales of agricultural and sideline products in the village and attracts more young people to return to their hometowns to start business.

3. Promote the integrated development of agriculture through tourism

With tourism at the core, Baihua Village links up agriculture and farmers, enabling farmers to directly engage in tourism product production and provide rural tourism services. In addition to leasing and storing farmers' houses for reconstruction and renovation, and developing homestays, Baihua Village has developed industries such as "Baihua Family" and "Tea Fragrance Valley Tea Cooperative" based on local agricultural specialties. The organic integration of agriculture and tourism jointly promotes rural economic growth.

Plans

Baihua Village closely focuses on the integration of agriculture and tourism, building up a layout of coordinated development of multiple industries such as leisure agriculture, cultural tourism, catering and accommodation. The village integrates the concept of "harmony" throughout the entire process and in all aspects of promoting rural modernization, striving to create a livable and beautiful countryside that highlights the charm of Anhui. Firstly, it is to add innovative elements. With the rise of demand for diversified experiences in rural tourism, especially

higher requirements for the safety performance of public facilities such as parent-child parks, it is necessary to innovate rural tourism carriers to prevent rural tourism from becoming a one-day tour or a one-time tour. Secondly, it is to actively build tea-themed tourism products, launch tea culture-themed tourism routes, promote the inheritance and innovation of tea culture, and enhance the potential of rural tourism. Thirdly, it is to continue to encourage the masses to develop household-based homestays and provide tourists with multi-type, cost-efficient and characteristic rural accommodation experiences. Baihua Village will continue to uphold the integrated development concept, and use green ecology, architectural art, agricultural tea gardens and other elements to promote the transformation and upgrading of rural tourism so that tourists can enjoy more than sightseeing as they can have leisure activities and in-depth experiences, too. As thus, efforts are made to keep empowering rural revitalization.

海南省五指山市水满乡水满村（方诺寨）：

茶文农旅融合蝶变美丽乡村

摘 要

海南省五指山市水满乡水满村（当地黎族方言也称"方诺寨"）美丽乡村项目以"政府+村委会+企业+农户"的利益联结模式实施投资建设及运营。三年来，水满村以水满古村1个村落旧址和水满上村、水满下村、新民村3个村庄为基点，依托独特的生态资源、民俗资源和产业资源，打造了雨林黎家民宿、田园民宿、雨林野奢木屋酒店、雨林氧吧露营、山盟梯田、山泉梯田、观光茶园、水满河溯溪画廊、雨林瀑布探险等10多个乡村旅游精品项目，建成2000亩茶叶、石斛、兰花、山兰稻等规模化、标准化农产品基地和1000多平方米的自动化茶厂，开发了"雨林生态红茶""野谷山泉米""石斛红茶"等特色农产品，成为闻名省内外的乡村旅游打卡胜地，走出了一条水满村的特色乡村振兴之路。

挑战与问题

水满村位于五指山市水满乡南部,紧邻五指山山脚,地处海南热带雨林国家公园核心圈,是海南省海拔最高、环境最优、生态最佳的村庄。水满村规划总面积4111.2亩,规划范围内共有4个自然村和1个水满古峒旧址,乡村建设用地约124.2亩,人口约468人,其中黎族人口约占80%,少量苗族和汉族。

水满村拥有茂密的原始雨林、壮观的山谷梯田、清澈的山泉河谷以及富含高密度负氧离子的优质空气。其位于稀缺的避暑长寿海拔区域,拥有神奇的黎族部落历史沿革。此外,村内还种植了优质的大叶红茶,并承载着深厚的黎苗文化底蕴。水满村虽然拥有得天独厚的资源优势,但长期缺乏统一的规划建设及运营,人们对"绿水青山就是金山银山"的认识不足,忽略了对原生态的保护。当前,乡村建设的推进需要政府、村委、村民和企业之间达成共识,解决产业培育过程中规模化发展及生态保护之间的矛盾。这些问题都是水满村在快速发展壮大之路上亟待解决的关键挑战。

措施

1. 政府主导,统一规划及指导建设

水满村美丽乡村项目在五指山市政府的主导下开展实施,引入海南百强企业富山集团,采用政府规划、企业投资、村委联合的合作方式进行建设。《水满村美丽乡村建设规划方案》被纳入市政府重点项目范畴,得到了政府层面的高度重视和政策支持,该方案旨在将市、乡、村、企等各级主体连成一体,统一理念,统一建设,共同推进项目发展。针对水满村的整村风貌改造,五指山市政府制定了方案及政策措施,由乡政府负责具体实施,通过"政府专项资金+企业自筹资金"的资金筹措模式,对乡村风貌进行了大规模的改造升级,确保了项目的顺利推进。

2. 利益联结，村企合作多维度开发

水满村采用"企业＋农户＋村集体"的合作模式，构建了利益共享、合作共赢、抱团共建的利益联结机制，共同致力于打造水满村美丽乡村的农文茶旅产业品牌矩阵。在此模式下，村民贡献出农田、林地及闲置房屋，村委会则利用荒弃校舍等闲置资源与企业合作，实现了资源的有效转化与利用。荒田变美景，空房变酒店，废弃的学校变研学基地，密林变树屋民宿……建成并运营了"山盟婚礼""山泉梯田""田园农舍民宿""雨林黎家村舍民宿"等项目。同时，水满村还建设了乡村旅游接待中心、服务驿站、雨林餐厅、雨林研学基地、雨林咖啡馆、雨林茶屋、雨林书屋、生态停车场等旅游配套设施。

3. 立足生态，打造乡村旅游目的地

水满村立足本村独特的生态资源，以热带雨林生态为主题，以田园生态为基底，以绿色产业为主导，以特色村寨为亮点，以农旅共享为目标，秉持"敬畏大自然，恢复原生态"的原则，开发了特色农田庄园、特色雨林民宿、雨林秘境露营、森林康养、研学旅行、亲子农耕体验等农文旅融合项目，构建了"农业＋旅游＋康养＋度假＋文创＋研学"的产业体系，让游客体验回归自然的黎族乡村生活，在天然氧吧中享受独特的康养之旅，打造"宜农、宜游、宜养、宜学、宜业"五位一体的热带雨林特色主题乡村旅游目的地。

4. 聚焦地标特色，全力打造五指山红茶品牌

水满村充分挖掘农业资源优势，大力发展远近闻名的地理标志产品"五指山红茶"：一是与农户合作，扩建大叶红茶标准化种植园近2000亩；二是与政府联合，共建海南第一个自动化制茶厂，可年产红茶3万千克以上，产品远销海内外。此外，水满村充分利用森林资源，大力发展林下经济，种植金钗石斛100余亩、兰花30余亩；同时租赁并有效管理了被农户废弃长达8年的138亩基本农田，恢复了当地特色水稻的种植，山兰米年产量达2.5万余千克。

成效

水满村发生了翻天覆地的变化，由一个默默无闻的黎族山寨，一跃成为全国知名的网红文旅小镇。2023年，水满村村集体经济收入达500多万元，与2020年相比增长了15倍；年游客接待量近30万人次，带动旅游总收入3000多万元。全村86%的村民投身于茶叶种植、槟榔种植、餐饮、山兰酒酿造及南药种植等产业。其中，五指山红茶产业农户人均年创收1.5万元，占全村产业收入的42%；槟榔产业人均年创收1.1万元，占全村产业收入的31%；农户人均可支配收入达65000多元，较2020年增长了35%。水满村与农户签订茶园合作协议、土地流转协议、基本农田租赁协议，每年农户能从土地租金中获得超过200万元的稳定收入。

经验与启示

1. 坚持共享理念

采用租赁、联营、入股、使用权经营权流转等多种共享方式，构建"公司＋农户＋村集体＋合作社"的利益联结方式，有效解决农户的顾虑，充分调动当地农户的积极性。农户通过农田合作获得租金，并额外获得再就业带来的劳务收入；在民房合作中，农户不仅获得股权，还实现了就业并享有提成收入等。这些合作模式确保农民切实分享了实质性的共享利益，农民参与的共享项目收入在农庄总收入中的占比超过38%。

2. 坚持品牌引领

水满村选定了最具潜力的农产品作为其主要推广的四大创意品牌 IP，分别是红茶、山兰米、野菜和雨林康养民宿。以品牌 IP 的塑造为核心驱动力，水满村申请并注册了"水满村"商标，并构建了全面的品牌视觉识别（Visual Identity, VI）系统，为水满村的核心产品打造具有地域特色的视觉标识系统，涵盖基地标识设计、产品包装定制、宣传画册编制以及电商平台页面优化等。以品牌 IP 为带动，充分发挥农庄创业创新平台的作用，赋能小微农人和返乡青年创业，打造水满新农人创业孵化基地和众创空间，建立共享直播、电商培训、技术培训、共享客服、公共展厅、共享前置仓等平台，为传统农人打开一扇互联网之窗。

3. 坚持生态打底

水满村依托森林、河流、山水、梯田、气候五大资源优势，深度挖掘富有雨林特色的自然文化，将"藏在深山无人知"的得天独厚的优势资源，塑造成自然学校、雨林研学基地、雨林探险基地、兰花幽谷、雨林康养等精品旅游线路，以生态为基底赋能文旅产业，打造"全庄、全域、全季"旅游新模式，大大提升了"诺寨何处、水满河谷"的知名度和影响力。

4. 坚持数字赋能

水满村通过打造数字化平台，实现农文旅三大板块智慧管理与服务。开发"携一码，游水满"数字平台，通过扫一码，实现生产过程管理与监控、农产品质量溯源、农产品电商交易；实现农耕田作一码知、加工包装一码知、营销交易一码办、预订游览一码办、雨林康养一码游、雨林黎家一码游。

5. 坚持民俗特色

一是依托水满黎族民俗文化，按照雨林黎家、千年古峒的 IP 定位，通过恢复重现黎家风情民俗，展示黎家村寨传统美食，留住黎家小山村的乡愁记忆，建成黎妈田园、黎家风情街、黎家风情民宿、黎家洞房、黎家美食街、黎家剧场、黎陶坊、黎锦坊、黎祖神鼓、黎母仙锣等多个汇集当地民俗风情的经典黎族民俗文旅项目。二是打造"雨林狂欢节""雨林戏瀑节""黎家购物节""黎家美食节"等节庆活动，让游客充分体验雨林文化和黎族民俗文化，打造"娱游乡村"。

下一步计划

未来五年，水满村将按照"绿水青山就是金山银山"理念，秉持"生态产业化，产业生态化"的建设原则，再追加 2 亿元投资，用三年时间，全面完成雨林黎家民宿、雨林康养、农业休闲观光、农耕体验、国家森林动物园、国家森林植物园、儿童公园、雨林研学、雨林探险、黎俗风情演绎、黎陶坊、黎家商业街、夜经济、旅拍网红打卡点、稻田山盟婚礼、黎哥大鼓、黎婆仙锣、观山台、溯溪咖啡、趣味漂流等乡村旅游设施建设，挖掘雨林文化，讲好乡村故事，写好联农文章，建好一流景区，实现水满村转型升级和将其打造成为最具特色、全省一流的热带雨林三产融合标杆项目。

Shuiman Village (Fangnuozhai), Shuiman Township, Wuzhishan City, Hainan Province:
The Integration of Tea Culture, Agriculture, and Tourism Transforms the Countryside

Abstract

The beautiful countryside project of Shuiman Village, Shuiman Township, Wuzhishan City, Hainan Province ("Fangnuozhai" in the local Li dialect) is invested in and implemented through the interest linkage model of "government + village committee + enterprise + farmers". Over the past three years, Shuiman Village has used the site of the ancient Shuiman Village and the three villages of Shuiman Upper Village, Shuiman Lower Village and Xinmin Village as the bases; launched more than 10 high-quality rural tourism projects, including Rainforest Lijia B&B, Pastoral B&B, Rainforest Wild Luxury Wooden House Hotel, Rainforest Oxygen Bar Camping, Shanmeng Terraces, Mountain Spring Terraces, Sightseeing Tea Garden, Water-Brimming Creek Gallery and Rainforest Waterfall Adventure by relying on its unique ecological resources, folk resources and industrial resources; built 2,000 *mu* large-scale and standardized agricultural product bases of tea, dendrobium, orchid, and Shanlan rice among other agricultural products, and an automated tea factory of more than 1,000 square meters; and developed specialty agricultural products such as "Rainforest Ecological Black Tea", "Wild Valley Spring Rice", and "Dendrobium Black Tea", becoming a well-known rural tourism destination. In a word, Shuiman Village has embarked on a distinctive rural revitalization path.

Challenges and Problems

Shuiman Village is located in the south of Shuiman Township, Wuzhishan City, at the foot of Wuzhi Mountain, in the core circle of the National Tropical Rainforest Park. It is the village with the highest altitude, the best environment and the best ecology in Hainan Province. The total planned area of Shuiman Village is 4111.2 *mu*. There are four natural villages and one Shuiman Gudong Site within the planned scope. The rural construction land covers about 124.2 *mu*. The population is about 468, of which the Li population accounts for about 80%, and there are a small number of Miao and Han people.

Shuiman Village has lush primitive rainforests, beautiful valley terraces, high-quality mountain springs and valleys, excellent air rich in high-density negative oxygen ions. Located at a scarce summer resort and longevity altitude, it has a magical history of Li ethnic tribe. In addition, the village has planted high-quality large-leaf black tea and bears a profound Li and Miao cultural heritage. Although Shuiman Village has unique resource advantages, it has long been lack of unified planning, construction and operation. Local people have insufficient understanding about "lucid waters and lush mountains are invaluable assets" and have neglected the protection of the original ecology. At present, rural construction requires the government, village committees, villagers and enterprises to reach a consensus, and industrial cultivation needs to solve the contradiction between large-scale development and ecological protection. These are the challenges and problems that Shuiman Village faces in the process of rapid development and growth.

Measures

1. Government-led, unified planning and construction guidance

The beautiful countryside project of Shuiman Village was carried out under the guidance of the Wuzhishan Municipal Government, with the introduction of Fushan Group, one of the top 100 enterprises in Hainan. It was built through a cooperative approach of government planning, enterprise investment, and village committee collaboration. The *Shuiman Village Beautiful Countryside Construction Planning Scheme* was included in the key projects of the municipal government, which supported the project construction by offering policy preferences. The city, township, village, enterprise and entities at other levels were integrated for unified conception and construction. In response to the transformation of the entire Shuiman Village, the Wuzhishan Municipal Government issued plans and policies, which were implemented by the township government through the model of "government special funds + enterprise self-raised funds". The rural landscape was greatly transformed to ensure the smooth progress of the project.

2. Benefit linkage, and multi-dimensional development via village-enterprise cooperation

Shuiman Village adopts the model of "enterprise + farmers + village collective", promotes the benefit linkage mechanism of benefit sharing, win-win cooperation, and joint construction, and is committed to creating a "brand matrix" for the beautiful rural agricultural, cultural, tea and tourism industries in Shuiman Village. The villagers cooperate with enterprises with farmland, forest land, and idle houses, and the village committee cooperates with enterprises with idle resources such as abandoned school buildings. In result the wasteland becomes beautiful scenery, the empty rooms become hotels, the schools turn into study tour bases, and the dense forests become tree house homestays. The "Shanmeng Wedding", "Mountain Spring Terraces", "Rural Farmhouse Homestays", "Rainforest Lijia Village Homestays" and other projects have been built and operated. Meanwhile, the rural tourism reception centers, service stations, rainforest restaurants, rainforest study tour bases, rainforest cafes, rainforest tea houses, rainforest bookstores, ecological parking lots and other tourism supporting facilities have been built.

3. Creation of an eco-friendly rural tourism destination

Shuiman Village on the strength of its unique ecological resources takes tropical rainforest ecology as the theme, rural ecology as the basis, green industry as the leading factor, characteristic villages as the feature, and agricultural tourism sharing as the goal. Upholding the principle of "respecting nature and restoring the original ecology", it develops agricultural, cultural and tourism integration projects such as characteristic farmland manors, characteristic rainforest homestays, rainforest secret camping, forest healthcare, study tours, and parent-child farming experiences; builds an industrial system of "agriculture + tourism + healthcare + vacation + cultural creation + study", enabling

tourists to experience the return to the natural Li rural life, and feel a different healthcare paradise in the natural oxygen bar; and creates a five-in-one tropical rainforest characteristic themed rural tourism destination suitable for agriculture, tourism, healthcare, study, and work.

4. Concentration on developing the GI product Wuzhishan black tea

Shuiman Village fully exploits its advantageous agricultural resources and vigorously develops the well-known geographical indication (GI) product Wuzhishan black tea. Firstly, it cooperates with farmers to expand the standardized plantation of large-leaf black tea by nearly 2,000 *mu*. Secondly, it cooperates with the government to build Hainan's first automated tea factory with an annual capacity of more than 30,000 kilograms of black tea, and its products are sold at home and abroad. In addition, Shuiman Village makes full use of forest resources and vigorously develops the forest economy, planting more than 100 *mu* of Dendrobium candidum and more than 30 *mu* of orchids; it leases and revitalizes 138 *mu* of basic farmland that has been abandoned by farmers for eight years, and resumes planting local specialty rice, with an annual output of more than 25,000 kilograms of Shanlan rice.

Results

Shuiman Village has undergone tremendous changes. It has transformed from an unknown Li village to a nationally renowned cultural and tourism town and a frequently mentioned place on Internet. In 2023, the village collective income stood at more than 5 million yuan, a 15-fold increase from 2020; it registered an annual number of tourists of nearly 300,000 and a total income of more than 30 million yuan. About 86% of the local villagers develop industries such as tea planting, betel nut planting, catering, Shanlan rice wine brewing and southern medicine planting. Among them, the per capita annual income of the farmers engaging in the Wuzhishan black tea industry is 15,000 yuan; the income in this regard accounts for 42% of the village's industrial income; the per capita annual income of those engaging in the betel nut industry is 11,000 yuan, the income in this regard accounts for 31% of the village's industrial income; the per capita disposable income of farmers is more than 65,000 yuan, an increase of 35% from 2020. Shuiman Village has signed tea garden cooperation agreements, land transfer agreements, and basic farmland leasing agreements with farmers, and the annual land rental income of farmers can reach more than 2 million yuan.

Experiences and Inspirations

1. Adhere to the concept of "sharing"

Shuiman Village uses a variety of sharing methods such as leasing, joint operation, equity investment, and transfers of use rights and operating rights to build a benefit connection mode involving "company + farmers + village collectives + cooperatives", effectively addresses farmers' concerns, and fully mobilizes the enthusiasm of local farmers. Farmers use farmland for cooperation to obtain rent and earn labor income from re-employment; farmers who cooperate with their private houses obtain equity while earning additional job income and commission income, etc. Each model also allows farmers to truly share visible and tangible dividends. The income from shared projects in which farmers participate accounts for more than 38% of the total income of the village.

2. Adhere to "brand" first

Shuiman Village selected the most promising agricultural products as the four main creative brand IPs: black tea, Shanlan rice, wild vegetables and rainforest healthcare homestay. Guided by the creation of brand IPs, the village has applied for registration of the "Shuiman Village" trademark; established a brand VI system; and built a regional visual identification system for Shuiman Village's knockout products, covering the base logos, product packaging, brochures, e-commerce pages, etc. Driven by brand IPs, the village gives full play to role of its entrepreneurship and innovation platforms; enables small and micro farm operators and returned youth to start business; builds up the Shuiman New Farmer Entrepreneurship Incubation Base and Public Innovation Space; establishes shared live broadcast, e-commerce training, technical training, shared customer service, public exhibition halls, shared forward warehouses and other platforms; and thus opens an Internet window for traditional farmers.

3. Adhere to the "ecological" basis

Relying on the five major resource advantages of forests, rivers, mountainous landscape, terraces, and climate, Shuiman Village deeply explores the natural culture with rainforest characteristics, and converts the unique advantages of "being hidden in the mountains" into high-quality tourism routes along nature schools, rainforest study bases, rainforest adventure bases, orchid valleys, and rainforest healthcare centers. It empowers the cultural and tourism industry with ecology as the foundation, and creates a new tourism model covering the "whole village, whole region, and all seasons", which greatly

enhances the popularity and influence of the village's tourism resources.

4. Adhere to "digital" empowerment

Shuiman Village has achieved intelligent management and service functions for the three major sectors of agriculture, culture and tourism through the construction of a digital platform, developed a digital platform to enable visitors to travel around Shuiman with one code, to realize production process management and monitoring, ensure agricultural product quality traceability, and conduct agricultural product e-commerce transactions by scanning a code; to know about farming, processing and packaging, to conduct marketing transactions, to book tours, to travel in the rainforest for healthcare and to visit the Lijia with one code.

5. Adhere to the local folk customs

Firstly, relying on Shuiman's "Li folk culture", in accordance with the IP positioning of the rainforest Lijia and the long-time Gudong, by restoring and reproducing the Lijia folk customs, displaying the traditional food of the Lijia mountain village, and keeping memory about the Lijia small mountain village, the Li Mom Farm, Lijia Customs Street, Lijia B&B, Lijia Bridal Chamber, Lijia Food Street, Lijia Theater, Li Pottery Workshop, Li Brocade Workshop, Li Ancestor God Drum, Li Mother Fairy Gong and many other classic Li folk cultural tourism projects that bring together local folk customs have been developed. Secondly, it is to launch the "Rainforest Carnival", "Rainforest Waterfall Festival", "Lijia Shopping Festival" and the "Lijia Food Festival" among other festive activities, enabling tourists to fully experience the rainforest culture and Li folk culture and enjoy much fun.

Plans

In the next five years, Shuiman Village will uphold the concept that "lucid waters and lush mountains are invaluable assets", adhere to the construction principle of "ecological industrialization and industrial ecology", and make an additional investment of 200 million yuan. In three years, it will fully complete the construction of rainforest Li homestays, rainforest healthcare, agricultural leisure and sightseeing, farming experience, National Forest Zoo, National Forest Botanical Garden, Children's Park, rainforest study, rainforest adventure, Li customs demonstration, Li pottery workshop, Lijia commercial street, night economy, photogenic spots, rice field "Shanmeng" (eternal love) wedding, Li brother drum, Li Po fairy gong, mountain viewing platform, stream tracing coffee, fun rafting and other rural tourism facilities, explore rainforest culture, do a good job in telling rural stories, write good articles about working with farmers, build a first-class scenic spot, realize the transformation and upgrading of Shuiman Village and make it the most distinctive and first-class benchmark project for the integration of the three industries in the province.

浙江旅游职业学院：
共富学院助推山区海岛县乡村振兴

摘　要

山区海岛县是浙江高质量发展建设共同富裕示范区的重要场景，其发展事关共同富裕示范区建设全局。文化产业和旅游业既是山区富民增收的主渠道，也是精神富裕的主动力。浙江旅游职业学院锚定"11519"行动目标（成立 1 个山区海岛县共同富裕学院、开展 100 项精准服务、实施 500 名教师助力计划、落实 1000 人次乡村管理者培训、完成 9000 人次专业培训），充分发挥学院人才、平台、资源、行业优势，成立山区海岛县共富学院，组建教授专家服务团队，实施万人培训计划，在服务项目、人才建设、工作机制上取得良好成效，形成了高校助推山区 26 县共同富裕的"浙旅模式"。

挑战与问题

山区海岛县,包括杭州市淳安县,温州市洞头区、永嘉县、平阳县、苍南县、文成县、泰顺县,金华市武义县、磐安县,衢州市、舟山市、丽水市所辖县区,台州市玉环市、天台县、仙居县、三门县等32个县(市、区),占浙江省行政区划约35.6%;县域总面积达4.8万平方千米,占全省区域总面积45.5%。山区海岛县乡村资源十分丰富,但产业转化相对不足、经济基础相对薄弱、人才流失相对严重,文化和旅游业高质量发展对推进山海协作、促进乡村振兴,缩小地区差距、城乡差距,实现浙江省共同富裕示范区建设具有重要意义。

措施

1. 成立共富学院,建立校地合作新机制

为确保助力山区海岛县共同富裕工作,浙江旅游职业学院有组织、有方向、有聚焦地采取措施,举全校之力,整合资源,在全省范围内率先成立"山区海岛县共同富裕学院",并在山区海岛各县分别设立共同富裕服务站。共富学院协调校地合作,推动项目发展,落实具体举措,夯实了助力共同富裕工作的组织基础。此外,共富学院还建立了"二级学院+专家团+团委+共富单元"的结对共建制度,即一个学院对接一个专家团所联系的山区县,开展师生社会实践等活动。

2. 组建专家服务团队,构建智力助富新模式

为精准助力山区海岛县文旅高质量发展,学校组建教授专家服务团,高起点、高标准、高质量指导地方发展。学校组建9支服务团队,由校领导挂帅,每个团队配备数名教授专家、行业能手,每个团牵头助力3至4个山区海岛县。专家团充分发挥专业优势,深入一线问诊把脉地方文旅发展,形成26个文旅发展报告,编写淳安县高品质饭店划分标准,指导姜家5A级景区镇、华西村4A级景区、灵鹫山国家旅游度假区的创建工作等。

3. 实施万人培训计划，探索技能人才培养新路径

为解决制约山区海岛县文旅发展人才短缺的问题，学校发挥教学培训优势，推出万人培训计划。组织山区海岛县400名中职教师开展成长培训计划，举办1000人次以上的乡村旅游运营与管理培训班，完成9000人次以上的景区村镇建设、乡村餐饮、新媒体与直播带货、品牌创建、服务礼仪与技能提升等业务培训班，全面夯实人才基础。

成效

经过持续探索和实践，学校针对性制定了助力山区海岛县共同富裕学院工作制度以及干部教师挂职、中高职衔接、师生社会服务和社会实践、业务人员培训、科研成果转化等工作方案。浙江旅游职业学院为服务山区海岛县"微改造、精提升"工作，累计共派出121支师生团队，团队成员700余名。"送教下乡"培训针对山区26县共安排41门课，派出教师30余名，培训人数超4000余人次。完成文化和旅游管理人员（从业人员）培训项目、景区创建和全域旅游发展等咨询指导项目30余项，充分发挥旅院师生的专业水平和职业素养，助力乡村振兴。

经验与启示

1. 以制度建设为依托，建立常态化运行机制

学校以助力山区海岛县工作领导小组为统领，健全共富学院、专家团、二级学院工作制度，完善工作流程，把工作例会、报告报备、沟通协调、结对共建、简报专报、成果转化六大制度落到各组织、各负责人上，使专家团、职能部门、二级学院明确自己的任务分工，使助力山区海岛县各项工作有章可循、有制可依。共富学院做好整项工作任务的组织保障、资金支持，以保障制度建设为核心，建立全方位综合服务机制。

2. 以专家团队为中枢，建立校地高效联动机制

学校推动以专家团为核心的工作机制建设，建立与地方、学校多元联动的常态化机制。专家团队一方面在共富一线走访调研、反馈需求、帮扶项目实施落实；另一方面联系学校职能部门、二级学院，作为桥梁纽带实现多方联动。

下一步计划

浙江旅游职业学院将聚焦"两个先行"奋斗目标，贯彻落实浙江省人民政府《关于推进文化和旅游产业深度融合高质量发展的实施意见》，进一步发挥学校特色优势，按照山区海岛县所需所盼，持续聚力构建助力山区共富五大工作体系：一是聚焦发展成效，完善助力山区海岛县共富学院常态化运行机制；二是聚焦发展主题，探索一县一主题活动，形成特色鲜明共建主题，系统推动校地合作深度开展；三是聚焦发展平台，打造共富工作站，依托乡村文旅振兴博士或大师流动平台，在地方美食发掘、非遗传承与保护、文旅项目指导等方面，探索文旅融合中的产业升级路径；四是聚焦发展路径，创新项目指导培育方式方法，推动产学研一体化发展，助力地方实施产品创牌、环境创优、文化创新、运营创效和模式创造行动；五是聚焦发展支撑，强化行业人才培养培训，增强山区海岛县文旅发展动能。

2024 世界旅游联盟：旅游助力乡村振兴案例（中英文双语版）
WTA Best Practices of Rural Revitalization through Tourism 2024 (Chinese-English Bilingual Edition)

Tourism College of Zhejiang:
The School for Common Prosperity Promotes Rural Revitalization in Mountainous Island Counties

Abstract

The mountainous island countries are important places for high-quality development and construction of a demonstration zone for common prosperity in Zhejiang Province, and their development concerns the overall construction of a demonstration zone for common prosperity. The cultural industry and the tourism industry are not only the main channels for enabling the people in mountainous areas to get rich by increasing their income, but also the main driving force for enriching their cultural life. The Tourism College of Zhejiang sets forth the "11519" action goals (establishing a school for common prosperity in mountainous island counties, providing 100 targeted services, implementing a plan to support 500 teachers, conducting training among 1,000 rural managers and completing professional training for 9,000 people); gives full play to the college's strengths in talents, platforms, resources, and the industry; establishes the School for Common Prosperity in mountainous island counties; builds a service team of professors and experts; and implements a 10,000-person training program. Good results have been achieved in service projects, talent development, and work mechanisms, and a "Zhejiang Tourism Model" in which the college promotes the common prosperity of 26 counties in mountainous areas has taken form.

Challenges and Problems

The altogether 32 mountainous island counties (cities, districts) include Chun'an County of Hangzhou City; Dongtou District, Yongjia County, Pingyang County, Cangnan County, Wencheng County, Taishun County of Wenzhou City; Wuyi County and Pan'an County of Jinhua City; the counties and districts under the jurisdiction of Quzhou City, Zhoushan City and Lishui City; Yuhuan City, Tiantai County, Xianju County and Sanmen County of Taizhou City, accounting for about 35.6% of the zone under the jurisdiction of Zhejiang Province; the counties have a total area of 48,000 square kilometers, accounting for 45.5% of the total area of the province. Mountainous island counties are rich in rural resources, but industrial transformation is relatively inadequate, the economic foundation is relatively weak, and the drain of talent is serious. Under such circumstances the high-quality development of culture and tourism is of great significance to promoting cooperation between mountainous areas and coastal areas, enhancing rural revitalization, narrowing regional and urban-rural gaps, and realizing the construction of a demonstration zone for common prosperity in Zhejiang Province.

Measures

1. Establish a College of Common Prosperity and a new mechanism of cooperation between the school and the locality

In order to ensure that the work of helping mountainous island counties to achieve common prosperity is well-organized, targeted, and focused, the college has gone all out and integrated resources to take the lead in establishing the "School for Common Prosperity in Mountainous Island Counties" in the province, and set up common prosperity service stations in various mountainous island counties. The

School for Common Prosperity coordinates school-locality cooperation, promotes project development, implements specific measures, and consolidates the organizational foundation conducive to common prosperity. At the same time, the School for Common Prosperity has established a pairing co-construction system made up of the "secondary colleges + expert groups + Youth League Committee + common prosperity units": one secondary college pairs with one mountainous county contacted by an expert group to carry out social practice and other activities involving teachers and students.

2. Establish an expert service team and build a new model of intellectual assistance

In order to provide targeted assistance to promote the high-quality development of cultural tourism in mountainous island counties, the school has established a professor and expert service team to guide local development with a high starting point, high standards and high quality. The school has established nine service teams led by school leaders. Each team has several professors, experts and leaders of the industry. Each team takes the lead in assisting three to four mountainous and island counties. The expert team gave full play to its expertise, went deep into the front line to investigate into the development of local cultural tourism, wrote up 26 cultural tourism development reports, compiled the classification standards for high-quality hotels in Chun'an County, and guided the creation of Jiangjia 5A-level scenic town, Huaxi Village 4A-level scenic spot, and Lingjiu Mountain National Tourism Resort.

3. Implement a 10,000-person training plan and explore new paths for cultivating skilled personnel

In order to address the bottleneck of talent shortage for the development of cultural tourism in mountainous counties, the school has given play to its teaching and training strengths and launched a

10,000-person training plan. It has organized 400 secondary vocational school teachers in mountainous counties to join in the growth training plans, held rural tourism operation and management training sessions involving more than 1,000 people, and offered more than 9,000 business training courses on scenic village and town construction, rural catering, new media and live streaming, brand creation, service etiquette and skills improvement, etc., to comprehensively consolidate the talent base.

Results

After continuous exploration and practice, the school has formulated targeted work systems to help mountainous island counties achieve common prosperity as well as work plans concerning temporary appointments of officials and teachers, connection between secondary and higher vocational education, social service and social practice for teachers and students, business-oriented training, and transformation of scientific research results. The Tourism College of Zhejiang has sent a total of 121 teams of teachers and students with more than 700 members to join in the "micro-transformation and fine improvement" work in mountainous island counties. The "bringing education to the countryside" training arranged a total of 41 courses for 26 counties in mountainous areas, dispatched more than 30 teachers, and trained more than 4,000 people. More than 30 consulting and guidance projects such as training projects for cultural and tourism management personnel (practitioners), scenic spot creation and global tourism development have been completed to give full play to the professional competence of the teachers and students of the Tourism College and thus to help rural revitalization.

Experiences and Inspirations

1. Establish a normalized operation mechanism by relying on system construction

The college is led by the leading group for assisting mountainous and island counties; improves the work system of the School for Common Prosperity, the expert group, and the secondary colleges; improves the work process; and ensures the six major systems of regular work meetings, report filings, communication and coordination, pairing and co-construction, briefings and special reports, and achievement transformation are implemented by specific organizations and persons in charge so that the expert group, functional departments, and

secondary colleges can clarify their own division of tasks and all the work in assisting mountainous and island counties has rules and regulations to follow. The School for Common Prosperity will do a good job in providing organizational guarantee and financial support for all the work and establish a comprehensive service mechanism with the guarantee system construction at the core.

2. Take an efficient linkage mechanism between the school and the locality with the expert team at the hub

The college promotes a working mechanism with the expert group at the core, and has established a normalized mechanism for multiple linkages between the locality and the school. On the one hand, the expert team visits and investigates the front line for common prosperity, reports on needs, and implements assistance projects. On the other hand, it contacts the school's functional departments and secondary colleges to serve as a bridge to achieve multi-party linkage.

Plans

The Tourism College of Zhejiang will focus on the "two-first" goals, implement the *Implementation Opinions on Promoting the Deep Integration and High-quality Development of the Cultural and Tourism Industries* of the People's Government of Zhejiang Province, further give play to its unique strengths, and continue to build five major work systems to help mountainous areas achieve common prosperity in accordance with the needs and expectations of mountainous island counties. Firstly, it is to focus on development results and improve the normal operation mechanism of the school to help mountainous island counties to achieve common prosperity. Secondly, it is to focus on the development theme, explore "one county, one theme" activities, develop distinctive co-construction themes, and systematically promote the in-depth development of school-locality cooperation. Thirdly, it is to focus on development platforms, build a common prosperity workstation, and rely on the rural cultural and tourism revitalization doctors or masters mobility platform to explore the path of industrial upgrading in the integration of culture and tourism in terms of local food discovery, intangible cultural heritage inheritance and protection, and cultural and tourism project guidance. Fourthly, it is to focus on development paths, innovate project guidance and cultivation methods, promote the integrated development of production, education and research, and help local governments implement product branding, strive for excellent environment, conduct cultural innovation, seek higher operational efficiency and implement model creation. Fifthly, it is to focus on development support, strengthen industry talent training, and enhance the cultural and tourism development momentum of mountainous island counties.

山东省济宁市邹城市大洪沟村：
激活沉睡文旅基因，探索乡村振兴新路

摘 要

山东省济宁市邹城市大束镇大洪沟村抓住打造乡村振兴齐鲁样板省级示范区的机遇，引进工商资本，与浙江中图文旅集团合作。大洪沟村采取村集体资产入股、群众资产租赁的模式，盘活了村内70套闲置宅院和周边460余亩低效闲置土地，激活了乡村生态环境、农耕文化、民居文化、民俗节庆等文化旅游资源。村企携手打造了大洪漫谷乡村旅游项目，形成了产业孵化、研学体验、民俗旅游、文化创意等多元旅游业态，实现了村民共创、共享、共富的发展目标，探索出一条大洪沟村农文旅融合发展的乡村振兴新路径。

挑战与问题

大洪沟村北依尼山圣境，南依峄山风景名胜区，村庄依山傍水，地理地貌起伏错落，生态环境绝佳，村内房屋古朴自然。由于村内无产业，大量青壮年外出务工，导致该村"空心化"现象严重，发展主要面临以下问题：一是土地闲置，由于留守老人、儿童较多，加之农耕地土质较差，从事农业生产投入产出低，导致绝大多数土地常年闲置；二是基础设施配套不完善，村庄道路条件较差，大多是砂石路、土路，交通相对闭塞，阻断了村庄与外界的交流和外来资源的引入；三是文化资源有待挖掘，村庄房屋依山而建，呈阶梯状分布，错落有致，具有典型的鲁西南地区乡村民居文化特点，但部分房屋年久失修，无人居住，开发难度较大。

措施

1. 打造特色民俗民宿村

大洪沟村坚持"保护传承传统文化、保留优化原生村貌、形成乡村特色产业"的原则，采取村集体资产入股、群众资产租赁、社会资本引入、专业团队运营的模式，盘活村内70套闲置宅院和周边460余亩低效闲置土地。坚持"一房一品、一院一景"设计理念，利用夯土墙、石块、茅草、木头等中国传统的建筑材料，建设高端民宿、乡风礼堂、艺术创作工坊等功能区，打造具有北方民居和农耕民俗文化特色的民俗民宿村。

2. 开展特色民俗体验项目

大洪沟村发挥优秀传统文化富集优势，深入挖掘孔孟文化、非遗民俗以及农耕文化，一是打造了灵泉春茶、汉服馆、浮生小酒馆、咖啡屋等15个休闲项目；二是建设15个民宿小院；三是建设6幢文创小院作为非遗传承人创作工坊；四是依托农耕种植地打造学农课堂、露营基地、户外拓展等研学基地，开展劳动教育、自然教育、美食制作、非遗手作、户外运动五大类研学课程；五是建设主题乐园，包含高空飞艇、单轨滑车、无动力乐园、越野车等多个游乐项目，为游客提供趣味性休闲体验。

3. 打造节庆活动IP

大洪沟村已经初步形成了"春季桃花节""夏季啤酒节""秋季月圆大洪沟""冬季民俗节"四大系列节庆活动。部分相关的节庆活动已经连续举办三届，单日游客量超过5000人次。节庆活动成为大洪沟村旅游发展的"活力密码"，吸引了大量客流。一年四季不间断的节庆活动提升了大洪沟村旅游热度，让大洪沟村特色主题文化在全年大放光芒，旅游产业的发展持续促进了经济增长。

4. 打造特色共享农庄

大洪沟村积极建设电商基地，一是通过将当地的冬桃、香菇、大枣、小米、芝麻油等农产品，开发成伴手礼产品，以展示、体验、讲解等方式进行产品宣传与销售；二是联合周边的各类果蔬种植基地，将当地沙地冬桃、特小凤西瓜等高档水果，作为山东本土特色农产品销往全国其他地区；三是将猪牙皂、峄山松墨、郭里土陶等农旅融合文创产品推向全国市场，盘活大洪沟村农业资源。

成效

大洪沟村现已经成为"文化民俗体验打卡地""乡村观光打卡地""乡土记忆怀念蓝本"。2023年，大洪沟村旅游接待人数突破50万人次，带动就业1100余人，从一个村集体年收入不到3万元的小村庄发展到现在140万元的突破，实现了村民土地流转有"租金"、房屋入股有"股金"、入园就业有"薪金"、干得好的有"奖金"、年轻人有"五险一金"的共富家园。

经验与启示

1. 盘活闲置资产，空心村变网红村

大洪沟村聚焦城市居民的差异化旅游度假需求，对闲置资源进行保护性开发，充分保留本村特有的环境和山水，在原有村庄肌理上进行翻修和修缮，开发大洪沟系列网红旅游产品，既满足了现代都市人回归自然、放松心灵的需求，又实现了乡村的发展与蝶变。

2. 推动村企共建，局外人变受益者

大洪沟村把维护乡村群众的最大利益作为发展乡村旅游的前提，创新"党支部+合作社+农户"模式，将村内剩余劳动力、闲置土地等资源整合融入产业发展和项目建设，通过固定租金收益、返聘岗位工资以及经营分红等举措，保障村民和村集体的长久收益，让乡村群众成为最大受益者。

下一步计划

一是探索新模式。大洪沟村摸索中国乡村经济发展新模式，计划打造涵盖乡村产业孵化、乡村研学课堂、非遗民俗复活、乡村休闲度假、乡村观光旅游五大主要板块于一体的超级乡村实验地。通过对村庄统一规划、统一招商、统一推广以及整体统一运营，实现年产值3000万元以上的富裕目标。二是丰富新业态。大洪沟村继续完善乡村产业孵化、高端民宿、会员体验等项目，提升农耕研学体验和休闲旅游观光效果，持续丰富拓展整个项目的经营业态，拓宽营收渠道，进一步增强带动强村富民的辐射能力。大洪沟村将持续为乡村振兴探索"大洪沟经验"，实现企业有活力、集体能增收、群众能致富的乡村旅游赋能乡村振兴新路径。

2024 世界旅游联盟：旅游助力乡村振兴案例（中英文双语版）
WTA Best Practices of Rural Revitalization through Tourism 2024 (Chinese-English Bilingual Edition)

Dahonggou Village, Zoucheng City, Jining City, Shandong Province:

Awake Dormant Cultural Tourism Genes and Explore New Paths for Rural Revitalization

Abstract

Dahonggou Village, Dashu Town, Zoucheng City, Jining City, Shandong Province seized the opportunity to build a Qilu provincial demonstration zone for rural revitalization, attracted industrial and commercial capital, and cooperated with Zhejiang Zhongtu Cultural Tourism Group. Dahonggou Village adopted the model of village collective assets investment and mass assets leasing, which brought into use 70 idle houses in the village and more than 460 *mu* of inefficient idle land in the surrounding area, and injected vitality into rural ecological environment, farming culture, folk house culture, folk festivals and other cultural tourism resources. The village and enterprises jointly launched the Dahong Mangu Rural Tourism Project, and developed a diversified tourism industry involving industrial incubation, research and study experience, folk tourism, and cultural creativity, realizing the development goals of villagers' co-creation, sharing, and common prosperity, and exploring a new path for rural revitalization in Dahonggou Village through the integrated development of agriculture, culture, and tourism.

Challenges and Problems

Dahonggou Village leans against the Nishan Holy Land in the north and the Yishan Scenic Area in the south. The village is surrounded by mountains and rivers, with undulating geographical features, excellent ecological environment, and simple houses. However, due to the lack of industry in the village, a large number of young and middle-aged people go out to work, which has led to serious "hollowing out" phenomenon in the village. The development mainly faces the following problems. Firstly, some land is idle. The large number of left-behind elderly people and children coupled with the poor soil quality of agricultural land led to low efficiency of agricultural production and some land staying idle all year round. Secondly, the supporting infrastructure is inadequate. The village road is in poor condition since there are mostly gravel roads and dirt roads of underdeveloped traffic, which hinders the communication between the village and the outside world and the inflow of external resources. Thirdly, cultural resources have yet to be excavated. The village houses are built on the mountains, and scattered in a stepped shape with typical rural residential cultural characteristics in southwestern Shandong. However, some houses have been in disrepair for a long time, dilapidated and uninhabited, making development difficult.

Measures

1. Create a characteristic folk homestay village

Dahonggou Village adheres to the principle of "protecting and inheriting traditional culture, preserving and optimizing the original village appearance, and developing rural characteristic industries". It adopts the model of village collective assets investment, mass assets leasing, social capital attraction, and professional team operation to bring into use the 70 idle houses in the village and more than 460 *mu* of inefficient idle land in the surrounding area. Adhering to the design concept of "one house, one product, one courtyard, one view", and using traditional Chinese building materials such as rammed earth walls, stones, thatch, and wood, the village endeavors to build high-end homestays, rural halls, art creation workshops and other functional areas, to create a folk homestay village with the characteristics of folk houses and farming culture typical of north China.

2. Carry out special folk experience projects

Dahonggou Village takes advantage of its excellent traditional culture and deeply explores Confucian culture, intangible cultural heritage and farming culture. Firstly, it has created 15 leisure projects of Lingquan Spring Tea, Han Dynasty Clothing Museum, Fusheng Bistro, and Coffee House. Secondly, it has built 15 homestay courtyards. Thirdly, it has built 6 cultural and creative courtyards as creative workshops for intangible cultural heritage inheritors. Fourthly, it has built agricultural classrooms, camping bases, outdoor development and other research and study bases on the basis of farming and planting land, and implemented five major research and study courses covering labor education, nature education, food production, intangible cultural heritage handicrafts, and outdoor sports. Fifthly, it has built theme parks, including high-altitude airships, monorails, non-powered parks, cross-country vehicles and other amusement projects to provide tourists with interesting experiences.

3. Create festival IP

Dahonggou Village has initially formed four major series of festivals, namely the "Spring Peach Blossom Festival", "Summer Beer Festival", "Autumn Full Moon Dahonggou" and "Winter Folk Festival". Some related festivals have been held for three consecutive sessions, with more than 5,000 tourists per day. Festivals have become the "vitality code" for the development of tourism in Dahonggou Village, attracting a large number of tourists. The continued festivals throughout the year have increased the popularity of tourism in Dahonggou Village, enabling the characteristic theme culture of Dahonggou Village to shine throughout the year. As thus, tourism continues to promote economic growth.

4. Create a characteristic shared farm

Dahonggou Village vigorously builds an e-commerce base. Firstly, it develops local winter

peaches, mushrooms, jujubes, millet, sesame oil and other agricultural products into souvenirs, and promotes and sells them through display, experience, explanation and other means. Secondly, it cooperates with various fruit and vegetable planting bases in the surrounding area to sell local sandy winter peaches, special small watermelons and other high-end fruits as Shandong characteristic agricultural products throughout the country. Thirdly, it promotes cultural and creative products integrating agriculture and tourism such as the pig tooth soap, Yishan pine ink, Guoli earthenware, etc. across the country, and revitalizes the agricultural resources of Dahonggou Village.

Results

Dahonggou Village has now become a "popular spot for cultural and folk experience", "popular rural tourism spot" and "a model place keeping rural memory". In 2023, the village received more than 500,000 tourists and created more than 1,100 jobs. It has grown from a small village with an annual collective income of less than 30,000 yuan to the current form with an income of 1.4 million yuan; it has built itself into a common prosperity home where villagers earn "rent" for land transfer, "dividends"

for house investment, "salary" for employment in the park, "bonus" for good work; moreover, young people enjoy "five insurances and one fund".

Experiences and Inspirations

1. Use idle assets and turn hollow villages into Internet-famous villages

Dahonggou Village focuses on the differentiated tourism and vacation needs of urban residents, leverages idle resources in a protective manner, fully preserves the village's unique environment and landscape, renovates and repairs the original village texture, and develops a series of Dahonggou internet-famous tourism products, which not only meets the needs of modern urbanites to return to nature and relax their minds, but also realizes the development and transformation of the village.

2. Promote village-enterprise co-construction and benefit outsiders

Dahonggou Village regards safeguarding the greatest interests of rural people as the premise for developing rural tourism, innovates the "Party branch + cooperative + farmer" model, integrating the village's surplus labor, idle land and other resources into industrial development and project construction, and through measures such as paying fixed rental, re-employment wages and operating dividends, it guarantees the long-term benefits of villagers and village collective, making rural people the biggest beneficiaries.

Plans

Firstly, it is to explore new models. Dahonggou

Village is exploring new models for the development of China's rural economy, and plans to create a super rural experimental site that covers five major sectors: rural industry incubation, rural study tour classrooms, the revival of intangible cultural heritage and folk customs, rural leisure and vacation, and rural sightseeing. Through unified planning, unified investment promotion, unified promotion, and overall unified operation of the village, the goal of building a wealthy country with an annual output value of more than 30 million yuan has been fulfilled. Secondly, it is to enrich the forms of business. Dahonggou Village continues to improve projects such as rural industry incubation, high-end homestays, and membership experience; enhance the agricultural research and study experience and leisure tourism and sightseeing effects; enrich and expand the business forms of the entire project; broaden revenue channels; and further enhance the radiation capacity of driving the development of villages and making people rich. Dahonggou Village will continue to explore the "Dahonggou Experience" for rural revitalization, and blaze a new path for rural tourism to empower rural revitalization by injecting vitality into enterprises, and increasing collective income and wealth for the masses.

2024 世界旅游联盟：旅游助力乡村振兴案例（中英文双语版）
WTA Best Practices of Rural Revitalization through Tourism 2024（Chinese-English Bilingual Edition）

河北省衡水市武强县周窝村：
用音乐奏响乡村振兴新乐章

摘　要

　　河北省衡水市武强县周窝村依托该村良好的产业基础和典型北方民居特色，按照"政府主导+市场运作"的模式，以及"一门一景、一户一品、体现灵性、各具特色"的原则，包装改造具有创意特色的民宿、咖啡屋、乐器体验馆等院落80多套，新建周窝音乐体验中心、世界乐器博物馆等场馆，打造了集文化旅游、音乐研学、休闲度假于一体的音乐小镇，用音乐奏响乡村振兴新乐章。

挑战与问题

周窝村位于河北低平原区,土地开阔平坦,属大陆性季风气候,为温带半干旱区。全村共256户959人,居住用房297套。周窝村虽然旅游自然资源相对较为匮乏,但它是河北金音乐器集团有限公司的所在地,这既为周窝村发展乡村旅游带来了机遇,也带来了挑战。一是如何发挥好周窝村在西洋乐器制造产业上的优势,进一步增强乐器制造和音乐产业聚合力,使周窝音乐小镇成为国内外知名的乐器生产、销售集散地和音乐主题文化旅游度假体验基地。二是如何整合周窝村文旅资源,丰富旅游业态,不断提升旅游产品品质,进一步提升周窝音乐小镇音乐旅游场景的独特吸引力。三是如何提升周窝音乐小镇文化旅游运营总体水平,提高运营质量和景区收益,变品牌优势为效益优势。

措施

1. 改造音乐村庄

一是基础设施改造工程。对村庄水、电、路、暖等基础设施进行升级改造,并新建了周窝音乐小镇服务中心、中心敬老院及污水处理厂、垃圾转运站等设施,全村家家户户普及了卫生厕所、健康厨房等。二是环境卫生保洁工程。在建设污水处理厂和垃圾转运站的基础上,购置垃圾箱、卫生转运车、洒水车等保洁设备;成立专职卫生保洁队伍,建立日常清扫和保洁制度,做到垃圾统收统运、日产日清、清扫保洁常态化,坚持软硬结合、双管齐下。三是对小镇民居院落主体、村庄的街角、墙面、电线杆、夜景衬托、绿化美化等进行音乐文化主题包装改造,塑造独具地域特色的音乐文化小镇风貌。

2. 打造音乐基地

周窝村以乡村旅游为突破口,大力发展文化创意产业,由单一从事乐器生产,转向从事音乐教育培训、音乐体验创作、音乐节目制作、音乐纪念品开发、音乐演艺活动、音乐休闲养生等多种业态。一是积极推进乡村旅游创客示范基地建设,完善了资金扶持、人才支持、免费场地、创业补贴等优惠政策,全力打造中国第一个乡村旅游与乐器产业相结合的文化创意旅游基地。二是周窝音乐小镇每年投资1000余万元,扶持音乐人创作、鼓励大学生创业、促进演奏家之间的研学交流,打造了小提琴体验工坊、DIY吉他制作等多个创客孵化器,吸引了国内外众多艺术家、青年人进入周窝音乐小镇创新创业。

3. 举办音乐活动

周窝村通过与中国音乐家协会吉他学会、北大青鸟集团、河北省音乐家协会等文化艺术机构开展合作,组织和承办各类国家级、省级音乐节和音乐活动,提升周窝音乐小镇的"名气、人气和商气",保持其内在动力和持久活力。周窝音乐小镇先后成功举办了中国大学生音乐节、中国吉他文化节、肖邦国际钢琴比赛、河北省管乐展演比赛等多项重大活动,音乐小镇还吸引了青春音乐学院和吉他中国博物馆的入驻,很多音乐人的音乐工作室也落户周窝。

成效

截至2020年，周窝村有乐器生产及加工配套企业近百家、文化创意小微企业百余家，从业人员达3000多人，有效促进了当地农村劳动力就地转移就业，带动了周边西辛庄村、李封庄村等6个村的发展。2023年，周窝音乐小镇吸引游客100万人次，实现旅游收入过亿元，当地村民年人均收入突破3万元。周窝音乐小镇先后被评为全国魅力新农村十佳乡村、全国最美村镇、全国生态文化村、全国乡村旅游重点村和国家4A级旅游景区。

经验与启示

1. 坚持守正创新

周窝村十字街将村庄划分为"和、谐、富、国"4个胡同区，每条胡同都有一个正能量的名字，如和谐、和善、和美、富强、富民、富国等，具有和美乡风的胡同文化影响着一代又一代周窝人。此外，村内还推行了"厕所革命""美丽庭院""星级文明户"等一系列村民们喜闻乐见、各具特色的评选活动，这些活动营造了比理想、比文化、比道德、比文明的社会主义新风尚。淳朴的周窝人在艺术的熏陶下更加热爱生活，勇于挑战、敢于追梦。

2. 突出主题特色

周窝村以音乐为主题，用音乐改变乡村，注重中西融合，坚持"政府主导+市场运作+村民参与"的建设模式，全方位、多层次地融合音乐文化元素，努力打造高品位的音乐特色名镇，探索出一条欠发达地区现代新农村建设新路子。

3. 加强相互赋能

2012年，周窝村以中国最大的管弦乐器生产企业——金音集团为龙头，引入文旅公司，将音乐教育与乐器生产相融合，打造以音乐为主题的特色小镇。周窝村现已成为集乐器展销、批发、零售、培训于一体的音乐旅游小镇、全国固定位置的乐器交易集散地、全世界乐器采购地。

下一步计划

一是引智借力，进一步提升小镇运营水平和效益。继续加强与中青旅控股股份有限公司、河北旅游投资集团股份有限公司等单位的沟通、洽商与合作，引入先进的管理运营经验、运营模式和市场推广渠道，进一步盘活小镇资源，实现资源优势向效益优势的最大转化。

二是打造常态化音乐演出活动，营造小镇浓厚的音乐氛围。一方面，依托小镇现有场地、器材资源，组织全县及周边市县的演艺队伍和文艺人才，每周末（周五夜至周日夜）在小镇举办多场景、多形态、多层面的各类文化演艺活动，盘活小镇的周末休闲游市场。另一方面，与专业团队合作，邀请知名艺术家及流量主播加盟，在小镇打造专场音乐演出活动，条件成熟时，可形成固定演出节目，吸引游客前来观看。

三是规划建设音乐创客街区，打造小镇高质量发展增长极。一方面，利用金音集团厂区临街位置，建设乐器展示、销售一条街，将金音集团展厅从厂区搬到厂外，便于游客参观和购买乐器，使之逐步成为全国的乐器生产、销售集散地。另一方面，在街区适当位置建设武强特色产品展示销售中心，集中展示、销售武强县的特色农产品、文创产品、非遗系列产品等，满足游客购物需求。

Zhouwo Village, Wuqiang County, Hengshui City, Hebei Province:
Play a New Chapter of Rural Revitalization with Music

Abstract

On account of the village's good industrial foundation and features of its residences typical of north China, Zhouwo Village in Wuqiang County, Hengshui City, Hebei Province, in accordance with the "government-led + market operation" model and the principle of "one door, one view, one household, one product, embodying creativity, and each with its own characteristics", has transformed more than 80 courtyards into homestays, coffee shops, and musical instrument experience halls with creative characteristics, and newly built venues such as the Zhouwo Music Experience Center and the World Musical Instrument Museum, forming a music town integrating cultural tourism, music research, and leisure and vacation and thus play a new chapter of rural revitalization with music.

Challenges and Problems

Zhouwo Village is located in the low plain area of Hebei Province. With open and flat land, it is a temperate semi-arid area under a continental monsoon climate. With 297 residential houses, the village has a total of 256 households of 959 people. Although Zhouwo Village is relatively short of natural tourism resources, it is home to Hebei Jinyin Musical Instrument Group Co., Ltd., and the development of rural tourism faces both advantages and challenges. Firstly, it is about how to give full play to the advantages of Zhouwo Village's Western musical instrument manufacturing industry, further enhance the cohesion of musical instrument manufacturing and music industries, and make Zhouwo Music Town a well-known musical instrument production and sales distribution center and music-themed cultural tourism holiday base. Secondly, it is how to integrate Zhouwo Village's cultural and tourism resources, expand the tourism industry, continuously improve the tourism products, and further build the unique attraction of Zhouwo Music Town's music tourism scene. Thirdly, it is how to improve the overall level of cultural tourism operations in Zhouwo Music Town, improve the quality of operations, increase scenic spot revenue, and turn brand strengths into benefits.

Measures

1.Reconstruct the music village

Firstly, it is the infrastructure reconstruction project. The village's water, electricity, roads, heating and other infrastructure were upgraded and reconstructed, and new facilities such as the Zhouwo Music Town Service Center, the Central Nursing Home, the sewage treatment plant, and the garbage transfer station were built. Every household in the village has access to sanitary toilets and healthy kitchens. Secondly, it is the environmental sanitation and cleaning project. On the basis of building a sewage treatment plant and a garbage transfer station, garbage bins, garbage transfer vehicles, sprinkler trucks and other cleaning equipment have been purchased; a full-time sanitation and cleaning team has been established, and a daily cleaning system has been set established to ensure that garbage is collected and transported, daily work is clarified, and cleaning is done as a routine, and a combination of soft and hard means is adhered to. Thirdly, it is to carry out music culture themed improvement and transformation of the main courtyards of the town's residential houses, the street corners, walls, telephone poles, night scenes, and greening of the village, to

create a unique regional style of the music culture town.

2. Create a music base

Zhouwo Music Town takes rural tourism as a breakthrough point and vigorously develops cultural and creative industries, shifting from single musical instrument production to music education and training, music experience and creation, music program production, music souvenir development, music performances, music leisure and health-related activities. Firstly, it is to actively promote the construction of a rural tourism maker demonstration base, improve preferential policies regarding financial support, talent support, free venues, and entrepreneurship subsidies, and endeavor to create China's first cultural and creative tourism base that combines rural tourism with the musical instrument industry. Secondly, Zhouwo Music Town invests more than 10 million yuan each year to support musicians' creation, encourage college students to start their own businesses, and promote the research and academic exchanges among performers. It has created a number of maker incubators such as violin experience workshops and DIY guitar production centers, attracting many artists and young people at home and abroad to come to Zhouwo Music Town for innovation and entrepreneurship.

3. Organize music events

Zhouwo Village cooperates with cultural and art institutions such as the China Society of Guitar, Beida Jade Bird Group, and the Hebei Provincial Musicians Association to organize and host various national and provincial music festivals and music events, etc., to enhance the town's reputation, popularity, and business atmosphere, and maintain the town's motivation and vitality. Zhouwo Music Town has

successfully held a number of major events, including the China College Students Music Festival, the China Guitar Culture Festival, the International Chopin Piano Competition, and the Hebei Provincial Wind Music Performance and Competition. The Music Town has also attracted the Youth Music Academy and the China Guitar Museum to settle down here, and the music studios of famous musicians have also successively settled in Zhouwo.

Results

By 2020, Zhouwo Village currently has nearly 100 musical instrument production and processing supporting enterprises, more than 100 cultural and creative small and micro enterprises with more than 3,000 employees, which effectively helped the local rural labor force to work locally, and contributed to

the effective poverty alleviation of some households in six impoverished villages around the town, such as Xixinzhuang Village and Lifengzhuang Village. In 2023, Zhouwo Music Town attracted 1 million tourists, earned a tourism revenue of over 100 million yuan, and the annual per capita income of local villagers exceeded 30,000 yuan. The town has been successively rated as one of the top ten charming new rural villages in the country, the most beautiful village in the country, a national eco-culture village, a national key village for rural tourism, and the national 4A-level scenic spot.

Experiences and Inspirations

1. Adhere to keeping up the fine tradition and making innovations

The cross street of Zhouwo Village divides the village into four hutong areas: "*He, Xie, Fu, Guo*". Each hutong has a name brimming with positive energy, signifying harmony, kindness, and beauty, prosperity, affluent people, and prosperous country, etc. The hutong culture with a positive ethos has influenced generation upon generation of Zhouwo people. In addition, "Toilet Revolution" "Beautiful Courtyards" "Star-rated Exemplary Households" and other commentary activities that are popular among villagers and have their own characteristics have given rise to a new socialist trend that puts a premium on ideals, culture, morality, and civility. Under the influence of art, the simple and honest Zhouwo people all the more love life, dare to challenge, and dare to pursue their dreams.

2. Highlight the themes

Zhouwo Village takes music as its theme, uses music to change the village, attaches importance to the integration of Chinese and Western cultures, adheres to the "government-led + market-based operation + villager participation" construction model, integrates music culture elements in an all-round and multi-level manner, endeavors to create a high-quality music town , and blazes a new path for the construction of modern new countryside in underdeveloped areas.

3. Strengthen mutual empowerment

In 2012, Zhouwo Village had China's largest orchestral instrument manufacturer Jinyin Group as the leader in bringing in cultural tourism companies and integrating music education with instrument production, with a view of building a characteristic town with music as the theme. Zhouwo Village has now become a music tourism town integrating instrument exhibition, wholesale, retail and training; a fixed-position instrument trading distribution center in China, and a global instrument procurement place.

Plans

Firstly, it is to attract talent and leverage our strength to further improve the town's operation level and increase benefits. We will continue to strengthen communication, negotiation and cooperation with professional teams such as China Cyts Tours Holding Co., Ltd. and Hebei Tourism Investment Group Co., Ltd.; adopt advanced management and operation experience, operation models and market promotion channels; further leverage the town's resources, to realize maximum transformation of resource strengths into benefits.

Secondly, it is to stage regular music performances and enhance the town's music atmosphere. For one thing, relying on the town's existing venues and equipment resources, we organize performing arts teams and literary talents from the county and surrounding cities and counties to hold various cultural performances in multiple scenes, forms, and levels at the music town every weekend (Friday night through Sunday night) to inject vitality to the town's weekend leisure travel market. For another, we cooperate with professional teams, invite well-known artists and popular anchors to join, and create special music performances in the town. When conditions are ripe, we can develop a fixed repertoire to attract a large number of tourists to come and watch.

Thirdly, it is to plan to build a music maker block and create a growth pole for the town's high-quality development. On the one hand, we will use the street-side location of the Jinyin Group factory to build a street for the display and sale of musical instruments, and move the Jinyin Group exhibition hall from the factory to somewhere outside the factory to facilitate tourists to look at and buy musical instruments, gradually turning it into a national musical instrument production and distribution center. On the other hand, we will build a Wuqiang specialty display and sales center at an appropriate location in the block to have a concentrated display and sale of Wuqiang's special agricultural products, cultural and creative products, intangible cultural heritage products, etc., to meet the shopping needs of tourists.

2024 世界旅游联盟：旅游助力乡村振兴案例（中英文双语版）
WTA Best Practices of Rural Revitalization through Tourism 2024 (Chinese-English Bilingual Edition)

重庆市丰都县包鸾镇：
整合资源，串点成线，旅游绘就乡村振兴新画卷

摘 要

习近平总书记2024年4月在重庆市考察时强调，重庆集大城市、大农村、大山区、大库区于一体，要大力推进城乡融合发展。重庆市丰都县包鸾镇立足于乡村旅游发展实践，探索以"镇政府搭台、村集体参与、公司运作、群众唱戏"的乡村旅游发展模式，聚焦高山、中山、低山自然资源禀赋，实行差异化发展，建成了包鸾坝、石里红枫、玉带山旅游一线，实现农文旅融合发展，助力乡村振兴。

挑战与问题

包鸾镇位于丰都县县城东南部，距县城20千米，总面积184.3平方千米，辖12个村、1个社区、103个村（居）民小组，总人口2.8万人。全镇海拔高度在180米至1846米之间，林地面积17.86万亩，森林覆盖率64.6%，南天湖自然保护区、世坪森林公园横跨全境，丰富的森林资源涵养了弹子台、梨子坪2座中型水库。群众多生活在高山或峡谷，交通不便，信息闭塞，发展难度大。目前面临的困难有以下几点。首先是缺乏发展资金，加上自然保护区、生态红线、基本农田保护等限制，村民在产业发展等方面遭遇重重挑战。其次，由于道路狭窄、坡陡、弯急，以及客运车辆不能通行等交通制约，包鸾镇无法充分利用其丰富的森林资源发展高山纳凉避暑、户外运动等旅游项目。最后，长期以来，包鸾镇的广大青壮年劳动力大量外出务工以维持生计，如何解决农民增收与农村"空心化"之间的矛盾，也是乡村振兴必须克服的一大难题。

措施

1. 做靓高山旅游品牌

玉带山位于包鸾镇红花坡村，海拔1800余米。玉带山拥有丰富的旅游资源，游客可以穿越原始森林、赏高山云海、观日出日落、采山菌野果等。该地还可以开发夏季露营、冬季冰雪、山地越野跑、越野骑行、徒步竞走等户外体验项目，以及骑马、射箭、山地摩托等特色项目，同时配套徒步旅游器材、越野体育竞技设备销售点、租赁站，让游客在徒步之余体验消费，逐步将"徒步过境游"变为"徒步目的游"。目前，玉带山徒步游线路已成为重庆市有名的户外运动基地，日均客流量近1000人次。

2. 做精低山乡村旅游品牌

包鸾坝平均海拔550米，面积9800余亩。包鸾坝作为连接石里红枫乡村旅游度假区、玉带山徒步游精品线路的"桥头堡"和游客集散地，旅游基础设施已基本完备，同时兴建了铜矿山红色研学基地、石里红枫避暑度假区、金竹寨山地运动公园等游乐设施。包鸾坝连续两年承办中国农民丰收节重庆主场活动，几千亩的油菜花和几百亩的彩稻景观每年吸引几万名游客前来打卡。一系列重大节庆活动的举办，助推了包鸾坝农家乐的广泛开展，有力促进了包鸾镇乡村经济的发展。

3. 擦亮中山旅游招牌

石里红枫乡村旅游度假区，为国家3A级旅游景区，由重庆市沐枫乡村旅游开发有限公司打造，位于包鸾镇飞仙洞村一组，海拔1100—1300米，园区占地面积10000余亩，其中一期4185亩、二期6000亩。度假区内种有日本红枫、樱花等观赏花开苗木50余万株。景区内现有游客接待中心、云端星空宾馆、亲子乐园、青少年校外拓展基地、露营基地、会议团建

中心、体育健身等完善的配套设施。景区内景点有四川二路红军游击队宣誓地遗址、元末宰相铁木键后裔墓葬群、天坑、猿家洞、铜矿山平原等。红枫乡村旅游度假区已成为重庆市民周末和假日游的理想旅游目的地。

成效

包鸾镇通过"企业+村集体+村民"的"共富模式",发展包鸾坝、石里红枫乡村旅游度假区和玉带山徒步游精品旅游线路。村民土地流转给企业,收取流转费;山地越野、露营等项目都由村民投资经营,收回成本后,再与企业利润分成;企业鼓励村民自建农家乐,缺资金的由企业无息借款。农用地经批准转为集体建设用地后,企业除按每年2000元/亩对村集体进行保底固定分红外,另将利润的1%分给村民;或是企业按照25万元/亩左右有偿使用农村集体建设用地。现在包鸾镇提供各类就业岗位150个以上,发展农家乐100户以上,每年至少有30万游客来包鸾旅游,有效带动包鸾镇约1.1万在家务农农民增收致富。

经验与启示

1. 整体规划,联动发展

包鸾镇聘请中冶赛迪工程技术股份有限公司编制《包鸾镇乡村振兴规划》,对全镇的旅游资源等进行详细的梳理,最大限度整合各类资源。规划提出,从农业现代化生产、高山特色产业、多元经营模式、科技创新引领、农文旅融合五个层面出发,发展西南区域高山平坝地形地貌下的乡村旅游。

2. 分部落实,扎根文化

包鸾镇深耕乡村文化,融合农文旅,将特色竹席文化发展为旅游项目,让游客体会乡土文化和民风习俗。同时利用优势气候发展各区域农业,做精产品,做活运营,做大企业,不断为乡村旅游添砖加瓦,为乡村振兴增光添彩。

3. 冲出限制,荒地变绿

包鸾镇政府和镇党委带领村民,充分利用荒地资源,合理规划旅游线路,突破交通限制,发挥高山高地资源优势和气候优势发挥,将无人问津的区域变为如今的徒步旅游胜地。

下一步计划

总体目标:以打造"红色水乡·诗画包鸾"为主线,全面推进"历史红镇、生态美镇、兴业强镇、创新活镇"建设,推动农文旅深度融合发展,激发乡村振兴新动能,努力将包鸾镇建成"生态美、环境美、经济美、形象美、生活美"的"五美"乡村。

具体做法:一是活用气候及地形优势,继续完善各区域基础设施设备建设,以点带线,促进县城和周围景区联系,推动项目发展和提档升级。二是明确功能定位,依托非遗文化、红色文化、生态景观等,打造集非遗研学、青少年实践、度假观光、生态农业、运动康养于一体的青少年社会实践基地和市级乡村振兴示范点。

Baoluan Town, Fengdu County, Chongqing City:

Integrating Resources and Tour Lines, Tourism Paints a New Picture of Rural Revitalization

Abstract

When General Secretary Xi Jinping visited Chongqing this in April 2024, he stressed that Chongqing should vigorously promote the integrated development of urban and rural areas as it is a megacity with a vast rural and mountainous area. Baoluan Town, Fengdu County, Chongqing City, based on the practice of rural tourism development, explored the rural tourism development model where "The town government is preparing the stage, the village collective is actively participating, local businesses are operating, and the masses are showcasing their talent". By focusing on the natural resource endowments of high mountains, middle mountains and low mountains and implementing differentiated development, the Baoluanba, Shilihongfeng and Yudai mountain tourism lines have been built; and integrated development of agriculture, culture and tourism is achieved to help rural revitalization.

Challenges and Problems

Baoluan Town is located in the southeast of Fengdu County seat, 20 kilometers away from the seat, with a total area of 184.3 square kilometers. Consisting of 12 villages, one community, 103 village (community) groups, it has a total population of 28,000. The town's altitude ranges between 180 meters and 1,846 meters, with a forest area of 178,600 *mu* and a forest coverage rate of 64.6%. The Nantian Lake Nature Reserve and Shiping Forest Park span the entire town. The rich forest resources have conserved two medium-sized reservoirs: Danzitai and Liziping. Most people live in high mountains or canyons, facing inconvenient transportation, information isolation, and grave difficulties in development. The current difficulties are as follows. Firstly, given the lack of development funds coupled with restrictions related to nature reserves, ecological red lines, and basic farmland protection, villagers have numerous difficulties in industrial development. Secondly, due to narrow roads, steep slopes, sharp bends, and traffic constraints against the pass of passenger vehicles, Baoluan Town cannot give full play to its resource advantages in developing high mountain cool summer vacation resorts and outdoor sports destinations. Thirdly, for a long time, the vast majority of young and middle-aged able-bodied people in Baoluan Town have left the mountains and worked outside to earn money. How to resolve the contradiction between increasing farmers' income and mitigating the rural "hollowing out" phenomenon is also a challenge to rural revitalization.

Measures

1. Make the alpine tourism brand more appealing

Yudai Mountain is located in Honghuapo Village, Baoluan Town, with an altitude of more than 1,800 meters. Yudai Mountain has abundant tourism resources, and tourists can cross the primeval forest, enjoy the sea of clouds in the mountains, appreciate sunrise and sunset, pick mountain mushrooms and wild fruits, etc. Moreover, outdoor experience projects such as summer camping, winter ice and snow sports, mountain cross-country running, cross-country cycling, hiking and racing should be developed. Featured projects such as horse riding, archery, and mountain motorcycling can be developed. Besides, sales points and rental stations of hiking equipment and cross-country sports equipment can be set up so that tourists can spend money after hiking, and the place gets changed from a transit spot into a destination for hiking. At present, the Yudai Mountain hiking boutique route has become the most famous outdoor sports base in the city, with an average daily passenger flow of nearly 1,000.

2. Build up the low-mountain rural tourism brand

Baoluanba is 550 meters average above sea level and covers an area of more than 9,800 *mu*. As a "bridgehead" connecting the Shilihongfeng Rural Tourism Resort and the Yudai Mountain hiking boutique route, Baoluanba is a tourist distribution center with basically complete tourism infrastructure. Moreover, recreational facilities such as the Tongkuangshan Red Study Tour Base, Shilihongfeng Summer Resort, and Jinzhuzhai Mountain Sports Park have been built. Baoluanba has hosted the Chongqing main venue event of the China Farmers' Harvest Festival for two consecutive years. Every year, thousands of *mu* of rapeseed flowers and hundreds of *mu* of colored rice landscape in Baoluanba attract tens of thousands of tourists. The series of major festivals have promoted the widespread development of Baoluanba farmhouses and has greatly contributed to the rural economy of Baoluan Town.

3. Polish the medium mountain tourism brand

Shilihongfeng Rural Tourism Resort, a national 3A-level scenic spot, was built by Chongqing Mufeng Rural Tourism Development Co., Ltd. It is located in Group 1, Feixiandong Village, Baoluan Town, with an altitude of 1,100-1,300 meters. The scenic spot covers an area of more than 10,000 *mu*, of which the first phase covers 4,185 *mu* and the second phase covers 6,000 *mu*. More than 500,000 flower seedlings are planted in the resort, such as Japanese red maple and cherry blossom. The scenic area currently has well-developed supporting facilities such as the tourist reception center, a cloud-starry sky hotel, a parents-children park, the youth extracurricular activity base, a camping base, a conference and team-bonding center, and a sports and fitness center. The

area has such scenic spots as the oath-taking site of the Sichuan Second Route Red Army Guerrillas, the tombs of the descendants of Chancellor Tiemujian in the late Yuan Dynasty, the Sinkhole, the Yuanjia cave, and the Tongkuangshan plain. Shilihongfeng Rural Tourism Resort has become an ideal tourist destination for weekend and holiday tours in Chongqing.

Results

Baoluan Town has developed Baoluanba, Shilihongfeng Rural Tourism Resort and the Yudaishan boutique hiking route by adopting the "common prosperity model" involving "enterprises + village collectives + villagers". The villagers' land is transferred to the company and a transfer fee is collected; mountain cross-country sports, camping and other projects are invested in and operated by villagers, and after recovering the costs, they share the profits with the company; the company encourages villagers to build their own farm stays, and those who lack funds can borrow interest-free from the company. After the agricultural land is approved to be converted to collective construction land, the company will distribute 1% of the profits to the villagers in addition to the guaranteed fixed dividend of 2,000 yuan/*mu* per year to the village collective, or the company shall use the rural collective construction land for a fee of about 250,000 yuan/*mu*. Now Baoluan Town provides more than 150 jobs of various types and has more than 100 farm stays; at least 300,000 tourists come to Baoluan every year, which effectively helps about 11,000 farmers in Baoluan Town to increase their income and become rich.

Experiences and Inspirations

1. Overall planning and interconnected development

Baoluan Town hired CISDI Engineering Technology Co., Ltd. to develop the *Baoluan Town Rural Revitalization Plan*, which made a detailed review of the town's tourism resources, integrated various resources to the maximum extent, and proposed to develop rural tourism in the high mountain and flat terrain of the southwest region from five aspects of modern agricultural production, high mountain characteristic industries, diversified business models, scientific and technological

innovation, and agricultural, cultural and tourism integration.

2. Develop sector by sector and take root in culture

Baoluan Town deeply taps into rural culture; integrates agriculture, culture and tourism; and develops the characteristic bamboo mat culture into a tourism project, enabling visitors to experience the local culture and folk customs. At the same time, it takes advantage of the supreme climate to develop agriculture, improve products, operate flexibly, and expand enterprises, constantly contributing to rural tourism and adding luster to rural revitalization.

3. Break restrictions and turn wasteland into green land

The Baoluan Town government and the town Party committee led the villagers to make full use of wasteland resources, rationally planned tourist routes, broke traffic restrictions, and give full play to the advantages of high mountain and highland resources and climate advantages, turning the otherwise hardly known area into today's popular hiking destination.

Plans

Overall goal: With the creation of "Red Water Town: Poetic and Picturesque Baoluan" as the main line, Baoluan Town comprehensively promotes the construction of "Historical Red Town, Eco-friendly and Beautiful Town, Industrially Competitive Town, and Innovative and Lively Town"; promotes the in-depth integration and development of agriculture, culture and tourism; stimulates new driving forces for rural revitalization; and endeavors to build Baoluan into a village with sound ecology, environment, economy, beautiful look and happy life.

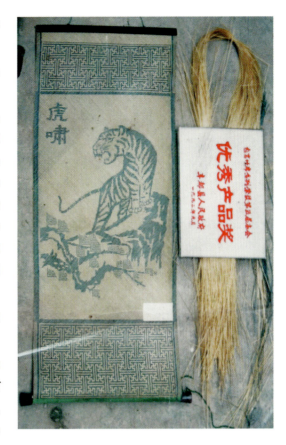

Specific measures: Firstly, Baoluan Town makes full use of the advantages of natural climate and terrain, continues to improve the construction of infrastructure and equipment in various regions, promotes the connection between the county seat and surrounding scenic spots, and promotes project development and upgrading. Secondly, Baoluan Town clarifies the functional positioning and relies on intangible cultural heritage, red culture, ecological landscape, etc., to create the youth social practice base and municipal rural revitalization demonstration site integrating intangible cultural heritage research, the youth practice, sightseeing, ecological agriculture, sports and healthcare.

福建省泉州市德化县佛岭村：
推动农文旅融合 打造和美乡村

摘　要

　　福建省泉州市德化县国宝乡佛岭村立足生态、地理、古厝、田地等独特的资源禀赋，坚持以旅兴农、文旅融合的发展模式，通过景区带动、资源盘活、环境整治等一系列措施，以"研学+"为主线，做深"研学+陶瓷""研学+农业""研学+红色""研学+拓展"等线路，推动研学与农业、文化、旅游等资源有机整合，打造研学康养农旅综合体。宜居宜业、和美乡村的"佛岭样板"被列入全国旅游精品线路，获评中国乡村旅游重点村等20多项荣誉，实现"空心村"向旅游度假村的蝶变。

挑战与问题

佛岭村地处"闽中屋脊"戴云山山麓和闽江、晋江两江源头腹地，是"中国天然氧吧"。省道206线贯穿其中，距厦沙高速公路九仙山互通口2千米，交通便利，地理优势明显。全村面积12平方千米，辖4个自然村12个村民小组，共有485户1496人。目前面临的挑战与问题有以下几点。一是缺乏乡村建设人才。由于城镇化的推进和农村大多数年轻人外出学习、务工，常住人口中超75%的是70岁以上老人，劳动生产力水平较低。二是产业链条没有得到延伸。农业产业几乎只进行粗加工，甚至不加工，抵御风险能力差、效益较低。三是部分基础设施不完善。

措施

1. 龙头景区带动，激发乡村活力

佛岭村紧抓辖区内云龙谷景区这个旅游拳头产品，构建"景区+村庄"的联合机制，累计投资6000余万元，全面进行提质升级，完成景区"福"文化、服务配套夜间景观等项目建设；打造小蛙露营基地；成功举办"山海泉州露营生活节""世界瓷都围炉煮茶文化生活节""世界瓷都·德化环云龙湖山地马拉松赛"等文旅热点活动。2023年，云龙谷景区成功获评国家4A级旅游景区。

2. 唤醒沉睡资源，做精农文旅品牌

佛岭村探索实施"统一流转，全面招商"发展模式，引导村民通过资产入股、政府购买和企业返聘村民等多种方式，实现农民和村集体双增收。一是村委会统一租赁收回闲置房屋、田地，由乡政府进行招商引资，引进厦门民宿专业运营团队，投入1000余万元，建设并运营"山有·福美""谷外云居""山有清欢""扬光堂"和"兰溪草堂"等5座精品民宿，"旅宿国宝"民宿聚集区初现规模。二是引进兴岩集团，打造集研学基地、自然教育、休闲采摘等功能于一体的田园综合体。

3. 深化"一清二整三美化"，扮靓乡村底色

佛岭村以入选"县级美丽乡村"为契机，持续深化"一清二整三美化"建设，累计投入2000余万元。一是完成滨溪公园、紫薇长廊、景观大道等美化绿化项目建设，倾力打造"遇见国宝"主题系列"微景观"，建成"一步一景、移步换景"的旅游景观带。二是完成"世界瓷都·国宝驿站"、龙山观景台、民居走廊、路灯工程及饮水工程等文旅配套基础设施项目建设。

成效

2023年，佛岭村成功获评国家4A级旅游景区，为当地村民增加就业岗位、经营摊位100余个，让村民在家门口就吃上了"旅游饭"。"旅宿国宝"民宿聚集区初现规模，年接待游客达2万人次，产值达1000余万元。佛岭村接待游客45余万人次，旅游收入4000余万元。

经验和启示

1. 聚焦资源整合，推动片区共建

一是整合优化山村行政资源，推动地域毗邻、宗族渊源较深的村落跨村联建，实行规划共用、项目共建、事务共管、利益共享。二是整合经费资源，结合片区发展规划，集中发展以休闲旅游、研学教育为代表的主导产业，以点带面，辐射带动佛岭国宝片区全面振兴发展。三是整合人力资源，共建护林员、保洁员等队伍，实行人员共用共管。

2. 聚焦业态融合，推动产业共创

一方面，推动农文旅深度融合。紧扣德化县陶瓷和旅游，立足自然资源禀赋和产业基础，发展陶瓷文创、红色研学和康养农旅等产业。另一方面，加大招商引资力度。坚持项目带动，多渠道、全媒体开展招商引资，成功引进兴岩集团来村发展文旅产业。

3. 聚焦民生汇合，推动服务共享

以佛岭"党建+"邻里中心建设为抓手，汇合兰花草志愿服务中心、德化县医院等机构力量，深入实施六邻里（邻里优质办、邻里帮帮团、邻里爱心餐、邻里关爱行、邻里文化圈、邻里乡村秀）特色服务，构建爱心幸福村，提升公共服务水平。

下一步计划

一是做强一个景区。围绕景区软硬件完善，引爆活动热点，不断提高"遇见国宝"文旅品牌影响力。深入挖掘消费需求，以"蛙"为核心文化元素，投资1880万元，着力推进水上游乐、丛林穿越赛道、彩虹秋千等7个游乐项目的建设，打造一批标志性、差异性景观IP，不断提升国家4A级旅游景区的品牌影响力。投资1700万元，新增太空舱、农业休闲体验园等项目，增加景区过夜游客数量；引入街景美食集装箱，为游客提供丰富多样的餐饮选择，满足游客多元需求。

二是做大一座民宿。以民宿培育为抓手，围绕佛岭精品民宿，加快推进"叶子家"在建民宿进度，争取2024年对外营业；积极探索政府、村委会、社会资本合资共建机制，力争每年新增2—3家精品民宿，逐步形成民宿聚集区。持续深耕"民宿+"多元开发模式，新建咖啡馆、棋牌室、乡村酒吧等一批服务设施，新增共享菜园、乡村垂钓、山地骑行等一批体验项目，推动民宿集群化、产业化和规范化，促进民宿培育、景观提升和业态培植。

Foling Village, Dehua County, Quanzhou City, Fujian Province:

Promoting the Integrated Development of Agriculture, Culture, and Tourism to Build a Harmonious and Beautiful Village

Abstract

Foling Village of Guobao Township, Dehua County, Quanzhou City, Fujian Province, makes use of its unique resources, including its ecological environment, geographical conditions, ancient houses, and farm fields, and continues to promote the integrated development of agriculture, culture, and tourism by developing scenic spots, making full use of resources, and improving the environment. With a focus on the "study tour+" approach, it has developed such thematic study tour programs as "study tour + ceramics", "study tour + agriculture", "study tour + CPC revolutionary history" and "study tour + outward bound" to combine study tours with local agricultural, cultural, and tourism resources and build an agricultural-tourism complex suitable for study tours and health preservation. The "Foling Model" for building a livable, harmonious, and beautiful village suitable for working in has won the village more than 20 honors, including the National Boutique Tourist Route and Key Village for Rural Tourism of China. Foling Village has successfully transformed itself from a hollow village to a tourist resort.

Challenges and Problems

Foling Village is located at the foot of the Daiyun Mountains, the "roof of central Fujian" and the hinterland of the headwaters of the Minjiang River and the Jinjiang River, and is reputed to be the "natural oxygen bar of China". It is run through by Provincial Highway 206 and is only two kilometers away from the Jiuxianshan interchange of the Shaxian-Xiamen Expressway. It is easily accessible and enjoys superior geographical conditions. The village covers an area of 12 square kilometers and has jurisdiction over 4 natural villages and 12 villager groups, with a population of 1,496 in 485 households. Its current challenges and problems are as follows. Firstly, there is a labor shortage. As the urbanization drive continues, most young people in the village have left for urban areas to study or to make a living, so more than 75% of the resident population is over 70 years old. The level of labor productivity is low. Secondly, there is a lack of a complete industrial chain. The agricultural products are only roughly processed, and some even go through no processing at all. The farmers are vulnerable to risks and the economic benefits are limited. Thirdly, there is poor infrastructure conditions.

Measures

1. Developing the Yunlong Valley Scenic Area to stimulate the vitality of the village

The Yunlong Valley Scenic Area is the most famous and popular tourist attraction in the village. Foling Village has built a "scenic area + village" mechanism, invested more than 60 million yuan, and comprehensively improved the scenic area, including adding the "Fu" (blessings) culture landscape and the nighttime landscape. It built a frog-themed camping base and held a camping festival, a tea-brewing festival, and a mountain marathon around Yunlong Lake, among other popular tourist events. In 2023, the Yunlong Valley Scenic Area was rated as a national 4A-level scenic spot.

2. Putting idle resources back into use and building up the brands of agriculture and tourism

Foling Village is piloting the development model under which the land use right is transferred collectively for investment attraction. The income of farmers and the village collective is increased by the villagers' asset investment, government purchase, and the hiring of locals by enterprises. Firstly, the village committee rents idle houses and fields, and the township government is responsible for investment promotion. The village introduced a professional homestay operation team from Xiamen and invested more than 1,000 yuan to build five boutique homestays. The homestay business cluster zone has begun to take shape. Secondly, the village has partnered with Xingyan Group to build a pastoral complex including a study tour base and U-pick farms, offering nature education and other leisure services.

3. Continuing to create a clean, tidy, and beautiful countryside

Foling Village was rated a beautiful village in Dehua County. Since then, it has continued to make the village environment cleaner, tidier, and more beautiful, and it has invested a total of more than 20 million yuan. Firstly, it completed such landscaping and greening projects as the Binxi Park, the Crape Myrtle Corridor, and the scenic avenue, striving to create a series of mini-landscapes with local characteristics and form a tourist belt full of such mini-landscapes. Secondly, it completed such supporting infrastructure projects as the Guobao Station, the Longshan Observation Deck, the Residential Architecture Corridor, the street lamp project, and the drinking water project.

Results

Foling Village was rated a national 4A-level scenic spot in 2023. The tourism industry has created more than 100 jobs for local villagers so that they can make a living without leaving their home village. The homestay business cluster zone is taking shape. It receives 20,000 tourists annually and produces an output value of more than 10 million yuan. In 2023, Foling Village received more than 450 thousand tourists and generated a tourism income of more than 40 million yuan.

Experience and Inspirations

1. Focus on resource integration and promote the collaborative development of the area

Firstly, integrate and optimize the administrative resources of the mountainous villages, and promote collaboration among villages that are close to each other in geography and lineage so that they can plan together, develop projects together, govern affairs together, and share the development benefits. Secondly, consolidate financial resources. As per the local development plan, Foling Village focuses on developing such leading industries as tourism and study tours and uses the spillover effect to drive the comprehensive revitalization and development of Guobao. Thirdly, share human resources. Local villages have jointly set up teams of forest rangers and sanitation workers for shared use and co-management.

2. Focus on the integration of different business forms and promote them to jointly create value

Firstly, promote the deep integration of agriculture, culture and tourism. Centering around Dehua's ceramics and tourism industry, and based on its natural resources and industrial foundation, Foling Village vigorously develops cultural and creative ceramic products, study tours themed on the CPC revolutionary history, health preservation, and agritourism industries. Secondly, increase efforts to attract investment. Foling Village adheres to the project-based approach and attracts investors via various channels and media platforms, successfully attracting Xingyan Group to invest in the village's tourism industry.

3. Gather forces to promote the sharing of public services and improve public well-being

While building the "Party Building +" Neighborhood Center, Foling Village brings together the Lanhuacao Volunteer Service Center and Dehua County Hospital and delivers six characteristic services: easier access to government services, dispute resolution, charitable meals, sympathy visits, cultural activities, and rural shows, to build a loving and happy village and improve public services.

activities, and continuously build up the tourism brand of "Meet Guobao". To further tap the consumer demand, it plans to invest 18.8 million yuan on seven amusement projects including the water park, the jungle crossing track, and the rainbow swing, with the frog as the core image, to create several iconic and differentiated landscape IPs, and continuously enhance the influence of the Yunlong Valley Scenic Area as a national 4A-level scenic spot. It also plans to invest 17 million yuan in the space capsule and the agritourism farm projects, to attract more overnight tourists. The food containers will be installed on the street to provide more dining options for tourists.

Secondly, expand the homestay industry. To cultivate more homestays, especially more boutique homestays, Foling Village will accelerate the "Yezijia" project, a homestay under construction, so that it can open to business by the end of this year. The village committee will actively seek cooperation with the government and social capital, strive to add two to three boutique homestays every year, and gradually form a homestay cluster zone. It will continue with the "homestay +" diversification model, build such service facilities as cafés, chess and card rooms, and rural bars, and introduce such experiential projects as shared vegetable gardens, angling, and mountain biking, to promote the clustering and standardized development of the homestay industry, cultivate more homestays and other business forms and improve the landscape.

Plans

Firstly, further improve the tourist attractions. Foling Village should focus on improving the tourist facilities and services, host more popular tourist

江苏省苏州市吴江区开弦弓村：
农文旅融合书写中国·江村新篇章

摘　要

江苏省苏州市吴江区七都镇开弦弓村，近年来紧抓乡村振兴建设的时代机遇，围绕讲好费孝通故事，擦亮"中国·江村"品牌建设，大力推进开弦弓村综合提升，高标准构建"一心、一廊、三村、四园"的空间格局，打造以文化为核心、系统运营为支撑的"中国·江村"。开弦弓村依托社会学文化的根脉，以乡村振兴"江村"品牌为引领，形成"研学＋产业＋生态"的江村旅游模式，走出了片区联动、组团发展、城乡融合的乡村振兴新路径，打造新时代"江村"新样板，成为观察中国乡村振兴战略实践和乡村旅游创新实践的重要窗口。

挑战与问题

开弦弓村地处长江三角洲太湖东南岸，南靠沪苏浙高速公路，东跨苏震桃一级公路，庙震公路穿村而过，交通便利。开弦弓村坐落于"吴头越尾"和优美的太湖风光带，吴越文化、太湖文化以及蚕桑文化、丝绸文化在此交融传承，发展繁荣；该地又因著名社会学家、人类学家费孝通先生的著作《江村经济》，而以"江村"的学名蜚声国际，成为世界了解和研究中国农村的窗口，也是国内外研究中国农村的首选样本。但是在开弦弓村新的发展阶段，仍然存在一些挑战与问题。一是资金、土地、人才等要素制约依然存在，资金渠道单一，现有收储土地转化存在产证归属等问题，集体经济增收渠道有限、人才流入不足等问题都限制了乡村发展潜力的释放。二是特色化产品生产与供给亟待增强，在吸引更多游客慢下来、停下来、住下来方面还缺乏系统策划和内容支撑。

措施

1. 坚持规划赋能

一是举全区之力高位统筹、系统开发，高标准编制《开弦弓村策划及概念规划》，组建江村综合提升专班，平台化、项目化推进开弦弓村综合提升项目建设。二是从全局视野描绘一张蓝图。依托全镇"一厅、两群、三园"的乡村振兴空间格局，高标准构建开弦弓村"一心、一廊、三村、四园"的空间框架，打造以文化为核心、系统运营为支撑的"中国·江村"客厅。三是以全域空间盘活闲置资源。以全域土地综合整治为抓手，推进低效厂房、闲置民房与田地、养殖池塘等各类资源的收储工作，为打造"江村文化空间"储力蓄能。

2. 坚持文化赋能

一是聚焦费孝通社会学文化标识，成功举办苏州市中国农民丰收节、江村发展大会、费孝通学术思想论坛、乡村振兴研讨会、乡村振兴江村行等一系列具有显著影响力的活动，进一步打响"中国江村"品牌。二是与清华大学、伦敦政治经济学院、华东师范大学、华东政法大学、西交利物浦大学、河海大学等一批高校合作，构筑学术联盟，开展文化和学术研究；与中国农业大学合作建成科技小院，依托市农科院打造亚夫工作站，开启乡村研究与农业科技探索新模式；与中小学、高校、国际智库等学校和机构合作，在开弦弓村建成超过49家挂牌基地。三是汇聚政学银企多方合力，实现资源共享，以项目化、研学式、合作型推动乡村振兴。

3. 坚持产业赋能

一是夯实发展基础。开弦弓村持续推进综合提升建设，建成运营江村1936系列的南园、山水桑田、嘉年华等园区项目，江村美食街完成改造开街运营，进一步完善农文旅融合载体。二是丰富旅游业态。开弦弓村打造了一批具有太湖特色、费老印记、江村味

道的文化旅游示范项目，如江村 Club、教授工作室、幸福凉茶铺、定胜高糕团店、"种豆得豆"臭豆腐店、三味蔬屋、乡建工作室等，形成大中小项目遍地开花、以点带面的文化旅游产业开发新格局，绘就美好江村生活。三是促进产业融合。开弦弓村通过高标准农田建设、主题农园的运营等勾画出有"江村"特色的休闲农业蓝图，农文旅融合发展，提升资源效应与经济效应，勾勒出乡村振兴的"江村"图景。

成效

开弦弓村通过统筹推进违法建设治理、农房风貌管控及人居环境整治提升，新建江村1936系列的南园、山水桑田、北园等综合性新园区，改造村内老旧建筑，建成江村市集、江村美食街、嘉年华、教授工作室、知源小院、足迹民宿、江村文化礼堂、江村Club等多功能公共空间，从乡村风韵、历史底蕴、生态原韵的角度微改造、精提升，呈现费老笔下的"江村记忆场景"，成为姑苏城外的乡村度假目的地。

开弦弓村培育电子商务、生态养殖、民宿经营、农家乐、村庄解说员等就业岗位和就业渠道，村内实现农户土地流转有租金、自主经营有收入、回乡创业有支持、就近务工有工资，全民共享乡村振兴成果。2023年，开弦弓村吸引旅客超过14万人次，带动超180人就业创业，旅游营收6000万元，村民人均可支配收入4.64万元，村集体收入较去年增长25%。

经验与启示

1. 坚持党建引领，凝聚合力推进乡村建设

突出党政主导、各方协同，将党建引领与基层"德治、自治、法治"深度融合，形成"三治融合"乡村治理新格局，营造良好稳定的发展环境。

2. 坚持统筹谋划，优化空间凸显载体优势

坚持"绿水青山就是金山银山"的理念，依托典型水乡风貌与生态系统，在打造特色田园乡村与整村特色康居村基础上，紧扣国家、省、市文旅品牌创建契机，优化村庄生态景观和人居环境，形成"景村互动"的景观风貌。

3. 坚持共建共享，探索兴业富民发展之路

"土"字谋突破，在继承土地资源的基础上，打造高标准稻田，建成太湖蟹园、香青菜基地和江村大米种植园等一批等精品休闲农业园区；"新"字谋发展，形成江村大米、香青菜、太湖蟹等一批新型绿色生态农产品，农业产业和"江村丰物"品牌内涵持续丰富。

下一步计划

一是提高站位。站在长三角生态绿色一体化发展示范区建设、"中国·江村"乡村振兴示范区建设等角度，以新质生产力促进农文旅深度融合，以系统化、战略性、市场化思维谋划江村发展全局。二是做优产业。紧扣文旅新市场、新趋势，加强要素保障，优化升级现有载体业态，推进江村学院、江村1936系列园区、江村姑苏小院等项目有序完成和投入运营。三是深挖文化。加快推进与中国社科院、长三角社会学联盟等科研院所合作，打造社会学实验室；做好各大院校社会学课程与实践调研落地落实，让开弦弓村成为社会学田野调查的必选实践点、中国乡村振兴的实景课堂，成为全国社会学研学第一村。

Kaixiangong Village, Wujiang District, Suzhou City, Jiangsu Province:

Promoting the Integrated Development of Agriculture, Culture, and Tourism to Write a New Chapter of Development

Abstract

In recent years, Kaixiangong Village of Qidu Town, Wujiang District, Suzhou City, Jiangsu Province, has seized the opportunity of rural revitalization, focused on the legacy of the great sociologist Fei Xiaotong, built up its brand as the "Jiangcun of China", and worked vigorously to improve the village environment in all respects. It has constructed a spatial layout according to high standards, consisting of "one core, one corridor, three villages, and four parks", with culture at the core and system operations as the support. Based on its sociological heritage and to build up the "Jiangcun" brand for rural revitalization, Kaixiangong Village has formed a tourism development model that brings together study tours, business development, and ecological conservation and embarked on a new path of rural revitalization characterized by regional linkage, clustering development, and urban-rural integration. It has set a new example for rural development in the new era and become an important window on China's practice of rural revitalization and rural tourism development.

Challenges and Problems

Kaixiangong Village is located on the southeast bank of Taihu Lake in the Yangtze River Delta, near the Shanghai-Jiangsu-Zhejiang Expressway in the south, and run through by the Suzhou-Zhenze-Taoyuan First Grade Highway in the east. Miaozhen Highway also runs through it. The village is thus easily accessible. This used to be where Wu and Yue states bordered during the Spring and Autumn Period about 2,500 years ago, so it inherited the cultures of Wu and Yue, and later integrated them into the Taihu culture, and nurtured the prosperous silkworm breeding and silk industries. It was also where the famous sociologist and anthropologist Fei Xiaotong conducted the fieldwork for his masterpiece *Jiangcun Jingji*, translated into English as Peasant Life in China, and thus established its international reputation among academics as the "Jiangcun". It has become a window for the world to study and understand rural China, and also the go-to place for Chinese and foreign academics to study China's rural areas. However, in this new stage of development, Kaixiangong Village faces several challenges and problems. Firstly, the constraints in capital, land, and labor, the lack of financing channels, the problem with the title deed of rural collective land whose use right has been transferred, the limited income source for the village collective, and the insufficient inflow of labor have all hindered rural development. Secondly, the production and supply of characteristic products need to be strengthened urgently, and there is still a lack of systematic planning, products, and services to attract and retain more tourists.

Measures

1. Empowering rural development with systematic planning

Firstly, the district coordinated the systematic development, compiled the *Conceptual Plan for the Development of Kaixiangong Village* up to high standards, set up a task force responsible for its implementation, and pushed ahead with relevant work on a platform-based and project-based basis. Secondly, the holistic approach to development was adopted. Based on the town's spatial layout of "one hall, two clusters, and three parks" for rural revitalization, Kaixiangong Village laid down the high-standard spatial framework of "one core, one corridor, three villages, and four parks" to build up the brand of "Jiangcun of China" with culture at the core and system operations as the support. Thirdly, the idle resources across the village were put to good use. While promoting comprehensive land consolidation, Kaixiangong Village purchased many low-efficiency plants, abandoned houses, fields, and breeding ponds, to pave the way for the "Jiangcun Cultural Space".

2. Empowering rural development with cultural heritage

Firstly, leveraging its association with Mr. Fei

Xiaotong and its status in China's sociological studies, Kaixiangong Village held several influential events, including the Chinese Farmers' Harvest Festival, Jiangcun Development Conference, Fei Xiaotong Academic Thought Forum, Rural Revitalization Seminar, and the Jiangcun Tour, increasing the visibility of the "Jiangcun of China" brand. Secondly, it works with Tsinghua University, London School of Economics and Political Science, East China Normal University, East China University of Political Science and Law, Xi'an Jiaotong-Liverpool University, and Hohai University, to form an academic alliance and carry out cultural and academic research. It has jointly launched a Science and Technology Backyard with China Agricultural University, and built the Yafu Service Station at the Suzhou Academy of Agricultural Sciences, introducing a new model of conducting rural research and developing agricultural science and technology. More than 49 primary and secondary schools, universities, and international think tanks have unveiled their bases in the village. Thirdly, Kaixiangong Village brings together government organs, academia, banks, and enterprises, and mobilizes them to share resources and jointly promote rural revitalization in a project- and research-based manner.

3. Empowering rural development with businesses

Firstly, it laid a solid foundation for development. Kaixiangong Village continued to make improvements in all respects. Projects such as Jiangcun 1936 series of parks including South Park, Shanshui Sangtian, and the Carnival were completed and put into operation. The Jiangcun Food Street was reopened after renovation, further improving the supporting facilities for the integration of agriculture, culture, and tourism. Secondly, it diversified the tourism industry. Kaixiangong Village has launched several demonstration tourism projects with the characteristics of Taihu Lake, with the marks of Fei Xiaotong, and of its flavor, including the Jiangcun Club, Professor Studio, Happy Herbal Tea Shop, local snacks shops, vegetable garden, and the Rural Development Workshop. At present, tourism projects of various sizes are blooming everywhere and help create a beautiful country life. Thirdly, it promoted the integrated development of local industries. Through the high-standard farmland initiative and the operations of theme farms, Kaixiangong Village has charted the development path for leisure agriculture with its characteristics, promoted the integrated development of agriculture, culture, and tourism, and improved resource utilization efficiency and economic benefits, presenting a scene of rural revitalization.

Results

Kaixiangong Village has coordinated efforts to remove illegal buildings, unify the look of residential houses and improve the living conditions. It has built new comprehensive parks such as the Jiangcun 1936 series of parks, including South Park, Shanshui Sangtian, and North Park; renovated old buildings, and built multi-purpose public spaces such as Jiangcun Market, Jiangcun Food Street, the Carnival, Professor Studio, Zhiyuan Courtyard, Footprint Homestay, Jiangcun Cultural Hall, and Jiangcun Club. Small-scale renovations were made to better preserve the countryside style, historical heritage, and ecological environment, and recreate the scenes penned by Mr. Fei. Kaixiangong Village has become a rural holiday destination in suburb Suzhou.

Kaixiangong Village has created many jobs by cultivating such businesses as e-commerce, eco-farming, homestays, farm stays, and tour guides. The villagers have all benefited and seen their income source diversify to include land rent, business revenue, and wages. Those returning to the village to start businesses can also get the support they need.

In 2023, Kaixiangong Village attracted more than 140,000 tourists and created more than 180 jobs, with tourism revenue of 60 million yuan. The per capita disposable income was 46,400 yuan, and the village collective income increased by 25% from the previous year.

Experience and Inspirations

1. Adhere to the guidance of the Party building work and gather forces to promote rural development

Kaixiangong Village highlights the leading role of the Party and government organs and the participation of stakeholders, and deeply integrates the Party building work with the "rule of virtue, autonomy, and rule of law" at the primary level in rural governance to create a good and stable development environment.

2. Adhere to holistic planning, optimize the spatial layout, and highlight the advantages of investment carriers

Kaixiangong Village upholds the belief that "lucid waters and lush mountains are invaluable assets" and works to build itself into a characteristic pastoral village and a characteristic health-preservation village based on its typical water town

look and ecosystem. Meanwhile, while working to apply for national, provincial, and municipal honors, it continuously improves its ecological landscape and living environment and brings the two closer to each other.

3. Adhere to the principle of joint contribution and development for all and develop local industries to enrich the people

Kaixiangong Village seeks breakthroughs from the soil. It has turned the stock land resources into high-standard paddy fields and built several high-quality leisure agricultural parks such as the Taihu Crab Garden, XiangQingCai Base, and Jiangcun Rice Plantation. Meanwhile, it also seeks innovation-driven development. It has developed many green eco-agricultural products such as Jiangcun rice, the vegetable XiangQingCai, and Taihu crabs. The agricultural industry and the brand "Jiangcun Fengwu" are producing more and more products.

Plans

Firstly, aim higher. Kaixiangong Village should strive to become a demonstration zone for the integrated green development of the Yangtze River Delta and a rural revitalization demonstration zone of China, promote the deep integration of

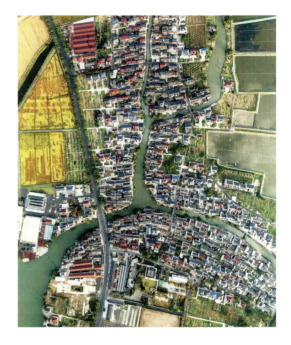

agriculture, culture, and tourism with new quality productive forces, and make systematic, strategic, and market-oriented development plans. Secondly, strengthen local industries. Kaixiangong Village should closely follow the new cultural and tourism markets and trends, increase the supply of factors needed, optimize and upgrade existing carriers and business forms, and orderly complete and put into operation such projects as Jiangcun College, Jiangcun 1936 series of parks, and Jiangcun Gusu Courtyard. Thirdly, dig deeper into the cultural heritage. Kaixiangong Village should accelerate cooperation with scientific research institutes such as the Chinese Academy of Social Sciences and the Yangtze River Delta Sociology Alliance to jointly build a sociology laboratory. It should do a good job in the implementation of sociology courses and practical research in major universities and become a must-visit place for sociological fieldwork, an off-campus classroom on rural revitalization, and the No. 1 village for sociological research in the country.

新疆维吾尔自治区阿克苏地区温宿县塔格拉克村：
景村融合描绘乡村振兴美丽画卷

摘 要

新疆维吾尔自治区阿克苏地区温宿县塔格拉克村依托得天独厚的生态旅游资源，围绕"景村融合"理念，通过实施"乡村振兴+乡村旅游+扶贫增收"发展战略，大力发展乡村旅游，打通"绿水青山"和"金山银山"的转化通道，打造宜居、宜业、宜游的美丽乡村，带动农牧民持续增收致富，描绘出"农业强、农村美、农民富"的乡村新画卷，为新疆乡村发展提供了可借鉴可复制的"塔村模式"。

挑战与问题

塔格拉克村辖区总面积5913.33平方千米，下辖3个村民小组，总人口239户738人，拥有耕地1712亩，草场306万亩，地处天山最高峰——托木尔峰脚下，环境优美，生态资源丰富。然而，塔格拉克村交通不便、基础设施落后、信息闭塞，农牧民思想观念保守，多数村民外出打工谋生，村庄空心化现象严重。整村可耕种土地稀少，村民以放牧为主，经济收入水平低，发展滞后。塔格拉克村优质的旅游资源没有得到合理开发利用。

措施

1. 改善村容村貌

塔格拉克村大力实施环境整治和美丽乡村建设，按照"宜建则建、宜改则改"的原则，一是统筹推进改水、改厨、改厕、改圈、改院、改线和拆违拆临；二是实施村委会大门及院落改造、村民房屋及庭院改造、道路亮化工程、修建人行道及围栏、打造村民广场及美食街、实施绿化美化工程等；三是掀起"美化提升""创意改造""文创设计"等行动热潮，用文字、绘画等方式，将传统文化、民俗文化等内容植入整村建设中，使美丽乡村从"一处美"向"处处美"转变，村容村貌焕然一新。

2. 完善基础设施

塔格拉克村充分借助天山托木尔景区创建国家5A级旅游景区的有利契机，先后完善了水、电、路、通信等基础设施，修建了通景公路、乡村公路、盘山公路、跨河大桥、游客服务中心、生态停车场、旅游厕所等，实施了山体护栏、标识标牌、木栈道、托木尔峰保护区展厅等项目建设，同时配套了区间车、智慧旅游、景区直通车等服务，极大完善了旅游设施。

3. 丰富旅游业态

塔格拉克村深度挖掘得天独厚的旅游资源，充分利用村集体土地、农家宅院及闲置草地，因地制宜发展新业态。先后开发建设火车主题公园、云中漫步乐园、天山托木尔滑雪场、餐饮步行街、云尚乐园、步步惊心游乐园、托峰大本营、舍得客栈、欢乐谷、天山花海、神仙湾等丰富多样的旅游业态，涵盖了休闲观光、露营体验、美食体验、农事体验、亲子采摘、婚纱摄影、民宿体验等文旅类型，丰富的旅游业态吸引无数游客前来观光游览。

4. 发展乡村产业

塔格拉克村大力发展家禽养殖和畜牧业，推进规模化、产业化、品牌化发展。一是党参炖土鸡、沙葱炒鸡蛋、牦牛肉火锅等特色美食走上游客餐桌，土鸡蛋、风干肉、羊奶粉等成为特色农产品，在景区销售网点、阿克苏好礼商超等对外销售。农牧民转型成为乡村旅游直接供应商，实现了本村产品从"自产自销"转变为"定期供销"。二是撬动土地价值，鼓励引导农牧民采取转包、租赁、折资入股等方式流转土地，将闲置的土地聚拢，集中连片进行规划提升改造，大规模种植芍药、向日葵、油菜花等"景观经济"作物，最大化提升土地价值。

成效

塔格拉克村借助天山托木尔景区创建国家5A级旅游景区的契机，依托当地得天独厚的自然资源、深厚的历史文化积淀和浓厚的民族风情，大力发展乡村旅游。这一系列举措促使该村在社会、经济、环境等多个领域实现了显著进步与变革，不仅有效促进了周边3个乡镇、7个村的一体化发展，还成功带动本地及周边地区5000余人实现就业，人均年收入增加5万元以上。2019年至2024年，塔格拉克村游客突破210万人次，旅游总收入达8000万元。塔格拉克村探索出了一条乡村旅游推动乡村振兴的有效路径，先后获得全国乡村旅游重点村、中国美丽休闲乡村、自治区乡村振兴示范村、地区文化润疆示范基地等荣誉。

经验与启示

1. 坚持科学规划

塔格拉克村紧扣乡村振兴战略总目标，抓好科学规划引领，避免大拆大建，保留乡村风貌，以人居环境整治为基础，打造以乡村旅游业态为核心，发展特色产业为支撑，保护绿色生态为优先，在"乡村振兴+美丽乡村建设+扶贫增收"的路上探索出了"产业振兴、人才振兴、文化振兴、生态振兴、组织振兴"的初步经验，谱写了"农村美、农业强、农民富"的乡村振兴新篇章。

2. 坚持绿色发展

塔格拉克村大牧场环境优美、生态良好，在推进旅游产业发展中始终践行"绿水青山就是金山银山"理念，秉承保护性开发原则，把保护和改善生态环境作为首要任务。一是在严格保护村庄及周围原有生态和自然景观的基础上，大力实施村庄绿化美化工程，植绿补绿、见缝插绿、栽花种草，突出体现自然生态脉络；二是配套建设污水处理和垃圾处理设施，实现污水、垃圾无害化处理，保持农村碧水蓝天、空气清新的生态环境。

3. 创新运营模式

发展乡村旅游必须坚持多元投入和市场运作，依靠独立个体难以支撑。塔格拉克村在乡村旅游发展过程中，采取"政府引导、企业参与、党员带动、农民受益"的理念，通过与社会资本方、村集体、农牧民合作经营，创新利益联结机制，不搞"一刀切"分红模式，实现各方共同受益，营造了全社会共同参与、共同推动的良好氛围。

下一步计划

下一步，塔格拉克村将遵循重创新、强引领的原则，致力于巩固和拓展脱贫攻坚成果，并同步推进乡村振兴工作，跑出"加速度"，倾力打造"乡村振兴+美丽乡村建设+乡村旅游+乡村扶贫+森林山地康养+亲子农场+研学基地+国家休闲旅游度假区"的乡村振兴"塔村模式"，奋力打造全国乡村振兴示范样板。

2024 世界旅游联盟：旅游助力乡村振兴案例（中英文双语版）
WTA Best Practices of Rural Revitalization through Tourism 2024 (Chinese-English Bilingual Edition)

Tagelake Village, Wensu County, Aksu Prefecture, Xinjiang Uygur Autonomous Region:

Promoting Rural Revitalization through Landscape-Village Integration

Abstract

Endowed with unique eco-tourism resources, Tagelake Village of Wensu County, Aksu Prefecture, Xinjiang Uygur Autonomous Region, focuses on promoting landscape-village integration and implements a strategy of developing rural tourism for poverty alleviation and rural revitalization. It vigorously develops rural tourism and opens up the channel for translating lucid waters and lush mountains into invaluable assets. In its drive to build a beautiful village suitable for living, working, and traveling, it helps farmers and herdsmen continue to increase their income, and depicts a new picture of the countryside with "a beautiful countryside, a strong agriculture, and a prosperous farmers". It offers a worthwhile and replicable "Tagelake model" for rural development in Xinjiang.

Challenges and Problems

Tagelake Village covers an administrative division of 5,913.33 square kilometers, with a population of 738 in 239 households divided into three villager groups. There are 1,712 *mu* of cultivated land and 3.06 million *mu* of grassland. The village sits at the foot of Tomur Peak, the highest peak of the Tianshan Mountains, enjoys a picturesque landscape, and is rich in biodiversity. Nevertheless, it had backward transportation conditions and a weak foundation, and its people had limited knowledge about what was going on in the outside world and failed to keep pace with the times. Most of the villagers left for urban areas to make a living, leaving the village seriously hollowed out. The arable land was scarce, and the land was mainly for grazing. The income of the villagers was meager and the development level was low. The high-quality tourism resources in the village were yet to be properly developed.

Measures

1. Improving the appearance of the village

Tagelake Village has worked vigorously to improve the environment and build itself into a beautiful village by launching construction or renovation projects depending on the actual conditions. Firstly, it has coordinated efforts to upgrade the water pipelines, kitchen, toilets, livestock pens, courtyards, and wiring system, and tear down illegal and makeshift buildings and structures. Secondly, it has renovated the gate and the courtyard of the village committee building, residential houses, and courtyards, installed or replaced road lights, built sidewalks, erected protective gratings, the villager square and the food street, and implemented greening and beautification projects. Thirdly, it has set off an upsurge of actions for beautification and upgrading, creative transformation, and cultural and creative design, and used texts and paintings to embed traditional culture and folk culture into the village development, create beauty everywhere, and give the village a facelift.

2. Improving infrastructure

As the Tomur scenic area of the Tianshan Mountains was working to apply for the status as a national 5A-level scenic spot, Tagelake Village has successively improved the infrastructure of water, electricity, roads, and communications and built a scenic highway, a rural road, a winding mountain road, a cross-river bridge, a visitor center, an eco-friendly parking lot, and tourist toilets. Besides, mountain guardrails and wayfinding signs were put up, wooden planks paved on the mountain, and the exhibition hall was opened for the Tomur Peak Conservation Area. In addition, tourists can also take the through bus to the Scenic Area, change to shuttle buses within it, and access smart tourism services. The tourist facilities are significantly improved.

3. Diversifying the tourism business scene

Tagelake Village has dug deeply into its unique

tourism resources and has made full use of the village collective land, farm houses, and idle grassland to develop new business forms in places where they are suitable. It has successively launched a great variety of tourism projects, including the train theme park, the hiking-in-the-cloud paradise, the Tomur Ski Resort, the pedestrian food street, Yunshang Paradise, an amusement park, the Tomur Base Camp, an inn, the Happy Valley, the Tianshan Flower Sea, and the Shenxian Bay, offering many categories of tourism products and services such as leisure sightseeing, camping, catering, farming experience, U-pick experience for parents and children, wedding photography, and homestays. The diverse tourism products have attracted countless tourists.

4. Developing rural industries

Tagelake Village works vigorously to expand the scale and build up brands of poultry breeding and animal husbandry. Firstly, local special dishes such as the codonopsis chicken soup, scrambled eggs with Allium mongolicum Regel, and the yak meat hot pot are served to the tourists, and characteristic brand products such as free-range kitchen eggs, air-dried meat, and goat milk powder are sold in the sales outlets in the Scenic Area and the Aksu Products Store. Farmers and herdsmen have become direct suppliers of products, but instead of selling what they have harvested, they regularly supply the products to the distributors. Secondly, to tap into the value of land, Tagelake Village encouraged and guided farmers and herdsmen to transfer their land use rights through subcontracting, leasing, and equity investment. It has consolidated the land, planned for the use of and improved the congruous area. Plants such as Chinese herbaceous peonies, sunflowers, and rape flowers are grown on a large scale to develop the "landscape economy" and maximize the economic returns of the land.

Results

As the Tianshan Tomur Scenic Area is working to apply for the status as a national 5A-level scenic spot, Tagelake Village makes full use of its unique natural resources, profound historical and cultural heritage, and rich and colorful ethnic customs, vigorously develops rural tourism.These initiatives have significantly advanced and transformed the village in various aspects including society, economy, and environment.It has not only effectively fueled the integrated development of the seven villages in three towns nearby, but also created more than 5,000 jobs, directly and indirectly, in the local and surrounding areas, with an average annual income increase of more than 50,000 yuan per person. Since 2019, Tagelake Village has received more than 2.1 million tourists, and generated a total tourism income of 80 million yuan, embarking on a workable path to promote rural revitalization through rural tourism development. It has successively won the honorary titles of the National Key Village for Rural Tourism Development, the Beautiful Leisure Village in China, the Rural Revitalization Demonstration

Village in Xinjiang, and the Demonstration Base for Strengthening Cultural Identity and Bonds in Xinjiang.

Experience and Inspirations

1. Adhere to scientific planning

Staying oriented to the ultimate goal of rural revitalization, Tagelake Village has planned scientifically in advance, avoided large-scale demolition and construction, and retained the original countryside flavor. On top of improving the living environment, it has focused on developing rural tourism businesses, which are supported by characteristic industries, and prioritized ecological conservation in the course. On the journey to rural revitalization by building a beautiful countryside and reducing poverty, it has gained some useful experience in "energizing rural industries, human resources, culture, ecology, and organizations", and written a new chapter of rural revitalization featuring "a beautiful countryside, a strong agriculture, and prosperous farmers".

2. Adhere to green development

Tagelake Village boasts expansive grassland, a beautiful environment, and a healthy ecosystem. While developing the tourism industry, it has always acted upon the belief that "lucid waters and lush mountains are invaluable assets", practiced conservation-oriented development, and prioritized environmental protection and improvement. Firstly, based on strictly protecting the original ecology and natural landscape in the village and surrounding areas, it has vigorously implemented the greening and beautification project, planting trees, flowers, and grass wherever there is space, and highlighting the texture of its natural ecology. Secondly, it has built supporting sewage and garbage treatment facilities for the harmless treatment of sewage and garbage, so that the village can stay as a natural oxygen bar with clear waters, a blue sky, and fresh air.

3. Introduce new operating models

The development of rural tourism requires diverse sources of input and market-oriented operations, and cannot be done singlehandedly. In its effort to build the rural tourism industry, Tagelake Village has established an approach featuring government guidance, business participation, the mobilization of Party members, and benefits for farmers. Through cooperation with social capital, village collectives, farmers, and herdsmen, it has established a new interests convergence mechanism and abandoned the "one-size-fits-all" dividend distribution model, so that everyone can benefit and is willing to contribute.

Plans

In the next step, Tagelake Village will focus on strengthening innovation and guidance and make every effort to do a good job in consolidating and building upon our achievements in poverty alleviation and in promoting rural revitalization. It will speed up to set a national model of rural revitalization, beautiful countryside, rural tourism, and rural poverty alleviation, and build a national leisure and tourism resort with forests and mountains for health preservation, parent-child U-pick farms, and study tour bases.

2024 世界旅游联盟：旅游助力乡村振兴案例（中英文双语版）
WTA Best Practices of Rural Revitalization through Tourism 2024（Chinese-English Bilingual Edition）

贵州省黔东南苗族侗族自治州榕江县：
"村超"文体旅融合发展助力乡村振兴

摘　要

　　贵州省榕江县立足比较优势和足球底蕴，选定新媒体和乡村足球文化 IP 作为新赛道，围绕"共享村超流量、共创人民足球、共造美好生活、共赢精彩未来"的目标，坚持守正创新、全民参与、共创共建，推动贵州"村超"火爆出圈，实现了现象级正能量传播，贵州"村超"成为贵州的又一张"新名片"。榕江县坚持以文塑旅、以旅彰文、以体促旅，充分用好自然珍宝和文化瑰宝，全力打造"村超"品牌，深入挖掘"村超"赛事的市场价值和产业潜力，大力发展超好吃、超好住、超好行、超好游、超好购、超好玩等"超能经济"，让活力四射的"村超"成为乡村振兴的催化剂，真正将村超"流量"转化为社会效益的"质量"和经济效益的"增量"，推动农文旅体商融合发展，助力乡村振兴。

挑战与问题

榕江县是全国最后一批脱贫县，属少数民族地区。榕江县基础设施虽然相比脱贫攻坚时要完善得多，但对标其他先进地区，榕江的基础设施难以满足"村超"火爆出圈所带来的接待和服务需求。在村超持续火爆过程中，需要大量资金来加强公共基础设施建设，以完善吃、住、行、娱、游、购、停等公共服务和旅游配套服务体系。

措施

1. 发挥资源优势

榕江县开展足球运动有着悠久的传统，榕江足球有80年历史，"村级赛事"有30多年历史，并一直保持着良好的足球氛围。苗、侗、水、瑶等少数民族人口占全县总人口的83.9%，多民族杂居赋予了榕江独有的民族风情。赛事本身所具有的乡土气息和赛场上多样的民族文化展示是"村超"的灵魂所在，文化是"村超"品牌的核心基因。

2. 讲好"村超"故事

榕江"村超"是一场村民足球比赛，更是一场民间文化活动大餐，全民参与，共创共建，乡土气息与民族风情融合，展现了人们对美好生活的向往。县域品牌打造要立足当地特色，讲好"村超"背后平凡人物的感人走心故事，探索有参与感和接地气的活动，做实、做真、做美，让品牌更具文化亲和力。

3. 加速新媒体传播

榕江县创新提出"让手机变成新农具，让数据变成新农资，让直播变成新农活"的"三新农"发展理念，建成新媒体电商产业园，积极发展和利用短视频、电商直播、线上营销等新业态，累计培育1.28万个新媒体账号，构建"村超"主账号+子账号新媒体传播矩阵，保持"村超"关注热度。榕江"村超"频频登上热搜，热度持续不减，短视频裂变传播已成为品牌传播的关键手段。

4. 举办活动造势

"村超"通过多种方式不断造势，发起全国美食足球友谊赛，邀请足球明星卡卡、范志毅、央视知名解说韩乔生和贺炜、水木年华等相继到榕江，举办贵州"村超村晚"展示活动、中法青年友谊赛、"逐梦"青少年女足公益赛等，持续为"村超"制造热点和话题。县域品牌不能成为昙花一现的"网红"，必须持续推进，不断延伸品牌的文化内涵和价值形象，让品牌产生持续影响力。

5. 促进体旅融合

榕江县将足球运动与神秘古朴多元民族文化、美食文化相结合，提出"超级星期六足球之夜"。"村超"现场群众不仅自发组织侗族大歌、苗族芦笙舞、齐跳多耶等民俗展演，村民还在比赛现场开展美食宠粉活动，让观众球迷免费试吃榕江牛瘪、塔石羊瘪、榕江卷粉、榕江西瓜等各类特色美食，自发践行文体旅深度融合。

成效

贵州"村超"与"英超"签署了战略合作协议，与中央广播电视总台"央视频"建立战略合作伙伴关系。榕江依托"村超"品牌影响力，深入挖掘村超赛事的市场价值和产业潜力，聚焦"吃、住、行、游、购、娱"六要素，推动榕江"超能经济"全面发展。2023年贵州"村超"期间（5月13日至7月29日），全县累计吸引游客338.42万人次，同比增长131.75%，实现旅游综合收入38.34亿元，同比增长164.05%，极大推动了旅游市场消费释放活力。"村超"入选2023中国旅游产业影响力案例、首批群众"三大球"精品赛事案例、2023中国公共关系优秀案例、2023抖音热点十大旅行目的地，并上榜2023年度乡村振兴十大新闻、2023年度十大流行语。

经验与启示

1.全民参与

榕江县立足比较优势和足球底蕴，将足球赛事与民族文化、非遗美食、淳朴民风等结合并进行融合式创新，尊重人民主体、人民主创、人民主推的群众共

创共建，推动"村超"火爆出圈。

2. 吸引人才

榕江县实施县域"聚才行动"，建立人才顾问、名誉村长、村超文化产业特派员等制度，组建的榕江县校友总会吸纳了1.8万多个优秀榕江籍的乡贤和校友，公益聘请水木年华成员缪杰、全国劳模张春丽、世界体操冠军刘榕冰和世界攀岩冠军龙见国等知名人士到各村担任"名誉村长"。

3. 借势造势

中国足球自带话题和流量。榕江"村超"本来是一场小地方的足球比赛，毫无新奇之处，但运用事件策划的手法，冠以超级联赛的名头，与"英超""中超"等知名赛事产生了联系。这样的策划激发了人们对乡村足球超级联赛的无限遐想，形成了巨大的热点话题效应，"村超"IP应运而生。

下一步计划

一是保护村超品牌。政府应做好服务保障工作，防止资本无序介入，对"村超"品牌实行公益化管理，将"村超"运营获得的收益用于乡村体育公益事业、村集体经济、球队和啦啦队活动经费、青少年足球发展、农村基础设施建设和民生保障等，确保"村超"品牌取之于民，收益用之于民。

二是优化村超赛事。坚持政治性、安全性、群众性、持续性、带动性的要求，秉持"策划有高度、平时有温度、假期有热度"的办赛理念，持续办好村超联赛，并开展全国美食非遗友谊赛暨全国女子足球友谊赛、全国青少年夏令营足球赛、村超"一带一路"国际友谊赛暨贵州—粤港澳大湾区足球友谊赛等赛事，实现"重要节点有大赛、周末有小赛、经常有外地球队交流赛"。

三是发展"超能经济"。深入挖掘"村超"赛事的文旅价值和消费潜力，大力发展超好吃、超好住、超好行、超好游、超好购、超好玩、超好招等"超能经济"，把文化瑰宝和自然珍宝转化为群众增收致富的金银财宝，持续推进农文体旅商融合发展，助力乡村振兴。

2024 世界旅游联盟：旅游助力乡村振兴案例（中英文双语版）
WTA Best Practices of Rural Revitalization through Tourism 2024 (Chinese-English Bilingual Edition)

Rongjiang County, Qiandongnan Prefecture, Guizhou Province:

The Village Super League Boosting Rural Revitalization through the Integration of Culture, Sports and Tourism

Abstract

Based on its comparative advantages and football tradition, Rongjiang County of Guizhou Province set its eyes on new media and rural football culture and proposed the goals of sharing the traffic brought by the Village Super League, establishing a football brand of the people and for the people, and creating a better life and a win-win future for all. Rongjiang County has upheld the fundamental principles while seeking innovation, engaged the whole village, and made Guizhou's Village Super League a household name all over the country, spreading positive energy in society. The Village Super League has become another "business card" of Guizhou Province. Rongjiang County continues to shape its tourism industry with cultural heritage, highlight its cultural heritage through tourist attractions, and promote tourism development through sports events. It makes full use of natural and cultural treasures, strives to build up the Village Super League brand, deeply taps its market value and commercial potential, and vigorously develops the "Super economy", covering catering, accommodation, transportation, travel, shopping, and entertainment, so that the energetic "Village Super League" becomes a catalyst for rural revitalization, and the traffic of the League can be truly translated into social and economic benefits, to promote the integrated development of agriculture, culture, tourism, sports and commerce, and contribute to rural revitalization.

Challenges and Problems

Rongjiang County is one of the last counties to be lifted out of poverty nationwide and is an ethnic minority area. Its infrastructure, though much improved thanks to the poverty alleviation assistance, is still insufficient to meet the soaring demand of football fans and tourists during the Village Super League season. As Rongjiang County continues to host the Village Super League events, it needs to invest heavily in the construction of public infrastructure to improve the public services and tourist services, covering such aspects as catering, accommodation, travel, entertainment, sightseeing, shopping, and parking.

Measures

1. Giving full play to the advantageous resources

The people in Rongjiang County have been playing football for a long time. The Rongjiang County football team has a history of 80 years, and the village-level football games could be dated back to more than 30 years. The football atmosphere here is always good. Miao, Dong, Shui, Yao, and other ethnic minorities account for 83.9% of the county's population and shape Rongjiang's unique ethnic customs. The simplicity and cultural diversity of the games are the soul of the League. Culture is the core gene of the Village Super League brand.

2. Telling the story of the Village Super League well

The League is a football game for villagers and a feast of folk cultural activities. It is by everyone and for everyone. It blends country life and ethnic customs and shows the people's aspiration for a better life. The brand of Rongjiang County should be based on local characteristics, the touching stories of the wonderful ordinary people behind the Village Super League, and engaging and easy-to-participate activities. The brand should advocate realness, authenticity, and beauty, and relate to the people psychologically.

3. Accelerating the dissemination of new media

Rongjiang County has proposed an original development philosophy of "turning mobile phones into agricultural tools, data into agricultural materials, and live streaming into a new form of farm work". It has built a new media e-commerce industrial park, and actively developed and used short videos, live streaming e-commerce, and online

marketing businesses. It has cultivated a total of 12,800 new media accounts, and built a new media communication matrix for the Village Super League, including main accounts and sub-accounts, to maintain the visibility and popularity of the League. The Village Super League has been a frequent trendy word on social platforms, and its popularity continues unabated. Viral marketing via short videos has become a key means of brand communication.

4. Hosting events to attract more traffic and exposure

The Village Super League has continuously increased its visibility by hosting activities in various forms. It initiated the National Food and Friendly Football Match, invited football stars including Kaká and Fan Zhiyi, the CCTV well-known sports commentators Han Qiaosheng and He Wei, and the pop duo Shuimu Nianhua, to Rongjiang County, and held the Village Super Village Evening Gala, the Sino-French Youth Friendship Match, and the Non-for-Profit Match of the Girls' Football Team, continuing to add contents to and create hashtags for the Village Super League. County brand building must not be short-lived but must be sustainable. Rongjiang needs to work constantly to enrich the cultural connotation, build up the value image of the brand, and let the brand have a sustainable influence.

5. Promoting the integrated development of sports and tourism

Rongjiang County has launched the Super Saturday Football Night event, which incorporates the mysterious, ancient multi-ethnic culture and food culture. At the event site, the villagers spontaneously staged folk cultural performances, including the Grand Song of the Dong Ethnic Group, the Lusheng Dance of the Miao Ethnic Group, and the Dance of Doye. The vendors also gave out free samples to the football fans, inviting them to try unique local flavors, including the Niubie hot pot, the Yangbie hot pot, roll noodles, and watermelons, spontaneously promoting the deep integration of culture, sports, and tourism.

Results

The Village Super League has signed a strategic cooperation agreement with the Premier League and established a strategic partnership with yangshipin.cn under China Media Group. Based on the brand influence of the Village Super League, Rongjiang County deeply digs into the market value and commercial potential of the League events and promotes the comprehensive development of the "Super Economy", with a focus on the six aspects of catering, accommodation, transportation travel, shopping and entertainment. During the Village Super League season in 2023 (May 13 to July 29), the county attracted a total of 3,384,200 tourists, a year-on-year increase of 131.75%, and generated comprehensive tourism income of 3.834 billion yuan, a year-on-year increase of 164.05%. Tourist consumption was greatly boosted. The Village Super League was voted among the Influential Practices in the Tourism Industry in China in 2023, the first batch of Boutique Mass Football, Basketball, and Volleyball Events, the Best Practices of Public Relations in China in 2023, and the Top Ten Tourist Destinations on Douyin in 2023. It was on the list of the 2023 Top Ten News Reports on Rural Revitalization and voted among China's Top Ten Buzzwords in 2023.

Experience and Inspirations

1. Engage the people

Based on its comparative advantages and football tradition, Rongjiang County combines football events with ethnic culture, local traditional cuisine, and folk customs, and lets the people play the main role in promoting the Village Super League to the rest of the country.

2. Attract talent

Rongjiang County has launched the county-wide talent gathering action and established such posts as talent consultants, honorary village heads, cultural industry commissioners of the Village Super League and the Rongjiang County Alumni Association, which has more than 18,000 members. It has hired Miao Jie, a member of the pop duo Shuimu Nianhua, Zhang Chunli, a national model worker, Liu Rongbing, a world gymnastics champion, and Long Jianguo, a world rock climbing champion, among other celebrities, to serve as honorary village heads.

3. Increasing visibility and popularity through event marketing

Chinese football is never short of traffic or

attention. The predecessor of the Village Super League was a small local football game; there was nothing special about it. But through event marketing and with the name "Super League", it has become something comparable to the Premier League and Chinese Super League, something of infinite possibilities, and thus a huge magnet of attention and discussion. The Village Super League brand thus came into being.

Plans

Firstly, protect the Village Super League brand. The government needs to provide the services needed, prevent disorderly intervention from social capital, and adopt a non-profit management for the brand. The income obtained from the operation of the Village Super League should be used to support rural sports undertakings, the village collective economy, football teams and cheerleading teams, youth football development, rural infrastructure construction, and other services essential to the people, to give back to the people.

Secondly, optimize the Village Super League event planning. Rongjiang County will continue to hold the 2024 Village Super League season by adhering to the political and safety requirements and engaging the general public to promote sustainable development and drive the development of related industries. The event planning should have the big picture in mind, and make sure that there are games and other activities on weekdays, weekends, and holidays alike. Rongjiang County plans to host the National Food and Intangible Cultural Heritage Friendship Match and the National Women's Football Friendship Match, the National Youth Summer Camp Football Match, "the Belt and Road" Village Super League Friendly Match and the Guizhou-Greater Bay Area Football Friendly Match. It will strive to make sure that there are major games on key dates, ordinary games on weekends, and friendly games with visiting teams from now and then.

Thirdly, develop the "Super Economy". Rongjiang County will further tap the cultural and tourism value and consumption potential of the Village Super League, vigorously develop the "Super Economy" covering catering, accommodation, transportation travel, shopping, entertainment, and investment promotion, cash on the cultural heritage and natural resources to enrich the people, continue the integrated development of agriculture, culture, sports, tourism, and commerce, and contribute to rural revitalization.

广西壮族自治区桂林市阳朔县：
国际乡村旅居地特色之路

摘 要

广西壮族自治区桂林市阳朔县秉承生态立县、绿色发展理念，依托得天独厚的山水田园、古镇古村、历史文化等文化旅游资源，坚持"+文旅"发展战略，围绕"国际化、标准化、品牌化、特色化"工作思路，大力培育新型文化旅游业态，打造国际乡村旅居地，助力乡村振兴，促进阳朔县社会经济高质量发展。

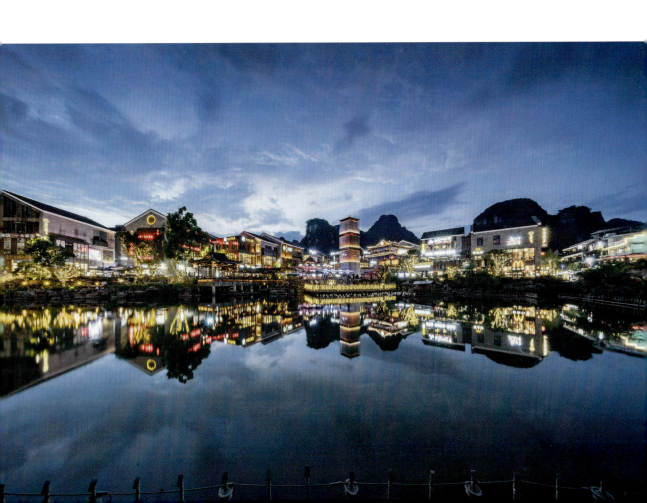

挑战与问题

阳朔在旅游发展过程中面临的最大挑战就是规划空间有限。阳朔县县域中的高价值、高人流量地区基本位于漓江风景名胜区保护范围内，漓江、遇龙河沿岸属于一二级保护区和特级保护区，可利用开发的空间较少。因此，项目资源开发需平衡好生态环境保护与政策规划之间的关系，实现"绿水青山"与"金山银山"的和谐共生，避免生态环境遭受破坏。

措施

1. 保护自然山水，推进阳朔乡村整体环境生态化

一是实施百里漓江绿化、彩化、花化、果化、生态护岸等工程，持续推进生态复绿、植树造林，率先实现自治区级"生态乡镇"全覆盖。二是扎实开展"美丽阳朔·生态乡村"建设、"五拆五清五建"专项行动，不断改善乡村生态环境。三是深入实施"绿满八桂"工程，对通道、城镇、村屯进行绿化美化，不断完善漓江、遇龙河生态保护区功能。四是积极探索漓江和遇龙河流域生态保障机制，实行生态奖补和财政保障，实现"保景富民"的生态目标。

2. 深化文旅融合，推进阳朔乡村旅游产品特色化

一是开发特色文化旅游产品，如壮族山歌会、瑶家坐歌堂、傩舞、舞牌灯、绣球制作、山水国画、画扇制作、仿古工艺、竹木根雕等，这些产品蕴含深厚的乡土情怀与本土文化特色，丰富了乡村文化的内容，推进乡村文化振兴。二是结合乡村人文景观，凸显"原始、古朴、真实、自然"的独特性，重点培育一批特色乡村旅游乡镇和特色旅游名村。三是自办节庆推陈出新，展示非物质文化风采，办好阳朔漓江渔火节、壮族"三月三"、白沙镇"六·廿三"、兴坪镇"九月十九"、福利镇"五月八"、普益乡"十月香"等传统民俗节庆，扩大宣传效果。

3. 整合文旅资源，推进阳朔乡村产业发展集聚化

一是全面实施"+文旅"战略，打造文旅产业集群，包括以大酒店品牌为核心的国际品牌酒店集群、以购物场所为核心的特色商业街区集群、依托特色村镇打造的精品旅游民宿集群、以大型演艺为代表的文

化演艺集群以及以休闲运动为主的户外运动产业集群等。二是引导文化和旅游与商业、体育、城镇化、农业等其他领域融合发展，打造低空飞行基地、茶艺课堂、古建文化、田园综合体、百里新村等一大批特色乡村旅游项目，塑造了阳朔独特的文旅品牌，形成了文旅融合发展的"阳朔模式"，助力实现乡村产业集聚化发展。

4. 接轨国际标准，推进阳朔乡村旅游服务规范化

一是提供国际化旅游服务与在线预订服务。游客可以通过景区、旅游度假区的官方网站、微信公众号、抖音等获得英语浏览、英文咨询、线上预订等服务，同时平台还提供电子门票。二是持续推动旅游标识国际化规范化。阳朔县对多语种旅游指示标识进行维护更新，开展多语种旅游标识标牌标准化规范化调查与整改，实现乡村旅游标识系统国际化。

5. 坚持共建共享，推进乡村旅游普惠全民化

阳朔旅游起源于20世纪80年代，民众早早便吃上了旅游饭。随着漓江排筏游、遇龙河漂流等旅游项目的落地生根，越来越多民众分享旅游发展红利。旅游发展能够给他们带来更多就业机会，大多数人实现了在家门口就业，如利用自家房产经营民宿、到旅游街区店铺工作、充当文化艺术演出演员等，本地居民在旅游发展中的幸福感、获得感不断增强。

成效

阳朔风光旖旎，处处是风景。阳朔县打造了山水观光产业、民俗文化演艺、康养民宿酒店、户外运动等产业集群。现有全国乡村旅游重点村2个，2023年全县全年接待游客2111.43万人次，同比增长75.92%；旅游总消费300.29亿元，同比增长79.76%。其中，入境游客9.8714万人次，同比增长899.84%。阳朔县先后获得全国休闲农业与乡村旅游示范县、中国乡村旅游创客示范基地、中国优秀乡村旅游目的地等荣誉称号。

经验与启示

1. 促进产业转型升级

阳朔县发展观光采摘农业及农产深加工，推动农

产品旅游商品化，发展有机生态产品，开发具有特色的伴手礼，构建旅游商品加工产业链，推动旅游商品加工产业规模化、品牌化、个性化发展，以旅促农，农旅融合发展，促进乡村振兴。

2. 举办体育赛事

阳朔县结合山水资源优势，大力开展户外运动，发展攀岩、登山、越野跑、徒步游、自行车骑行、房车露营、低空飞行、热气球、滑翔伞、漂流、铁人三项等几十种休闲运动体育健身项目，打造特色运动休闲旅游、山地户外体育旅游、老龄休闲养生旅游等旅游示范基地，为乡村振兴创造发展机遇。

3. 依托生态资源优势

阳朔县充分依托山清水秀的自然生态环境优势，加强对河湖水系的生态化、旅游化治理，把景区开发、乡村旅游、休闲农业等与乡村振兴工作相结合，走出一条产业优、百姓富、生态美、人民群众幸福感高的绿色发展道路。

下一步计划

一是将乡村旅游发展与传统村落保护深度融合，使乡村旅游融入更多的古镇文化、农耕文化、自然遗产和文化遗产元素。二是充分挖掘阳朔县独特的乡土人文景观，包括村落建筑、古镇古桥、观光采摘等乡村优质旅游资源，全面推动现代特色农业（核心）示范区和农业生态园、养生园、观光园、精品园的发展。三是重点培育一批特色乡村旅游乡镇和特色旅游名村，如骥马村、旧县村等。四是优化国际乡村旅居地的环境及服务，进一步促进观光农业与特色乡村旅游的蓬勃发展。

Yangshuo County, Guilin City, Guangxi Zhuang Autonomous Region:

A Path towards the International Rural Living Destination with Distinctive Characteristics

Abstract

Yangshuo County in Guilin City, Guangxi Zhuang Autonomous Region, adheres to the concept of ecological development of the county to seek green growth. By leveraging its unique cultural and tourism resources, including natural landscapes, ancient towns, villages, and history and culture, the county embraces the "+ Cultural Tourism" development strategy. Centering around the principles of "internationalization, standardization, branding, and specialization", Yangshuo County is vigorously cultivating new types of cultural tourism industries, building an international rural living destination to drive rural revitalization, and promoting the high-quality socio-economic development of the county.

Challenges and Problems

The biggest challenge Yangshuo County faces in its tourism development is the limited planning space. The high-value, high-traffic areas of the county are mostly within the protected areas of the Li River Scenic Area. The areas along the Li River and Yulong River fall largely within primary and secondary protection zones and special protection zones, leaving little space for development. Therefore, in the development of project resources, it is necessary to balance the relationship between ecological environment protection and policy planning, achieve the harmonious coexistence of lucid waters and lush mountains with gold and silver mountains, and prevent the ecological environment from being destroyed.

Measures

1. Protecting natural landscapes and promoting the overall ecological environment change of Yangshuo's rural areas

Firstly, it is to implement projects for greening, coloring, flowering, fruiting, and ecological riverbank protection along the hundred-mile stretch of the Li River; to continually advance the ecological restoration and afforestation; to take the lead in achieving full coverage of "ecological towns" at the autonomous region level. Secondly, it is to substantially carry out the "Beautiful Yangshuo and Ecological Rural Areas" campaign and the "Five-Demolition, Five-Cleanup, and Five-Construction" special action for continuous improvement in the rural ecological environment. Thirdly, it is to deepen the implementation of the Guangxi afforestation project, greening and beautifying corridors, towns, and villages, and continually improving the functions of the Li River and Yulong River ecological protection

zones. Fourthly, it is to explore the mechanisms for ecological protection in the Li River and Yulong River basins, and implement ecological compensation and financial guarantees to achieve the ecological goal of "protecting the scenery and bringing wealth to the people".

2. Deepening the integration of culture and tourism, and promoting the development of Yangshuo's rural tourism products with distinctive characteristics

Firstly, it is to develop distinctive cultural tourism products such as Zhuang ethnic group mountain song singing, Yao People performance, Nuo dance, lantern dancing, embroidered ball making, landscape painting, fan making, antique crafts, and bamboo and wood root carving. These activities are deeply rooted in local culture, enriching rural culture and promoting cultural revitalization in rural areas. Secondly, it highlights the uniqueness of the rural areas being primitive, ancient, authentic, and natural by combining cultural landscapes, with the focus put on the endeavor to foster a series of special rural tourism towns and famous villages. Thirdly, it is to innovate festive activities that showcase the intangible cultural heritage, such as the Yangshuo Li River Fishing Fire Festival, Zhuang People's "March 3rd", Baisha Town's "June 23rd", Xingping Town's

"September 19th", Fuli Town's "May 8th", and Puyi Township's "October Fragrance", expanding their promotional impact.

3. Integrating cultural and tourism resources to promote the clustering of Yangshuo's rural industries

Firstly, it is to fully implement the "+ Cultural Tourism" strategy and create clusters of cultural and tourism industries, including the international brand hotel clusters centering on major hotel brands, characteristic commercial street clusters centering around shopping venues, boutique homestay clusters based on distinctive villages and towns, cultural performance clusters represented by large-scale performances, and outdoor sports industry clusters with leisure sports as the mainstay. Secondly, it is to guide the integration of culture and tourism with other fields such as commerce, sports, urbanization, and agriculture. This includes advancing unique rural tourism projects like low-altitude flight bases, tea ceremony classes, ancient architecture culture, pastoral complexes, and the long stretch of new villages, creating a distinctive cultural tourism brand

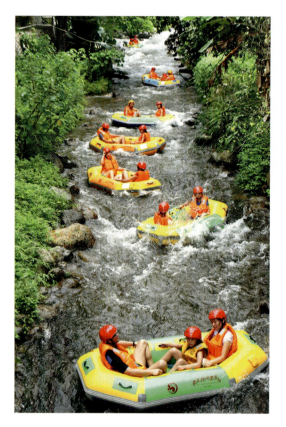

for Yangshuo County and developing the "Yangshuo Model" of integrated cultural tourism development, which contributes to the clustering of rural industries.

4. Aligning with international standards and promoting the standardization of Yangshuo's rural tourism services

Firstly, it is to provide internationalized tourism services and convenient online booking. Visitors can access English browsing, consultation, booking, and electronic ticketing services through the official websites, WeChat public accounts, and Douyin pages of scenic spots and resorts. Secondly, it is to continuously improve tourism signage to make it up to the international standard. Yangshuo County has maintained and updated multilingual tourist signs and conducted inspections and rectifications of multilingual tourism signage to internationalize the rural tourism signage system.

5. Promoting shared development and ensuring rural tourism benefits all

Yangshuo County's tourism industry began in the 1980s, and the local people have long benefited from tourism. With the establishment of tourism projects like Li River bamboo rafting and Yulong River drifting, more and more locals enjoy the benefits of tourism development as they have growing job opportunities. Most people can now work near home, whether by operating homestays in their own homes, working in the shops on tourist streets, or performing in cultural and artistic shows. Amid tourism development residents have an ever-growing sense of happiness and fulfillment.

Results

The scenery of Yangshuo is enchanting, and everywhere is picturesque. Yangshuo County has created clusters of industries centering around landscape sightseeing, folk culture performances, wellness homestays, and outdoor sports. The county currently has two of the National Key Villages for the Development of Rural Tourism. In 2023, the county received 21.1143 million tourists, a year-on-year increase of 75.92%, with total tourism revenue reaching 30.029 billion yuan, a year-on-year increase of 79.76%. Among them, 98,714 were inbound tourists, registering a year-on-year increase of 899.84%. Yangshuo County has been awarded titles such as the National Demonstration County for Leisure Agriculture and Rural Tourism, the Rural Tourism Maker Demonstration Base of China and the Excellent Rural Tourism Destination of China.

Experiences and Inspirations

1. Promoting industrial transformation and upgrading

Yangshuo County has developed sightseeing and picking agriculture, conducted deep processing of agricultural products, made agricultural products into tourism goods, developed organic ecological products, and created distinctive souvenirs. It has built a tourism product processing industry chain, promoting the industrialization, branding, and personalization of tourism product processing, thereby facilitating the integration of agriculture and tourism and promoting rural revitalization.

2. Hosting sports events

Leveraging its natural resources, Yangshuo County has vigorously developed outdoor sports such as rock climbing, mountaineering, trail running, hiking, cycling, RV camping, low-altitude flight, hot air ballooning, paragliding, rafting, and triathlons. The county has established demonstration bases for leisure sports tourism, mountain outdoor sports tourism, and elderly wellness tourism, creating development opportunities for rural revitalization.

3. Leveraging ecological resources

Yangshuo County has fully utilized its beautiful natural ecological environment and stepped up the ecological and tourism-based management of rivers and lakes. By integrating scenic area development, rural tourism, and leisure agriculture with rural revitalization efforts, Yangshuo County has paved a green development path that fosters industrial excellence, brings wealth to the people, beautifies the environment, and enhances the happiness of the locals.

Plans

Firstly, it is to conduct an in-depth integration of rural tourism development with traditional village protection and incorporate more of the ancient town culture and farming culture, natural heritage and cultural heritage elements into rural tourism development. Secondly, it is to fully utilize Yangshuo County's unique rural cultural landscapes, develop the county's unique rural resources, such as village architecture, ancient towns and bridges, sightseeing and picking activities, and promote the development of modern characteristic agriculture (core) demonstration zones, agricultural ecological parks, wellness parks, sightseeing parks, and boutique parks. Thirdly, it is to focus on cultivating a series of characteristic rural tourism towns and villages, like the Jima Village and Jiuxian Village. Fourthly, it is to optimize the environment and services of the international rural living destination. By so doing, thriving agritourism and distinctive rural tourism shall be generated.

2024 世界旅游联盟：旅游助力乡村振兴案例（中英文双语版）
WTA Best Practices of Rural Revitalization through Tourism 2024（Chinese-English Bilingual Edition）

中国国家铁路集团有限公司：
铁路旅游赋能乡村振兴

摘　要

中国国家铁路集团有限公司（以下简称国铁集团）深入贯彻习近平总书记对铁路工作的重要指示批示精神，依托路网和运输优势，结合帮扶县区资源禀赋和旅游市场需求，创新构建"铁路＋旅游＋乡村振兴"新模式，不断织密铁路旅游乡村振兴服务网，加大脱贫地区旅游专列和"慢火车"开行力度，培育铁路特色文旅产业集群，提升铁路乡村旅游产品竞争力，加强脱贫地区旅游资源引流赋能，推进铁路与脱贫地区农文旅融合发展，激发乡村旅游新经济新动能，助力帮扶县区经济社会发展步入快车道。

挑战与问题

"铁路+旅游+乡村振兴"是一种全新的帮扶模式，存在的主要问题如下。一是交通基础设施落后，一些旅游资源禀赋较好的帮扶县区没有铁路通达，或者开行车次较少，出行不便成为制约帮扶县区开拓旅游市场的主要障碍。二是铁路企业未能充分发挥自身的力量和优势，在与旅游资源的深度融合发展方面缺乏深度，在打造铁路旅游品牌、拓展文旅产品、带动帮扶县区引流赋能等方面还有差距。三是创新不足，运输方式较为传统，运输服务质量参差不齐，不能满足快捷、舒适的高品质旅行需求。

措施

1. 发展与优化铁路旅游乡村振兴服务网

一是加大帮扶县区铁路投资建设力度，进一步提升铁路网通达性、均衡性和可及性。二是优化丰富帮扶县区客运列车产品种类，增加帮扶县区途经车次，完善乡村旅游综合交通服务网，为帮扶县区吸引客流提供运输服务保障。三是大力推进帮扶县区客运基础设施提档升级，创新推动铁路沿线地区生态建设和站城融合发展，将县乡车站打造成乡村振兴的靓丽窗口。

2. 设计开行谱系化旅游列车

实施铁路文旅产品精准投放，吸引高端消费群体赴帮扶县区旅游消费，实现"东人西游""西物东送"。例如，国铁哈尔滨局集团公司推出以"林都号"为代表的高端旅游专列产品，以东西环线专列为代表的精品旅游专列产品，以点对点城际专列为代表的普惠旅游专列产品，覆盖旅游热点方向，打造具有东北特色的全季旅游产品；国铁乌鲁木齐局集团公司在和田站举办铁路旅游兴疆行动，开行新疆高端专列、精品专列和普惠专列等谱系化旅游列车，加大"引流入疆"工作力度，助力新疆旅游高质量发展。

3. 创新开行跨区域主题旅游专列

发挥不同项目的区域优势和资源禀赋，组合设计旅游线路，组织开行跨区域主题旅游专列，例如"淄博烧烤""京和号""林海雪原号""环西部火车游"等主题专列，促进多区域旅客资源流通。济南局在"淄博烧烤"网红旅游专列基础上创新推出了"高铁环游齐鲁"旅游套票，凡购买该套票的乘客，到相关景区游览，可在五日内多次预约乘坐指定列车，极大促进了山东地区乡村旅游提质升级。

4. 启动并推广"乡村振兴列车+"服务品牌

一是通过优化旅游列车组织结构，探索"直通+管内"创新运营模式，以提高游客出游效率。二是针对帮扶县区旅游资源的季节性、周期性特征，优化安排列车开行时表，统筹普通车底资源及高端车底资源。国铁集团在打造"乡村振兴列车+"服务品牌上已取得显著成效，成功构建了一系列红色旅游、研学旅游、文化遗产旅游、康养旅游等广受欢迎的"网红列车""网红线路"和"网红打卡地"，带动了沿线旅游、消费、服务业的整体升级。

5. 促进铁路与旅游项目深度融合，全面激活并充分挖掘帮扶县区旅游资源潜力

通过融合多种要素，创新铁路旅游项目，如"铁路旅游+文化""铁路旅游+体育""铁路旅游+康养""铁路旅游+网红打卡地"等，这些创新举措旨在实现铁路旅游与景区板块化联动、各类旅游资源串珠型互联、产品项目定制化联动，吸引了更多消费群体。

6. 助力帮扶县区引流赋能

统筹路内 18 个铁路局集团公司形成宣传矩阵齐发力，并联合中央和国家机关工委、农业农村部、文化和旅游部等部门在全国高铁车站和列车联合开展乡村旅游宣传推介，加大抖音、微博、小红书等社交平台宣传产品投放力度，打造"网红打卡+帮扶特产+铁路文旅攻略绘本+铁路特色文创产品"复合型引流模式，累计覆盖旅客流量 25 亿人次，减免广告宣传费用近 2 亿元。

成效

2023 年，中国国家铁路集团有限公司聚焦"打基础、利长远、补短板、调结构"，实施 24 个联网、补网、强链项目，丽香铁路、川青铁路、贵南高速铁路等 34 个项目建成投产，新建 102 座车站投入运营，极大改善了帮扶县区铁路客运服务基础设施水平。2023 年，面向老少边及帮扶县区铁路基建投资完成 4076 亿元，占全国 80.2%；新投产铁路 2776.7 千米，占全国 76.4%，覆盖 77 个老少边及帮扶县，其中 22 个帮扶县结束了不通铁路的历史，年运送帮扶县区旅客 2.1 亿人次。全路累计开行途经脱贫地区乡村旅游专列 486 列，发送游客 26.8 万人次，实现人均消费 2000 余元。公益性"慢火车"覆盖全国 21 个省区 100 多个脱贫县。铁路旅游项目促进了"吃、住、行、游、购、娱"的消费链升级，相关产业如酒店、餐饮、文化、休闲、特产等集聚壮大。

经验与启示

1. 完善基建

一是通过加大对贫困地区铁路基础设施的投资力度，提升铁路网络的覆盖广度、均衡性与可达性，推动铁路沿线地区的生态建设和站城一体化发展，将县乡车站打造成乡村振兴战略的示范窗口，展现地方特色与活力。二是增加途经帮扶县区的列车班次，完善乡村旅游的综合交通服务体系，确保为吸引游客到帮扶县区旅游消费提供坚实的运输服务保障。

2. 整合资源

一方面，充分利用乡村地区丰富优质的旅游资源，因地制宜，精细化和差异化地开发铁路特色旅游项目，推动铁路旅游与乡村旅游业深度融合，有效带动沿线群众收入的增长。另一方面，结合"快慢"列车运营优化开行方案，打通乡村旅游"最后一公里"，引导旅客在铁路沿线地区参与旅游、购物、游学和商务等多元化活动，从而激发乡村振兴的新动力和活力。

下一步计划

一是持续推进帮扶县区铁路规划建设。持续加大老少边和脱贫地区特别是西部地区铁路规划投资倾斜力度，强化出疆入藏等战略骨干通道建设，高质量推进川藏铁路、"百项交通扶贫骨干通道工程"等重点铁路建设项目，集中实施一批联网补网强链工程，大力推进脱贫地区物流基础设施建设提档升级。

二是拓展提升"乡村振兴列车"服务品牌。统筹提升路网运输能力和列车开行品质，扩大"复兴号"

动力集中型动车组开行范围，提高夕发朝至等普速列车开行质效，整体优化高铁和普速客车运行时点和停站安排，增加县城站客车停靠，进一步拓展延伸公益性"慢火车"服务内容，联合沿线乡村打造列车大集、列车巴扎、主题文化车厢等，组织开好"务工专列""助学专列""健康专列""科技专列"等特色列车。

三是不断提升客运服务品质。推动普速客站改造升级，对既有县级及以下车站老旧服务设施进行补强，深入开展列车餐饮提质专项行动，优化提升"无轨站"交通接驳、旅游咨询、物流配送等服务功能，让脱贫地区群众更多享受低成本、高品质的出行服务，进一步增强幸福感和获得感。

四是创新拓展铁路旅游助力乡村振兴帮扶成效。发挥"高铁+普速+旅游列车"等成网互补优势，依托乡村地区丰富旅游资源，持续推进旅游列车改造提升、优化开行、闲置开发与乡村旅游产业深度融合，联合沿线脱贫地区打造一批网红线路、网红列车、网红文创IP、网红打卡地等，助力脱贫地区大力发展旅游经济。

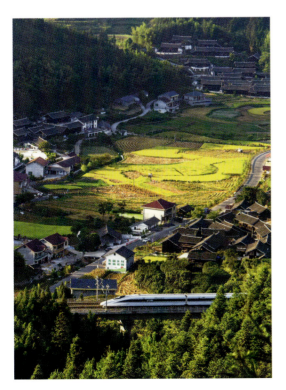

2024 世界旅游联盟：旅游助力乡村振兴案例（中英文双语版）
WTA Best Practices of Rural Revitalization through Tourism 2024 (Chinese-English Bilingual Edition)

China State Railway Group Co., Ltd.:
Rail Tourism Empowers Rural Revitalization

Abstract

Following President Xi Jinping's important instructions on railway affairs and exploiting its strengths in transport networks and transportation, China State Railway Group Co., Ltd., hereinafter referred to as "China Railway", has developed a new model of "railway + tourism + rural revitalization" in light of the resource endowments of the underserved counties and districts it is paired with and based on the tourism market demand. China Railway has constantly strengthened the "railway + tourism + rural revitalization" service network, increased special tourist trains and "slow trains" in areas lifted out of poverty, fostered cultural tourism industry clusters with railway characteristics, enhanced the competitiveness of rural rail tourism products, redoubled efforts in promoting and empowering tourism resources in areas lifted out of poverty, and advanced the integration of railways with the agricultural, cultural, and tourism sectors of areas lifted out of poverty. Such efforts have injected new impetus into the rural tourism industry and helped the economic and social development of the paired assistant counties and districts get on the fast track.

Challenges and Problems

"Railway + tourism + rural revitalization" is a new model of support for paired assistant areas. The main problems are as follows. Firstly, due to the weak transportation infrastructure, some counties and districts endowed with rich tourism resources are inaccessible by railway or have fewer trains, resulting in inconvenience in travel. This has posed a major obstacle to the tourism sector of these counties and districts. Secondly, railway enterprises fall short in fully exploiting their own strengths and advantages to promote the integrated development with tourism resources, and need to double down on building rail tourism brands, expanding the cultural tourism product mix, and helping the paired counties and districts increase their visibility. Thirdly, a lack of innovation in the modes of transport and the patchy quality of transportation services make it difficult to meet the people's demand for fast, comfortable, and high-quality travel.

Measures

1. Improve the "railway + tourism + rural revitalization" service network

Firstly, scale up railway investment and construction in the paired assistant counties and districts, and further enhance the accessibility, balance, and reachability of the rail transport network. Secondly, optimize and enrich the varieties of products on passenger trains, increase the number of trains passing through the paired assistant counties and districts, improve the comprehensive rural tourism transport service network, and provide transport services to support the paired assistant counties and districts in attracting tourists. Thirdly, make a big push to upgrade the passenger transport infrastructure in the paired assistant counties and districts, advance ecosystem building and integrated development of stations and localities along the way, and build county- and township-level stations into a showcase of rural revitalization.

2. Design and launch trips run by special tourist trains

Rail tourism products are marketed in a targeted manner to attract high-end consumers to travel in the paired assistant counties and districts and achieve the purposes of "bringing tourists from the eastern regions to the western regions" and "transporting goods produced in the western regions to the eastern regions". For example, the Harbin branch of China Railway has launched high-end tourist trains represented by "Lindu", premium tourist trains represented by the east-west ring rail, and inclusive tourist trains represented by point-to-point intercity rails. These trains connect popular tourist attractions and are all-season tourism products with the characteristics of northeast China; the Urumqi branch of China Railway has carried out the rail tourism campaign aimed at prospering Xinjiang at Hotan

Railway Station. It has launched a series of tourist trains such as high-end special trains, high-quality special trains, and inclusive special trains in an effort to attract tourists to Xinjiang and support the high-quality development of Xinjiang's tourism sector.

3. Creatively launch cross-regional themed tourist trains

Capitalizing on the regional advantages and resource endowments of different projects, China Railway has designed tourist routes in combination and launched cross-regional themed tourist trains, such as "Zibo Barbecue", "Jinghe", "Linhai Xueyuan", and "Rail Tour Around the West", facilitating the travel of passengers across multiple regions. On the basis of the "Zibo Barbecue" tourist train, the Jinan branch of China Railway innovatively released the "High-Speed Rail around Qilu" travel package that allows passengers to travel around the province by high-speed rail within five days, boosting the upgrading of rural tourism in Shandong.

4. Build and promote the "Rural Revitalization Train Plus" service brand

Firstly, optimize the arrangements for tourist trains and explore the innovative operational model integrating direct trains and trains under the jurisdiction model to improve the efficiency of travel for tourists. Secondly, according to the seasonal and periodic characteristics of tourism resources in the paired assistant counties and districts, optimize the train schedules and coordinate regular and high-end undercarriage resources. China Railway has achieved remarkable results in building the "Rural Revitalization Train Plus" service brand, and rolled out a series of popular trains, routes, and attractions such as red tourism, study tours, cultural heritage tourism, and wellness tours, driving the upgrading of tourism, consumption, and service industries along the route.

5. Promote further integration of rail and tourism projects, fully unleash and tap into the potential of tourism resources in the paired assistant counties and districts

Carry out innovative rail tourism projects by integrating various elements, such as "rail tourism + culture", "rail tourism + sports", "rail tourism + healthcare", "rail tourism + influencer hotspot". These innovative measures aim to form synergy between rail tourism and scenic areas, link various tourism resources, and synergize custom products and projects to attract a broader range of consumers.

6. Help the paired assistant counties and districts increase their visibility

China Railway has coordinated its 18 branches for joint promotional efforts, and worked with the Work Committee for Departments Directly Under the CPC Central Committee, the Ministry of

Agriculture and Rural Affairs, the Ministry of Culture and Tourism, and other departments to carry out rural tourism promotional campaigns at high-speed rail stations and trains across the country. Efforts have been increased to promote products on social platforms such as TikTok, Weibo, and Xiaohongshu, and develop an integrated promotion model of "influencer trips + specialties in paired counties and districts + cultural and creative products with railway characteristics", covering a total of 2.5 billion passengers and reducing advertising costs by some 200 million yuan.

Results

In 2023, China Railway concentrated its efforts on "laying the foundation, delivering long-term benefits, addressing areas of weakness, and adjusting the structure". It implemented 24 projects aimed at connecting and strengthening the rail transport network and reinforcing the chain, completed and put into operation 34 projects including the Lijiang-Shangrila Railway, the Sichuan-Qinghai Railway, and the Guiyang-Nanning High-speed Railway, and built 102 new stations, greatly improving the level of railway passenger transport service infrastructure in the paired assistant counties and districts. In 2023, China Railway invested 407.6 billion yuan in railway construction in old revolutionary areas, areas with large ethnic minority populations, and border areas and the paired assistant counties and districts, accounting for 80.2 percent of the country's total. New railways of 2,776.7 kilometers came into operation, accounting for 76.4 percent of the country's total, covering 77 old revolutionary areas, areas with large ethnic minority populations, border areas, and paired counties and districts, of which 22 paired counties ended the history of being inaccessible by rail. A total of 210 million passengers were transported in the paired assistant counties and

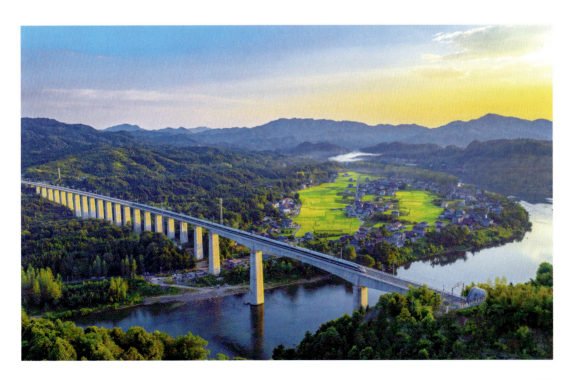

districts in the year. the number of trips run by rural tourism trains by way of areas lifted out of poverty reached 486, and transported 268,000 tourists, with per capita consumer spending of more than 2,000 yuan. The public-interest "slow trains" covered more than 100 counties lifted out of poverty in 21 provinces and autonomous regions. The rail tourism program has propelled the upgrading of the consumption chain of "catering, accommodation, transportation, travel, shopping, and entertainment", and facilitated the growth and agglomeration of related industries such as hospitality, catering, culture, leisure, and specialty products.

Experiences and Inspirations

1. Improve the infrastructure

Firstly, increase investment in railway infrastructure in areas lifted out of poverty, improve the coverage, balance, and accessibility of the rail network, promote ecosystem building and integrated development of stations and localities along the way, and develop county- and township-level stations into a window for the rural revitalization strategy that showcases local features and vitality. Secondly, increase trips passing through paired assistant counties and districts, improve the comprehensive transport service system for rural tourism, and provide good transport services for tourists to those areas.

2. Integrate resources

On the one hand, make full use of the rich and high-quality tourism resources in rural areas, develop distinctive rail tourism projects in a refined and differentiated manner based on local conditions, and promote further integration of rail tourism and rural tourism, thus raising the incomes of people living in areas along the way. On the other hand, optimize the operational plans for high-speed and slow trains, solve the "last mile" problem of rural tourism, and guide passengers to participate in diverse activities such as tourism, shopping, study tours, and business activities in areas along the way, thus injecting new impetus and vitality into rural revitalization.

Plans

Firstly, continue with the planning and construction of railways in the paired assistant counties and districts. More railway investments will be steered towards old revolutionary areas, areas with large ethnic minority populations, border areas, and areas lifted out of poverty, especially in the western region. Efforts will be made to strengthen the construction of strategic main arteries such as that

connecting Xinjiang and Xizang, promote key railway construction projects such as the Sichuan-Tibet Railway and "100 main artery projects for poverty alleviation", and carry out a number of projects that strengthening the rail transport network and chain, and vigorously upgrade logistics infrastructure in areas lifted out of poverty.

Secondly, strengthen and upgrade the "Rural Revitalization Train" service brand. China Railway will further improve both the transportation capacity of the transport network and the quality of trips run by trains, expand the coverage of the power-concentrated Fuxing EMU, improve the quality and efficiency of regular-speed overnight trains, optimize the schedules of high-speed and regular-speed trains in a coordinated way, increase the number of trains at county-level stations, further expand the service of public-interest "slow trains", work with areas along the way to launch "marketplace on train" and themed culture carriages, and do a better job in special trains for migrant workers, special trains for students, "healthcare-themed trains", and "technology-themed trains".

Thirdly, continuously improve the quality of passenger services. Efforts will be made to advance the renovation and upgrading of regular-speed railway stations, strengthen the service facilities of existing stations at and below the county level, carry out special campaigns to improve the quality of rail catering, and upgrade the service functions of "trackless stations" such as shuttering, travel consultation, and logistics and distribution. Moreover, people in areas lifted out of poverty will be given better access to affordable yet high-quality travel services, and further enhance their sense of happiness and gain.

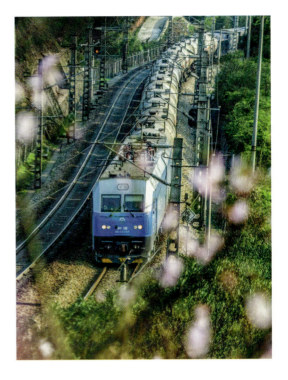

Fourthly, innovatively improve the effects of rail tourism empowering rural revitalization. The complementary advantages of the "high-speed train + regular-speed train + tourist train" networks will be fully exploited. Based on the rich tourism resources in rural areas, continued efforts will be made to upgrade tourist trains, improve operations, and make good use of idle resources in coordination with the rural tourism industry, and work with the areas lifted out of poverty to develop popular routes, trains, cultural and creative products, and attractions, in an effort to help them bolster the tourism economy.

2024 世界旅游联盟：旅游助力乡村振兴案例（中英文双语版）
WTA Best Practices of Rural Revitalization through Tourism 2024（Chinese-English Bilingual Edition）

山西省高平市河西镇苏庄村：
"喜"文化赋能古村活化

摘　要

山西省高平市河西镇苏庄村借助省、市大力发展文旅康养产业的强劲东风，依托文化资源和区位优势，持续盘活古院落等民居，开发"喜产品"、延伸"喜业态"、讲好"喜故事"、壮大"喜产业"，走出"喜"文化赋能古村振兴的特色之路。

挑战与问题

山西省高平市河西镇苏庄村地域面积3.31平方千米，全村共524户，常住人口1830人，60周岁以上的418人。苏庄村在乡村振兴过程中面临两大困扰：一是缺乏思路，对于从哪做、怎么做毫无头绪；二是缺乏动力，人口大量流失，同时全体干部群众齐心向前谋发展的合力不足。

措施

1. 整治环境

苏庄村从2021年开发建设以来，重点实施了"拆迁亮村、环境整治、古院修缮、居所集中"四大行动，累计拆迁、置换旧房5万多平方米，在镇区新建的住宅楼安置村民226户，苏庄村实现了改水改污、改厕供气全覆盖，村庄变成了景区，村民也享受到了与城市居民同等的基础设施和公共服务。

2. 植入文化

高平市的传统文化底蕴深厚，婚俗文化更是特色鲜明。苏庄村以"喜"为切入点，确立了"喜镇苏庄"的发展定位，全力打造中国婚庆体验地，吸引年轻人到古村举办中国式传统婚礼，接受中国传统文化的滋养，婚庆民俗成为开发古村、吸引人流、壮大产业、推动乡村发展的核心要素和强大力量。

3. 引入国企

为了解决镇村两级投资难的问题，苏庄村和国投集团村企共建，共同开发古村。

4. 导入产业

苏庄村依托古房古院和新建的婚礼堂，全链条引入传统婚礼仪式举办、婚庆用品定制和婚庆服务，以及吃、住、娱、购等业态，发展壮大"喜文化"产业。

成效

通过实践探索，苏庄村取得了"村美、民富、前景广"的良好成效。苏庄村建立了"国企+村集体+农户"的联农带农富农机制，国投集团投资建设运营，占股60%；村集体用建设用地和古院入股，占股40%，分红增收；村民通过"民房出租、股金分红、景区就业、自主经营"四条渠道增收致富。2023年，喜镇苏庄接待游客120万人次，带动村集体增收130万元，带动村民人均增收4500元，人均收入达到24000元。苏庄村被评为中国历史文化名村、首批中国传统村落、国家3A级旅游景区、中国婚庆旅游目的地。

经验与启示

1. 坚持党建引领是关键

县级党委政府在产业规划、政策扶持、资金支持、

服务管理等层面给予大力支持；乡镇党委坚持示范引路、试点先行的理念，由点及面地有序抓好具体实施；村级党组织带领农民群众摒弃等、靠、要的思想，敢于和善于承接党和政府的各项优惠政策，带领群众闯市场、搞经营、引资本、助发展。通过市、镇、村三级联动，齐抓共管，推动村级集体经济良性发展。

2. 坚持整合资源是基础

苏庄村将传统文化资源、古建资源与政策资源、组织资源等有机结合，充分利用古建资源、民俗文化打造文旅康养产业，坚持走乡村旅游业、康养产业、种养殖业等多元化联动发展的路子，撬动沉睡资源，释放出最佳经济效益。

3. 坚持共同富裕是核心

壮大村集体经济，必须充分激发村民的创造性和内生动力，坚持以群众为主体，与相关利益方构建产权明晰、成员稳定的现代管理体制和利益联结机制，实现平等协商、民主管理、利益共享。因地制宜推动人才、技术、资本、农户等要素进入产业发展链条，多渠道增加群众的劳务工资收入和财产性收入等。

下一步计划

一是继续围绕传统"喜"文化，将传统的"八礼四节"等民俗文化植入旅游业态，成功解锁传统与时尚、古典与流行的搭配，实现古村院落的活化升级和创新融合。二是深度挖掘古建文化内涵，不断植入新的业态，提升古院落的舒适度和吸引力，打造有情怀、有特色、有品质的规模化精品院落。苏庄村将致力于成为一流的一站式中国传统特色"喜"文化体验目的地，吸引更多的游客来苏庄村添喜纳福，赏中国古建筑之美，品传统"喜"文化之礼。

Suzhuang Village, Hexi Town, Gaoping City, Shanxi Province:

An Ancient Village Given a New Life by the Reviving Wedding Traditions

Abstract

Suzhuang Village of Hexi Town, Gaoping City, Shanxi Province, rides on the trend of the province and the city vigorously developing the cultural, tourism, and healthcare industries, leverages its cultural resources and regional advantages, and renovates ancient courtyards and other dwellings one after another. It has developed wedding products, expanded the traditional wedding ceremony industry, extended the industrial chain, and promoted the traditional wedding culture, embarking on a characteristic road of rural revitalization.

Challenges and Problems

Suzhuang Viiage covers an area of 3.31 square kilometers, with a registered population of 524 households and a permanent population of 1,830, including 418 over the age of 60. It faces two major problems in the pursuit of rural revitalization. Firstly, it has no ideas about what to do or how to do it. Secondly, it lacks inner drive as many of its young and middle-aged people have left elsewhere for better livelihoods and the remaining villagers and village officials are not of one mind on how to develop the village.

Measures

1. Improving the environment

Since 2021, Suzhuang Village has launched four actions to demolish illegal buildings and light up the village, improve the village environment, repair and renovate ancient courtyards, and relocate dwellings to designated areas. So far, a total of more than 50,000 square meters of old houses have been demolished and swapped, and 226 villagers have been relocated to the newly built residential buildings in the town. Suzhuang Village has achieved full coverage of safe drinking water, sewage treatment facilities, flush toilets, and gas supply. The village has become a scenic area, and the villagers now enjoy the same infrastructure and public services as urban dwellers.

2. Tapping into cultural heritage

Gaoping City boasts a profound cultural heritage and is particularly known for its distinct wedding customs and traditions. Hence Suzhuang Village positions itself as a "Wedding Town" and strives to build itself into a place of choice for traditional Chinese weddings, to attract young couples to hold traditional Chinese weddings in it and carry forward traditional Chinese culture. Wedding customs have become the core element and a strong magnet for attracting people, growing the wedding industry, and promoting the development of this ancient village.

3. Introducing a state-owned enterprise (SOE)

To solve the financing difficulties facing the village and township governments, Suzhuang Village and State Development & Investment Corporation (SDIC) have partnered up to jointly develop the ancient village.

4. Diversifying business forms

Based on the ancient dwellings and courtyards and the newly-built wedding hall, Suzhang Village has introduced a wide range of service suppliers covering traditional wedding ceremonies, wedding supply customization, and wedding services, as well as catering, accommodation, entertainment, and shopping, to grow and expand the wedding industry.

Results

The above practices have brought Suzhuang Village a beautiful environment, higher income, and broad development prospects. Suzhuang Village has established a mechanism of "SOE + village collective + rural households" to engage farmers and increase their income. SDIC takes up 60% of the shares with capital investment, project construction, and operation, and the village collective takes up the remaining 40% with construction land and ancient courtyards, and is entitled to dividends. The villagers have also seen their income increase from housing rental, stock dividends, employment in the scenic area, or their own business. In 2023, Suzhuang Village received 1.2 million tourists, the income of the village collective increased by 1.3 million yuan, and the per capita income of villagers increased by 4,500 yuan, bringing the per capita income to 24,000 yuan. Suzhuang Village has been rated as the Famous Historical and Cultural Village of China, the first batch of Traditional Chinese Villages, the national 3A-level scenic spot, and the Wedding Tour Destination of China.

Experience and Inspirations

1. Adhere to the guidance of party building work

The county-level Party committee and government provide strong support in industry planning, policy, financing, service, and management. The township Party committee values the demonstration role of pilot areas, and orderly and gradually expands the project coverage. The village-level Party organization guides the villagers to abandon the attitude of

"passively longing for government assistance, expecting government grants and claiming for poverty reduction funds", and instead leads them to leverage various preferential policies, develop the market, start businesses, and attract investment to boost development. Hence the city, the town, and the village work together, promoting the healthy development of the village collective economy.

2. Consolidate resources

Suzhuang Village organically combines traditional cultural heritage, ancient buildings, policy support, and organizational resources. It makes full use of ancient buildings and folk culture to develop the cultural, tourism, and wellness industries. It adheres to the diversification path featuring the integrated development of rural tourism, wellness, and breeding industries, to maximize the economic output from idle resources.

3. Pursue common prosperity

To strengthen the village collective economy, it is necessary to fully stimulate the creativity and initiative of villagers and let them play the main role. It is also important to jointly build with stakeholders a modern management system and an interest linkage mechanism with clearly defined property rights and stable memberships, which promote equal consultation, democratic management, and benefits for all. Based on local conditions, rural households, technology, capital, and other factors shall be introduced into the industrial chain, to increase the labor wage income and property income of the villagers through multiple channels.

Plans

Firstly, Suzhuang Village will continue to focus on the wedding traditions, implant the "Eight Rites and Four Customs" of traditional weddings into the tourism industry, blur the boundary between tradition and fashion, classical and popular, and upgrade ancient village courtyards with innovations. Secondly, Suzhuang Village will dig deeply into the cultural heritage of ancient buildings, continuously introduce new business forms, enhance the comfort and appeal of ancient courtyards, and create large boutique courtyards with profound historical heritage, characteristics, and quality services. Suzhuang Village will strive to build itself into a first-class destination featuring one-stop services for traditional Chinese weddings and attract more couples to the village to appreciate ancient architecture and experience wedding customs and traditions.

山东省潍坊市青州市桐峪沟村：
景村共建谱写乡村振兴新篇章

摘　要

　　山东省潍坊市青州市弥河镇桐峪沟村在保持原真性的同时，深入挖掘传统老村内涵，创新性地融合现代休闲养生、农事体验、生态观光等多种元素，实现了从泥泞破旧的小山村向中国美丽休闲乡村的绚丽蝶变，打造了集湖光山色、农事体验、特色美食、手工作坊、红色教育、精品民宿、休闲养生于一体的乡村旅游综合体，年接待游客120万人次，走出了一条景村共建、农旅深度融合发展的乡村振兴之路。

挑战与问题

桐峪沟村地势低洼，逢雨必涝，交通闭塞，生产生活极为不便，居住条件较差。村内2400亩土地全部为荒山坡地，资源长期闲置，由于曾经的过度砍伐和人为损坏，区域内森林覆盖率不到20%。桐峪沟村缺乏统一规划，村内开设的农村合作社规模较小，村集体收入较低。

措施

1. 土地流转，打通村庄发展门路

桐峪沟村本着"先保护、后开发"的原则，将2400余亩荒山坡地尽数流转给九龙峪景区开发公司，由开发公司将部分荒山坡地开发为旅游景区。通过发展乡村旅游，形成"三变"生"四金"的发展模式。"三变"即荒山变景区、旧村变新村、旧房变民宿；"四金"即流转土地生"租金"、村民务工赚"薪金"、股份合作分"股金"、乡村旅游挣"现金"。

2. 景村共建，提升村庄公共基础设施

一是桐峪沟村的大街小巷全部硬化、绿化、亮化，交通标志、路灯、停车场等交通设施配备齐全。二是打造特色游览线路，开通旅游专线，配套完善的信息咨询、智慧旅游、旅游投诉、宣传展示、公共休息、便民服务、公共厕所等公共服务设施。三是坚持护绿与植绿并重，开展"增绿工程"，绿化总面积达2200余亩，绿化覆盖率达到90%以上，实现了生态循环和可持续发展。

3. 产业推动，厚植村庄发展内涵

一是桐峪沟村在对原生态景观风貌进行保护的基础上，融合乡村文化元素，打造"桐峪里"特色民宿，现已建成精品民宿60家、房间超200间，形成民宿产业集群。二是依托优质原生态资源，利用万亩农田，建设柿子、葡萄、山楂等有机种植园，开发高端农业衍生品，开展山楂酒、柿饼等农产品深加工，发展休闲采摘观光游，年接待游客120万人次。三是充分利用景区内部土壤基质，开发占地1200亩的中草药种植基地，打造集中药种植、加工、康养于一体的药王谷。四是建成约4万平方米的九龙峪大酒店，打造集中医传承、温泉疗养、享老养生于一体的颐养健康综合体。

成效

首先，桐峪沟村依托九龙峪乡村旅游综合体，全力构建乡村休闲、度假体验、精品民宿为主导的旅游村落，直接吸纳1000多名村民就业，分散在景区管理、绿化、安保、民宿服务等各个岗位，越来越多的村民吃上了旅游饭。其次，桐峪沟村统一规划、分片承包、自主经营，引导村民种植樱桃、玫瑰、中草药等特色农产品，集中发展集种植、观光、采摘、休闲于一体的乡村旅游业。最后，桐峪沟村不断开展职业农民、文化传承人、乡村旅游经营主体等新型主体培育，开展农业种植、科技运用、商户经营、园区务工等多元化培训活动，真正实现了村民全就业、共发展。村民

人均收入由原来的 0.89 万元发展到现在的 3.5 万元，村集体收入由 3 万元发展到 100 多万元。桐峪沟村先后获得中国美丽休闲乡村、山东省乡村振兴示范村、山东省美丽乡村示范点、山东省景区化村庄、山东省乡村旅游重点村等荣誉称号。

经验与启示

1. 发展特色优势产业是旅游助推乡村振兴的关键路径

桐峪沟村以九龙峪景区为依托，以发展旅游经济为抓手，立足本土特色优势产业，通过引入大量社会资本，将乡村闲置资源转变为优质资产，通过"景区引流+吃住在农家+产业群共建"的模式助力兴村富民，有效推进乡村三产融合发展。

2. 开发绿色生态产品是旅游助推乡村振兴的必要补充

桐峪沟村大力优化乡村生态环境，以生态养身、中草药养生、禅意养心为主线，打造集现代生态农业、农业文化研学、农耕田园体验、山地康养度假等于一体的综合型康养休闲产业样板园区，构建生态文明建设与乡村振兴协同联动机制，走出了一条"禅意康养+生态产业+现代农业"的和谐发展之路。

3. 创新乡村治理机制是旅游助推乡村振兴的重要保障

桐峪沟村通过整合资源和村企合作，形成以政府为主导，多方面主体协同推进的旅游发展模式，形成了包括党组织、政府、村集体、社会组织、乡贤、农民在内的多元治理主体良性互动关系，使其在治理目标上高度趋同、治理功能上协调互补，共同服务于乡村社会的全面发展。

下一步计划

一是打造农文旅融合发展示范样板。在保护原生态景观风貌基础上，以农为主、多业并举，融入丰富乡村文化元素，推动一二三产业融合发展，丰富农业观光、农事体验、生态休闲、中医药康养等业态供给，打造集"农、文、旅"多功能于一体的综合园区，全面满足游客需求，持续发展美丽乡村新经济。二是打造精品民宿集聚区。提升桐峪里民宿基础设施和管理服务质量，全力培育以休闲旅游体验、度假住宿为主的乡村旅游新地标，满足不同游客消费需求。三是推动村庄智慧化建设。借助数字科学技术，发展智慧旅游，开发"一站式、智能化、个性化"智慧服务系统，推出具有交互性、体验性特点的数字乡村旅游产品，推出"一键订单""一键投诉""无接触入园"等便捷服务。

2024 世界旅游联盟：旅游助力乡村振兴案例（中英文双语版）
WTA Best Practices of Rural Revitalization through Tourism 2024 (Chinese-English Bilingual Edition)

Tongyugou Village, Qingzhou City, Weifang City, Shandong Province:

A New Chapter in Rural Revitalization through Integrated Scenic and Village Development

Abstract

　　Tongyugou Village, located in Mihe Town, Qingzhou City, Shandong Province, has undergone a remarkable transformation. By preserving its original style while deeply exploring the traditional values of the old village, the village has creatively integrated modern elements such as leisure, wellness, agricultural experiences, and ecological tourism. This transformation has turned the once muddy and dilapidated mountain village into a beautiful and restful rural destination, known as a comprehensive rural tourism hub that now attracts 1.2 million visitors annually. Tongyugou Village has become a model for rural revitalization, where scenic and village development go hand in hand with the deep integration of agriculture and tourism.

Challenges and Problems

Tongyugou Village faced significant challenges due to its low-lying terrain, frequent flooding during rain, and poor living conditions. The village's 2,400 *mu* of land was largely on the barren hillside, with resources remaining idle for a long time. Due to excessive logging and human damage, the forest coverage rate in the area was less than 20%. The village lacked unified planning, the rural cooperatives were small in scale, and the village collective income was low.

Measures

1. Land transfer to open development pathways

Following the principle of "protect first, develop later", Tongyugou Village transferred its 2,400-plus *mu* of barren hillsides to the Jiulongyu Scenic Area Development Company. The company developed part of the land into a tourist attraction. This approach created a development model that transformed barren hills into scenic areas, old villages into new ones, and old houses into homestays. The model generated income through land rental, wages from employment, dividends from cooperative shares, and direct cash earnings from rural tourism.

2. Scenic and village development is implemented to improve public infrastructure

Firstly, the village streets and alleys were all hardened, greened, and illuminated. Traffic signs, streetlights, and parking lots were fully equipped. Secondly, the village established special tourist routes, opened dedicated tourist lines, and improved public service facilities such as information consulting, smart tourism, tourist complaints, promotion displays, public rest areas, convenience services, and public toilets. Thirdly, the village implemented a "Greening Project", with a total greening area of over 2,200 *mu*, reaching a green coverage rate of more than 90% and achieving ecological sustainability.

3. Industrial development helps to enrich the connotations of village development

Firstly, the village preserves its original ecological landscape while incorporating rural cultural elements to create "Tongyuli" distinctive homestays. Currently, there are 60 boutique homestays with over 200 rooms, forming a homestay industry cluster. Secondly, leveraging high-quality ecological resources, the village has developed organic orchards of persimmon, grape, hawthorn by utilizing large areas of farmland and established high-end agricultural derivative products, such as hawthorn wine and dried persimmons, while promoting leisure picking and sightseeing tours. The village receives 1.2 million tourists annually. Thirdly, the village developed a 1,200-*mu* traditional Chinese medicine herb planting base, creating a "Herb King Valley" that is focused on planting, processing, and wellness. Fourthly, the village has built the 40,000-square-meter Jiulongyu Grand Hotel, creating a comprehensive wellness facility that integrates traditional Chinese medicine heritage, hot spring therapy, and eldercare.

Results

Firstly, Tongyugou Village has leveraged the Jiulongyu rural tourism complex to develop a tourism village centering on rural leisure, vacation experiences, and boutique homestays. It has directly employed over 1,000 villagers in various roles, from landscape management to security and hospitality, enabling more villagers to benefit from tourism. Secondly, the village has unified its planning, segmented land for contracting, and guided villagers to grow specialty agricultural products like cherries, roses, and medicinal herbs, bringing about a thriving rural tourism industry that integrates farming, sightseeing, picking and leisure. Thirdly, the village continuous training programs have been implemented to train new professional farmers, cultural heritage inheritors, and rural tourism operators, significantly boosting employment and village collective income. The villagers' per capita income has increased from 8,900 yuan to 35,000 yuan, and the village collective income has grown from 30,000 yuan to over 1 million yuan. Tongyugou Village has been recognized with honors such as the Beautiful Leisure Village of China, Shandong Province Rural Revitalization Demonstration Village, Shandong Province Beautiful Village Demonstration Site, and Shandong Province Key Rural Tourism Village.

Experiences and Inspirations

1. Developing distinctive advantageous industries is the key to leveraging tourism to promote rural revitalization

By relying on the Jiulongyu Scenic Area and focusing on tourism economics, Tongyugou Village has transformed its idle resources into valuable assets. The "scenic attraction draws visitors, farming sustains visitors, and industries grow together" model has effectively integrated the three industries and boosted village development and prosperity.

2. Developing green and ecological products is a necessary complement to leveraging tourism to promote rural revitalization

The village has optimized its rural ecological environment, focusing on eco-friendly agriculture, health-keeping with traditional Chinese medicine, and Zen and mind healing. It has created a comprehensive wellness and leisure industry park that integrates modern ecological agriculture, agricultural education, rural experience, and mountain wellness vacationing, establishing a synergistic relationship between ecological civilization and rural revitalization and blazing a path of harmonious development of health-keeping, ecological industries, and modern agriculture.

3. Innovative rural governance mechanisms are crucial to leveraging tourism to promote rural revitalization

By integrating resources and fostering village-

enterprise cooperation, Tongyugou Village has established a tourism development model led by the government and supported by various stakeholders, including the Party organization, government, village collective, social organizations, able villagers, and farmers. This collaborative approach ensures that governance objectives align, strategies are coordinated, and functions complement each other, collectively driving comprehensive rural development.

Plans

Firstly, it is to create a model for integrated agricultural, cultural, and tourism development. While preserving the original ecological landscape, the village will focus on agriculture, diversify industries, and incorporate rich rural cultural elements to promote the integration of primary, secondary, and tertiary industries. This will enrich offerings such as agricultural sightseeing, farming experiences, ecological leisure, and health-keeping with traditional Chinese medicine, creating a comprehensive park that integrates agricultural, cultural, and tourism development, meets tourists' needs and fosters a new rural economy. Secondly, it is to develop a boutique homestay cluster. The village will improve infrastructure and management services for the Tongyuli homestays, establishing a new landmark for rural tourism centered on leisure tourism and vacation accommodation that caters to diverse tourist demands. Thirdly, it is to advance smart village construction. Leveraging digital technology, the village will develop smart tourism by creating an "all-in-one, intelligent, and personalized" service system. The system will offer digital rural tourism products with interactive and experiential features, including services like "one-click orders", "one-click complaints", and "contactless entry".

2024 世界旅游联盟：旅游助力乡村振兴案例（中英文双语版）
WTA Best Practices of Rural Revitalization through Tourism 2024（Chinese-English Bilingual Edition）

湖北省恩施土家族苗族自治州咸丰县彭家沟村：

湖北文旅集团助力"穷沟沟"变"金窝窝"

摘 要

2021年，湖北文旅集团开始帮扶大山深处的恩施土家族苗族自治州咸丰县彭家沟村，充分发挥文旅主业优势，坚持推动产业振兴、促进农旅融合，着力培育"一黑一白一绿"（恩施黑猪、唐崖白柚、工商贸旅）当家产业，走出一条"村强民富、人和景美"的"彭家沟新路"，"一户一处景、一村一幅画"的美丽画卷正在变为现实。

挑战与问题

彭家沟村发展过程中面临以下问题。一是产业亟须转型升级。彭家沟村的支柱产业主要是家家户户的黑猪养殖,以及因地制宜推广种植的有机白柚。近几年,受市场周期影响,黑猪和白柚的市场销售面临低价调整,销售渠道有限,村民收入锐减,村集体收入深受影响。二是环境治理问题。黑猪养殖导致污水横流、臭气熏天,解决环境问题迫在眉睫。三是农旅融合问题。乡村旅游基础设施和交通条件都需要改善,同时缺乏标志性旅游产品和活动品牌。

措施

1. 做强黑猪产业

一是湖北文旅集团会同村两委成立"咸丰县唐崖镇恩施黑猪养殖专业合作社",建立"党支部+专业合作社+农户+集体经济"模式,统一生猪品种、饲养标准,并与市场经营主体签订生猪购销合同,既为生猪养殖提供技术支撑,又确保了以保底价格收购生猪,稳定了养殖户的收入。二是湖北文旅集团出资帮助村里开办土特产加工车间和销售中心,生产腊肉、香肠等农产品,由传统产业逐步向精深加工转型。三是彭家沟村通过组织产销对接、开展爱心消费、利用互联网直播、在湖北文旅集团展陈点设专柜推介等方式,拓宽销售渠道,多渠道解决村里农产品滞销问题,实现提销量助增收的效果。

2. 开展人居环境整治

一是高质量编制彭家沟村村庄规划。重点对农村宅基地、新建房屋风貌、强弱电线路布局、新建牲畜圈舍等进行管控,坚决遏制乱搭乱建、乱排放、乱占耕地、乱堆放等现象。二是推动村里打造"一队三会"(志愿者服务队、乡贤联谊会、乡风文明理事会、村民议事会)。志愿者服务队每天在村里巡逻,监督每家每户的环境卫生,并义务打扫村里的公共环境卫生;乡贤联谊会、乡风文明理事会、村民议事会让村民充分参与乡村治理,营造向上向善向美、共建共治共享的社会氛围。

3. 发展庭院经济

一是彭家沟村实施畜禽粪污资源化利用项目,推动养殖户把生猪粪便干燥处理成有机肥料,把生猪尿液发酵成沼液统一运输存储;建设沼液中转池和田间管道,实行沼液还田还土,种养循环,让村容村貌绿起来、净起来,保护生态环境。二是彭家沟村结合自身农产品,谋划田园农业、民俗风情等农旅活动,实现以旅带农、以农助旅。

成效

2021年以来,湖北文旅集团帮扶彭家沟村积极推进农旅融合、村景融合。彭家沟村全村建成标准化圈舍150栋,全年出栏生猪超过2.5万头,产值突破1.2亿元,全村农户年收入超20万元的达112户,超50万元达76户,超100万元达41户,人均纯收入超4万元,村集体经济年收入达到20万元以上,形成了"一黑一白"(恩施黑猪、唐崖白柚)支柱产业强根基、"一宴一节"(土司刨汤宴、白柚采摘节)特色节庆兴文化、"一院一廊"(土家风情院落、生态产业观光走廊)土家景观活生态,接待游客8万人次,带动村民收入1700万元以上。全村获评全国"一村一品"示范村、民主法治示范村、示范性老年友好型社区、湖北省乡村振兴示范村等。

经验与启示

1. 做法切合实际

一是富裕工程。先让村民"富",大力培育当家产业;后让村民"服",积极倡导与培育优良的家风民俗。二是便民工程。村组建黑化路、农户建硬化路;村组建照明灯、农户修花果园;村里修产业园、农户修种养场。三是最美工程。评比表彰最美致富带头人、最美媳妇、最美婆婆、最美老人、最美志愿者、最美庭院。

2. 经验朴实管用

一是产业支撑。优先养殖恩施黑猪,循环种植唐崖白柚,适时启动工商贸旅,稳步推进农旅融合。二是夯实堡垒。建强党的组织,建优自治组织,建好经济组织,建实群众组织。三是共同缔造。提振自力更生、向富向美之志,激发艰苦奋斗、向善向和之智。

3. 目标鼓舞人心

一是筑牢乡村振兴基本盘,建成强富美高示范村,实现产业和造血强、村民和集体富、环境和生态美。二是以市场为导向抓经济,以人民为中心善治理,争创国家级乡村振兴示范村、全国文明村。

下一步计划

一是实施智慧赋能。建设智慧农业和农产品展销中心,为"土家腊肉、土法皮蛋、唐崖白柚"三款特色农产品搭建展示馆、销售厅和电商营销平台,有效推动"山货出山"。二是培养新型农民。对农民开展农技、农销等专业化培训,举办各级乡村振兴现场教学、新型农民实用人才培训和中小学生课外研学等活动,预计每年培训50余场5000余人次,带动村集体经济增收10万元以上。三是推进农业升级。建设冷库和肉品清洗、分解、腌制、烘烤、包装一体化、标准化腊肉加工生产线。项目建成后,可形成年加工100万斤腊肉制品的产能,推动"恩施黑猪"产业由传统养殖向精深加工转变,带动村集体经济增收50万元以上。四是发展乡村旅游。建设乡村旅游标识系统、旅游配套设施,串联世界文化遗产——唐崖土司城址景区,预计年接待游客2万人次以上,实现旅游综合收入1000万元以上。

Pengjiagou Village, Xianfeng County, Enshi Tujia and Miao Autonomous Prefecture, Hubei Province:

The Path to Prosperity with the Help of Hubei Cultural Tourism Group

Abstract

In 2021, Hubei Cultural Tourism Group began to provide targeted assistance for Pengjiagou Village, which nestles in the depths of mountains in Xianfeng County, Enshi Tujia and Miao Autonomous Prefecture, Hubei Province. Relying on its strengths in cultural tourism, Hubei Cultural Tourism Group has helped the village develop pillar industries (Enshi black pig, Tangya white pomelo, and industry and commerce, trade, and tourism). The beautiful picture of "one household, one scene, one village, one picture" is becoming a reality.

Challenges and Problems

Pengjiagou Village was faced with the following problems. Firstly, the village was in urgent need of industrial transformation and upgrading. The pillar industries of Pengjiagou Village are black pig breeding and organic white pomelo growing according to local conditions. In the last couple of years, due to the market cycles, pig and pomelo prices were on a decrease, and there were limited sales channels, resulting in a sharp drop in the income of villagers and exerting sizable influence on the village collective income. Secondly, environmental governance was a big concern. Black pig breeding was imperative to address environmental issues such as sewage and bad odor from pig breeding. Thirdly, how to promote integration of agriculture and tourism was a great challenge. Rural tourism infrastructure and traffic conditions needed to be improved, and there were no signature tourism products and flagship activities.

Measures

1.Consolidate the black pig industry

Firstly, Hubei Cultural Tourism Group worked with the village committee and village Party branch committee to set up the Enshi Black Pig Breeding Specialized Cooperative, establish the model involving the Party branch, specialized cooperative, farmers, and the collective economy, set unified standards for pig breeds and raising, and sign pig purchase and sale contracts with market operators. This not only provides technical support for pig breeding but also offers guaranteed prices, which stabilized the income of villagers. Secondly, Hubei Cultural Tourism Group provided financial support for the village's specialities processing workshops and sales centers, which produce and sell agricultural products such as bacon and sausages. This facilitates the village's shift from traditional industries to deep processing. Thirdly, Pengjiagou Village has broadened the sales channels of agricultural products through supply and demand matchmaking, charitable consumption activities, live streaming, and promotional counters at the exhibition area of Hubei Cultural Tourism Group. These various channels address the problem of agricultural surpluses, thus increasing sales and raising the people's incomes.

2. Improve the living environments

Firstly, draw up a rational spatial plan for Pengjiagou Village, focus on the management of rural residential land, new housing styles, the layout of strong and weak current lines, and new livestock pens, and firmly curb unregulated buildings, discharges, occupation of cultivated land, and stacking. Secondly, help the village set up a volunteer service team, an able villagers' association, a cultural-ethical progress council, and a villagers' council. The volunteer service team patrols the village every day, checks the environmental sanitation of each household, and cleans the public spaces in the village. The able villagers' association, the cultural-ethical

progress council, and the villagers' council allow villagers to fully participate in rural governance and foster a positive atmosphere based on collaboration, participation, and shared benefits.

3. Develop the courtyard economy

Firstly, Pengjiagou Village has implemented the manure recycling project which requires farmers to dry pig manure into organic fertilizer and ferment pig urine into biogas slurry for unified transportation and storage. The biogas slurry tanks and field pipelines have been built to use biogas slurry on the fields, forming a closed loop of planting and breeding and making the village greener and cleaner. Secondly, revolving around its own agricultural products, Pengjiagou Village has organized pastoral agriculture, folk customs, and other agritourism activities so that tourism and agriculture and agriculture promote each other.

Results

Since 2021, Hubei Cultural Tourism Group has helped Pengjiagou Village promote the integration between agriculture and tourism and between the village and scenic areas. Pengjiagou Village has 150 standard pig barns which breed more than 25,000 pigs for market annually, with an output value exceeding 120 million yuan. Up to 112 households in the village earn more than 200,000 yuan per year, 76 households earn more than 500,000 yuan per year, and 41 households earn more than 1 million yuan per year. Per capita net income exceeds 40,000 yuan, and the annual income of the village collective surpasses 200,000 yuan. The village now has a strong foundation of pillar industries including the Enshi black pig and the Tangya white pomelo, and holds

distinctive festivals including the Tusi pork festa and the white pomelo picking festival. The Tujia ethnic residential courtyards and the eco-friendly industry sightseeing corridor in the village receive about 80,000 tourists per year, bringing an income of more than 17 million yuan to the villagers. Pengjiagou Village has been honored as the Demonstration Village for the "One Village, One Product" Initiative, the Democracy and Rule of Law Demonstration Village, the Model Age-Friendly Community, and the Rural Revitalization Demonstration Village in Hubei.

Experiences and Inspirations

1. Practical actions

Firstly, vigorous efforts are made to help the villagers get rich and foster pillar industries with local features. This gains support and trust from the villagers. In addition, activities are carried out to strengthen family values and traditions and improve folk customs. Secondly, greater convenience is delivered to the people. The village has built roads with the asphalt concrete surface, installed street lamps, and established industrial parks. The villagers have contributed to the construction of paved roads and built courtyards with flowers and fruit trees and planting and breeding facilities. Thirdly, exemplary figures are selected and recognized, including exemplary entrepreneurial individuals, daughter-in-laws, mother-in-laws, seniors, and volunteers, and the most beautiful courtyards.

2. Simple yet effective experience

Firstly, strengthen industrial support. Priority is given to breeding Enshi black pigs, along with the planting of Tangya white pomelo. Great efforts are made to develop industry and commerce, trade, and tourism at an appropriate time, and steadily promote the integration of agriculture and tourism. Secondly, reinforce the organizations. The measures include strengthening Party organization, improving autonomous organizations and economic organizations, and solidifying people's organizations. Thirdly, work together and motivate the people to create a better and more prosperous life through self-reliance, keep working hard, and uphold the values of beauty, goodness, and harmony.

3. Inspiring goals

Firstly, lay a solid foundation for rural revitalization to build a demonstration village that is prosperous beautiful and has thriving industries and a beautiful environment. Secondly, pursue market-oriented economic development, implement people-centered governance, and strive to build a national demonstration village for rural revitalization and a national civility village.

Plans

Firstly, harness the power of smart technology. It is planned to establish a smart agriculture and agricultural products exhibition center, and set up an exhibition hall, sales hall, and e-commerce marketing platform for the three agricultural specialities, namely, the Tujia bacon, indigenous preserved eggs, and Tangya white pomelo, so as to bring the village's products to consumers in other regions. Secondly, train new-type farmers. Specialized training on agricultural technology and marketing will be provided for the farmers, and a range of activities will be organized in the village, such as on-site education on rural revitalization at all levels, practical training for new-type farmers, and study tours for primary and secondary school students. It is estimated that over 50 sessions of training will be carried out for more than 5,000 participants annually, which will bring an additional income of over 100,000 yuan to the collective. Thirdly, advance agricultural upgrading. A standardized bacon processing line will be built, including cold storage and integrated operations for cleaning, disassembling, salting, roasting, and packaging. When completed, the project with an annual processing capacity of 500,000 kilograms of bacon products is expected to extend the Enshi black pig industry chain from breeding to deep processing, generating an income of more than 500,000 yuan for the collective. Fourthly, boost rural tourism. The rural tourism signage system and supporting facilities will be built to connect the village with the Site of Tangya Tusi Domain, a World Cultural Heritage site. It is estimated to receive more than 20,000 tourists annually and bring in tourism revenue of more than 10 million yuan.

安徽省黄山市休宁县齐云山镇：
祥源·齐云山生态文化旅游度假区助力乡村振兴

摘　要

　　祥源控股集团于 2011 年落户安徽省齐云山镇，先后累计投入 10 亿元打造祥源·齐云山生态文化旅游度假区。祥源控股集团根植于中华传统沉浸式养生"隐"文化，利用齐云山绝美的自然资源及独厚的文化资源，将道家养生、徽州风韵、状元之乡等在地文化融入旅游实践，引入索道交通、观山酒店、人文小镇等核心内容进行投资、建设、运营，打造集沉浸式主题旅游、休闲度假、精品住宿、风味餐饮、文化消费等于一体的文旅目的地。祥源控股集团积极践行"绿水青山就是金山银山"的发展理念，成功构建了山上"齐云山景区"与山下"齐云小镇"的互补联动模式，将自然景观与人文特色深度融合，实现了产业布局与乡村振兴战略的有效对接。此举不仅为文旅行业高质量融合发展提供了鲜活的创新案例，更促使祥源·齐云山生态文化旅游度假区成为山岳型旅游目的地休闲度假产业项目的标杆之作。

挑战与问题

安徽省黄山市休宁县齐云山镇，因镇区内齐云山而得名，全镇面积107.97平方千米，下辖7个行政村，总人口1.32万人。镇区内的齐云山，凭借其独特的丹霞地貌和千年道家文化的沉淀，构筑了得天独厚的旅游资源优势，1994年被批准为国家重点风景名胜区。然而，因内有交通和基础设施薄弱、旅游开发深度欠缺、旅游功能及配套不足、旅游人才匮乏等限制，外有黄山强势景区形成冲击，内外因素相交导致齐云山旅游发展增速迟缓，当地居民及周边村落未能享受旅游红利，区域可持续的发展动力不足。

措施

1. 成立合资企业平台

2011年，祥源控股集团联手安徽省休宁县人民政府联手打造祥源·齐云山生态文化旅游度假区，建设齐云山景区、祥源·齐云旅游小镇、祥富瑞精品客栈、自由家营地及树屋世界、横江·太极竹筏漂流等旅游业态，共同打造集景区游玩、休闲度假、康养旅居、山景住宿、户外娱乐等功能于一体，服务与设施一流的国际文旅游憩目的地。

2. "山上+山下"发展结构

山上，以齐云山景区为核心，进行完善基础设施、优化游览配套、更新交通体系、保护历史风貌等保护性开发，打造"山水人文"的旅游名片；山下，以齐云小镇为载体，引入标准的旅游配套设施和推陈出新的消费场景，关联周边田园农耕体验内容，实现文旅商业的可持续发展。

3. 向内挖掘在地文化

祥源·齐云山生态文化旅游度假区确立"以文养心，以医养身"为项目核心定位，在文化塑造上引入剪纸、铁画、木雕、竹雕、砚雕等徽州传统非遗技艺；在养生主体上，孵化以睡眠谷、丹房为代表的康养业态，将传统中医、中医心理学、新安医学三者融合形成康养产业基地，打造徽州健康生命生活方式。

4. 向外突破营销边界

祥源·齐云山生态文化旅游度假区以"来齐云山，做逍遥客"为主题，上午时间推出"复古游齐云"，涵盖五福拜年、状元擂台、新春雅集、白岳趣谈和真仙祈福五大场景；下午时间安排"风雅徽州集"，通过货郎游街、文人书房、乡俗展演和匠心好物，还原古徽州烟火市集；晚上时间推出"白岳夜逍遥"，包括齐云山打铁花、横江舞金龙、鱼灯游园会和横江烟花秀等，流光溢彩、热闹非凡，为每位游客提供全天候的沉浸式度假体验。此外，度假区还创新性地引入了以"摩崖石刻数字博物馆"为代表的全息场景技术，将旅游数字化发展融入现实。同时，借助"祥源旅行"一站式旅行服务平台，有效地实现

了本地旅游产品与本地优选山货"齐货出山"。

成效

祥源·齐云山生态文化旅游度假区从"山上"走向"山下"，有效利用地方资源进行旅游要素转化，完成齐云山文旅产业搭建和融合发展全过程。这一过程不仅促使齐云山从传统景区转型升级为综合性旅游目的地，还极大地提升了齐云山的品牌价值，实现了品牌重塑和增值，为项目和产业的可持续发展奠定了坚实的核心支撑。目前齐云小镇年接待游客300余万人次，实现旅游综合收入8000万余元。项目开发直接和间接带动就业500人，为周边村落提供岗位100个，协助镇区20户家庭转型从事旅游经营活动（农家乐、民宿客栈、山村土特产销售、农村电商等），引导返乡就业创业村民150人。当地居民创收累计约2000万元，村民年人均收入从2017年的2万元增长至2023年的约4万元。

经验与启示

1. 顶层设计因地制宜

祥源·齐云山生态文化旅游度假区项目从前期策划、功能分区、业态计划到动线设计都围绕齐云山项目文商旅融合进行，文化上注重深度挖掘及二次创意，使抽象的文化转化成受市场欢迎的体验场景；商业上思考流量及转化效率，并及时调整灵活变化；旅游上不过度依赖原生资源，积极探寻新增长点。度假区坚持"山上、水上、镇上"整体谋划定位，以活化"白岳"文化为方向，围绕"古风逍遥 日游夜娱"主题，不断进行度假产品创新升级。

2. 在地关系良性平衡

项目从立项到交付运营的全过程中，祥源控股集团、地方政府以及当地居民村民这三方群体均深度参与并贯穿始终。地方政府提供良好的营商环境及政策支持，为企业预留更多的发挥空间；祥源控股集团在扶持业务及带动就业方向上，尽量吸收更多当地村民参与到小镇经营中来，配合政府实施"回家工程"，发展"归雁经济"，成为推进乡村振兴的重要力量；政府、企业、农民三者相互支持，形成区域发展的持久动能。

下一步计划

在文旅融合、文化复兴、乡村振兴的时代背景下，在长三角一体化、融杭接沪区域发展契机下，祥源·齐云山生态文化旅游度假区将继续借势政策东风及区域发展机遇，聚焦"大黄山世界级休闲度假康养旅游目的地"项目定位及产业融合发展方向，"山上"坚持保护性运营，侧重于软性内容植入及呈现；"山下"以持续的国内头部康养资源、徽州在地代表文化资源嫁接实现商业赋能，通过配套设施更新、多元经营政策、在地内容再造、营销杠杆加码、深度运营支持、重点项目投资6大发展路径，继续积极探寻小镇全新的增长点和增值内容。祥源控股集团将秉承战略升级后的"文旅产业服务商"企业使命，持续为中国文化旅游产业的高质量融合发展、祥源文旅产品和服务的提质升级、黄山全域旅游工作的高效建设，以及乡村振兴战略的施行全力以赴。

2024 世界旅游联盟：旅游助力乡村振兴案例（中英文双语版）
WTA Best Practices of Rural Revitalization through Tourism 2024 (Chinese-English Bilingual Edition)

Qiyunshan Town, Xiuning County, Huangshan City, Anhui Province:

Promoting Rural Revitalization with Qiyunshan Eco-Cultural Resort

Abstract

Sunriver Holdings Group started to invest in Qiyunshan Town of Anhui Province in 2011 and has accumulatively spent 1 billion yuan developing Qiyunshan Eco-Cultural Resort. Sunriver is deeply rooted in the hermit-style immersive health preservation culture of ancient China, uses Mount Qiyun's beautiful natural landscape and unique cultural resources, and integrates local cultural elements such as the Taoist way of health preservation, ancient buildings, and scholarly tradition into its tourism development practice. It has funded, built, and put into operation cableways, mountain-viewing hotels, and cultural-heritage towns, and built Qiyunshan Town into a tourist destination offering immersive theme tours, leisure and holidaymaking services, boutique hotels and homestays, catering, and cultural consumption products and services. Upholding the belief that "lucid waters and lush mountains are invaluable assets", Sunriver strengthens the connectivity between the natural landscape of Mount Qiyun and the town at the mountain foot, plans tourism development to promote rural revitalization, and provides a living example of the high-quality integrated development of the cultural and tourism industries. The Qiyunshan Eco-Cultural Resort has set a model for other mountain destinations to develop the leisure and holidaymaking business.

Challenges and Problems

Qiyunshan Town is named after Mount Qiyun. It covers an area of 107.97 square kilometers and has seven administrative villages under its jurisdiction, with a population of 13,200. Mount Qiyun boasts the unique Danxia landform and a millennium-old Taoist culture, giving it a unique advantage in developing tourism. It was approved as a national key scenic area in 1994. Its development back then, however, was constrained by poor transportation and other infrastructure, underdeveloped tourism resources, and a lack of tourist services and supporting facilities as well as tourism professionals. Its proximity to the famous Mount Huangshan did not help, either. These internal and external factors combined resulted in slow tourism development in Mount Qiyun. Without tourism dividends, residents and surrounding villages lacked the motivation to drive regional sustainable development.

Measures

1. Establishing a joint venture platform

In 2011, Sunriver joined hands with the People's Government of Xiuning County to develop the Qiyunshan Eco-Cultural Resort, including the Mount Qiyun Scenic Area, the Qiyun Tourist Town, Xiangfurui Boutique Inn, a campsite, tree houses, and bamboo rafting. They are working together to build it into an international destination equipped with first-class services and facilities ranging from sightseeing, leisure and holidaymaking, health preservation, rooms with mountain views, and outdoor entertainment.

2. Coordinating the development of the Mount Qiyun Scenic Area and the tourist town

Centering around the Mount Qiyun Scenic Area, Sunriver has improved infrastructure, including tourist facilities and the transportation system, and conserved historical heritage, to highlight the natural landscape and cultural heritage. At the foot of the mountain is the Qiyun Town where standard tourist facilities are introduced and consumption scenarios keep updating. Experiential farming activities are also available near the town, in a bid to realize the sustainable development of local cultural, tourism, and commercial industries.

3. Tapping into local culture

Qiyunshan Eco-Cultural Resort is positioned to cultivate the mind with culture and physical health with medicine. To cultivate the mind, it has introduced intangible cultural heritage handicrafts such as paper-cutting, iron painting, wood carving, bamboo carving, and inkstone carving, and to cultivate the body, it has incubated a health preservation business represented by the Sleep Valley and the House of Elixirs. A health preservation industry base is built by integrating traditional Chinese medicine (TCM), TCM-based psychology, and traditional medicine of Anhui, to continue to promote local healthy lifestyles.

4. Blurring the boundaries of marketing

With the theme of "Be Free and Unfettered at Mount Qiyun", Qiyunshan Eco-Cultural Resort

has launched an immersive tour package covering the whole day: in the morning, visitors can visit Mount Qiyun where five traditional cultural scenes are recreated, including New Year's Blessings, the Number One Scholar competition, and Taoist rituals; in the afternoon, visitors can go to the ancient-style market to watch the merchants' parade and folk customs performances, visit traditional studies, and appreciate exquisite handicrafts; at night, colorful and lively activities will be staged to entertain tourists, including the molten iron fireworks performance, the dragon dance, the fish-shaped lantern show, and the fireworks show. The holographic scenes represented by the "Digital Museum of Cliff Carvings" make digital tours a reality. Local tourism products and select characteristic goods are available on the one-stop travel service platform represented by "Sunriver Travel".

Results

Qiyunshan Eco-Cultural Resort has expanded from the mountain to its foot, effectively translated local resources into tourism resources, built the cultural and tourism industries from scratch, and promoted their integrated development. By turning Mount Qiyun from a traditional scenic area to a tourist destination, Qiyunshan Town has reshaped and enhanced its tourist brand value, underpinning the sustainable development of related projects and industries. At present, Qiyun Town receives more than three million tourists annually and generates a comprehensive tourism income of more than 80 million yuan. It has, directly and indirectly, created 500 local jobs and 100 jobs in surrounding villages, and assisted 20 households in starting their own tourism business (e.g. farm stays, homestays, the sale of local mountain goods, and rural e-commerce). It has lured back 150 migrant workers to start their business. The project has cumulatively increased the income of residents by about 20 million yuan, and the annual per capita income of villagers was raised from 20,000 yuan in 2017 to about 40,000 in 2023 yuan.

Experience and Inspirations

1. The top-level design is adapted to local conditions

From early-stage planning, functional zoning, business planning, and flow design, Qiyunshan Eco-Cultural Resort has kept its focus on the integration of cultural, commercial, and tourism business. Culturally, it digs deeply into local culture and makes secondary creations to turn the abstract culture

into experiential scenes welcomed by tourists. Commercially, it values traffic and traffic conversion efficiency and adjusts flexibly and promptly. The tourism industry does not rely too much on native resources, but instead actively explores new growth points. The Resort adheres to the holistic planning of "the mountain, waters and the town", and continuously develops new and upgrades tourism products including day travel and night entertainment activities featuring local cultural heritage.

2. The relations of local stakeholders are well-balanced

From project approval to delivery and operation, the Qiyunshan Eco-Cultural Resort project has always been the fruit of the concerted effort of Sunriver, the local government, and the local people. The local government provides a good business environment and policy support, reserving space for Sunriver. In terms of supporting business and driving employment, Sunriver hires as many local villagers as possible in the operation of the town, assists the government in implementing the Homecoming Project and developing the "returnee economy", and becomes an important force in promoting rural revitalization. The government, the company, and farmers support each other to form a lasting driving force for regional development.

Plans

As China works to promote the integrated development of culture and tourism, cultural rejuvenation, and rural revitalization, Qiyunshan Eco-Cultural Resort will continue to leverage policy support and seize opportunities brought by the integrated development of the Yangtze River

Delta and the regional development of areas near Hangzhou and Shanghai, and adhere to its positioning as a world-class leisure and wellness destination in the greater Huangshan area and the integrated development of local industries. It will continue the conservation-oriented operation of the mountain area, with a focus on soft content placement and presentation. At the mountain foot, it will continue to introduce domestic heading health preservation businesses and local representative cultural resources to empower the commercial scene, and actively explore new growth points and value-added content through six development paths: the upgrade of supporting facilities, business diversification, reshaping of local content, marketing leverage, in-depth operational support, and investment in key projects. Sunriver will adhere to its new mission of becoming "a service supplier in the cultural and tourism industries" and continue to go all out to promote the high-quality integrated development of China's cultural and tourism industries, develop higher-quality cultural and tourism products and services, efficiently develop all-area-advancing tourism in Huangshan, and implement the national strategy of rural revitalization.

2024 世界旅游联盟：旅游助力乡村振兴案例（中英文双语版）
WTA Best Practices of Rural Revitalization through Tourism 2024（Chinese-English Bilingual Edition）

山西省大同市云州区：
黄花新质生产力赋能区域高质量发展

摘　要

山西省大同市云州区深刻践行习近平总书记"让黄花成为乡亲们的'致富花'"的重要指示，依托黄花特色产业资源，引导农户全面参与，由单一种植产业、初加工产业向"种植基地＋加工基地＋电子商务＋观光旅游＋文创体验"全产业链体系发展，联村成片发展乡村旅游，探索黄花农业新质生产力，擦亮"忘忧云州"乡村品牌，推动形成产业链条完整、功能多样、业态丰富、利益联结紧密的"小黄花·大产业"格局，带动区域高质量发展。

挑战与问题

大同市是山西省黄花的主要产区之一,从明朝开始就享有"黄花之乡"的盛名。2011年以来,大同市云州区把黄花产业确立为"一县一业"的主导产业和农民脱贫致富的支柱产业,采取"公司+农户""合作社+农户"等运作模式,不断扩大种植面积,配套出台土地流转、资金扶持、技术服务、招商引资等一系列扶持黄花产业发展的政策,全力跟进服务,推动黄花产业向规模化种植、集约化加工、品牌化销售的现代农业发展。在发展过程中仍然存在以下问题:一是产业体系建设不足,黄花产业的第一产业产值占比较高,黄花产品的精深加工、"特""优"品牌建设仍处于发展阶段,商业贸易、物流集散、科研开发和文化展示等产业链条不强,制约黄花产业发展壮大;二是资金筹措投入不足,制约项目发展和推进;三是专业人才支撑不足,制约了产业管理和运营水平。

措施

1. 一二三产业融合

云州区为了将黄花产业真正做成大产业,突出黄花优势主导产业,一是建设慧农科技产业园区,构建集黄花"标准种植—精深加工—电商销售—仓储物流—旅游观光—乡村度假"于一体的现代农业园区,加快产业集群集聚发展。二是积极探索"黄花+旅游"发展模式,打造"火山黄花田园综合体"和"火山下的忘忧村",建成火山天路、忘忧农场、吉家庄旅游小镇等以黄花为媒介的23个乡村旅游点。三是创新探索"交旅融合"新业态,提升忘忧大道为音乐公路,打造一条集特色黄花产业、忘忧休闲农业、快乐旅游观光于一体的旅游道路,现已成为游客热衷的网红打卡体验地。

2. "产学研"深度对接

一是以国内权威黄花产业专家颉敏昌教授为核心构建团队,先后引进了农业、食品等专业的研究生13人投入黄花产业发展。二是与中国农业大学食品学院等多所院校及研究机构合作,研究开发出黄花菜和其根茎叶副产品两大系列、六大品类的130余种黄花农产品,如黄花精酿啤酒、黄花酱、黄花脆、黄花饼、忘忧酒、黄花酥和黄花油茶等,不断提升黄花产业的产业创新力和人才贡献率。

3. 打响"忘忧云州"品牌

为了进一步宣传和打响"大同黄花"和"忘忧云州"品牌知名度,云州区一是邀请成龙代言;二是积极参加山西文化产业博览交易会;三是举办"大同黄花专场推介"活动,通过产业发展论坛、美食大赛、忘忧音乐节等,实现产销对接;四是常态化组织形式多样的电商直播带货,先后参与主办央视"秦晋之好""大同黄花晋京城""星光行动·大同好粮助农专场"等大型直播活动,为黄花发展增值赋能。

4. 扶持"返乡创业"模式

政府积极扶持"乡村经纪人"模式,按照"农业+科技、农业+旅游、农业+生态、农业+康养、农业+文化、农业+教育和农业+互联网"七大板块将返乡创业的青农们分类培训,发挥他们的各自专长,深耕精品种植、科技研发、产品销售和研学旅游等,这些"乡村经纪人"成为产业致富能手、返乡乡贤。截至目前,项目区共培育"乡村经纪人"90余人,规模较大的约15户,全年资金流水300万元以上。

成效

2023 年，云州区荣获国家乡村振兴示范县，西坪镇（黄花菜）荣获第十二批全国"一村一品"示范村镇，坊城新村荣获 2023 全国乡村治理示范村，唐家堡黄花旅游度假区获省级旅游度假区。项目区内有效增加本地就业岗位约 1500 个，优势特色农业产值从 3000 万元增长至 3603.4 万元，文旅产业产值从 3500 万元提升至 3820 万元，唐家堡、坊城新村集体经济收入突破 100 万元，其他村村集体经济突破 30 万元以上。村集体经济收入总额由 213 万元提升至 313 万元，居民人均可支配收入由 13500 元提升至 15881 元。

经验与启示

1. 强化资源要素保障

重视发挥地方政府的引导作用，系统谋划，综合施策，吸引更多资源、资金向乡村聚集和落地生根，催生"聚合效应"。项目从规划设计、要素保障、财政支持、人才培育等多渠道入手，形成全方位政策支持体系，推动产业稳步建设。

2. 坚持产业融合赋能

项目区全力用好"大同黄花"金字招牌，以"品牌化、电商化、数字化"为支撑，2023 年举办首届世界黄花大会，并连续六年开展黄花丰收活动月活动，建设"黄花 e 镇"，推进唐家堡民俗体验区电商文化街项目，对接快手、抖音、一亩田、天猫、京东、拼多多等电商平台，用数字化理念引领业态发展，推动优质农产品搭上"数字快车"，实现产业共育，激发"共富效应"。

3. 坚持文化活化利用

项目区进一步发挥文化对产业的带动作用，深度挖掘萱草"母亲花""忘忧草"的文化概念，塑造"忘忧云州"文旅品牌，打造串联忘忧大道忘忧农场等多个精品景点的乡村休闲旅游线路，开展以黄花为主的科普、自然、食农、生活等文化研学教育活动，实现文化与产业互融互促。

下一步计划

一是加快推进项目落地见效。充分发挥领导小组和工作专班统筹协调作用，持续顶格推进、顶格调度，强化各部门协同联动，加快工程竣工、资产移交等合规程序办理，推动项目尽快投产。二是加强梳理总结。提炼在振兴工作和产业发展方面的经验做法，充分发挥项目区典型示范和辐射带动作用，将振兴模式提炼、推广、运用到全区甚至全省乡村振兴工作中，通过组织现场观摩、经验交流等方式，带动周边乡镇、经济薄弱村发展进步，通过理论提升指导实践，为全省乡村振兴工作贡献力量。三是乡村旅游与康养、生态、科技、教育等行业形成更广泛更深入的融合，逐渐形成多主题多层次要素服务以及丰富多彩的夜游和节庆活动等，推动乡村旅游市场规模持续扩大、产业链条不断延展，综合带动乡村振兴作用不断增强。

Yunzhou District, Datong City, Shanxi Province:

Empowering Regional High-Quality Development with the Daylily Industry

Abstract

Yunzhou District of Datong City, Shanxi Province earnestly implements President Xi Jinping's call to make the daylily a "gold flower" for the villagers. With its characteristic daylily industry, it guides farmers to fully participate and extends the industrial chain from planting and primary processing to plantations, processing bases, e-commerce, sightseeing tours, and cultural and creative experiences. It also promotes village-wide rural tourism, taps into the economic potential of the daylily industry, and burnishes the rural brand of "Sorrow-Forgetting Yunzhou". It is working to form a complete industrial chain centering around daylilies, with diverse functions and business forms and strong interest linkages, and promote high-quality regional development.

Challenges and Problems

Datong City is one of the main daylily growers in Shanxi Province and has been reputed as "the Hometown of the Daylily" since the Ming Dynasty. Since 2011, Yunzhou District has established the daylily industry as the dominant industry for the "One County, One Industry" initiative and the pillar industry for increasing farmers' income. Through the operation modes of "company + farmer" and "cooperative + farmer", it continuously expands the planting area and has introduced several favorable policies concerning the transfer of land use rights, financial support, technical services, and investment promotion. It also provides follow-up services and urges the daylily industry to evolve into modern agriculture with a large planting area, intensive processing, and brand-based sales. In this development process, however, it still faces the following problems. Firstly, the industrial system is not balanced. For the daylily industry, the output value of the primary sector is still too high, and it is still in the infancy of developing deep-processed products and "characteristic" and "high-quality" brands. The weaknesses in commercial trade, logistics and distribution, research and development, and cultural display also restrict the development and growth of the daylily industry. Secondly, a lack of investment hinders project implementation. Thirdly, a lack of professionals restricts the management and operation level.

Measures

1. Promoting the integrated development of primary, secondary, and tertiary sectors

In order to truly expand the daylily industry and highlight it as an advantageous dominant industry, Yunzhou District firstly built the Huinong Science and Technology Park, a modern agricultural park offering one-stop services ranging from standardized daylily planting, deep processing, e-commerce sales, warehousing, and logistics, to tours and rural holidaymaking, and accelerated the clustering development. Secondly, it actively explores the development model of "daylily + tourism". It has built a complex featuring daylily plantations at the foot of the volcano and "The Sorrow-Forgetting

Village at the Foot of the Volcano", and added 23 rural tourist attractions featuring the daylily landscape, such as the Heavenly Way to the Volcano, the Sorrow-Forgetting Farm, and the Jijiazhuang Tourist Town. Thirdly, it explores new business forms that integrate transport facilities and tourism resources. Wangyou Avenue was upgraded into a Music Highway, to turn it into a scenic road featuring the characteristic daylily industry, leisure agriculture, and sightseeing businesses. It has become a must-visit for tourists.

2. Strengthening cooperation with universities and research institutes

Firstly, Yunzhou District has built a team with Professor Jie Minchang, an authoritative expert in the daylily industry, at the core, and has successively recruited 13 graduate students specialized in agriculture and food science to develop the daylily industry. Secondly, it has worked with many universities and research institutes such as the College of Food Science and Nutritional Engineering of China Agricultural University, and jointly developed more than 130 kinds of daylily products which are divided into six categories of two series: the daylily flowers, and the daylily roots, stems and leaves, including the daylily craft beer, daylily sauce, daylily crisp, daylily cake, daylily wine, daylily shortbread, and daylily oil tea, continuously improving the innovation capacity and the talent contribution rate of the daylily industry.

3. Building the brand "Sorrow-Forgetting Yunzhou"

To further raise the brand visibility of "Datong Daylily" and "Sorrow-Forgetting Yunzhou", Yunzhou District hired Jackie Chan as the brand ambassador, actively participated in the Shanxi Cultural Industry Expo, and held a special marketing event for its

daylily industry, including an industrial development forum, a food competition, and a music festival to match supply and demand. It also regularly organizes various forms of livestreaming e-commerce sessions and has participated in some organized by China Media Group, to increase the added value of daylilies.

4. Support villagers to return to their hometown to start a business

The government actively cultivates the "rural broker" model and organizes training for the returnee farmers in seven categories: "agriculture + science and technology", "agriculture + tourism", "agriculture + ecology", "agriculture + health preservation", "agriculture + culture", "agriculture + education" and "agriculture + Internet", so that they can give play to their respective skills in planting techniques, research and development, sales, and study tours. These brokers have the backbone of local industrial development. Up to now, the project areas have cultivated more than 90 brokers, including about 15 in the largest area, and the annual capital flow is more than 3 million yuan.

Results

In 2023, Yunzhou District was awarded the National Rural Revitalization Demonstration

County, Xiping Town (Daylily) was voted among the 12th batch of National Demonstration Villages and Towns for the "One Village, One Product" Initiative, Fangcheng New Village was awarded the 2023 National Rural Governance Demonstration Village, and Tangjiabao Daylily Resort was awarded a Provincial-Level Tourism Resort. The project areas have created about 1,500 local jobs, the output value of advantageous and characteristic agriculture has increased from 30 million yuan to 36.034 million yuan, and the output value of the cultural and tourism industries from 35 million yuan to 38.2 million yuan. The income of village collectives of Tangjiabao and Fangcheng New Village has each exceeded 1 million yuan, and that of other villages has exceeded 300,000 yuan. The total income of the village collectives has increased from 2.13 million yuan to 3.13 million yuan, and the per capita rural disposable income has increased from 13,500 yuan to 15,881 yuan.

Experience and Inspirations

1. Strengthen the guarantee of resources and production factors

Yunzhou District values the guiding role of local governments, plans systematically, and adopts a package of policies to attract more resources and funds to rural areas and produce the "clustering effect". From planning and design, factor supply, and financial support, to talent cultivation, there is a complete set of policies supporting the steady development of the industry.

2. Leveraging the empowering role of integrated industrial development

The project areas make full use of the reputation of "Datong Daylily". With the purposes of branding, e-commerce, and digitalization, Yunzhou District held the first World Daylily Congress, and has hosted the Daylily Harvest Month for six consecutive years, and developed the "Daylily E-Town" and the E-Commerce Street in the Tangjiabao Folk Customs Experience Zone. It has also opened stores on such e-commerce platforms as Kuaishou, Douyin, ymt.com, Tmall, JD.com, and Pinduoduo, driven development through digitalization, and pushed high-quality agricultural products onto the "digital express", to jointly cultivate the industry and stimulate the "common prosperity effect".

3. Exploring cultural connotation

The project areas give culture a bigger role in developing the daylily industry. In China, the daylily is a symbol of love for one's mother and is also known as the Sorrow-Forgetting ("wangyou") Grass. On this basis, the cultural and tourism brand of "Sorrow-Forgetting Yunzhou" is established, and a rural scenic route is developed to connect many high-quality scenic spots such as Wangyou Avenue and the Sorrow-Forgetting Farm. Study tours and other educational activities are also staged with themes on popular science, nature, food, agriculture, and lifestyles, to integrate and promote cultural and industrial development at the same time.

Plans

Firstly, Yunzhou District will accelerate the

implementation of the project. It will give full play to the coordinating role of the leading group and the working group, continue to advance the project and allocate resources from the top level, strengthen inter-departmental coordination and linkage, and speed up the handling of compliance procedures for project completion and asset transfer, so that the project will be put into operation as soon as possible. Secondly, it will increase efforts to summarize the best practices in rural revitalization and industrial development, give full play to the exemplary and leading role of the project areas, and promote the development model to the rest of the district and even the entire province. It will organize field observation trips and experience exchange sessions to help surrounding towns and underdeveloped villages develop, guide practices with theories, and contribute to rural revitalization across the province. Thirdly, it will integrate rural tourism with health preservation, ecological conservation, science and technology, education, and other industries in more areas and at a deeper level, gradually developing multi-theme and multi-level element services, and launching colorful night tours and festivals, so that it will have an ever-expanding rural tourism market, an ever-extending industrial chain, and an ever-enlarging role in promoting rural revitalization.

海南省东方市三家镇红草村：
鳄珍科技助力乡村振兴

摘　要

　　海南鳄珍鳄鱼科技有限公司（以下简称鳄珍科技）遵循国家创建特色产业小镇的总体要求，根据海南省委、省政府建设特色产业小镇的总体部署，立足东方市三家镇红草村独特的自然条件和鳄鱼特色产业发展的新理念，深度开展农旅融合实践，集鳄鱼养殖、研发、深加工、销售、原料供应、旅游观光六位一体，涵盖鳄鱼全产业链，采取"公司＋合作社＋农户"的模式，带动农户持续增收致富，有效推动了红草村经济、文化和社会的全面进步，走出了一条特色旅游产业带动乡村振兴的新路子，为广大偏远地区的乡村振兴事业提供了宝贵的经验和启示。

挑战与问题

红草村地处海南省东方市三家镇东部边缘地带，是一个典型的经济欠发达地区。红草村交通设施建设严重不足，村容村貌状况差，通常是"雨天一身泥，晴天一身灰"。村内产业单一，村民大多依靠种植辣椒、香蕉等传统农作物艰难度日，许多适龄的男青年因村子条件落后，娶妻成家都成了难题。面对这样的困境，如何结合本村的实际情况，发掘和利用好村里的优势资源，因地制宜发展特色产业，带动乡亲们脱贫致富，成为红草村干部和群众面临的重大课题。

措施

1. 项目落地

鳄珍科技的鳄鱼养殖产业项目严格按照海南省扶贫产业项目的实施流程，即先纳入项目库后审批执行，全面完成了包括农户需求调查、产业项目考察、村级评议申报、镇级审定上报等在内的所有规定环节。该项目承担了超过 600 万元的产业帮扶资金，主动积极参股红草村村委会合作社的投资，帮助村集体经济从事鳄鱼养殖，确保每年向各参与投资的村委会提供固定 10% 的分红回报，有效促进了村集体经济的价值创造与财富积累。

2. 土地流转

鳄珍科技通过与红草村委会签订《东方市农村土地外包合同书》，流转了三家镇的村集体及农户土地 237 亩建成鳄鱼养殖基地，公司按每年每亩约 650 元的标准向村民支付土地租金，年租金总额约为 15 万元。至今，鳄珍科技已累计支付了土地流转费用达 462 万元。

3. 人才培养

鳄珍科技配合各级政府成功举办了超过 40 场针对鳄鱼养殖技术及电商直播带货的培训活动。惠及人数超过 1600 余人次。在此过程中，公司全程提供鳄

鱼苗和鳄鱼饲料，培养了一大批技术熟练、眼界开阔的鳄鱼养殖工人和电商直播人才。据估算，一对夫妻在一年内可养殖 1500 条鳄鱼，每年出栏达到 500 条，年收入不低于 10 万元。展望未来 5—10 年，该鳄鱼养殖项目有望带动整个小镇 300 户村民实现增收，预计增收总额可达 1 亿—2 亿元。

4. 产业带动

一是带动上游鳄鱼饲料产业发展。鳄珍科技每年向周边采购大量的鳄鱼饲料用鱼，从根本上解决了村民养鱼的销路问题，带动村民通过养殖罗非鱼和各种杂鱼实现增产增收，四年来累计采购金额近 3000 万元。二是带动餐饮、住宿及仓储物流等配套产业的发展。随着鳄珍科技产业规模和品牌影响的不断扩大，加上环岛旅游公路的开通，驻地涌入了大量的人流、物流和资金流，附近村民充分利用地理优势与自然资源，积极开展餐饮、住宿和农副产品经营。

成效

红草村在上级党委政府的大力支持和广大村民的齐心协力下，借助鳄珍科技的引领带动，各项事业实现了跨越式发展。红草村不仅成了全球存栏鳄鱼数最多的生态养殖中心，更在产业发展、旅游开发、村民生活等多个方面取得了显著成果。红草村的鳄鱼养殖业迅速崛起，其养殖数量在全国占比达 37%，全球占比超过 15%，并成为全国 80% 鳄鱼种苗的供应源。此外，红草村也吸引了大量游客前来观光旅游，年游

客数近8万人，为村集体经济注入了新的活力。

鳄珍科技协助红草村争取项目财政扶持资金700万元用于公共基础设施建设，使村里的道路和村容村貌焕然一新。村里两层以上的小洋楼从2019年的2栋激增到180多栋，许多家庭都购置了小轿车，村民的生活水平得到了显著提升。鳄珍科技雇佣大量村民从事劳务活动获取收入，支付劳务费超过1500万元，累计向东方市上缴税收近3000万元。

经验与启示

1. 农旅融合

鳄珍科技在充分利用红草村自然资源的基础上，不仅发展了鳄鱼养殖业，还巧妙地将农业与旅游业相结合，打造了一系列鳄鱼主题的旅游项目。游客们可以近距离观赏鳄鱼，了解鳄鱼的生活习性，体验鳄鱼产品的制作过程。农旅融合的模式增加了红草村的知名度和吸引力。

2. 精准扶贫

鳄珍科技始终坚持以人为本，通过提供技术培训、就业机会和创业支持等方式，帮助村民参与到鳄鱼产业链中来。这不仅提高了村民的收入水平，也增强了他们的自我发展能力。同时，鳄珍科技还积极参与到村里的公益事业中，为村民提供更好的教育、医疗和文化服务，进一步提升了村民的生活质量。

3. 协同发展

鳄鱼产业的发展不仅带动了饲料、加工、销售等相关产业的发展，还促进了当地交通、通信等基础设施的完善。这些相关产业的协同发展，进一步提升了红草村的产业竞争力，为乡村振兴注入了新的活力。

下一步计划

鳄珍科技将依托现有鳄鱼特色产业农旅融合发展的良好基础，深耕鳄鱼特色文化，积极创建海南5椰级乡村旅游点和国家4A级旅游景区，并在生鲜、营养品、养生酒、皮具、生物医药和日化等领域全面发力，讲好故事，做强产业，引领中国（东方）鳄鱼小镇在未来5—8年鳄鱼存栏量增加到100万条，年产值突破50亿—100亿元，纳税逾2亿—5亿元，建成世界领先的鳄鱼特色旅游体验中心、鳄鱼养殖中心、鳄鱼产品交易中心、鳄鱼博物馆、鳄鱼研究院、鳄鱼产业高峰论坛、鳄鱼嘉年华等项目，产品辐射全球，引领世界鳄鱼产品时尚消费潮流，成为全球鳄鱼从业者和爱好者向往的胜地。同时将红草村打造成全国乡村振兴的典范，为海南自贸港的建设增光添彩。

Hongcao Village, Sanjia Town, Dongfang City, Hainan Province:

Hainan CR&TPB Crocodile Industry Technology Co., Ltd. Boosting Rural Revitalization

Abstract

Hainan CR&TPB Crocodile Industry Technology Co., Ltd. follows the national requirements for building characteristic industrial towns and the relevant plan of the Hainan Provincial Party Committee and Provincial Government and advances the integrated development of agriculture and tourism in Hongcao Village of Sanjia Town, Dongfang City based on local natural conditions and crocodile industry. It has built a complete industrial chain covering crocodile breeding, research and development, deep processing, sales, raw materials supply, and tourism, and adopted the "company + cooperative + farmer" model to help farmers increase income. By doing so, it has effectively promoted economic, cultural, and social progress in Hongcao, embarked on a new path of rural revitalization driven by the characteristic tourism industry, and provided valuable references for the rural revitalization of remote areas.

Challenges and Problems

Hongcao Village is located on the fringes of Sanjia Town and is economically underdeveloped. It is seriously short of transportation facilities, and the village environment is so bad that it is muddy on rainy days and dusty on sunny days. Most villagers struggle to make a living by planting peppers and bananas, and many young men are so poor that they cannot afford marriage to start a family. In the face of such a predicament, the village officials and villagers need to figure out how to develop characteristic industries according to local conditions and make good use of advantageous resources, to increase the farmers' income.

Measures

1. Project implementation

The crocodile breeding project of Hainan CR&TPB Crocodile Industry Technology Co., Ltd. was included in the province's list of industrial projects for poverty alleviation before it got the approval for implementation. The project team has gone through all the required procedures including a survey on farmers' demand, a survey on local business projects, village-level evaluation and declaration, and town-level approval and reporting. The company contributed more than 600 yuan in assistance funds and made an active equity investment in the cooperative of Hongcao Villagers' Committee. It helps the village collective economy breed crocodiles and pays 10% of the fixed returns as dividends to each investing villagers' committee on time every year, to create value and wealth for the village collective.

2. Circulation of land use rights

The company signed the Contract on Rural Land Use Rights Transfer in Dongfang City with the Hongcao Village Committee, built a crocodile breeding base covering 237 *mu* of collective and farmers' land in Sanjia Town, and rented land from the villagers at about 650 yuan per *mu* per year, totaling 150,000 yuan. So far, it has paid 4.62 million yuan for land use rights circulation.

3. Talent training

The company assisted local governments at all levels in holding more than 40 training sessions on crocodile breeding techniques and livestreaming e-commerce for more than 1,600 participants. It also supplies crocodile hatchlings and crocodile feed and has cultivated a large number of skilled and broad-minded crocodile breeding and livestreaming e-commerce specialists. It is estimated that a couple can normally raise 1,500 crocodiles a year, with 500 sold per year, and earn not less than 100,000 yuan. It is expected to increase the income of 300 rural households in the town by 100-200 million yuan in the next five to ten years.

4. Driving the development of related industries

Firstly, the upstream crocodile feed industry.

Hainan CR&TPB Crocodile Industry Technology purchases a large quantity of crocodile feed fish from surrounding areas every year, spending nearly 30 million yuan in the past four years and increasing the income of farmers breeding tilapia and miscellaneous fish. Secondly, catering, accommodation, warehousing, and logistics industries. With the ever-growing scale and brand influence of the project, plus the opening of the Hainan Coastal Scenic Highway, large flows of people, goods, and capital have flooded into the project area, and the nearby villagers have made full use of geographical advantages and natural resources to provide catering and accommodation services and sell agricultural and sideline products.

Results

With the strong support of the higher-level Party committee and government and the concerted efforts of the villagers, and with the guidance of Hainan CR&TPB Crocodile Industry Technology, Hongcao Village has achieved leapfrog development on various fronts. It has become an eco-breeding center with the most crocodiles in the world and achieved remarkable results in developing industries including tourism and improving living standards. The crocodile breeding industry has grown fast; it accounts for 37% of the national market and more than 15% of the global market and supplies up to 80% of the country's baby crocodiles for farming. In addition, Hongcao Village has also attracted a large number of tourists, with nearly 80,000 of them per year, injecting new vitality into the village's collective economy.

Hainan CR&TPB Crocodile Industry Technology has assisted Hongcao Village in securing 7 million yuan in government funds for infrastructure construction and improving the roads and the village's appearance. The number of Western-style residential buildings with more than two floors has surged from two in 2019 to more than 180, and there are many cars in the village. The living standards have been significantly improved. The company also employs many villagers and has paid more than 15 million yuan for labor and nearly 30 million yuan in taxes to Dongfang City.

Experience and Inspirations

1. Agriculture-tourism integration

Making full use of local natural resources, Hainan CR&TPB Crocodile Industry Technology has developed the crocodile breeding industry and

agritourism, with several crocodile-themed tourism projects launched. Visitors can see crocodiles up close, learn about their living habits, and make crocodile products on their own. The agriculture-tourism integration model has increased Hongcao's visibility and appeal.

2. Targeted poverty alleviation

Always putting the people first, the company provides related technical training and employment opportunities to villagers and supports those who want to start their crocodile-related business. It has not only raised the villagers' income but also enhanced their development ability. At the same time, it actively participates in philanthropic undertakings and provides better educational, medical, and cultural services for the villagers, further improving their quality of life.

3. Coordinated development

The booming crocodile industry has not only stimulated the development of feed, processing, sales, and other related industries but also led to better transportation, communications, and other infrastructure. The coordinated development of related industries has further enhanced Hongcao's industrial competitiveness and injected new vitality into rural revitalization.

Plans

Hainan CR&TPB Crocodile Industry Technology will build on the good foundation of the integrated agricultural and tourism development, continue to grow the characteristic crocodile breeding industry and work actively to make Hongcao Village a five-coconut rural tourist attraction in Hainan and a national 3A-level scenic spot. It will extend its business into the fields of fresh produce, nutrition, pro-health wine, leather goods, biomedicine, and daily chemicals, double down on public communication, and strengthen the industry. It will lead China (Oriental) Crocodile Town to increase the number of crocodiles to 1 million in the next five to eight years, with an annual output value of more than 5-10 billion yuan and a tax payment of more than 200-500 million yuan. It plans to build a world-leading crocodile-themed tour center, a crocodile breeding center, a crocodile product trading center, a crocodile museum, a crocodile research institute, and host the crocodile industry forum and crocodile carnival, among other projects. It will ship products to the rest of the world, boost the consumption of crocodile products worldwide, and make Hongcao a must-visit place for global crocodile farmers and enthusiasts and a national model of rural revitalization, contributing to the development of Hainan Free Trade Port.

浙江省江山市廿八都镇：
农文旅融合助千年古镇蝶变

摘　要

　　浙江省江山市廿八都镇立足新发展阶段、贯彻新发展理念，围绕"商帮文化"和"高端民宿"两大主题，按照"镇村搭台、文化唱戏、旅游助力"的发展模式，大力推进"旅游富民"工程，深化农文旅多产业融合发展，培育打造古韵浔里、长寿兴墩、边界林丰、运动浮盖、霞客坚强等主题村落，成功打造国家级历史文化名镇、国家5A级旅游景区、国家4A级旅游景区各1个，省3A级景区村庄7个，实现村集体总收入1579万元，探索出一条农文旅融合助力共同富裕的新路径。

挑战与问题

廿八都镇位于江山市西南端，浙、闽、赣三省交界处，凭借独特的地理位置和屯兵重镇、商贸枢纽等历史因素，素有"东南锁钥、入闽咽喉"之称。廿八都镇由于偏居浙西南边陲，经济社会发展相对滞后，主要原因如下。一是基础配套落后，设施老化，人居环境不佳；二是产业结构以农业为主，文旅业态几乎为零；三是人才出现空档，大量年轻人外出务工，空心化问题突出。

措施

1. 赋予文化新活力

一是坚持文化保护，廿八都镇历经五载发掘古镇历史文化资源，出版《廿八都镇志》，投资1.2亿元建成廿八都古镇景区，投资额占当年市级财政的六分之一。二是坚持文化传承，培育木偶戏等国家级非遗传承人，保护优秀民俗，以场景化、互动化的方式提供沉浸式体验。三是坚持文化活化，打造国家5A级旅游景区廿八都古镇，多角度、全方位展现"生活着的古镇"历史文化积淀。

2. 营造体验新场景

修编《廿八都历史文化名镇保护规划》，以进一步加强镇域风貌管控，强化环境改造。项目先后投入近8000万元，拆除不协调建筑5000多平方米，完成300多幢房屋的仿古改造，实现了4.5千米管线的下埋，并对20多处重要节点区域进行了绿化美化及景观改造。此外，还打造了200多处美丽庭院，并建成了"仙霞探古"省级城乡风貌样本区，将美好人居环境打造成游客体验新场景。

3. 开创共赢新模式

一方面，坚持项目带动，"景镇合一"，结合小城镇、美丽乡村、历史文化村落保护等工作，先后实施古镇一期开发、美丽城镇建设、未来乡村建设，推出"旅游＋写生""旅游＋研学""旅游＋运动"等深受游客喜爱的旅游线路产品。另一方面，实施政策叠加，出台《廿八都古镇保护管理专项资金管理办法》，制定餐饮、民宿运营等补助政策，建立景区共建共享共融机制，成立餐饮、民宿、农特产品等行业协会，搭建景区收益与镇村企共享的分配渠道。

4. 构建和谐新局面

创新出台《关于加强廿八都古镇保护管理的实施意见》，建立古镇管理的多部门联动机制，妥善化解群众住房、建房难题，有效防范农户私拆乱建现象。引导古镇、景区、所在村三方合力，推进古镇景区居民庭院整治改造、衣物晾晒点以及非机动车停放点建设等工作，有效破除景区发展与周边村民生活产生纠纷的困境。

成效

廿八都镇持续推进农文旅深度融合，成功培育了包括古韵浔里在内的5个主题村落。全镇建有农家乐

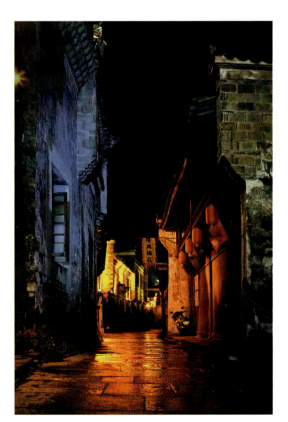

民宿128家，餐位数3000多个，床位数1431张，其中银宿5家，另建成银鼎级文化主题酒店2家、三星级旅游饭店1家。2023年，全镇接待游客43万人次，旅游经营收入超5700万元。2024年春节期间，全镇累计接待游客3.2万人次，同比增长137.4%，带动古镇旅游消费1000万元，实现新春旅游"开门红"。2023年全镇村集体经营性收入达50万元以上的行政村有4个，达30万元以上的行政村实现全覆盖。2023年度古镇农民人均收入达2.61万元，镇金融机构人民币储蓄存款4.88亿元，较2018年增长54%，大幅快于全市城镇人均存款增幅。

经验与启示

1. 注重借势借力

廿八都镇全力抓住江山全域旅游发展契机，借助乡村建设的力量，积极推动业态的多元化和特色化发展。一批新业态如闽菜赣菜馆、洋货店主题咖啡馆、"江山味道"展陈馆等相继呈现。同时，浔里未来乡村演武校场、水战乐园、二十四节气体验馆等研学游项目也相继建成，为"研、学、旅、行"产业的蓬勃发展奠定了坚实的基础。

2. 注重共建共享

廿八都镇实施微改造、精提升，发动本地非遗传承人参与镂空艺术馆、木偶剧场等业态打造经营，实现原住民、新商业共融发展；搭建"古镇特色名小吃

大赛"等活动载体,挖掘本土美食技能人才创业;筹划历史文化研究会,集聚"文人墨客"共探文化活态传承、文化创意产业新路径。

3. 注重合作共赢

廿八都镇与福建蒲城盘亭乡、江西上饶铜钹山镇积极推进落实浙闽赣三省边界全域旅游战略合作框架协议,进一步深化协同发展机制,共同策划、包装、打造浙闽赣边界全域旅游精品线路,共同打造"一日游三省"旅游品牌。与绍兴市柯桥区签订的山海协作文旅合作协议,也将进一步推动廿八都旅游业发展,并对乡村振兴和共同富裕产生积极影响。

下一步计划

一是做好产业升级提质行动。加快推动廿八都古镇一期提升工程,实施业态焕新计划、商帮文化标识建设工程;有序推进二期建设,持续抓好未来乡村场景落地、提升公共设施水平、提速数字赋能治理等关键事项,奋力打造浙闽赣三省边际文化旅游中心镇。二是深化强村富民共建行动。充分发挥本地生态和旅游资源优势,做大做强"一村一品"特色产业,大力推进规模化、标准化、品牌化建设,挖掘培育各村市场潜力大、区域特色明显、附加值高的主导产品和产业。三是开展商帮经济培育行动。采取"融投资带动片区开发、全域土地综合整治"模式,与第三方企业集团合作推进廿八都国际商帮小镇建设,引入一批文化旅游、新型能源、生态环保、生命健康等超百亿投资项目,力争将廿八都打造成为国际商帮大会永久举办地、国家乡村振兴和区域共富的示范窗口。

Nianbadu Town, Jiangshan City, Zhejiang Province:

Integration of Agriculture, Culture, and Tourism Transforms the Thousand-Year-Old Town

Abstract

Based on the new development stage and implementation of the new development concept, Nianbadu Town, Jiangshan City, Zhejiang Province focuses on the two major themes of "merchant culture" and "high-end homestays". Following the development model where "towns and villages set up the stage, culture performs, and tourism helps", it vigorously promotes the "tourism to enable the people to live a better-off life" project, deepens the integrated development of agriculture, culture, and tourism, and cultivates and creates themed villages such as Xunli with ancient charm, Xingdun scenic spot at Changshou, Linfeng scenic spot at the provincial border, Sports Fugai, and Xiake Spirit. It has successfully created one national historical and cultural town, one national 5A-level scenic spot, one national 4A-level scenic spot, and seven provincial 3A-level scenic spot villages, achieving a total collective income of 15.79 million yuan for the villages, and exploring a new path for the integration of agriculture, culture, and tourism to promote common prosperity.

Challenges and Problems

Nianbadu Town is located in the southwest of Jiangshan City, at the junction of Zhejiang, Fujian, and Jiangxi provinces. With its unique geographical location and history that it once was a military stronghold and a commercial hub, it is known as "the key to the southeast and the gateway to Fujian". Due to its location on the southwestern border of Zhejiang, Nianbadu Town lags in economic and social development, the main reasons are as follows. Firstly, the basic supporting facilities are backward, the equipment is aging, and the living environment is poor. Secondly, there is predominantly agriculture while the income from cultural and tourism industries is nearly zero. Thirdly, there is a talent gap, with a large number of young people going out to work, and the problem of hollowing out is protruding.

Measures

1. Inject new vitality to culture

Firstly, Nianbadu Town insists on cultural protection. After five years of exploring the historical and cultural resources of the ancient town, Nianbadu Town published the *Nianbadu Town Chronicles* and invested 120 million yuan to build the Nianbadu Ancient Town Scenic Area, which accounted for one-sixth of the city's fiscal revenue that year. Secondly, Nianbadu Town insists on cultural inheritance, train inheritors for national intangible cultural heritage such as puppet shows, protect excellent folk customs, and provide immersive experiences in a scenario-based and interactive way. Thirdly, Nianbadu Town insist on cultural revitalization to build the national 5A-level scenic spot—Nianbadu Ancient Town, showing the historical and cultural accumulation of the "living ancient town" from multiple angles.

2. Create a new experience scene

The Nianbadu Historical and Cultural Town Protection Plan was revised to further strengthen the town's landscape control and environmental transformation. Nearly 80 million yuan was invested to demolish more than 5,000 square meters of non-conforming buildings, complete the transformation of more than 300 houses in the antique style, bury 4.5 kilometers of utility lines, green and beautify more than 20 important node areas, and transform the landscape. More than 200 beautiful courtyards were created, and the "Xianxia Ancient Exploration" provincial urban and rural landscape sample area was built to turn the beautiful living environment into a tourist experience scenario.

3. Build a new win-win model

On the one hand, Nianbadu Town insists on project-driven development and the integration of scenic spots and towns. Nianbadu Town combines the protection of small towns, beautiful villages, and historical and cultural villages; successively implement the first phase of ancient town development, beautiful town construction, and future village construction; and launch popular route

products such as "tourism + sketching", "tourism + study", and "tourism + sports". On the other hand, Nianbadu Town implements multiple policies, issue the *Management Measures for Special Funds for the Protection and Management of the Nianbadu Ancient Town*, formulate subsidy policies for catering and homestay business, establish a mechanism for the co-construction, sharing, and integration of scenic spots, establish industry associations of catering, homestays, and agricultural products, and build a distribution channel for the sharing of scenic spot revenue with the town, village, and enterprise enterprises.

4. Create a new harmonious situation

Nianbadu Town innovatively issues the *Implementation Opinions on Strengthening the Protection and Management of the Nianbadu Ancient Town*, establish a multi-department linkage mechanism for the management of the ancient town, properly resolve the housing and construction problems of the masses, and effectively prevent farmers from arbitrarily demolishing and building houses. We guide the ancient town, scenic area, and the village to work together to promote the renovation of the courtyards of residents in the ancient town scenic area, and the construction of clothing drying points and non-motor vehicle parking points, to effectively resolve the contradiction between the development of the scenic area and the living of surrounding villagers.

Results

Nianbadu Town continues to promote the deep integration of agriculture, culture, and tourism,

successfully fostering five themed villages including Guyun Xunli. The town has 128 rural homestays, more than 3000 dining spaces, and 1431 beds. Specifically, it has five silver inns, two silver-ding-themed hotels, and one three-star tourist hotel. In 2023, the town received 430,000 tourists and earned a tourism income of more than 57 million yuan. During the 2024 Spring Festival, the town received a total of 32000 tourists, a year-on-year increase of 137.4%, driving up local tourism consumption by 10 million yuan and achieving a "good start" for Spring Festival tourism. By 2023, there were four administrative villages in the town, each with a collective operating income of over 500,000 yuan, and all administrative villages each had an income of over 300,000 yuan. In 2023, the per capita income of farmers in the ancient town reached 26,100 yuan, and the RMB savings deposits of the town's financial institutions reached 488 million yuan, an increase of 54% compared to 2018, significantly faster than the growth rate of per capita deposits in urban areas throughout the city.

Experiences and Inspirations

1. Focus on leveraging opportunities and strengths

Nianbadu Town will fully grasp the opportunity

of Jiangshan's holistic tourism development and leverage rural construction to do a good job of developing diversified businesses with distinctive characteristics. A number of new businesses have sprung up one after another, such as the Fujian and Jiangxi cuisine restaurant, the foreign goods themed cafe, and the "Jiangshan Taste" exhibition hall. Meanwhile, Xunli Future Rural Martial Arts Training Ground, Water Battle Park, Twenty-Four Solar Terms Experience Park and other research and study tourism projects have also been launched one after another, laying a solid foundation for vigorous development of the "research, study, travel, and transportation" industry.

2. Focus on co-construction and sharing

Nianbadu Town implements micro-transformation and fine improvement and mobilizes local intangible cultural heritage inheritors to participate in the creation and operation of hollow art galleries, puppet theaters, and other businesses, to realize the co-development of aboriginals and new businesses. Moreover, we hold various activities such as the "Ancient Town Specialty Snack Competition", support local talents in command of cooking skills to start businesses, plan historical and cultural research associations, and gather "literati and poets" to explore new paths for cultural inheritance and development of cultural and creative industries.

3. Focus on win-win cooperation

Nianbadu Town, Panting Township, Pucheng Town, Fujian Province, and Tongbashan Town, Shangrao City, Jiangxi Province actively promote the implementation of the strategic cooperation framework agreement on the border tourism of Zhejiang, Fujian and Jiangxi provinces, further deepen the coordinated development mechanism,

jointly plan, package and create high-quality tourism routes for the border tourism of the three provinces, and jointly create the tourism brand of "one-day tour of three provinces". The mountain-sea cooperation and cultural tourism cooperation agreement signed with Keqiao District, Shaoxing City will also further promote the development of Nianbadu's tourism industry, and have a positive impact on promoting rural revitalization and common prosperity.

Plans

Firstly, it is to advance industrial upgrading. Nianbadu Town will accelerate the Phase I upgrading project of the Nianbadu ancient town; implement the business renewal plan and the business group cultural logo construction project; advance the Phase II construction in an orderly manner; continue to focus on the key issues such as the implementation of future rural scenes construction, the improvement of public facilities, and the acceleration of the governance empowered by digital technology; and endeavor to build a cultural tourism town at the borders of Zhejiang, Fujian and Jiangxi provinces. Secondly, it is to deepen joint construction to strengthen villages and enable locals to live a better-off life. Nianbadu Town should give full play to the advantages of local ecological and tourism resources, build up the "one village, one product" characteristic industries, vigorously promote standardized construction of brands on a certain scale, and explore ways to foster leading products and industries with great market potential, notable regional characteristics and high added value in each village. Thirdly, it is to boost the business group economy. Nianbadu Town should adopt the model of "investment and financing to drive regional development and comprehensive land improvement in the whole region"; cooperate with third-party enterprise groups to promote the construction of the Nianbadu International Business Group Town; bring in many cultural tourism, new energy, ecological and environmental protection, life and health, and other investment projects each involving more than 10 billion yuan; and endeavor to build Nianbadu into a permanent venue for the International Business Group Conference and a demonstration window for national rural revitalization and regional common prosperity.

2024 世界旅游联盟：旅游助力乡村振兴案例（中英文双语版）
WTA Best Practices of Rural Revitalization through Tourism 2024（Chinese-English Bilingual Edition）

广东省清远市清新区三坑镇：
三禾·稻里民宿项目助力乡村振兴

摘　要

　　广东省清远市三坑镇充分利用打造"特色温泉康养+"全域旅游特色小镇的契机，深化农村土地制度改革，充分盘活农村宅基地和闲置农房，经过镇经济总公司"整体打包流转"，成功引入清远市稻里酒店管理有限公司进行民宿项目投资建设，百年老宅经过保护和修缮，成为特色古宅、民宿古院，三和村被打造成具备地方乡土风情的三禾·稻里民宿。项目建成后，清远市稻里酒店管理有限公司与广州白天鹅酒店管理有限公司签订合作协议，由专业团队负责项目整体运营及管理。三禾·稻里民宿项目的成功建设，为同类型的项目在建设方式和经营模式上打开了新思路、贡献了新方案，为推动全镇乡村旅游转型升级提供了新样板。

挑战与问题

三坑镇三禾·稻里民宿项目在推进过程中主要存在两点挑战与问题。一是项目整村出租工作推进难度大。三坑镇三和村和红心村"空心化"严重，为高效活化利用农民承包地、宅基地和村集体经营性建设用地资源，工作组进村入户开展土地资源整合宣教工作，梳理出三和村30亩闲置用地、30户旧农房，红心村70亩耕地和鱼塘。二是土地房屋租赁的租期问题。清远市稻里酒店管理有限公司需要长期稳定的房屋土地租借，以保障自身的持续发展和稳定收益，计划租期为25年。但是村民担忧太长的租期会对后续收益造成影响，双方意见不一致。

措施

1. 连片整合闲置资源

三和村作为全镇第一个"整村出租"的案例，通过镇政府、清远市稻里酒店管理有限公司和社会各方面的共同努力，整合村中连片闲置土地和房屋，重新盘活处于"休眠"状态的土地资源，为后续引进社会资本及项目建设提供了充分的资源要素保障，打出了"旅游+"盘活农村闲置用地和旧农房资源的"组合拳"，有效助力乡村振兴，同时为其他谋求取得发展的"空心村"、闲置土地房屋资源提供了有效发展的新思路。

2. 实行政府风险兜底机制

工作组提出实行政府风险兜底机制。由镇属经济发展公司与三和村集体及村民签订土地、房屋租用合同，先行垫付租金，彻底打消村民因企业征地带来的法律纠纷、经济损失等顾虑。再由镇属经济发展公司与企业签订土地租赁合同，对闲置用地、旧农房、耕地、鱼塘等资源整体"打包流转"，坚定了社会资本深度参与乡村民宿运营的信心。

3. 乡贤助力项目建设

在项目筹备过程中，面对村民对工作的配合意愿不高等问题，三坑镇发挥"乡贤助力乡村振兴、推动乡村发展"作用，通过发掘乡村运营人才库，积极动员乡贤及乡村带头人主动参与项目，协助厘清权属边界、解决民事纠纷，为项目的顺利推进发挥不可或缺的作用。

4. 积极整合社会资源

三禾·稻里民宿积极引进社会公共资源，与清远市图书馆建立合作关系，选取三禾书院成功打造"粤书吧"项目。"粤书吧"独立成栋，共三层，建筑面积850平方米，藏有成人、青少年儿童读物8000余册，配备智能设备和多样数字资源，具备商务会客、阅读工作、咖啡休闲等多种功能。

成效

三坑镇引进建设三禾·稻里民宿项目，将旧农房打造成具有地方乡土风情的温泉民宿，让古村落焕发新颜，实现了从"空心村"到"民宿村"的美丽蝶变。

2023年，三坑镇吸引了超过60万游客前来游玩，带来了超2亿元的经济效益，并在2024年继续保持同比增长。项目的成功运营为当地带来多个就业岗位，吸纳九子里、沙溪等周边村小组约40位村民就业，村民每年工资收入可达5万元。三和村村民通过出租闲置旧房屋收取租金，每年房屋租金收益超20万元，房屋租金每五年提升10%。村中耕地、池塘、空地等公共区域的村集体经营性建设用地租金纳入村集体经济收益，三和村年集体收益超8万元、红心村年集体收益达9万元，收益每五年提升10%。

源要素投入乡村，结合现有闲置资源和当地独特的温矿泉资源，因地制宜发展乡村文旅产业。

3. 发展文旅

三坑镇大力推动温矿泉旅游综合发展区基础设施建设和村居人居环境整治，建设村史馆、村公共服务中心、旅游驿站等设施，做好精神文明和基础设施建设，搭好文旅舞台。对外讲好三坑文旅故事，吸引更多优质企业和游客来到三坑镇，推动三坑镇文旅经济蓬勃发展。

经验与启示

1. 盘活资源

除盘活"空心村"的三禾·稻里民宿项目外，三坑镇还有本土知名品牌民宿7家，呈现5种不同的运营模式。这些模式在有效利用闲置房屋土地基础上，依托于三坑镇富含各种微量元素、有效助眠的温矿泉资源，吸引游客。

2. 引入资本

三坑镇政府主动搭台，与村委、村集体通过土地流转，进行现有闲置资源整合。镇政府通过招商引资的方式吸引优质社会资本参与乡村振兴，带动更多资

下一步计划

三坑镇将继续发挥党建引领作用，一是以"温泉民宿+"为主业态，进一步做好农村闲置资源的整合盘活工作，扎实做好自身资源和民宿产业的匹配支撑，抓招商、抓服务、抓保障，结合当地独特的温矿泉资源，保持本地旅游产业的迅猛发展势头，带动乡村旅游、现代农业发展。二是开展乡村民宿装备产业基地建设，促进一二三产业融合发展。三是做好镇内优质旅游项目的对外推广，通过案例的对外宣传，为谋求发展旅游经济的企业注入"强心剂"，吸引更多清远市及大湾区优质民宿企业等社会资本进驻三坑镇，进一步推进旅游助力乡村振兴，为三坑镇经济社会发展带来新机遇。

Sankeng Town, Qingxin District, Qingyuan City, Guangdong Province:

Promoting Rural Revitalization with the Sanhe Daoli Homestay Project

Abstract

While working to build a tourist town specializing in "hot springa wellness+", Sankeng Town of Qingyuan City, Guangdong Province reforms the rural land use system and has leased the idle rural homesteads and dwellings as a package via the township economic development company. It has introduced Qingyuan Daoli Hotel Management Co., Ltd. to invest in the homestay project which turns century-old houses into characteristic mansions and homestay courtyards, and Sanhe Village into the characteristic Sanhe Daoli Homestay. After the completion of the project, Qingyuan Daoli Hotel Management signed a cooperation agreement with Guangzhou White Swan Hotel Management Co., Ltd. which will assign a professional team to take charge of project operation and management. The successful construction of the Sanhe Daoli Homestay project has opened up new ideas and contributed new solutions for similar projects in terms of construction methods and business models, providing a new model for transforming and upgrading the rural tourism industry across the town.

Challenges and Problems

Sankeng Town faced two main Challenges and Problems while implementing the Sanhe Daoli Homestay project. Firstly, whole-village leasing was difficult to achieve. In the "hollow" villages of Sanhe Village and Hongxin Village, to efficiently consolidate farmers' contracted land, homesteads, and village collective's construction land, the project team visited villagers door by door to explain the land consolidation policy, and eventually identified 30 *mu* of idle land, 30 old farmhouses in Sanhe Town, and 70 *mu* of cultivated land and fish ponds in Hongxin Village. The second problem concerned the lease term of land and houses. The lessee Qingyuan Daoli Hotel Management demanded a long lease to ensure its sustainable development and profitability, and planned for a 25-year lease, while the villagers were worried that the long lease would hurt their future income, and thus disagreed.

Measures

1. Consolidating idle resources on a large scale

Sanhe Village was the first in the town to lease the whole village. Through the concerted efforts of the township government, Qingyuan Daoli Hotel Management Co., Ltd., and other stakeholders, Sanhe Village consolidated the contiguous idle land and houses, putting these "dormant" land resources back into use for the subsequent introduction of social capital and future project construction. Through the "tourism +" approach, it has leveraged rural idle land and old dwellings, effectively promoting rural revitalization. At the same time, it has provided a new way out for other similar "hollow" villages seeking development.

2. Leveraging the government's role in cushioning against risks

The project team proposed that the government should be the cushion against risks. The township economic development company signed a land and house lease contract with Sanhe Village collective and villagers, and paid the rent in advance, thus dispelling the villagers' concerns about any legal disputes and economic losses that might arise due to land acquisition. Then, the township economic development company signed a land lease contract with Qingyuan Daoli Hotel Management Co., Ltd., and leased out the idle land, old dwellings, cultivated land, and fish ponds as a package, which bolstered the company's confidence in deeply participating in the operation of rural homestays.

3. Engaging the capable and widely respected villagers in project development

In the preparation stage, in response to the villagers' lack of interest in the project, Sankeng Town actively mobilized the capable and widely respected villagers to participate in the project and contribute to rural development and revitalization. It built a talent pool for project operation and assisted in clarifying the land ownership boundary and resolving civil disputes, playing an indispensable role in the smooth progress of the project.

4. Actively pooling social resources

Sanhe Daoli Homestay actively introduces public resources from outside the village. It has established a partnership with Qingyuan City Library which has opened the Reading Bar at Sanhe Academy. The Reading Bar is a standalone three-floor building with a construction area of 850 square meters and a collection of more than 8,000 books for adults, teenagers, and children. It is equipped with smart devices and a variety of digital resources. Here you can have a business meeting, read, work, have some coffee, or simply relax.

Results

The Sanhe Daoli Homestay project has turned the old rural houses into hot-spring homestays with distinct characteristics, giving the ancient village a new look and transforming it from a "hollow" village to a homestay village. In 2023, Sankeng Town attracted more than 600,000 tourists and generated a tourism revenue of more than 200 million yuan, and the year-on-year growth continues in 2024. The project has created many local jobs, including about 40 for villagers from surrounding Jiuzili Village and Shaxi Village, who can earn 50,000 yuan each a year. The villagers of Sanhe Village earn more than 200,000 yuan from their rent which will increase by 10% every five years. The rent of the village collective construction land in public areas such as cultivated land, ponds, and vacant land is included in the collective's economic income. The annual income of Sanhe Village collective exceeds 80,000 yuan, and that of Hongxin Village collective reaches 90,000 yuan, and the rent will grow by 10% every five years.

Experience and Inspirations

1. Make good use of local resources

In addition to the Sanhe Daoli Homestay project, there are seven well-known local homestay brands in Sankeng Town, with five different operating models. Based on the effective use of idle houses and land, they all attract tourists with the various trace elements, hot springs, and minerals the town is richly endowed with.

2. Introduce social capital

Sankeng Town government took the initiative to set up a platform for village committees and village collectives to consolidate idle resources through the transfer of land use rights. The town government has attracted high-quality social capital to participate in rural revitalization through investment promotion. As more resources and factors flow into the countryside, the rural cultural and tourism industries are developed based on existing idle resources, hot springs, and minerals.

3. Develop cultural and tourism business

Sankeng Town vigorously improves the infrastructure and the living environment in the Comprehensive Development Zone for Hot Spring and Minerals Tourism. The village history gallery, the public service center, and the tourist service station are built. In addition to infrastructure, cultural-ethical progress is advanced to promote tourism development with cultural development. Sankeng Town also steps up to tell the story of its cultural and tourism development to the outside world, attract more high-quality enterprises and tourists, and promote the vigorous development of its cultural and tourism economy.

Plans

Sankeng Town will continue to follow the guidance of Party-building work. Firstly, based on "hot spring homestay +" as the principal business, it will continue to consolidate and leverage rural idle resources, solidly develop local resources to match the homestay industry, promote investment, and improve services. It will make good use of its unique hot springs and mineral resources, maintain the strong momentum of the local tourism industry, and drive the development of rural tourism and modern agriculture. Secondly, it will build a rural homestay equipment industry base and promote the integrated development of primary, secondary, and tertiary industries. Thirdly, it will promote high-quality tourism projects and success cases to external investors, boost their confidence in tourism development, attract more high-quality homestay enterprises and other social capital in Qingyuan and the Greater Bay Area, further promote rural revitalization through tourism, and bring new opportunities for the economic and social development of Sankeng Town.

宁夏回族自治区石嘴山市大武口区龙泉村：

农文旅融合赋能乡村振兴

摘　要

　　宁夏回族自治区石嘴山市大武口区龙泉村被誉为"贺兰山下第一村 塞北长城古村落"。近年来龙泉村抢抓乡村振兴战略发展机遇，坚持"规划引领 因地制宜"的原则，突出地域性、独特性、时效性和前瞻性，深入挖掘文化遗产资源、自然生态资源，依托贺兰山形成"山、庄、田"错落有致的地理形态，大力发展乡村旅游。通过开发贺兰山生态保护修复、长城国家文化公园建设、天然富硒土地认证等项目，非遗工坊、主题民宿、特色农庄等产业，果蔬采摘、休闲观光、研学体验等活动，龙泉村将生态旅游、文化旅游和社区旅游进行了有机结合，共同绘就了乡村旅游新图景，成为文化旅游促进乡村振兴的生动案例。

挑战与问题

龙泉村位于被誉为中国"波尔多"的贺兰山东麓葡萄酒产区北部，紧邻国家4A级旅游景区贺东庄园，距国家5A级旅游景区沙湖20千米。具有百年历史的9个泉眼涌出清澈的泉水滋养着乡间小溪，古老的贺兰山岩画、明长城、古汉墓群遗址近在咫尺。在发展乡村旅游的过程中，龙泉村面临以下问题。一是治理体系不够完善。乡村治理体系还不能很好地适应经济社会发展节奏和消费需求变化，对本地居民的引导还不够，村集体经济中村民的参与率较低，产业转化率不足。二是服务质量还有待提高。乡村旅游的服务主要由本地村民提供，他们的年龄偏大，整体文化素养不高，服务意识和水平相对较低。三是运营管理人才缺乏，尤其缺乏景区运营人才和产业融合中的复合型人才。

措施

1. 生态优先，扮靓环境

龙泉村以乡村振兴为契机，将贺兰山生态修复、大气污染防治和山水林湖草综合整治有效衔接，实施村居环境、行洪沟道整治，完善基础设施，建成"桃花源"、百果园和田园景观项目，科学布局景观，全方位融合生态建设和农村产业发展。

2. 传承文化，丰富内涵

一是依托明长城、贺兰山岩画等历史古迹，打造天使文创街、非遗工坊、研学基地等文化业态，丰富乡村旅游体验和内涵。二是在旅游开发中保护与传承中华优秀传统文化，展现具有中国特色的农事节气、各具特色的宅院民居、自然朴实的农业景观、耕读传家的祖传家训和邻里守望的乡风民俗。三是促进历史文化挖掘和遗产保护，推动岩画等历史文化遗产的保护和修复工作，采取"非遗传承+残疾人培训"模式，定点培养传承人，推广木雕、剪纸等非遗产品。

3. 盘活资源，兴旺产业

一是依托合作社共赢模式，引进厚德酒坊、马来风情等20余家商户投资兴业；二是利用土壤富硒、泉水富锶优势，发展草莓、香菇、大樱桃等设施农业；三是借助葡萄酒庄园，开发研学旅游、酿酒体验、品鉴休闲、观星露营等活动；四是利用民居果园开展农家乐、特色采摘等旅游项目。

成效

龙泉村发展"吃住行游购娱"全要素旅游新业态，2023年接待游客147.01万人次，收入达到1366.37万元；建设了工艺葫芦非遗工坊，打造集设计、生产、观摩、体验、销售于一体的产业链条，资产达到125.6万元；农业种植效益由2017年的2000元增至2023年的12000元，增长了5倍。龙泉村通过发展旅游业创造了就业机会，农民在家乡扎根，增收致富渠道由单一的农业生产收入转变为资产性收入、务工收入、经营性收入等相互补充的多元方式，人均纯收入由2017年的1.4万元增加到2023年的2.1万元，

村集体经济收入也达到了 34 万元。

经验与启示

1. 转变发展思路

秉持"小组团 + 多风格 + 低成本 + 乡土化"的发展策略，龙泉村利用古村落优势，盘活现有资产，并集中打造了田园采摘区、休闲商业街、示范创业街、百草园、烧烤娱乐区、民宿休闲区六大功能街区，农户房屋空置率由原来的 50% 下降到不足 10%。同时，这一发展模式带动了乡间别墅、田园香居等 50 余户村民的返乡创业热情，并成功吸引了厚德酒坊、龙泉山庄等 20 余家经营实体前来投资兴业。

2. 展现乡村文化

发展旅游业不仅加深了居民和游客对文化的理解，还通过展示丰富的历史文物、艺术品和手工艺品，有效增强了居民的文化自信。游客通过体验乡村生活、品尝当地特色美食、参与民俗文化活动等方式，深度体验当地特色文化，更加有力地保护和传承地方传统文化，助推龙泉村由传统村落向乡村文化旅游名村转变。

下一步计划

一是分享旅游实践。龙泉村将继续借助文旅新媒体，联动中央电视台、人民网、新华网、"学习强国"等官方媒体平台，推送各类推文、短视频；通过文化和旅游部门、国家公共文化云平台的直播与录播，将龙泉村的生态、文化、美食展现在全国乃至世界人民眼前；与宁夏卫视、幸福大武口等当地官方媒体合作推出专题节目，参与自治区"两晒一促"大型文旅宣传推介活动，将龙泉村乡村建设新成就和乡村旅游新面貌向大众充分展现。二是举办主题活动。每年依托百年葡萄古藤举办"展藤节"和葡萄酒主题活动，邀请来自世界各地的葡萄酒爱好者，参观酒庄、品鉴美酒、摄影写生、体验非遗，感受龙泉村独特的自然风光、丰富的文化底蕴和民俗文化的无限魅力。

Longquan Village, Dawukou District Shizuishan City, Ningxia Hui Autonomous Region:

Integration of Agriculture, Culture, and Tourism to Empower Rural Revitalization

Abstract

Longquan Village in Dawukou District, Shizuishan City, Ningxia Hui Autonomous Region, is known as "The Top Village under Helan Mountain, an Ancient Village along the Great Wall in the Northern Frontier". In recent years, Longquan Village has seized the development opportunities brought along by the rural revitalization strategy, adhering to the principle of "being guided by planning and tailored to local conditions", and emphasizing regional characteristics, uniqueness, timeliness, and foresight in its work. The village deeply digs into cultural heritage and natural ecological resources. Leveraging the geographical morphology of "mountains, villages, and fields" formed in Helan Mountain, it has vigorously developed rural tourism. By developing projects such as the ecological protection and restoration of Helan Mountain, the construction of the Great Wall National Cultural Park, and the certification of naturally selenium-rich, together with the industries concerning intangible cultural heritage workshops, themed homestays, and distinctive farms as well as activities like fruit and vegetable picking, leisure sightseeing, and study tours, Longquan Village has organically integrated ecological tourism, cultural tourism, and community tourism, creating a new landscape of rural tourism. This serves as a vivid case of cultural tourism promoting rural revitalization.

Challenges and Problems

Longquan Village is located in the northern part of the Helan Mountain East Slope Wine Region, known as China's "Bordeaux", adjacent to the national 4A-level scenic spot Hedong Manor, and 20 kilometers away from the national 5A-level scenic spot Shahu Lake. The village is nourished by clear spring water from nine century-old springs, with ancient Helan Mountain rock paintings, the Ming Great Wall, and ancient Han tomb sites nearby. In the process of developing rural tourism, Longquan Village faces the following problems. Firstly, the governance system is inadequate. The rural governance system cannot yet fully adapt to the pace of economic and social development and changes in consumer demand, and there is insufficient guidance for local residents such that the level of involvement of villagers in the collective economy is low, and the rate of industrial transformation is inadequate. Secondly, the quality of service needs improvement. The services in rural tourism are mostly provided by local villagers who are generally old and with a low education level, and their service awareness and level are relatively low. Thirdly, there is lacking in operational management talent, especially in terms of scenic area operation and integrated industrial development.

Measures

1. Prioritize ecology to beautify the environment

Longquan Village takes rural revitalization as an opportunity to effectively link up Helan Mountain ecological restoration, air pollution prevention, and comprehensive improvement of mountains, rivers, forests, fields, lakes, and grass. It improves the village environment and the flood channel, upgrades infrastructure, completes the "Peach Blossom Spring", Various Fruit Garden, and rural landscape projects, and scientifically arranges landscapes, fully integrating ecological construction and rural industrial development.

2. Inherit culture to enrich connotations

Firstly, relying on historical sites such as the Ming Great Wall and Helan Mountain rock paintings, the village has created cultural businesses as seen in the Angel Cultural Creative Street, intangible cultural heritage workshops, and educational bases to enrich rural tourism experiences and connotations. Secondly, in tourism development, the village protects and inherits excellent traditional culture, showcasing the characteristics of Chinese agricultural festivals, distinctive residential courtyards, natural and simple agricultural landscapes, family teachings that emphasize both farming and studying as well as rural customs of neighborly support. Thirdly, the village promotes the exploration and protection of history and culture, advancing the protection and restoration of cultural heritage such as rock paintings. Adopting the model of "intangible cultural heritage inheritance + training for people with disabilities" has helped to

train designated inheritors and promote intangible cultural heritage products like wood carving and paper cutting.

3. Use resources to drive the development of industries

Firstly, using the win-win model of cooperatives, the village has attracted over 20 businesses, including Houde Distillery and Malai Style, to invest and start businesses. Secondly, utilizing the advantages of selenium-rich soil and strontium-rich spring water, it has developed controlled environmental agriculture for strawberries, shiitake mushrooms, and cherries. Thirdly, leveraging wine estates, it has developed study tours, offered tourists winemaking experiences, leisure tasting, stargazing camping, and organized other activities. Fourthly, it has utilized residential orchards to develop agritourism and specialty picking projects.

Results

Longquan Village has developed a new tourism model integrating all elements of "eating, housing, traveling, shopping, and entertainment". In 2023, the village received 1.4701 million tourists, earning an income of 13.6637 million yuan. It has established a handicraft gourd intangible cultural heritage workshop; and built an industrial chain integrating design, production, observation, experience, and sales, with assets reaching 1.256 million yuan. The benefits of agricultural planting have increased from 2,000 yuan in 2017 to 12,000 yuan in 2023, a five-fold increase. Longquan Village has creat opportunities by developing tourism, which enables farmers to take root in their hometowns; people's income comes from multiple sources that are mutually complementary, like the income from assets, labor, and business, instead of just agricultural production.

The per capita net income has increased from 14,000 yuan in 2017 to 21,000 yuan in 2023, and the village collective economy has earned 340,000 yuan.

Experiences and Inspirations

1. Transform development thinking

Adhering to the development strategy of "small groups+diverse styles+low costs+localization", Longquan Village used existing assets to concentrate on creating six functional zones: the orchard picking area, leisure commercial street, demonstration entrepreneurial street, herbal garden, barbecue, and homestay leisure area. The vacancy rate of farmers' houses has dropped from 50% to less than 10%. At the same time, this development model has sparked the enthusiasm of more than 50 villagers, such as those from Countryside Summer Retreats and Rural Fragrant Residences, to return home for entrepreneurship. It has also successfully attracted over 20 business entities like Houde Distillery and Longquan Manor to invest and start businesses.

2. Showcase rural culture

The development of tourism not only deepens the understanding of culture among residents and tourists, but also effectively enhances residents' cultural confidence by showcasing rich historical artifacts, artworks, and handicrafts. Tourists deeply

experience local culture by participating in rural life, tasting local specialties, and engaging in folk cultural activities. This effectively protects and inherits local traditional culture, promoting Longquan Village's transformation from a traditional village to a village famous for rural cultural tourism.

Plans

Firstly, it is to share tourism practices. Longquan Village will continue to leverage culture and tourism new media, linking with official media platforms such as CCTV, People's Daily Online, Xinhua Net, and "Xuexi Qiangguo" to spread various articles and short videos. Through live and recorded broadcasts by cultural and tourism departments and the national public culture cloud platform, it will showcase Longquan Village's ecology, culture, and cuisine to people nationwide and even worldwide. It will also cooperate with Ningxia TV, Happiness Dawukou, and other local official media to launch special programs and participate in the Ningxia Autonomous Region's "Two Shows and One Promotion" large-scale cultural and tourism promotion activities, fully displaying Longquan Village's new achievements in rural construction and new features of rural tourism to the public. Secondly, it is to hold themed activities. With century-old grape vines, the village annually hosts the "Exhibition Vine Festival" and wine-themed activities, inviting wine enthusiasts from around the world to visit wineries, taste fine wines, engage in photography and sketching, experience intangible cultural heritage, and enjoy Longquan Village's unique natural scenery, rich cultural heritage, and infinite charm of folk culture.

2024 世界旅游联盟：旅游助力乡村振兴案例（中英文双语版）
WTA Best Practices of Rural Revitalization through Tourism 2024 (Chinese-English Bilingual Edition)

重庆市酉阳土家族苗族自治县：
"酉女织梦"：绣出一片桃花源

摘　要

"酉女织梦"项目由酉阳县妇联与子月苗族文化传播有限责任公司共同实施，在县妇联、县农业农村委、县乡村振兴局、县商务委、县文化旅游委等部门扶持下，坚持把助推手工产业发展作为服务大局、服务贫困妇女的一项重要举措，从"强帮扶、搭平台、重带动"发力，采取"公司＋扶贫＋乡村妇女工坊＋乡村绣娘"的帮扶模式，着力培育酉阳"巧姐"，打造"酉女织梦"品牌，示范带动全县手工编织产业良性发展。项目先后在20余个乡镇设立苗绣工坊，通过免费培训苗绣技艺、公司承接订单、原料委托加工，以工坊就业、居家就业、零散加工等方式，带动乡村留守妇女及残疾人通过苗绣创收致富。自2013年来，项目累计培训乡村留守妇女及残疾人6500余名，唤回5200余名外出打工的年轻妈妈返乡就业，实现了年人均增收15000—30000元的显著成效。这一转变不仅让17000余名留守儿童有了妈妈的陪伴，还使得22000名空巢老人得到了子女的照顾与陪伴。

挑战与问题

酉阳县地处重庆市、湖北省、湖南省、贵州省四省（市）结合部，辖区面积5173平方千米，辖39个乡镇（街道）、278个行政村（社区），总人口86万人，是重庆市辖区面积最大、少数民族人口最多的县。酉阳县是土家族、苗族最集中的聚居地，有大量形式多样、内容丰富、弥足珍贵的文化遗产，以及丰富的原生态土家族苗族文化资源，被誉为"中国土家摆手舞之乡""中国著名民歌之乡"。全县共有女性39.8万人，妇女待就业者人数庞大，可供选择的就业岗位不多，人岗匹配难，就业形势严峻。

措施

1. 培育酉州苗绣特色产业

酉阳县结合悠久的民族历史文化，组织农村留守妇女、贫困妇女学习酉州苗绣技术。酉阳县依托1个国家5A级旅游景区、5个国家4A级旅游景区、2个国家森林公园和2个湿地公园等丰富的旅游资源大力发展手工产业，打造旅游产品。通过引导酉州苗绣技艺的开发与创新，该县成功推出了一系列具有酉阳特色的旅游文创产品，助力实现"用苗绣吸引游客，以旅游带动苗绣"的产业发展愿景。

2. 做亮"酉女织梦"产业品牌

"酉女织梦"品牌积极参与了由重庆市妇联举办的手工编织产品展示展演活动，以及渝洽会、中华民族风情展等各类展会。同时，在桃花源、叠石花谷等网红旅游景区设立产品展销点；在车田乡、花田乡等乡村旅游示范乡镇建立苗绣产品展示厅，在重庆文化产业园设立"酉阳民族文化产品展销厅"，在北京园博园设立"重庆酉阳苗绣馆"，以扩大在全国范围内的市场影响力。为了进一步推广"酉女织梦"品牌，还举办了"巴渝网姐邀你购——爱在桃花源·巾帼助脱贫"妇联主席直播带货活动，通过专场带货酉州苗绣，助力创优"酉女织梦"品牌。

3. 推动苗绣妇女全面发展

酉阳县采取了不交学费、不分年龄、不论性别、不管远近、不限身体素质的"五不"原则和乡村学员自发的"联、帮、带"模式，采用集中授课、现场教学实践相结合的方式，开展了苗绣工艺理论知识培训、基础绘图知识培训和基础编织技艺培训，通过劳务用工和苗绣手工培训相结合的方式，有效激发村民主观能动性，使他们能够学习并掌握苗绣刺绣技艺，培养发展了一批苗绣技艺能手和非遗项目传承人，部分员工还参加了抖音直播带货培训和商品销售技巧培训。

4. 完善酉州苗绣产业链

子月苗族文化传播有限责任公司建成酉州古城总部旗舰店、桃花源苗绣坊、龚滩古镇苗绣坊、何家岩苗绣坊、车田乡苗绣坊等，拓展了湖南张家界、重庆磁器口等实体连锁店，并通过实体连锁店、对外供货批发、广交会外贸订单、抖音橱窗、淘宝店铺、阿里巴巴批发网等渠道进行销售，实现酉州苗绣非遗文化产业产销一体化、产供销一条龙。

成效

子月苗族文化传播有限责任公司投资近1000万元先后在酉州古城建立手工实践基地，升级改造集产供销于一体的11个苗绣妇女手工坊，设立2个扶贫车间，构建"公司＋扶贫＋乡村妇女工坊＋乡村绣娘"脱贫带动机制，培训贫困、留守、残疾妇女6500多人次，并免费提供原材料，保底回收产品，把贫困妇

女吸附到产业链上，带动妇女实现居家灵活就业。全县发展苗绣、西兰卡普、剪纸、十字绣、毛线鞋等多类型手工企业、工坊等 40 余个，从事手工的妇女达 5286 人，带动酉阳县花田乡、车田镇、浪坪乡、龚滩镇、酉酬镇等乡村脱贫户实现就近就地就业，年增收 15000—30000 元不等。2023 年，酉州苗绣实现年销售 3700 万元以上，成为酉阳乡村振兴示范产业。

"酉女织梦"全面深入挖掘酉州苗绣文化，提升苗绣文创作品技艺质量和文化内涵，实现非遗产品生活化、时尚化、创意化、精品化发展。2020 年苗绣妇女手工坊被评为"国家高新技术企业"。2021 年以来，苗绣妇女手工坊与各高校合作成功申报 2 项发明专利、5 个软著、9 个商标、15 个外观设计专利、300 余个版权。苗绣产品"绣出一片桃花源"系列团扇从 2019 年到 2021 年连续三年获得"重庆好礼"金奖，入选重庆外事礼品；2022 年 20 多件苗绣产品作为"上合组织"国礼走向 80 多个国家。从 2013 年至今，酉州苗绣参加各种大型文化旅游大赛及展会，获得各类奖项 50 余个，酉阳苗绣非遗产品走出国门、走向世界。

等主题宣教活动，大力开展理想信念教育，弘扬"四自"精神，引领广大妇女坚定感党恩、听党话、跟党走的信念信心。

2. 抓巾帼行动

持续深入推进"乡村振兴巴渝巾帼行动"，聚焦"宜居宜业和美乡村"目标，引领乡村妇女积极投身巾帼心向党、巾帼建新功、巾帼暖人心系列行动，在实现全面小康、推进乡村振兴中主动作为，在推进移风易俗、立足岗位创新创优中提升本领，积极引导广大妇女做伟大事业的建设者、文明风尚的倡导者、敢于追梦的奋斗者，激发广大妇女干事创业热情。

3. 抓典型示范

积极开展三八红旗手（集体）、巾帼建功标兵示范宣传工作，培树一批乡村振兴中涌现的女性先进典型，使全县妇女学有榜样、赶有目标，引导广大妇女学赶先进、见贤思齐、岗位建功。

经验与启示

1. 抓思想引领

以习近平新时代中国特色社会主义思想团结引领广大妇女，子月苗族文化传播有限责任公司在日常工作中携手各位绣娘和从事手工艺的农村妇女广泛开展"巾帼心向党 奋进新征程""酉女织梦""酉女爱家"

下一步计划

一是突出何家岩村苗绣产业优势，充分发挥以苗绣文旅、苗绣研学为核心的产业优势，结合村里的万亩梯田，探索文旅融合新路径；二是进一步与国家非遗馆、故宫文创进行合作，依托苗绣为更多景区量身定制文旅、文创产品，扩大苗绣品牌影响力；三是全面提升以何家岩村为中心的生态旅游产业带，为成功申报国家 4A 级旅游景区创造有利条件，持续助推酉阳县旅游经济发展。

Youyang Tujia and Miao Autonomous County, Chongqing City:

"You Women Embroidering Dream": To Embroider a Land of Peach Blossoms

Abstract

The "You Women Embroidering Dream" project is jointly implemented by the Youyang Women's Federation and Ziyue Miao Culture Communication Co., Ltd., with support from various county departments such as the County Women's Federation, County Agricultural and Rural Affairs Committee, County Rural Revitalization Bureau, County Commerce Commission, and County Culture and Tourism Commission. The project prioritizes promoting the development of the handicraft industry as an important initiative to serve the general development and support impoverished women. Through efforts to "strengthen assistance, build platforms, and emphasize empowerment", the project adopts a support model of "company + poverty alleviation + rural women's workshops + rural embroiderers". It focuses on training "Qiao Jie" (skilled women) in Youyang and building the "You Women Embroidering Dream" brand to demonstrate and drive the healthy development of the county's handicraft industry. The project has established Miao embroidery workshops in over 20 towns and townships, providing free training in Miao embroidery techniques, accepting company orders, and processing materials by commission. Through workshop employment, home-based employment, and scattered processing, the project enables rural left-behind women and people with disabilities to generate income and achieve prosperity through Miao embroidery. Since 2013, over 6,500 rural left-behind women and people with disabilities have been trained, and more than 5,200 young mothers who had left for work have returned home for employment, resulting in an annual income increase of 15,000—30,000 yuan. As a result, more than 17,000 once left-behind children now have their mother's company, and 22,000 once "empty nesters" have the companionship of their children.

Challenges and Problems

Youyang County is located at the junction of Chongqing City, Hubei, Hunan, and Guizhou provinces (municipalities) and covers an area of 5,173 square kilometers. It comprises 39 towns (subdistricts), and 278 administrative villages (communities), with a total population of 860,000, which makes it the largest county by land area and the county with the highest ethnic minority population in Chongqing City. Youyang County is the most concentrated settlement area for the Tujia and Miao ethnic groups. With a rich and diverse cultural heritage that includes valuable cultural resources, it is known as the "Hometown of Chinese Tujia Hand Waving Dance" and the "Famous Hometown of Chinese Folk Songs". The county has 398,000 women, a large number of whom are unemployed, and facing limited job opportunities. The employment situation is grim.

Measures

1. Cultivate the Youzhou Miao embroidery specialty industry

Youyang County leverages its rich ethnic history and cultural characteristics to organize rural left-behind and impoverished women to learn Youzhou Miao embroidery techniques. The county capitalizes on its abundant tourism resources, including one national 5A-level scenic spot, five national 4A scenic spots, two national forest parks, and two wetland parks, to develop the handicraft industry and create tourism products. By guiding the development and innovation of Youzhou Miao embroidery techniques, the county has successfully launched a series of tourism cultural and creative products with Youyang characteristics, contributing to the realization of the industrial development vision of "attracting tourists with Miao embroidery and promoting Miao embroidery through tourism".

2. Enhance the "You Women Embroidering Dream" brand

The project actively participates in various exhibitions such as the handicraft product exhibition and performance activities organized by Chongqing

Women's Federation, the Western China International Fair, and the Chinese National Folk Culture Exhibition. Meanwhile, it has established product display and sales points in popular tourist spots such as Taohuayuan and Die Shi Huagu, set up Miao embroidery product exhibition halls in rural tourism demonstration towns like Chetian Village and Huatian Village, and established a "Youyang Ethnic Cultural Products Exhibition Hall" in the Chongqing Cultural Industry Park and a "Chongqing Youyang Miao Embroidery Pavilion" in the Beijing Garden Expo. The project has also hosted live-streamed sales events such as "Bayu Net Sisters Invite You to Buy - Love in Taohuayuan: Women Helping Poverty Alleviation", focusing on promoting Youzhou Miao embroidery and enhancing the "You Women Embroidering Dream" brand.

3. Promote all-round development of Miao embroidery women

Youyang County follows the "five no's" principles: no tuition fees, no age limits, no gender restrictions, no distance limitations, and no physical fitness requirements associated with a "connect, help, and lead" approach initiated by rural students. The project provides Miao embroidery craft theoretical training, basic drawing knowledge, and foundational

weaving skills through a combination of centralized instruction and hands-on practice. The combination of employment and Miao embroidery handcraft training effectively stimulates the villagers' initiative to learn and master Miao embroidery techniques, fostering a group of Miao embroidery artisans and intangible cultural heritage inheritors. Some employees have also participated in Douyin live-streaming sales training and product sales techniques training.

4. Improve the Youzhou Miao embroidery industry chain

Ziyue Miao Culture Communication Co., Ltd. has established the flagship store in Youzhou Ancient City as well as bricks-and-mortar stores like the Taohuayuan Miao Embroidery Workshop, Gongtan Ancient Town Miao Embroidery Workshop, Hejiayan Miao Embroidery Workshop, Chetian Township Miao Embroidery Workshop, and has expanded the bricks-and-mortar chain stores in places like Zhangjiajie City, Hunan Province, and Ciqikou Ancient Town, Chongqing City. The products are sold through bricks-and-mortar chain stores, wholesale to external suppliers, foreign trade orders from the Canton Fair, Douyin showcases, Taobao shops, Alibaba wholesale networks, and other channels. In this way, integrated production and sales are realized for the Youzhou

Miao embroidery intangible cultural heritage industry.

Results

Ziyue Miao Culture Communication Co., Ltd. has invested nearly 10 million yuan to establish a handicraft practice base in Youzhou Ancient City, upgrade and renovate 11 Miao embroidery women's workshops where production, supply, and sales are integrated, set up two poverty alleviation workshops, and establish a "company + poverty alleviation + rural women's workshops + rural embroiderers" poverty alleviation mechanism. Over 6,500 impoverished, left-behind, and disabled women have been trained, with free materials provided and product buyback guaranteed, integrating impoverished women into the industry chain and enabling them to gain flexible home-based employment. The county has developed more than 40 handicraft enterprises and workshops, covering Miao embroidery, Xilankapu (a traditional Tujia brocade), paper-cutting, cross-stitching, and woolen shoes. Over 5,286 women are engaged in handicrafts, and the poverty-stricken households in towns like Huatian Village, Chetian Village, Langping Village, Gongtan Village, and Youchou Village find local employment and increase their annual income by 15,000-30,000 yuan. In 2023, Youzhou Miao embroidery achieved annual sales of over 37 million yuan, becoming a demonstration industry for rural revitalization in Youyang County.

The "You Women Embroidering Dream" project thoroughly explores the culture of Youzhou Miao embroidery, enhancing the quality and cultural connotations of Miao embroidery cultural and creative works, and achieving high-quality development of intangible cultural heritage products that are closely related to daily life and meanwhile stylish and creative. Miao Embroidery Women's Workshop was recognized as a "National High-Tech Enterprise" in 2020. Since 2021, Miao Embroidery Women's workshops have successfully applied for two invention patents, five software copyrights, nine trademarks, 15 design patents, and over 300 copyrights in cooperation with universities. The "Embroidery of a Taohuayuan" series of Miao embroidery round fans won the "Chongqing Gift" Gold Award for three consecutive years from 2019 to 2021 and was selected as a Chongqing gift for foreign guests. In 2022, over 20 Miao embroidery products were presented as state gifts to more than 80 countries at the Shanghai Cooperation Organization summit. Since 2013, Youzhou Miao embroidery has participated in various cultural tourism competitions and exhibitions, winning over 50 awards, and Youyang Miao embroidery intangible cultural heritage products have been showcased worldwide.

Experiences and Inspirations

1. Emphasizing proper ideological guidance

The company unites and guides women with Xi Jinping's Thought on Socialism with Chinese

Characteristics for a New Era, carrying out extensive thematic education and advocacy activities such as "Youyang Women Weaving Dreams" and "Youyang Women Love Their Families", promoting ideals and beliefs, and upholding the spirit of self-respect, self-confidence, self-reliance, and self-improvement. Such guidance instills in the women a deep sense of gratitude to the Party and a commitment to follow its leadership.

2. Enhance women's drive

The project continuously advances the "Bayu Women's Action for Rural Revitalization", focusing on the goal of building "Livable and Workable Beautiful Villages", leading rural women to actively participate in activities such as "Women Follow the Party's Lead", "Women Build New Achievements", and "Women's Heart-warming Actions". Women are encouraged to contribute proactively to achieving comprehensive well-being, promoting rural revitalization and advancing social customs; to innovate and excel in their roles; and to position themselves as builders of great causes, advocates of exemplary practices, and dream chasers.

3. Promoting exemplary roles

The project actively promotes the recognition of "March 8th Red Banner Bearers" (both individuals and groups) and exemplary women figures in making contributions. It highlights outstanding female role models who have emerged in rural revitalization, providing examples for the women across the county to learn from and aspire to, and encouraging them to pursue excellence and achieve success in their roles.

Plans

Firstly, it is to highlight Hejiayan Village's strengths in the Miao embroidery industry, fully leverage its industrial advantages centered on Miao embroidery culture and tourism and Miao embroidery research tours, and explore new paths for integrating culture and tourism based on the village's ten thousand mu of terraced fields. Secondly, it is to expand cooperation with national intangible cultural heritage museums and the Palace Museum, to customize cultural and creative tourism products for more scenic spots based on Miao embroidery, and to further expand the brand influence of Miao embroidery. Thirdly, it is to all-roundly enhance the Eco-Tourism Industry Belt Centering on Hejiayan Village, and continue to support the development of Youyang County's tourism economy by creating favorable conditions for the successful application of He Jiayan Village as a national 4A-level scenic spot.

福建省南平市武夷山市五夫镇：
农文旅融合发展赋能乡村振兴

摘 要

福建省南平市武夷山市五夫镇立足实际，以农业产业为基础、朱子文化为灵魂，围绕农文旅融合高质量发展主线，推进和美乡村"1+1"建设，以兴贤村为1个示范村，串联五夫、五一、兴贤、翁墩、典村等环国家公园1号风景道的5个村，打造1条乡村振兴精品线路，"串点连线成片"，着力建设优美五夫、和美五夫、富美五夫，全域推进乡村振兴。

挑战与问题

五夫镇开埠于晋代中期，距今已有1700余年。五夫镇距南平市40千米，下辖11个行政村，总人口1.59万，总面积175.76平方千米，距武夷山国家旅游度假区45千米，是中国历史文化名镇、旅游开发古镇、生态保护重镇和特色农业大镇，素有"朱子故里""白莲之乡"的美誉。在乡村振兴进程中，五夫镇要着力解决好产业发展、文化展示、环境优化、人才聚集这四大问题。

措施

1. 提升基础农业

白莲、水稻是五夫镇特色农产品，五夫镇种植白莲已有上千年历史，种植面积达万亩。五夫镇为进一步提升产业附加值，一是积极倡导荷稻轮作创新种植模式，发展莲螺鱼立体养殖技术，打造"田螺湾"、科力兴种业、稻香世界等示范项目。二是建成五夫农产品精深加工园区、五夫莲肆白莲交易中心，进一步延伸水稻、白莲产业链，全力做好土特产文章，提升乡村产业发展水平。

2. 挖掘文化内涵

五夫镇自古名人学者云集，素有"邹鲁渊源"之称，一代理学大师朱熹在此生活近50年，创立了朱子理学，造就五夫镇"理学之邦"的美誉。五夫镇现有朱子故居紫阳楼、兴贤古街、兴贤书院、朱子社仓、连氏节孝坊等30多处古文化景观，文化旅游资源丰富，是武夷山"双世遗"中文化遗产的重要组成部分。五夫镇围绕朱子文化历史遗存，一是构建"一像、一庙、一楼、一院、一仓"的朱子文化景观打卡点，形成朱子文化研学旅游线路；二是结合朱子四礼、龙鱼戏打造非遗文化体验项目，常态化开展朱子文化节、荷花节系列活动，联合朱子学校、同文书院固定开展"非遗文化演出"。

3. 优化生态环境

五夫镇持续聚焦"水美乡村"建设，开展潭溪中小河流域治理。一是邀请中国环境科学研究院、省环保设计院开展潭溪流域水环境溯源分析，研究并实施农田退水等提升水质措施，切实提高水环境质量。二是积极开展"森林生态银行"项目建设，打造到秋天来五夫赏红叶的"枫林晚"文化主题山体公园，推动形成"春回大地菜花黄，夏日戏水赏荷塘，秋风送爽翻稻浪，冬月梅花阵阵香"的四季美景。

4. 创新人才机制

五夫镇深化下派书记与科技特派员"双派联动"机制，建立科特派示范站6个、科特派示范基地16个，先后选派了42个科技特派员团队、216名科技特派员、29名下派书记、5名流通助理，以及18名引进生、选调生、大学生村官助力五夫乡村振兴发展战略实施。袁隆平杂交水稻专家工作站、"中国—联合国开发计划署合作项目科特派减贫示范区"落户五夫镇。

成效

五夫镇拥有林地21万亩，生态林4.2万亩，森林覆盖率达75.19%。全镇耕地3.2万亩，每年种植优质稻2万余亩、白莲1万余亩，白莲年产可达100万斤，产值4000万元。2023年五夫镇农业总产值4.47亿元，同比增长10.6%；农村人均可支配收入25421元，同比增长7%；财政各项收入6187.15万

元。五夫镇先后获评中国历史文化名镇、全国特色小镇，被列为"国家级田园综合体试点区""国家农业综合开发现代农业园区"，被国台办授予"朱子故里南平海峡两岸交流基地"的称号。

3. 建设闽台融合发展示范乡镇

五夫镇以朱子文化为纽带，发挥国家级海峡两岸交流基地优势，招引优质台商台胞入驻五夫，吸引台湾青年到五夫创业落户，打造"台湾一条街"，在闽台融合上起到先锋作用。

经验与启示

1. 建设特色农业全产业链示范乡镇

五夫镇依托农产品精深加工园区，延伸水稻、白莲、哈密瓜等特色农产品加工产业链，开发"稻香世界""瓜果飘香""四季花海"等农旅融合体验项目，有力推动特色农业全产业链建设。

2. 建设国家级优秀传统文化研学营地

五夫镇加快朱子文化园项目建设，开设研学课程，持续举办研学体验活动，常态化开展朱子文化节、荷花节等文化节庆活动，形成"月月有活动、季季有惊喜"氛围。

下一步计划

一是镇村联动强化组织保障。整合镇村资源和社会力量，推行"群众夜话""诸事合议"等民主议事决策制度，全面形成党委抓总、镇村联动、村企共建、群众参与的党建引领乡村振兴工作新格局。二是政策支撑。研究制定白莲产业奖补政策，推动白莲产业"做深做精"、规模化全链条化发展。三是人才支撑。完善政策吸引台湾青年和研学文创团队落户，优化"科技特派员+"服务模式，充分发挥农业技术、文旅策划、项目运营等人才和团队优势，充实和加强乡村振兴人才队伍。

Wufu Town, Wuyishan City, Nanping City, Fujian Province:

Empowering Rural Revitalization through the Integration of Agriculture, Culture, and Tourism

Abstract

Given actual circumstances, Wufu Town in Wuyishan City, Nanping City, Fujian Province, by basing its development on agriculture and taking Zhuzi culture as the core, focuses on high-quality integrated development of agriculture, culture, and tourism. The town is advancing the construction of harmonious villages through the "1+1" model. It is taking Xingxian Village as a demonstration village to link up the five villages of Wufu, Wuyi, Xingxian, Wengdun, and Dian along the No. 1 scenic route of the National Park. This strategy aims to create a boutique rural revitalization route, linking points, and connecting lines to form a comprehensive development area, thereby building a beautiful, harmonious, and prosperous Wufu and promoting rural revitalization throughout the area.

Challenges and Problems

Wufu Town was established in the mid-Jin Dynasty, over 1,700 years ago. It is located 40 kilometers from Nanping City, and 45 kilometers from the Wuyishan National Tourist Resort. With a population of 15,900, the town covers an area of 175.76 square kilometers and has 11 administrative villages under its jurisdiction. It is known as a historical and cultural town in China, a town with significant tourism potential, an ecological protection town, and a town with distinctive agriculture. It is also renowned as the "hometown of Zhu Xi" and the "land of white lotus". In the process of pursuing rural revitalization, Wufu Town faces four major challenges concerning industrial development, cultural display, environmental improvement, and talent aggregation.

Measures

1. Enhancing the agricultural foundation

White lotus and rice are characteristic agricultural products of Wufu Town. The town has a thousand-year history of white lotus cultivation, with a planting area of over 10,000 *mu*. To further enhance the added value of the industry, Wufu Town actively promotes crop rotation innovation, develops integrated techniques like lotus-snail-fish farming, and establishes demonstration projects like "Tianluowan", Kelixing Seed Industry, and Daoxiang World. It has also built an agricultural product deep-processing park and a white lotus trading center, extending the industrial chain of rice and white lotus to do well in developing the specialty-related industry and improving the level of rural industrial development.

2. Exploring cultural connotations

Wufu Town is home to many scholars and has been called the "origin of Zou and Lu" (a reference to Confucius and Mencius' places of origin). The great Neo-Confucian philosopher Zhu Xi lived here for nearly 50 years and established Zhuzi philosophy, giving Wufu the reputation of "the land of Neo-Confucianism". Wufu Town is rich in cultural tourism resources, with more than 30 ancient cultural sites, including Zhu Xi's former residence Ziyang Tower, Xingxian Ancient Street, Xingxian Academy, Zhu Xi Shecang, and the Lian Clan's Archway of Chastity. It is an important part of Wuyishan's dual World Heritage. Wufu Town has developed Zhu Xi-centered cultural heritage by creating key cultural views encompassing the statue, the temple, the tower, the

yard, and the storage and establishing a Zhu Xi study tour route. The town also, based on the four rituals prescribed by Zhu Xi and the local Longyu Dance, organizes cultural experience projects and festive activities such as those on the Zhuzi Culture Festival and the Lotus Festival and collaborates with Zhuzi School and Tongwen Academy to regularly put on intangible cultural heritage shows.

3. Improving ecological environment

Wufu Town continues to focus on the construction of a "Waterside Beautiful Village" by improving the environment at the Tanshi River basin. This involves inviting experts from the Chinese Academy of Environmental Science and the Provincial Institute of Environmental Protection to conduct water environment analysis and implement measures like farmland drainage to improve water quality, significantly enhancing the local water environment. The town is also developing the "Forest Ecological Bank" project, creating the "Maple Forest Evening" themed mountain park, and promoting the formation of seasonal scenic landscapes: In spring, the earth awakens with yellow rapeseed flowers; in summer, one can play in water and admire the lotus ponds; in autumn, the cool breeze sweeps through the rolling waves of rice fields; and in winter, the air is filled with the fragrance of blooming plum blossoms.

4. Innovating talent mechanism

Wufu Town is deepening the dual-deployment mechanism of sending out party secretaries and technology specialists, and establishing six demonstration stations and 16 demonstration bases for technology specialists. The town has deployed 42 teams of technology specialists totaling 216, 29 party secretaries, 5 circulation assistants, 18 recruits, and college graduate village officials to support the

implementation of the rural revitalization strategy. The town also hosts the Yuan Longping Hybrid Rice Expert Workstation and China-UNDP Cooperation Project Technology Specialist Demonstration Area for Poverty Alleviation.

Results

Wufu Town has 210,000 *mu* of forest land including 42,000 *mu* of ecological forest, with a forest coverage rate of 75.19%. The town has 32,000 *mu* of arable land, with over 20,000 *mu* planted with high-quality rice and over 10,000 *mu* planted with white lotus annually. The annual output of white lotus reaches 1 million jin or 500,000 kilograms, generating a production value of 40 million yuan. In 2023, Wufu Town's total agricultural output value reached 447 million yuan, a year-on-year increase of 10.6%; the per capita disposable income of rural residents was 25,421 yuan, a year-on-year increase of 7%; and various fiscal revenues amounted to 61.8715 million yuan. Wufu Town has been recognized as a Chinese historical and cultural town, a national characteristic town, a "National Pastoral Complex Pilot Area", and a "Modern Agricultural Park for National Comprehensive Agricultural Development". It has also been designated as a "Zhu Xi Hometown

Nanping Cross-Strait Exchange Base" by the Taiwan Affairs Office of the State Council.

Experiences and Inspirations

1. Building a demonstration township with a full industrial chain for agricultural products

Wufu Town relies on its agricultural product deep-processing park to extend the processing chain of characteristic agricultural products like rice, white lotus, and Hami melon, and develop agriculture-tourism integrated projects like "Fragrant Rice World", "Fragrant Fruits Orchard", and "All-year Flower Sea", thereby strongly promoting the construction of a full industrial chain of agricultural products.

2. Building a national excellent traditional culture study camp

Wufu Town is accelerating the construction of the Zhuzi Cultural Park, offering study tour courses, continuously holding experience-based research activities, and regularly organizing cultural festivals such as the Zhu Xi Culture Festival and the Lotus Festival, creating a vibrant atmosphere of "have activities every month and bringing surprises each season".

3. Building a demonstration township for Fujian-Taiwan integrated development

Using Zhuzi culture as a link, Wufu Town takes advantage of the national cross-strait exchange base to attract qualified Taiwan's businesses and residents to settle in Wufu Town, drawing in Taiwan's youth to start businesses and live in the town, and thereby creating a "Taiwan Street". Thus, it is playing a vanguard role in Fujian-Taiwan integration.

Plans

Firstly, it is to strengthen organizational support through town-village linkage. By pooling the town and village resources and social forces, the town will implement democratic decision-making systems such as "Night Talks with the Public" and "Joint Consultation on Affairs", to develop a new pattern of party leadership in rural revitalization where the party committee takes overall responsibility, the town-village linkage is in place, villages and enterprises engage in co-construction, and the people participate. Secondly, it is to provide policy support. Wufu Town will conduct research and formulate reward and subsidy policies for the white lotus industry to promote the deep and fine development of the white lotus industry, to achieve large-scale and full-chain development. Thirdly, it is to ensure talent support. Wufu Town will improve policies to attract Taiwan's youth and study tour-oriented creative teams to settle, improve the "Technology Specialist+" service model, and fully bring into play the strengths of agricultural technology, cultural and tourism planning, and project operations to build up the rural revitalization talent team.

新疆维吾尔自治区伊犁哈萨克自治州特克斯县琼库什台村：

打造国家级哈萨克族文化名村

摘　要

　　新疆维吾尔自治区伊犁哈萨克自治州特克斯县紧紧围绕习近平总书记提出的"文化润疆"思想，充分发挥国家历史文化名城和自治区全域旅游示范区等综合资源优势，积极探索琼库什台村高质量发展路径。琼库什台村依托具有特色的哈萨克族游牧民族传统木制房屋群落和保留的乌孙古道等优势旅游资源，因地制宜，着力打造哈萨克特色民宿、哈萨克风味美食、哈萨克马术表演、哈萨克歌舞表演、哈萨克村寨、草原美景等特色旅游产品；培育创意观光农业、采摘农业、果蔬庭院等乡村旅游业态及家庭牧场、牧场体验、牧家风情等民俗体验旅游业态。通过大力发展民俗旅游，盘活村级资产，琼库什台村旅游业成为壮大村集体经济和实现农牧民致富增收的主导产业。

挑战与问题

琼库什台村位于特克斯县喀拉达拉镇东部，距县城 90 千米。作为牧业村，琼库什台村的发展主要面临以下问题。一是农业生产落后，村集体收入来源单一，村民生活水平得不到改善；二是虽有历史悠久且保存完整的少数民族特色村寨，但开发和保护的力度不够，而且基础设施不完善，无法为当地旅游经济发展提供有力载体；三是村落位置相对闭塞，部分村民受教育水平不高，专业技能缺失，就业问题突出。

措施

1. 开展人居环境整治

一是 2023 年投入 638 万元，新建供水主管网 7000 米、支管网 3000 米；新建水源地 300 立方米蓄水池、路面硬化 2000 平方米、公共照明设施 20 盏。二是 2024 年实施基础设施建设项目，琼库什台村新建 500 kV 箱式变电器 1 座、箱变基站 5 个、电力接入 2400 米。三是持续在做好道路保护的基础上，采用鹅卵石对村庄内道路进行整修。四是按照设施外观、色彩与历史建筑风貌相协调的要求，在保护区外新建垃圾转运站 1 座，在村庄内设置分散式垃圾收集箱，在保护区内主街道、河流以及其他开放空间，栽种当地植物，美化街区和村庄环境。

2. 引进企业打造民宿

一是针对牧民群众无资金、缺技术等问题，引进"西游文旅"大型企业投资 4300 万元，流转宅基地 69 套和租赁老年活动场所打造集中民宿连片区；二是政府先后投入资金 200 万元对 105 户特色民居进行改造，投入 150 万元对 30 户民居进行内部装修；三是充分利用闲置资产，将琼库什台村的老学校开发利用，建设成乌孙古道旅游驿站，引进社会企业运营，收益 30% 用于脱贫户和困难群众分红，70% 用于壮大村集体经济。

3. 促进文旅产业融合

一是民俗文化厚植传播。琼库什台村以游牧民族文化和特色传统村寨为主题，将哈萨克族传统游牧特色文化与库什台自然风光结合起来，将草原石人、乌孙古道的传说等故事融入旅游推广中，与游客手拉手共同开展丰富多样的"民族团结一家亲"活动，将多姿多彩的哈萨克族文化展示在广大游客眼前。二是着眼民宿、宾馆、餐饮等行业一次性用品，整合镇村两级闲置资源，开办小型加工厂。三是组织闲暇在家的妇女制作红马甲、迷你冬不拉、骨雕、小帽、木雕及包尔扎克等民族特色产品，景区增设民俗文化产品展示摊位，发挥泰通物流作用，让更多群众干上旅游的活、吃上旅游的饭、挣上旅游的钱。

4. 加大服务质量提升

琼库什台村2024年通过冬季大培训开展乡村课堂，围绕旅游业、养殖业、农产品加工、电子商务、餐饮服务等，培养懂技术、善经营的新型职业牧民，共开展培训16种24场次，参加人数达到246人，农牧民服务水平进一步提高。

成效

琼库什台村成立琼库什台村股份制经济合作社，村民全覆盖入股，借助旅游资源，下设马队合作社、马术表演合作社、歌舞演艺合作社、蜜蜂养殖合作社，通过资源入股，抽取合作社收入20%为村集体经济增收，每年增收16万元。2023年，全村村集体收入达到77.05万元，村民实现户均收入3.7万元。截至2023年，琼库什台村牧家乐、民宿、超市、文创店等数量达到145家。全村336户1398人的住房已享受富民安居工程。琼库什台村相继获得中国历史文化名村、第一批全国乡村旅游重点村、中国美丽休闲乡村、中国首批传统村落和非物质文化遗产生态保护村、中国少数民族特色村寨等荣誉称号。琼库什台村秀美的自然环境、独特的木构建筑群、浓郁的民俗风情不仅为当地村民创造了一个宜游宜居、干净美丽的绿色生态环境，更吸引大量游客慕名前来，逐步成为摄影、写生、探险爱好者的旅游胜地。

经验与启示

1. 文旅融合

依托极具代表性的少数民族农牧乡村旅游资源，逐步推动"文化+生态""文化+旅游""文旅+农业"等新型联动发展工程落地生根。

2. 加强宣传

持续加强与各级媒体的交流合作，以拍摄宣传视频、开展节庆活动、发布旅游信息等方式加强新媒体旅游营销，制作宣传折页，手绘地图、画册等文化旅游宣传资料，多种渠道扩大宣传推广范围。

3. 全民参与

政府的大力支持和合作社的建立，使村民经济融合为一个整体，极大调动了全体村民的创业积极性，增强了村民脱贫致富的信心和决心，上下一体、齐心协力，共同为琼库什台村旅游发展、农牧民增收致富提供坚实有力的保障和持久的动力。

下一步计划

一是继续强化琼库什台村保护基础设施建设，建设完善配套道路、供水管网、排水管网等基础设施，以琼库什台村为中心，规划总长约100千米的精品旅游线路，沿途修建游客休憩站、房车营地等旅游设施，构建全域旅游新格局。二是实施好哈萨克族特色民居改造，持续挖掘旅游民宿新形势、新亮点，科学推动高端民宿建设。三是打造旅游产品电商销售站点，提高"库什台""山花养蜂"等系列野生蜂蜜产品、黑小麦、奶制品、肉制品加工和民族特色刺绣等产品流通效率。四是规范旅游专业合作社，强化旅游马队、穿越导游、服务接待等规范化建设，持续提升琼库什台村民宿游客接待能力，促进旅游人均收入不断提高。

Qiongkushitai Village, Tekes County, Ili Kazak Autonomous Prefecture, Xinjiang Uygur Autonomous Region:
Build a National Kazak Cultural Village

Abstract

Following the instructions of President Xi Jinping's thought of "ebriching Xinjiang with culture",Tekes County, Ili Kazak Autonomous Prefecture, Xinjiang Uygur Autonomous Region has given full play to the comprehensive advantages as a city rich in history and culture and the autonomous region's all-in-one tourism demonstration zone, and made active explorations in the high-quality development path of Qiongkushitai Village. Relying on the traditional wooden house clusters of Kazak nomads, the Wusun Ancient Road, and other tourism resources, Qiongkushitai Village has focused on developing featured tourism products according to the actual conditions, such as Kazak homestays, Kazak cuisine, Kazak equestrian performances, Kazak song and dance performances, Kazak village, and grasslands. It has fostered diverse business forms of rural tourism such as creative sightseeing agriculture, fruit and vegetable picking, and fruit and vegetable courtyards, and business forms of folk tourism such as family pastures, pastoral experiences, and pastoral customs. By boosting folk tourism and putting its assets to good use, Qiongkushitai Village has made tourism a pillar industry that underpins its collective economy and raise the incomes of farmers and herdsmen.

Challenges and Problems

Located in the east of Karadala Township of Tekes County and 90 kilometers away from the county seat, Qiongkushitai Village specializes in animal husbandry village, and mainly faces the following challenges and problems. Firstly, the village lags behind in agricultural production, has limited sources of income of the collective economy, and finds it difficult to improve the living quality of villagers. Secondly, although there are well-preserved ethnic minority villages with a long history, development and protection efforts are not enough, and the infrastructure is inadequate to support the development of tourism. Thirdly, the location of the village is isolated, and many villagers are not highly educated and lack specialized skills, making it difficult for them to find jobs.

Measures

1. Improve the living environments

Firstly, funds of 6.38 million yuan were allocated in 2023 to build a primary water supply system of 7,000 meters and of a branch water supply system of 3,000 meters; a new reservoir with a storage of 300 cubic meters was built, road surfaces of 2,000 square meters were paved, and 20 public lighting facilities were installed. Secondly, infrastructure construction projects have been implemented since the beginning of 2024. A 500 kV box-type transformer, five box-type transformer base stations, and power transmission lines of 2,400 meters have been newly built. Thirdly, cobblestones were used to renovate the roads in the village. Fourthly, to match the appearances and colors of the facilities with historical architectures, a new waste transfer station was built outside the nature reserve, decentralized waste collection boxes were set up in the village, and native species were planted in the main streets, rivers, and other open spaces in the nature reserve to beautify the environment.

2. Engage enterprises in the construction of homestays

Firstly, to help herdsmen solve their difficulties in funding and techniques, the village introduced Xiyou Cultural Tourism, a large tourism enterprise, to invest 43 million yuan to utilize 69 housing sites and rent the activity facility for the elderly to build contiguous homestays. Secondly, the government spent 2 million yuan in renovating 105 residential buildings with local features and 1.5 million yuan in decorating 30 buildings. Thirdly, make full use of idle assets, develop and utilize the former school of the village to build a tourist station along the Wusun Ancient Road, engage enterprises in operations, and use 30% of the income as dividends to poverty-stricken households and people and 70% used to strengthen the village's collective economy.

3. Promote the integration of culture and tourism

Firstly, foster and promote folk culture. Revolving around the theme of nomadic culture and traditional villages, Qiongkushitai Village combines the Kazak nomadic culture with the natural scenery of Kushitai, integrates stories such as the grassland stone human and the folklore of the Wusun Ancient Road into tourism promotion, and works with tourists to hold diverse activities on national unity and family, immersing tourists in the colorful Kazak culture. Secondly, the town and the village set up a small processing plant for disposable products

in homestay, hotel, catering, and other industries. Thirdly, organize women at home to make ethnic products such as red vests, mini Dongbula, bone carvings, small hats, wood carvings, and traditional Kazakh fried buns; set up stalls displaying and selling folk cultural products in scenic areas, and bring into full play the role of Taitong Logistics so more people can engage in tourism and get more incomes from tourism.

4. Improve the service quality

In 2024, Qiongkushitai Village implemented a winter training program for rural classrooms, focusing on tourism, animal husbandry, agricultural product processing, e-commerce, catering services, and other topics. The program trained new-type professional herdsmen who are highly skilled and good at management. A total of 24 sessions of 16 types of training with 246 participants were carried out, helping farmers and herdsmen to improve their skills and services.

Results

The Qiongkushitai Village Joint-stock Economic Cooperative covers all villagers as shareholders. Based on the village's tourism resources, it consists of a horse tourism cooperative, an equestrian performance cooperative, a song and dance performance cooperative, and a bee breeding cooperative. By contributing resources as equity investment, 20% of the cooperative's income is allocated to the village's collective economy, increasing its annual revenue by 160,000 yuan. In 2023, the revenue of the collective economy reached 770,500 yuan, and per household income was 37,000 yuan. As of 2023, there were 145 pastoral homestays, agritainment operators, supermarkets, and cultural and creative stores in Qiongkushitai Village. The project aimed at improving the housing conditions had benefited 336 households with 1,398 people. Qiongkushitai Village has been honored the Village Rich in History and Culture in China, the Beautiful Village for Leisure of China" and the Ethnic Minority Villages of China and selected into the first batch of the National Key Villages for Rural Tourism Development and the China's First Batch of Traditional Villages and Villages in Intangible Cultural Heritage Protection. With a picturesque natural landscape, unique wooden buildings, and rich folk customs, Qiongkushitai Village not only provides a clean and beautiful environment for villagers, but also attracts a large number of tourists, making it a popular destination for photography, sketch, and adventure enthusiasts.

Experiences and Inspirations

1. Integrate culture and tourism

Relying on its agricultural, animal husbandry, and rural tourism resources of ethnic minorities, the village has taken steps to implement integrated development projects such as "culture + ecology", "culture + tourism", and "cultural tourism + agriculture".

2. Strengthen publicity

The village has maintained close communication and cooperation with media organizations at all levels, strengthened tourism marketing on new media by producing promotional videos, holding festivals, and releasing tourism information, distributed promotional leaflets, hand-drawn maps, photo albums, and other promotional materials, and expanded the scope of publicity and promotion through various channels.

3. Engage in the people

With the strong support of the government and the establishment of cooperatives, the village economy has become a unified whole, inspiring villagers to engage in business and entrepreneurial activities and enhancing their confidence and determination to get rid of poverty and live a better life. By working together, Qiongkushitai Village has provided solid guarantee and lasting impetus for tourism development and raised the incomes of farmers and herdsmen.

improve basic infrastructure such as roads, water supply systems, and sewerage systems, plan a high-quality tourist route with a total length of about 100 kilometers centered on Qiongkushitai Village, build tourist facilities such as tourist rest areas and recreational vehicle (RV) campsites along the route, and foster a new pattern of all-in-one tourism. Secondly, continue with the renovation of Kazak dwellings, explore the new dynamics and highlights of homestays, and methodically promote the construction of high-end homestays. Thirdly, build an e-commerce platform for tourism products, and improve the circulation efficiency of local products such as the "Kushtai" and "Shanhua Yangfeng" series of wild honey products, black wheat, dairy products, meat processing, and embroidery with ethnic characteristics. Fourthly, exercise more regulation over specialized tourism cooperatives, horse tourism teams, tour guides, and tourist reception and services, and further improve the reception capacity of homestays in Qiongkushitai Village, so as to increase the per capita tourism revenue.

Plans

Firstly, continue to strengthen the construction of village protection infrastructure, build and

2024 世界旅游联盟：旅游助力乡村振兴案例（中英文双语版）
WTA Best Practices of Rural Revitalization through Tourism 2024 (Chinese-English Bilingual Edition)

甘肃省甘南藏族自治州舟曲县土桥子村：
庭院小葡萄助力乡村大振兴

摘　要

　　甘肃省甘南藏族自治州舟曲县大川镇土桥子村立足依山傍水、生态宜居的资源禀赋和生态优势，大力发展乡村旅游、林果培育等绿色产业，努力把绿水青山转变为促进群众增收致富的金山银山。2012年开始，该村在中共中央组织部的定点帮扶下，综合利用江、湖、田、园等自然优势，以文化为灵魂、观光休闲康养旅游为引力，逐步构建起以土桥子村为中心，涵盖荷花鱼塘、江景游步道、湿地公园、康养中心、桑茶基地、葡萄长廊、绿色产业基地、农家乐、民宿等一系列项目的乡村旅游发展模式。该模式不仅促进了本村的发展，还对周边村庄产生了显著的辐射带动效应，共同形成了一条乡村旅游示范带。如今土桥已不"土"，旧貌换新颜，土桥子村成为全县乃至全州乡村旅游发展的"先行区"和"示范区"，2016年被评选为"中国美丽乡村百佳范例"，2017年被中央文明办列入"2017年度全国文明村名录"，享有"康养小镇·葡萄之乡"的美誉，引领广大农民走上乡村振兴的康庄大道。

挑战与问题

舟曲县大川镇土桥子村位于舟曲县东南部，距县城 12 千米，现为镇政府所在地，平均海拔高度 1200 米，环境优美、气候湿润、生态宜居。全村共有 3 个村民小组，总人口 112 户 420 人，占地面积 1.73 平方千米，土地总面积 450 余亩，葡萄种植 270 余亩，年产量约 14 万公斤，农户自酿葡萄酒约 6900 公斤。土桥子村在日益蓬勃发展的同时也出现了以下问题：一是随着种植面积的逐渐扩大，葡萄树龄老化和部分品种葡萄易裂果、糖分过高不耐贮运，葡萄产业效益低下，果农面临丰产不丰收困境；二是村庄虽大力发展庭院经济，但之前村庄的发展主要以政府投入为主，村集体、村民的自我发展意识和自我造血功能依然较弱，制约了村庄发展潜力；三是土桥子村虽然旅游文化基础设施基础较好，但没有形成产业链综合效应，产业发展动力不足；四是由于两河口至舟曲县高速连接线的改道通车，大量外地过境游客绕过土桥子村直奔舟曲县城，大幅度降低了土桥子村的游客量，造成该村旅游经济效益和收入直线下降骤减。

措施

1. 党建引领促发展

土桥子村在大川镇党委、政府的正确指导下，坚持党建引领，大力发展特色葡萄产业和村级旅游业，探索出一条建强支部促发展、发展产业助党建的良性循环发展道路。在发展过程中，党员率先让地造景、迁坟让路，带动群众买苗种葡萄和开发经营农家乐、民宿等乡村旅游产业，以实际行动践行"舟曲模式"的"尖兵排头行动"，共同描绘出一幅美丽乡村旅游崭新画卷。

2. 多措并举促建设

大川镇"以党建为引领、以群众为基础、以产业为支撑、以致富为目标"，一是加强旅游基础设施建设，集中实施水、电、路、排污系统等基础设施建设，建成停车场 3 处、星级公厕 4 座，完成村容绿化和环境美化，改善了农村发展环境；二是建成生态公园和康养中心，升级改造乡村记忆博物馆、水磨坊、农家乐、民宿等工程。

3. 庭院经济促旅游

土桥子村深耕"庭院经济+观光旅游"的发展模式，有效推动了庭院经济与乡村旅游业的深度融合与协同发展。一是依托独特的田园风光，合理打造具有农家韵味、乡土气息，与地域特色和村庄规划相协调的小微景观；二是打造集休闲度假、地方美食、露营基地、自然风光体验等于一体的观光旅游模式。

成效

土桥子村通过控产提质，走上了精品化葡萄种植道路，市场占有率大幅提高。同时，该村已建成并启用一条预计年产量为120吨的葡萄果饮加工销售生产线，该生产线每年可收购农户葡萄约20吨，惠及农户超过300户1200余人。土桥子村每年定期举办葡萄节、马拉松大赛等乡村游体验活动，将农户的葡萄、花椒、土蜂蜜等特色农产品打造为旅游商品，有效带动农户增收0.2万—5万元，户均增收0.9余万元，实现了群众"家门口就业、家门口赚钱"的发展模式，成功实现了旅游富民的发展目标。

经验与启示

1. 科学规划

土桥子村基于优良的资源禀赋，通过总体合理规划布局，建造一个集田园观光休闲、乡村社会实践、自然文化教育、家庭亲子教育、户外拓展运动、健康养生度假等功能于一体的国家3A级旅游景区，以旅游区建设带动全村人文、环境、经济的可持续发展，打造美丽乡村旅游休闲新天地。

2. 农旅融合

休闲旅游产业作为土桥子村的绿色产业，对带动乡村发展、促进农民致富、辐射周边发展的作用极为明显。农旅深度融合使彼此实现了深层次促进和发展，景区的发展因此得到了农民更为广泛的支持和积极参与，形成了推动当地持续发展的活力源泉。

3. 弘扬文化

土桥子村通过发展乡村旅游，成功挖掘并展现了乡村独特的生态美景、田园风光以及民俗风情的价值，同时促进了乡村特有的传统工艺、文物古迹、节庆文化、农耕文化等非物质文化遗产的传承和发扬，让游客真切体会到"望得见山，看得见水，记得住乡愁"的乡村情怀，实现了文化、生态与经济的和谐共生。

下一步计划

大川镇将按照中国农科院专家量身打造的产业发展规划，遵循全县以党建引领乡村振兴的总体战略部署，继续发展土桥子村集餐饮、住宿、休闲、娱乐于一体的文化旅游产业。土桥子村将进一步发挥水上乐园、民宿温泉酒店、藏医理疗馆、桑茶体验馆等项目的经济作用，进一步拓展乡村旅游发展空间，吸引更多的游客前来休闲娱乐、康养度假，不仅能带动大川镇经济发展，也将吸收更多当地及周边的剩余劳动力从事第三产业，全面拓宽增收渠道，切实增加大川镇群众劳务收入。

Tuqiaozi Village, Zhouqu County, Gannan Tibetan Autonomous Prefecture, Gansu Province:
Small Vineyards Drive Great Rural Revitalization

Abstract

Tuqiaozi Village, located in Dachuan Town, Zhouqu County, Gannan Tibetan Autonomous Prefecture, Gansu Province, has capitalized on its advantageous location of being nestled in a scenic and eco-friendly environment to develop green industries like rural tourism and fruit cultivation. Since 2012, with the targeted assistance from the Organization Department of the Central Committee of the Communist Party of China, Tuqiaozi Village has utilized its natural resources, including rivers, lakes, fields, and gardens, with culture as its soul and leisure tourism and wellness as its attraction, gradually establishing a rural tourism pattern centered on Tuqiaozi Village that encompasses a series of projects such as lotus ponds, riverside walkways, wetland parks, wellness centers, mulberry tea plantations, grape corridors, green industry bases, farm stays, and homestays. This model has not only promoted the development of the village itself, but also had a significant radiating and driving effect on surrounding villages, collectively forming a demonstration belt for rural tourism. Nowadays, Tuqiaozi Village has shed its former rustic image and taken on a new look, becoming a "pioneer" and "demonstration area" for rural tourism development in the entire county and even the prefecture. Tuqiaozi Village has been recognized as one of the "Top 100 Beautiful Villages in China" in 2016, listed as a "National Exemplary Village" in 2017, and awarded the titles "Wellness Town" and "Hometown of Grapes". Such transformation has pushed the village onto a path of rural revitalization, leading local farmers toward prosperity.

Challenges and Problems

Tuqiaozi Village is situated 12 kilometers southeast of Zhouqu County, at an average altitude of 1,200 meters. The village, which serves as the seat of the town government, covers 1.73 square kilometers, with 450 *mu* of land, of which 270 *mu* is dedicated to grape cultivation with an annual yield of approximately 140,000 kilograms, and the farmers brew about 6,900 kilograms of wine by themselves. However, several challenges have emerged alongside the village's growth. Firstly, aging grapevines and quality problems. As the vineyard area has expanded, aging grapevines and certain varieties prone to cracking and over-sweetness have led to low profitability, causing a paradox where high yields do not bring high incomes. Secondly, poor capabilities in self-development. Despite the village's efforts to develop a courtyard economy, earlier development was primarily government-funded, leading to poor self-development and self-sustaining capabilities on the part of the villagers and the village collective. Thirdly, lack of comprehensive industrial integration. The village's tourism and cultural infrastructure is well-developed, but the lack of an integrated industrial chain has limited the overall economic gains. Forthly, reduced tourist traffic. With the rerouting of the highway connecting Lianghekou to Zhouqu County, a significant portion of tourists now bypass the village, which leads to a sharp decline in the number of tourists and corresponding economic benefits.

Measures

1. Party leadership in development

Under the guidance of the Dachuan Town Party Committee and government, Tuqiaozi Village has leveraged Party leadership to vigorously develop its grape industry and village tourism, creating a virtuous cycle where strong Party branches promote development and thriving industries strengthen the Party. The Party members led the endeavor in making land available for scenic spots, relocating ancestral graves, and encouraging villagers to plant grapes and open farm stays, embodying the "Zhouqu Model" and drawing a new picture of beautiful rural tourism.

2. Multi-faceted construction

Guided by the principle of "Party leadership, public participation, and industrial support towards prosperity", Dachuan Town has strengthened tourism infrastructure by implementing projects for water, electricity, roads, and sewage systems, building three parking lots and four-star toilets, and conducting village greening and beautification, thereby

enhancing the rural development environment. It has also developed ecological parks and wellness centers; and upgraded village museums, water mills, farm stays, and guesthouses.

3. Promoting courtyard economy and tourism

Tuqiaozi Village has effectively integrated "courtyard economy + sightseeing tourism" to boost the growth of both. The first is to reasonably build small and micro landscapes with a farmhouse charm and a rustic atmosphere, which are coordinated with regional characteristics and village planning, relying on the unique rural scenery. The second is to create a tourism model that integrates leisure, vacation, local cuisine, camping bases, natural scenery experience, etc.

Results

By controlling yields and improving quality, Tuqiaozi Village has embarked on a path of high-end grape cultivation, significantly increasing its market share. A new grape juice production line with an annual capacity of 120 tons has been established, purchasing approximately 20 tons of grapes from 300 local farmers and benefiting over 1,200 people. The village regularly hosts events like the Grape Festival and Marathon, turning local products such as grapes, Sichuan pepper, and honey into popular tourist goods, boosting farmers' incomes by 2,000 to 50,000 yuan, with an average increase of 9,000 yuan per household. This has successfully created a development model where villagers can find jobs and earn money locally, achieving the goal of increasing the wealth of the community through tourism.

Experiences and Inspirations

1. Scientific planning

Tuqiaozi Village has leveraged its excellent resources to develop a comprehensive plan that

integrates rural sightseeing, social practice, cultural education, family activities, outdoor sports, and wellness tourism. This has led to the establishment of national 3A-level scenic spot, driving the sustainable development of the village's culture, environment, and economy, and establishing a new model of rural tourism.

2. Agriculture-tourism integration

The integration of agriculture and tourism in Tuqiaozi Village has demonstrated the power of green industries to drive rural development, increase farmers' incomes, and benefit surrounding areas. The deep integration of agriculture and tourism has gained strong support from farmers for the development of the scenic area, generating momentum for continued growth.

3. Cultural promotion

Through the development of rural tourism, Tuqiaozi Village has highlighted and capitalized on the value of its ecological scenery, rural landscapes, and folk customs. At the same time, it has promoted the inheritance and promotion of the intangible cultural heritage of traditional crafts, historical sites, festive culture, and agricultural heritage, allowing tourists to truly experience the rural feelings of "see the mountains, see the water, and feel homesick", and achieving the harmonious coexistence of culture, ecology, and economy.

Plans

Dachuan Town, following the industrial development plan tailored by experts from the Chinese Academy of Agricultural Sciences and in line with the overall county strategy of promoting rural revitalization through Party leadership, will continue to develop Tuqiaozi Village's cultural tourism industry, which integrates dining, accommodation, leisure, and entertainment. The village will further develop projects such as a water park, guesthouses with hot springs, Tibetan medicine treatment centers, and mulberry tea experience centers to expand the space for rural tourism. These efforts aim to attract more visitors, promote economic development in Dachuan Town, and create jobs for locals to increase their incomes.

国家电网辽宁省电力有限公司：
助力中国万里海疆第一岛走出绿色产业致富路

摘　要

　　国网辽宁省电力有限公司丹东供电公司聚焦辽宁沿海经济带和辽东绿色经济区发展格局，在电网建设、电力保供、产业支撑、优质服务等方面积极发挥电网行业优势和基础保障作用，促成辽宁省丹东市獐岛村在特色乡村建设、旅游开发经营、居民生产生活等领域高水平融入电气化元素，打造"全电海岛"清洁用能示范项目，有效解决边陲海岛公共基础设施薄弱、电气化发展滞后、民生保障不足等痛点问题，推动獐岛村由传统农业逐步向观光农业、生态农业和休闲农业方向转型升级，实现旅游业从传统服务业向现代服务业转变，为海岛经济发展树立了典范。

挑战与问题

辽宁省丹东市獐岛村地处鸭绿江与黄海交汇处，与朝鲜、韩国、日本隔海相望，是我国1.8万千米大陆海岸线最北端起点第一岛。獐岛村陆地面积只有1平方千米左右，岛上居民800余人，祖祖辈辈以海谋生。獐岛村有发展旅游业得天独厚的自然资源和人文资源，但岛上公共服务设施极度缺乏，道路、电力、淡水等基础设施无法适应旅游业的发展。20世纪90年代，村民赖以生存的6千亩蚬子滩涂海产品养殖遭遇赤潮，损失惨重，村集体负债2800万元，獐岛村"靠天吃饭"的生存模式难以为继。

措施

1. 统筹政府资源，首创电力服务"三农"新模式

国网辽宁省电力有限公司与辽宁省农业农村厅、乡村振兴局强化政企协同联动，聚焦高标准农田建设、农业重点产业链建设、乡村电气化发展、乡村治理体系建设和定点帮扶5大重点任务，签署国内首个省级电力公司与省级政府部门服务乡村振兴战略合作协议，国网辽宁省电力有限公司全力做好优质供电服务和保障，政企合力推进惠农政策与电力服务有效衔接，为辽宁沿海经济带和辽东绿色经济区实施电气化提升工程提供政策支撑。

2. 优化服务模式，打造"村网共建"模式新样板

一是在獐岛村设立辽宁省首个"村网共建"海岛电力便民服务示范点，签订政企网格化服务合作协议，实施服务点与村委会合署办公模式，聘请村干部兼任电力联络员，遴选专职电力网格员24小时驻岛服务，有效提升边陲海岛服务响应质效，网格员到达现场时间由原来的跨海登岛2小时缩减至10分钟以内。二是针对海岛冬季燃煤取暖效率低、污染重、燃料运输不便等难题，建立政、电、民三方代表议事制度，确定政府出资采购电暖设备、供电公司建设配套设施、村民仅需承担电费支出的全岛电采暖改造实施方案，开辟"全电海岛"报装接电绿色通道，完成獐岛村全量157户居民电采暖改造，全岛清洁取暖率达到100%。

3. 带动产业升级，激活"全电海岛"发展新动能

国网辽宁省电力有限公司丹东供电公司围绕"红色旅游、绿色发展、全电驱动"工作理念，将供电服

务与地方经济发展和生态建设相融合，主动对接獐岛村发展需求，联合属地政府出台乡村电气化及产业清洁用能支持政策，配套制定覆盖海岛旅游业、深海捕捞业和滩涂养殖业的电网规划方案，实施"全电海岛"乡村电气化提升工程，优化獐岛村内外10千伏配电网架，促成实施全岛亮化景观改造、海水滩涂养殖产业升级等4项乡村电气化项目，为獐岛村修建旅游码头、环岛步道、民宿客栈、网络宽带、垃圾焚烧厂和污水处理厂等旅游基础及配套设施提供强有力的电力保障，助力獐岛村成功打造以旅游业为"龙头"、捕捞业和养殖业为"两翼"的绿色产业。

水活源"。乡村的脱贫致富需要结合乡村特点，打造主导产业，找准产业是产业扶贫的关键。从"绿水青山"通往"金山银山"的道路不会是千篇一律的，只有充分挖掘利用自身资源禀赋，找到适合自己的生态发展道路，才能在乡村振兴的大道上越走越稳、越走越宽。

成效

獐岛村坚持绿色发展，全岛植物覆盖率达到65%以上，深入发掘和保护獐岛村古建筑、古树名木和民俗文化等历史文化遗迹10处，新建（改造）生活垃圾分类房（亭）2个，配置分类运输等环卫机动车辆4辆，城乡生活垃圾无害化处理率维持在100%，垃圾焚烧处理率达80%以上，自来水普及率达到100%，清洁取暖率达到100%，3年以来减少碳排放2835吨，达到"户户都是美丽庭院"的目标。

獐岛村成功晋升为国家4A级旅游景区，从昔日闭塞落后的小渔村蝶变成"中国最美渔村"，年接待游客达20万人次，带动周边农民就业人口近万人，实现旅游综合收入4000多万元。獐岛村的村集体资产超过2.2亿元，村集体经济年收入超过2000万元，村民人均年收入超过7万元。獐岛村荣获全国休闲农业与乡村旅游示范点、全国休闲渔业示范基地等9个国家级荣誉称号，已成为中国北方海岛旅游的主要景区，其发展模式已经辐射带动周边区域经济。

经验与启示

1. 产业带动是脱贫致富之源

产业是脱贫之基、致富之源，兴办产业才能"引

2. 政企合力是乡村振兴之路

乡村振兴需要充分发挥政府、企业、村委、村民等各个方面的作用，需要通过合理的权利赋予、利益分配等增强各方的参与度，尤其是要发挥村委、村民的内生主体意识，凝聚合力，提高产业扶贫的组织化程度，培育新型合作关系，推动产业升级优化。

3. 公共服务是持续发展之基

乡村治理和公共服务体系建设是关系到群众切身利益和乡村振兴全局的重要问题，具体包括乡村基层组织建设、提升乡村治理水平、乡村公共设施建设、提升乡村电力普及水平、提升乡村用能电气化水平等。加强乡村公共服务体系建设，带动产业发展，推动乡村文化和经济产业高质量发展。

下一步计划

国网辽宁省电力有限公司丹东供电公司将持续把休闲农业与清洁能源有机融合，通过优化海岛用能结构，助力海岛开发旅游资源、改善生态环境、策划特色品牌，做好海岛经济发展的典型示范，为乡村振兴战略实施积累宝贵经验，打造宜居、宜业、宜游的美丽海岛。

2024 世界旅游联盟：旅游助力乡村振兴案例（中英文双语版）
WTA Best Practices of Rural Revitalization through Tourism 2024（Chinese-English Bilingual Edition）

State Grid Liaoning Electric Power Co., Ltd.:

Assisting China's First Island along the Vast Coastline in Blazing a Path to Prosperity through Green Industrial Development

Abstract

Given the development pattern of the Liaoning Coastal Economic Belt and the Eastern Liaoning Green Economic Zone, State Grid Liaoning Electric Power Co., Ltd. Dandong Power Supply Company plays the advantages of the power grid industry and provides foundational support in areas such as grid construction, power supply security, industrial development, and quality service. This endeavor has integrated electrification into various aspects of Zhangdao Village, Dandong City, Liaoning Province, including characteristic rural construction, tourism development, and locals' production and living. The company has created a "fully electrified island" model project for clean energy use, effectively addressing the challenges of poor public infrastructure, sluggish development for electrification, and insufficient livelihood security on the remote island. This effort has facilitated Zhangdao Village's transition from traditional agriculture to agritourism, ecological agriculture, and leisure agriculture, making its tourism industry shift from traditional services to modern services. Zhangdao Village has become a model for the island's economic development.

Challenges and Problems

Zhangdao Village in Dandong City, Liaoning Province, is located at the intersection of the Yalu River and the Yellow Sea, facing Democratic People's Republic of Korea, Republic of Korea, and Japan across the sea. It is the starting point of China's 18,000-kilometer mainland coastline, known as the first island at the northernmost point. With a land area of only about 1 square kilometer and a population of over 800, the village has traditionally made a living on the sea. Despite its rich natural and cultural resources ideal for tourism, the island's public service facilities were severely lacking. Basic infrastructure like roads, electricity, and freshwater was inadequate for tourism development. In the 1990s, the villagers' 6,000 *mu* clam farming area suffered significant losses due to red tides, leaving the village collective in debt by 28 million yuan. The survival mode of "relying on nature to eat" of the village was not sustainable.

Measures

1. Coordinating government resources to pioneer a new model of power service for issues of agriculture, farmers and rural areas

State Grid Liaoning Electric Power Co., Ltd. has strengthened government-enterprise collaboration with the Department of Agriculture and Rural Affairs Liaoning Province and the Rural Revitalization Bureau, focusing on five key tasks: high-standard farmland construction, key agricultural industry chain development, rural electrification, rural governance system construction, and targeted assistance. The company signed the country's first provincial-level strategic cooperation agreement with government departments to support rural revitalization, ensuring quality power supply services. This government-enterprise partnership has effectively linked agricultural policies with power services, providing policy support for electrification upgrades in the

Liaoning Coastal Economic Belt and the Eastern Liaoning Green Economic Zone.

2. Optimizing service models and creating a new "village-grid co-construction" model

Firstly, the first "village-grid co-construction" island power service demonstration point in Liaoning Province was established in Zhangdao Village. A government-enterprise grid service cooperation agreement was signed, and a joint office model was implemented, where village officials also serve as power liaisons, and dedicated power grid staff provide 24-hour island service. This effectively reduced the response time from the previous two hours to under 10 minutes. Secondly, to address issues such as low efficiency, pollution from coal heating in winter, and difficulty in fuel transportation, a tripartite decision-making system involving government, electricity, and residents was established. The system developed an all-island electric heating renovation plan where the government funds the purchase of electric heating equipment, the power company builds supporting facilities, and villagers only bear the electricity costs. This initiative completed the electric heating renovation for all 157 households on the island, achieving 100% clean heating.

3. Driving industrial upgrading and activating new development drivers of the "fully electrified island"

State Grid Liaoning Electric Power Co., Ltd. Dandong Power Supply Company, following the concept of "red tourism, green development, being fully electricity-driven", integrated power supply services with local economic development and ecological construction. They actively aligned with Zhangdao's development needs and collaborated with the local government to issue policies supporting rural electrification and clean energy use in industries. The company implemented the "fully electrified island" rural electrification upgrade project, optimized the 10 kV distribution network both within and outside the island, and facilitated the implementation of four rural electrification projects, including island-wide lighting, seawater and beach aquaculture industry upgrading, and others. These efforts provided strong power support for building tourism infrastructure such as docks, coastal walkways, guesthouses, broadband networks, garbage incinerators, and sewage treatment plants, helping Zhangdao Village successfully embrace a green industry led by tourism, with fishing and aquaculture as supporting industries.

Results

Zhangdao Village adheres to green development, with a vegetation coverage rate of over 65% across the island. The village has uncovered and protected 10 historical and cultural relics concerning ancient buildings, famous trees, and folk culture. Two garbage sorting houses (pavilions) were newly built or renovated, and four sanitation vehicles for classified transportation were equipped. The urban and rural garbage harmless treatment rate has remained 100%, with an incineration rate of over 80%. The island's tap water coverage and clean heating rate have both reached 100%. Over the past three years, carbon emissions have been reduced by 2,835 tons, achieving the goal that "every household has a beautiful courtyard".

Zhangdao Village has been successfully upgraded into a national 4A-level scenic spot, transforming from a once isolated and backward fishing village into "the China's Most Beautiful Fishing Village". The village now attracts 200,000 tourists annually, generating jobs for nearly 10,000 surrounding farmers and achieving a total tourism income of over 40 million yuan. The village collective assets have exceeded 220 million yuan, with an annual income of over 20 million yuan, and the per capita annual income of the villagers has exceeded 70,000 yuan. Zhangdao Village has received nine national honors, including the National Demonstration Spot for Leisure Agriculture and Rural Tourism, and the National Leisure Fishery Demonstration Base, becoming a major scenic spot for northern China's island tourism. Its development model has also radiated to and driven the economic growth of surrounding areas.

Experiences and Inspirations

1. Industrial development underpins poverty alleviation and prosperity

Industry is the foundation of poverty alleviation and the source of wealth. Promoting industrial development is key to "divert water and broaden sources". Rural poverty alleviation and prosperity

require tailoring the dominant industry to local characteristics. Finding the right industry is crucial for poverty alleviation through industrial development. The path of earning benefits by leveraging the lush mountains and lucid water is not the same everywhere. Only by fully exploiting and utilizing local natural resources and finding a suitable ecological development path can we steadily advance on the road to rural revitalization.

2. Government-enterprise collaboration is the path to rural revitalization

Rural revitalization requires fully leveraging the roles of government, enterprises, village committees, and villagers. It is necessary to enhance the participation of all aspects through reasonable rights conferment and benefit distribution, especially encouraging village committees and villagers to be active participants. Such collaboration fosters new cooperative relationships, promotes industrial upgrading, and makes the endeavor for poverty alleviation through industrial development better organized.

3. Public services are fundamental to sustainable development

Rural governance and the construction of public service systems are vital issues affecting the well-being of the people and the overall rural revitalization. These include grassroots rural organization building, governance level promotion, public facility construction, electricity access promotion, and rural electrification promotion. Strengthening the rural public service system can drive industrial development and promote high-quality development of rural culture and economic industries.

Plans

State Grid Liaoning Electric Power Co., Ltd. Dandong Power Supply Company will continue to integrate leisure agriculture with clean energy, optimize the island's energy structure, help develop tourism resources, improve the ecological environment, and plan distinctive brands. This initiative will serve as a model for island economic development, providing valuable experience for implementing the rural revitalization strategy and creating a beautiful island that is livable, business-friendly, and tourist-friendly.

湖北省咸宁市通城县内冲瑶族村：
文旅融合助力乡村振兴

摘　要

湖北省咸宁市通城县内冲瑶族村联合通城城发隽达文旅投资有限公司，全面贯彻落实乡村振兴战略，立足本地旅游资源，将瑶乡风情、山水田园、中医药文化融合，打造吃瑶家饭、住瑶家院、观自然景、赏民俗情、享田园乐的国家4A级旅游景区。内冲瑶族村因地制宜发展乡村旅游，促进旅游新业态产业链延伸、价值链提升、增收链拓宽，助力乡村振兴。

挑战与问题

通城县内冲瑶族村坐落在闻名遐迩的药姑山脚下，杭瑞、京港澳、武深高速公路依境而过，村庄占地总面积13.5平方千米，全村人口1482人，是中国传统村落，湖北省内唯一的国家级瑶族特色保护自然行政村。内冲瑶族村着力打造药姑山内冲瑶族村景区，在发展乡村旅游的过程中也面临诸多挑战与问题。一是过快地进行商业化开发，传统的乡村生活、手工艺技艺等特色因商业化而受到冲击，原有的瑶文化逐渐被淡化。二是景区虽交由旅游公司运营，但是建设规划、招标等工作由政府负责，两方工作的脱节导致基础设施经营管理效率低下。三是政府机构、旅游企业、村委会和村民利益分配机制不完善，各方诉求演变成各方矛盾，旅游公司无法运用先进的管理经验，无法凸显经营模式的优势。

措施

1. 促进瑶文化资源传承

内冲瑶族村促进和保护其独特的、真实的瑶文化资源，一是对大风磅、石神庙、瑶民居等遗址遗迹进行保护；二是发掘有文艺特长的本土人才，把"拍打舞""锣鼓赛"等本地文艺品牌进一步做响；三是发挥瑶文化研究会等民间学术组织的作用，加强与各地瑶学会沟通交流，整理和编排瑶文化相关的民间习俗，为古瑶文化建设提供学术依据和参考。

2. 促进生态可持续发展

内冲瑶族村牢固树立"绿水青山就是金山银山"理念，以生态为本，让绿色成为美丽乡村发展靓丽的底色。内冲瑶族村落实古村落保护性建设制度，划出"五道红线"，对村内卫生保洁，村民文明礼仪、野生动物保护等提出明确要求，村容村貌发生翻天覆地的变化，生态环境不断改善。

3. 促进文旅融合

内冲瑶族村以市场为导向，以政策为牵引，以种植养殖业与旅游产业融合发展为重点，因地制宜，精准施策，大力发展优势特色产业，着力打造一批采摘园和示范基地，实现四季有花、田里有瓜、树上有果、园中有药，坚持文化特色、产业发展、农民增收和旅游发展结合，打造美丽乡村。

成效

如今的内冲瑶族村群山环抱，古井、神台、梯地等瑶族历史遗迹随处可见，古瑶文化气息扑面而来。吃农家饭、住萌萌屋、赏民俗演艺、登山踏青、吸氧润肺……越来越多的游客来药姑山古瑶村景区旅游打卡，一个名不见经传的小山村逐渐转变为"网红村"。截至2023年12月，内冲瑶族村累计接待游客200余万人。预计2024年全年接待游客将接近60万人。

该村共带动村民 300 余人从事演艺、保洁、民宿餐饮等涉旅行业，村民人均从旅游业中获得年收入近 30000 元。内冲瑶族村先后获评国家 4A 级旅游景区、中国传统村落、中国美丽休闲乡村、国家森林乡村、第三批全国乡村旅游重点村、中国古瑶文化传承展示基地。

经验与启示

1. 旅游业促进乡村经济发展

内冲瑶族村通过开发农家乐、民宿、农产品深加工等旅游产品，为村民提供就业机会，促进村民增收。同时旅游业的发展带动了相关产业链的发展，如农产品销售、交通运输、文化创意等，形成乡村经济的良性循环。通过旅游业的发展，乡村实现资源转化，促进乡村经济的繁荣。

2. 旅游业促进乡村文化传承和保护

乡村地区拥有丰富的传统文化和历史遗迹，而旅游业的发展可以为这些文化资源提供展示和传承的平台。内冲瑶族村通过打造特色乡村旅游线路和景点，吸引游客前来参观和体验，促进传统文化的传播。同时，旅游业的需求也激发了乡村居民对自身文化的认同和自豪感，推动乡村文化的传统与创新相结合，实现乡村文化的活力焕发，促进了乡村文化的传承与保护。

3. 旅游业促进乡村生态保护和绿色发展

乡村地区的自然环境和生态资源，是旅游业吸引

力的重要组成部分，而旅游业的发展也需要依赖于良好的生态环境。通过发展生态旅游，游客能接触自然和农田，增加对自然生态的认知，并提高环保意识。同时，旅游业的发展带动了乡村地区的生态修复和环境治理，推动乡村绿色发展，实现乡村生态保护与经济发展的双赢。

下一步计划

内冲瑶族村将不断完善和优化旅游产业结构，提升旅游发展质量。2024 年 4 月 1 日，药姑山古瑶村景区面向大众实施免票政策。内冲瑶族村把打破"门票经济"、加快推进全域旅游目的地建设作为首要任务，顺应观光经济转向体验经济、单点旅游转向全域旅游的发展趋势，把发展模式由门票经济转向产业经济，大力发展文化休闲、沉浸式演艺体验、特色餐饮、药膳食疗康养、购物娱乐等产业。通过提档升级引流促消费和整合资源，推出瑶族特色餐饮、建立商户管理平台、村企合作打造民宿样板间等，完善景区文旅产业要素、延长游客消费时间、并增强产业的带动力；延伸吃、住、行、游、购、娱相关旅游产业链条，为游客提供差异化、有内涵的产品和服务，培育新的旅游消费热点，为本地区的经济和社会人文发展作出贡献。

2024 世界旅游联盟：旅游助力乡村振兴案例（中英文双语版）
WTA Best Practices of Rural Revitalization through Tourism 2024 (Chinese-English Bilingual Edition)

Neichong Yao Village, Tongcheng County, Xianning City, Hubei Province:

Promoting Rural Revitalization through Culture-Tourism Integration

Abstract

Neichong Yao Village of Tongcheng County, Xianning City, Hubei Province, in cooperation with Tongcheng Chengfa Junda Culture and Tourism Investment Co., Ltd., fully implements the rural revitalization strategy on all fronts. Based on local tourism resources, it integrates Yao ethnic customs, idyllic landscapes, and traditional Chinese medicine culture to create a national 4A-level scenic spot where visitors can enjoy Yao food, live in Yao-style courtyards, appreciate natural scenery and folk customs, and live a simple country life. Neichong Yao Village develops rural tourism according to local conditions, extends the industrial chain and the value chain of tourism, and diversifies the income sources to promote rural revitalization.

Challenges and Problems

Located at the foot of the famous Yaogu Mountain, Neichong Yao Village covers a total area of 13.5 square kilometers and has a population of 1,482 people. It is a traditional village and the only natural administrative village under state protection for Yao ethnic features in Hubei Province. In its effort to develop rural tourism and build a scenic area at the foot of the Yaogu Mountain, the village faces many challenges and problems. Firstly, the commercial development rush dealt a blow to traditional country life, handicraft business, and other local characteristics, and the original Yao culture was gradually diluted. Secondly, while the scenic area is operated by a tourism company, the government is responsible for its construction planning and tendering, and a lack of communication and coordination between the two results in inefficient infrastructure operation and management. Thirdly, the mechanism for interest distribution among government agencies, the tourism company, the village committee, and villagers is poorly designed, intensifying the contradictions among all parties involved, and the tourism company cannot promote its advanced management experience or give play to the advantageous business models.

Measures

1. Promoting the inheritance of Yao culture

Neichong Yao Village promotes and protects its unique and authentic Yao culture. Firstly, the relics of Dafengbang, Stone God Temple, and traditional Yao dwellings are put under conservation. Secondly, villagers with artistic talent are identified and encouraged to build up local artistic brands of the Patting Dance and the Gong and Drum Competition. Thirdly, via non-governmental academic organizations such as the Yao Culture Research Association, it strengthens communication and exchanges with Yao culture-themed societies in other places, sort out the folk customs of Yao people, and provide academic basis and reference for the study of ancient Yao culture.

2. Promoting ecologically sustainable development

Neichong Yao Village firmly believes that "lucid waters and lush mountains are invaluable assets", and works to build a beautiful countryside based on ecological conservation. It has implemented the conservation-oriented development policy for the ancient village, drawn five red lines for ecological conservation, and put forward clear requirements for environmental sanitation, civilized etiquette of villagers, and wildlife protection. As a result, the appearance of the village has completely changed, and the ecological environment has been continuously improved.

3. Promoting the integration of culture and tourism

Following the guidance of government policies, the village vigorously develops advantageous and characteristic industries in a market-oriented manner,

with a focus on the integrated development of the planting and breeding industry and the tourism industry, and by adopting targeted measures based on local conditions. It strives to build several u-pick farms and demonstration bases where flowers are booming throughout the year, in addition to all sorts of melons, fruits, and medicinal herbs. It highlights its cultural characteristics and develops local industries including tourism to increase farmers' income and build a beautiful village.

Results

Nowadays, Neichong Yao Village, still surrounded by mountains, is full of elements of ancient Yao culture, including historical relics such as ancient wells, shrines, and terraces. Here visitors can enjoy country food, live in characteristic homestays, enjoy folk performances, hike mountains, or just relax and breathe in the fresh air... As more and more tourists come, the once little-known mountainous village has gradually established its reputation as a popular destination on social platforms. Till December 2023, Neichong Yao Village had received more than two million tourists, and it is expected to receive nearly 600,000 tourists in 2024 alone. The tourism industry has created, directly and indirectly, more than 300 local jobs, such as performing arts, sanitation, homestay, and catering, and increased the villagers' income by nearly 30,000 yuan per person. Neichong Yao Village has been rated as a national 4A-level scenic spot, the Chinese Traditional Village, the Beautiful Leisure Village of China, a National Forest Village, among the third batch of the National Key Village for Rural Tourism Development, and a Display Base for Ancient Yao Cultural Heritage of China.

Experience and Inspirations

1. Promote rural economic development through tourism

Neichong Yao Village creates employment opportunities and raises farmers' income by developing tourism products such as farm stays, homestays, and deep processing of agricultural products. At the same time, the booming tourism industry has stimulated the development of related industrial chains, such as agricultural product sales, transportation, and the cultural and creative industry, forming a virtuous cycle of rural economy. The development of tourism has capitalized on local resources and promoted the development of the rural economy.

2. Promote the inheritance and conservation of rural culture through tourism

Rural areas are rich in traditional culture and have many historical sites, and the tourism industry can provide a platform for displaying and inheriting these cultural resources. Neichong Yao Village attracts tourists with its characteristic rural tourism routes and attractions and promotes its traditional culture at the same time. Meanwhile, the arrival of tourists has also enhanced the villagers' identity with and pride in local culture, stimulated them to preserve and innovate in the traditional culture, breathed life into the rural culture, and promoted its inheritance and protection.

3. Promote rural ecological conservation and green development through tourism

The natural environment and ecological resources in rural areas are a major magnet for tourists, and the development of tourism also depends on a good ecological environment. The eco-tourism industry can lead tourists close to nature and farmland, increase their understanding of natural ecology, and raise their environmental awareness. At the same time, the development of tourism has driven the ecological restoration and environmental governance of rural areas and promoted their green development, leading to a win-win situation of ecological conservation and economic development.

Plans

Neichong Yao Village will continue to improve the composition of the tourism industry for higher-quality development. On April 1, 2024, the Ancient Yao Village Scenic Area of Yaogu Mountain officially launched the free admission policy. By giving up on

the ticket revenue, Neichong Yao Village accelerates to build the whole village into a tourist destination, which is its No.1 priority. Following the tourism development trend of shifting focus from sightseeing to experiential activities, from fixed-point tourism to all-area-advancing tourism, Neichong Yao Village has shifted from the ticket economy to the industrial economy, and is vigorously developing cultural and leisure, immersive performing arts experience, characteristic catering, herbal cuisines for health preservation, shopping, and entertainment industries. By upgrading the facilities to boost consumption and consolidating resources, it will launch traditional Yao dishes, establish a merchant management platform, and jointly build model homestays with enterprises, to add more content to the tourism industry, keep the consumers longer, and better stimulate the development of related industries. It will extend the industrial chains of catering, accommodation, travel, sightseeing, shopping, and entertainment, provide tourists with differentiated products and services with local characteristics, cultivate new tourism consumption hotspots, and contribute to local economic, social, and cultural development.

2024 世界旅游联盟：旅游助力乡村振兴案例（中英文双语版）
WTA Best Practices of Rural Revitalization through Tourism 2024（Chinese-English Bilingual Edition）

黑龙江省齐齐哈尔市铁锋区查罕诺村：
推进旅游高质量发展，构建宜居宜业美丽新乡村

摘　要

在乡村振兴的实践和探索过程中，黑龙江省齐齐哈尔市铁锋区查罕诺村克服了资源和资金等困难，创造性开发休闲旅游景点，塑造乡村旅游名片。如今，查罕诺村已经发展成为集观光度假、生态保护、农事体验、乡土美食于一体的乡村旅游目的地，走出了一条乡村振兴的特色之路。

挑战与问题

查罕诺村辖查罕诺、哈拉马、东三家子三个自然屯，全村总人口1430人，辖区面积23.8平方千米。查罕诺村交通便利，水源丰富，土地肥沃，草原广袤，有着得天独厚的乡村旅游自然资源，有利于发展乡村休闲旅游业。随着乡村旅游发展规模的不断增大，查罕诺村面临着许多困境。一是乡村旅游发展建设用地供给不足的问题日益凸显，旅游开发难度大；二是招商引资难度大，效果不明显；三是乡村旅游人才匮乏，对旅游产品开发、经营管理、市场营销等缺乏了解。

措施

1. 加快配套设施建设

查罕诺村为扩大旅游业规模，带动村域经济发展，增加新亮点，一是建设了水上公园南湖金三角花岛，花岛的三面栽植花开50000株，并修建微型仿古长城和6个龙头喷泉；二是修建了水上烧烤长廊；三是陆续开设了56家农家乐，初步完善了产业体系，为游客提供休闲、游乐、饮食、度假一条龙服务，让游客吃得满意、住得舒服、玩得开心。

2. 打造休闲旅游景点

2012年，查罕诺村投资500万元建设村西水上公园。水上公园包括人工湖水面面积500亩，陆岛面积15亩。岛上修有仿古式木制防腐二层凉亭、铁质凉亭、长廊，水面上架设有九曲桥、风雨桥，湖边种植了各种花草树木。2015年以后，水面上逐步增设"水战船"、竹排、快艇、水上碰碰船、水上自行车、水上闯关等水上游乐项目。同时，水上公园还开发了10000平方米的游玩区，包含76项游乐设施，建有各种热门游玩项目，如网红桥、网红秋千、七彩滑道、碰碰车、滑世界等，深受游客喜爱，景点游客络绎不绝。

3. 打造乡村特色名片

查罕诺村利用自然资源优势，建设具有农村特色、体现古朴农村气息的农家乐56家。农家乐没有山珍海味，只有溜达鸡、野生鱼、田园菜，厨师将健康、绿色、安全的原材料精心烹饪成美味佳肴。农家乐的老板们热情周到，营造出温馨的氛围，让顾客感受到舒适和惬意。农家乐成为查罕诺村的特色名片。

成效

自 2010 年起，查罕诺村逐年开发建设乡村休闲旅游产业，经过 10 多年的发展，现在乡村休闲旅游产业初具规模，取得了较好的经济效益。如今，查罕诺村的乡村旅游从业人员达到 180 人，年接待游客 30 万人，年旅游收入 800 万元。村民通过出售自家农产品包括蔬菜、水果、溜达鸡、大鹅、野生鱼、河蟹等，实现了超过 80 万元的收入。村集体累计增收 230 万，每年村民人均增收超 3000 元。乡村旅游业的发展不仅增强了村集体经济，也使村民走上了致富之路。近年来，查罕诺村获得了多项荣誉称号，先后被评为国家 3A 级旅游景区、全国乡村旅游重点村、中国美丽休闲乡村、全国文明村镇和"一村一品"示范村镇等。

经验与启示

1. 突出科学规划

查罕诺村的村党总支、村委会把乡村旅游建设工作当作头等大事来抓，建立了"政府指导，村屯主导，全民参与"的乡村旅游建设发展机制。乡村旅游工作按照规划提出的工作思路和预定的工作目标任务顺利推进，取得较好的效果。

2. 强化服务意识

查罕诺村注重提升旅游业经营者的服务意识，并强调遵守法律法规和规范经营的重要性，热情接待和服务来村观光的游客，展现文明乡村的良好风貌，做大做好娱乐、休闲、食宿、度假旅游品牌，推动乡村旅游业的发展。

3. 加强管理力度

查罕诺村强化旅游市场规范化管理，推进旅游行业诚信体系、标准体系、管理体系建设。一是通过正面引导，积极营造旅游业发展的良好氛围，提升查罕诺村的知名度，并塑造良好的整体形象；二是强化乡村旅游点的安全设施建设，明确安全责任人员，制定安全管理制度，加强对乡村旅游点的安全督查；三是加强卫生管理，制定环境卫生公约，设专门保洁员，创造良好的公共卫生环境。

下一步计划

一是开发"扎龙硕果系列大米""碧水湖畔粘豆包""查罕诺有机大米""查罕诺村农户有机蔬菜、瓜果""查罕诺有机鱼"等特色农副产品；二是围绕争创国家 4A 级旅游景区的目标，加大投资，进行高起点的查罕诺村景观节点开发、建设及生态保护；三是按照新农村"美丽家园"的标准，建立长效管理机制，坚持长效治理，落实美丽休闲乡村建设工作任务。

Chahannuo Village, Tiefeng District, Qiqihar City, Heilongjiang Province:
Promoting High-Quality Tourism Development and Building a Beautiful, Attractive Village to Live and Work in

Abstract

  In the pursuit of rural revitalization, Chahannuo Village of Tiefeng District, Qiqihar City, Heilongjiang Province, has overcome the resource and financing challenges, developed leisure tourist attractions, and established its reputation as a rural destination that offers tourists and holidaymakers a picturesque landscape, a sound ecological environment, farming experience, and delicious country food, embarking on the road of rural revitalization with its characteristics.

Challenges and Problems

Chahannuo Village has jurisdiction over three natural villages: Chahannuo, Halama, and Dongsanjiazi, with a population of 1,430 and an area of 23.8 square kilometers. It has convenient access to transport, abundant water sources, fertile land, and vast grassland — all are unique natural resources for developing the rural leisure tourism industry. With the continuous expansion of the scale of rural tourism development, Chahannuo Village faces many difficulties. Firstly, the undersupply of land for rural tourism development has become increasingly prominent, making it difficult to develop tourism. Secondly, investment promotion is difficult, with no obvious effect. Thirdly, there is a lack of rural tourism professionals who know how to develop, operate, and promote tourism products.

Measures

1. Accelerating the construction of supporting facilities

To expand the scale of tourism, drive economic development, and create more attractions, Chahannuo Village has built the Golden Triangle Flower Island on the South Lake of the Water Park, with 50,000 flowers planted on three sides of the island, in addition to a miniature Great Wall and six dragon-head fountains. There is also a water barbecue promenade. Moreover, 56 farm stays have been opened in succession. The tourism industry has been initially improved, offering one-stop services for tourists ranging from leisure, amusement, catering, and holidaymaking to guarantee a comfortable, enjoyable stay in the village.

2. Creating more leisure tourist attractions

In 2012, Chahannuo Village invested 5 million yuan to build the Water Park in the west of the village, including an artificial lake with a water surface area of 500 *mu* and an island area of 15 *mu*. On the island covered with all sorts of flowers and trees, there is an antique-style wooden antiseptic two-story pavilion, an iron pavilion, a gallery, a zigzag bridge, and an all-weather bridge across the water. After 2015, more water amusement facilities were added, including "water blazers", bamboo rafts, speedboats, water bumper boats, water bicycles, and a water obstacle course. A 10,000-square-meter playground has also been added, including 76 amusement facilities for a variety of popular programs, including the photogenic bridge, swings and colored slides, bumper cars, and the Slide World. These programs are beloved by tourists, attracting an endless stream of them.

3. Highlighting rural characteristics

Making use of its advantageous natural resources, Chahannuo Village has opened 56 farm stays with rural characteristics and simplicity, which offer no rare delicacies, but free-range chicken, wild fish, and backyard vegetables. With these healthy, green, safe ingredients, delicious dishes, hospitality, and a comfortable living environment, the farm stays have become the characteristic magnet of Chahannuo Village.

Results

Since 2010, Chahannuo Village has been developing the rural leisure tourism industry, which, more than 10 years on, has begun to take shape and generated considerable economic benefits. At present, the tourism industry hires 180 people, receives 300,000 tourists, and earns 8 million yuan a year. Villagers have earned more than 800,000 yuan from selling their agricultural products, including vegetables, fruits, free-range chicken, geese, wild fish, and river crabs. The income of the village collective has increased by 2.3 million yuan and the per capita income of the villagers by more than 3,000 a year. The village collective and villagers alike have benefited from tourism development, which has strengthened the village collective economy and enriched the villagers. In recent years, Chahannuo Village has won several honorary titles, including the national 3A-level scenic spot, the National Key Village for Rural Tourism Development, the Beautiful Leisure Village of China, the National Civilized Village/Town, and the Demonstration Village/Town for the "One Village, One Product" Initiative.

Experience and Inspirations

1. Highlight scientific planning

The general Party branch and the village committee of Chahannuo Village promote tourism development as a top priority and have established a mechanism that features government guidance, the principal roles of villages, and the participation of all villagers. The tourism work has been smoothly carried out per the plan and toward the objectives, achieving good results.

2. Raise the service awareness

Chahannuo Village strengthens tourism operators' awareness of service and compliant

operations, warmly receives and serves tourists, and embodies the good features of a civilized village in the course. It works to build up brands of entertainment, leisure, accommodation, and holidaymaking, and promote the development of rural tourism.

3. Strengthen management

Chahannuo Village strengthens the standardized management of the tourism market and works to build the integrity system, standards system, and management system of the tourism industry. The first is to actively create a good environment for the development of tourism, enhance Chahannuo's popularity, and create a good overall image. The second is to improve safety facilities at tourist attractions, appoint safety personnel, formulate safety management policies and rules, and strengthen safety supervision at tourist attractions. The third is to strengthen sanitation management, formulate environmental sanitation and public health conventions, appoint cleaning staff, and create a good public health environment.

Plans

Firstly, it will develop characteristic agricultural and sideline products, such as "ZhalongShuoguo Rice", "Bishui Lakeside Sticky Bean Bun", "Chahannuo Organic Rice", "Chahannuo Organic Vegetables, Melons and Fruits" and "Chahannuo Organic Fish". Secondly, while striving for the status of the national 4A-level scenic spot, it will increase investment, develop more high-quality attractions, and improve the ecological environment. Thirdly, it will establish a long-term management mechanism following the criteria of a "beautiful homeland" for the village, adhere to long-term governance, and truly build Chahannuo into a beautiful leisure village.

广东省广州市花都区塱头村：
文化振兴助力古村蝶变

摘 要

2021年，广东省广州市花都区政府与唯品会签订塱头乡村振兴项目战略合作协议，创新实施"政府＋企业＋村集体"的合作模式，以古村落文化振兴为切入点，探索农村高质量发展新路径，打造实现共同富裕的可持续模式。合作企业公益性投入超2亿元，引进国内顶级规划团队做保护性规划，建成春阳台艺术文化中心、"和春住"精品民宿、"心画中国"沉浸式光影艺术展、塱那头草地、市集商铺等多元化业态设施，推动塱头文化和产业双振兴。2023年，塱头村入选广东省首批"百千万工程"典型村，政企村合作的"塱头模式"也入选广东省"千企帮千镇，万企兴万村"典型案例。

挑战与问题

塱头村位于广州市花都区炭步镇，是一个拥有超过七百年历史的科甲古村，也是广州市仅有的两座国家级历史文化名村之一。塱头村系统地保留了"耕读传家"的文化传统，保存着完整的明清青砖建筑逾300座，村中还有20多座祠堂书室，与古代民居一起组成了占地约6平方千米的气势恢宏的古建筑群，堪称岭南宗祠与民居博物馆。塱头村有着辉煌的历史和深厚的文化底蕴，但多年也面临发展困境。一是古村"空心化"制约发展，二是古村的活化利用未形成可持续发展的模式。在推进乡村振兴的过程中，塱头村需要以文化为发力点，充分利用区位及历史文化优势寻找到适合自身的振兴之路。

措施

1. 保护与传承并举

春阳台艺术文化中心位于塱头村村口，总面积8602平方米，集岭南风貌、乡村特色、现代气息于一体，融合了文博展馆、藏书楼、善本室、阅览室、剧场与艺博活化等多样空间，在充分尊重地方文化的基础上，为古村的多元文化活动提供全新场所。"和春住"民宿作为岭南乡居新体验的亮点，总面积约3100平方米，共包含21座独栋院落，这些院落全部改建自古村旧屋，在保持民居"三间两廊"布局的基础上，修缮原有民居的青砖肌理、瓦作纹样，修旧如旧，并运用现代技术进行了结构加固、基础设施升级，在确保风貌原真性的同时，打造符合现代居住需求的高品质精品民宿，体现活化保护。

2. 文化与产业并重

一是打造聚焦塱头历史与传统的村落常展，包括"太阳永照"，展示塱头人家的安居与乐业；"与道大适"，展示中国读书人的安身与立命；"奕叶"，展示塱头古村的传承往事等。二是规划发展露营营地、古村展览、文化市集等业态。利用闲置零散土地改造形成超3万平方米的公共绿地，打造了一个传统文化、民间艺术与现代潮流充分融合的综合性户外园区，为塱头项目提供多元化场景的可观、可玩、可赏的度假休闲区。三是整合古村落、农业园区、精品民宿、乡村绿道等资源，完善道路交通、休闲憩、旅游公厕、停车场等公共基础设施，着力打造独具文化传承底蕴的产学研一体化文旅目的地和乡村振兴新引擎。

3. 品牌与渠道并行

充分发挥唯品会企业平台优势，联合多方力量组建新媒体团队，构建全渠道的宣传矩阵，共同打造塱头文化IP。一是打造特色文旅活动，与广州画院、广州雕塑院联合举办"晴耕雨读"乡村振兴作品展系列活动，开展美术、书法、雕塑等各类艺术展、大咖讲座50多场次。联合政府举办炭步镇首届村居美丽乡音PK赛，各渠道传播量近1000万人次，提高古村

美誉度、知名度。二是利用微信视频公众号、抖音号，搭建群众身边的宣传平台，对塱头古村音乐会、主题市集、艺文展集、灯光秀等系列活动进行全方位、多层次正面宣传，提高塱头古村知名度。

成效

文化浸润乡土，奋斗谱写未来。塱头村以文化振兴为项目总体设计基调，延续岭南文脉。通过政企村联手，深挖古村落文化资源，与现代潮流充分融合打造独具文化底蕴的IP，让乡韵"活"起来，让文化传承生生不息。自项目启动以来，已带动200多个就业岗位；古村周末客流量由原来的日均200—300人提升至目前的日均7000人，而且还在持续上升，该项目有望带动村集体年收入和村民人均年收入持续增加。

经验与启示

1. 文化资源为乡村振兴"铸魂"

文化是传统村落得以传承延续的核心和灵魂。塱头村诗礼传家、耕读文化气息浓厚，是中国农耕文明的文化标本。塱头乡村振兴项目以文化立魂，围绕塱头村"耕读传家"的文化内核，溯源古村发展脉络，让文化遗产回归生活，激发古村保护与发展的内生动力。

2. 创新模式为乡村振兴"强基"

塱头村创新实施"政府+企业+村集体"三方

同频发力的合作模式。当地政府主动跟进项目建设，争取各级财政资金2亿元以上，完善基础配套设施。唯品会进行公益性投入，负责项目整体规划设计建设与运营，无偿投入公益资金超2亿元，全部收入用于回馈村民及乡村振兴事业发展。村民积极参与共治共建，塱头村与广东省唯品会慈善基金会共同成立公司，负责项目运营管理，创新项目消费业态，培养塱头村自发"造血"能力。

3. 旅游载体为乡村振兴"引流"

围绕游客需求、市场变化，塱头乡村振兴项目持续发力，提质扩容打造炭步文化IP，擦亮塱头村特色文旅品牌。利用"互联网+"做好古村推介，关注文旅热点爆点，举办更多古村特色文旅体活动，以活动为媒，引流聚客，凝聚人气，推动古村旅游体验升级。

下一步计划

下一步塱头村将继续坚持文化引领、公益赋能的理念，以文化振兴为笔，绘就乡村振兴新图景。一是与省、市、区教育局及中小学合作，开展青少年研学活动。通过与中山大学等高校联动，重点打造新耕读研学基地。二是推进建设富有岭南文化特色的商业区二期，着力丰富塱头村吃、住、行、娱、游、购、学全业态，努力将其打造成"最传统·最活力"且具有文化传承底蕴的文旅新地标。

Langtou Village, Huadu District, Guangzhou City, Guangdong Province:

Transforming the Ancient Village through Cultural Revitalization

Abstract

In 2021, the Huadu District Government of Guangzhou City, Guangdong Province, signed a strategic cooperation agreement with vip.com on the rural revitalization project in Langtou Village. The project adopts the "government + enterprise + village collective" cooperation model and starts with cultural revitalization, to explore a new path for high-quality rural development and a sustainable model for common prosperity. The company vip.com has invested more than 200 million yuan in charitable funds, brought a top-tier planning team in the country to plan the village's conservation-oriented development, and built diverse business facilities, including the Chunyangtai Arts and Cultural Centre, the "Hechun Stay" boutique homestay, the "Painting China" immersive light show, the Langnatou Lawn, and the marketplace, to promote cultural and industrial revitalization in Langtou Village. In 2023, Langtou Village was voted among the first batch of typical villages of the "High-Quality Development of Villages, Townships and Counties" initiative in Guangdong. The "Langtou Model" of government-enterprise-village cooperation was also selected as a "Best Practice for Enterprise Assistance to Villages and Towns" in the province.

Challenges and Problems

Located in Tanbu Town, Langtou Village has a history of more than 700 years and was known for its excellent performance in the imperial exams in ancient China. It is also one of the only two national historical and cultural villages in Guangzhou City. Langtou Village systematically retains the cultural tradition that values both farming and scholarship. There are more than 300 well-preserved Blue bricks buildings of Ming and Qing Dynasties, and more than 20 ancestral halls and study rooms; together with ancient dwellings, they form a magnificent ancient building complex covering an area of about 6 square kilometers, making it a museum of Lingnan-style ancestral halls and residential museum. Despite its glorious history and profound cultural heritage, Langtou Village has been troubled by the following two constraints for many years. Firstly, it is too hollow to develop. Secondly, the current way of resource utilization and development is not sustainable. To promote rural revitalization, Langtou Village needs to start with culture and make full use of its location, and historical and cultural advantages to find its path to revitalization.

Measures

1. Attaching equal attention to both conservation and inheritance

Chunyangtai Arts and Cultural Centre is located at the village entrance, with a total area of 8,602 square meters. This modernist Lingnan-style building with rural characteristics includes an exhibition hall, a library, a rare-book room, a reading room, a theater, and a cultural and creative zone. It gives the village a new place for hosting colorful cultural activities with full respect for local culture. The "Hechun Stay" homestay covers a total area of about 3,100 square meters and consists of 21 stand-alone courtyards, which are all repurposed from old houses in the village. They kept the original layout of three rooms and two hallways and restored the original patterns of blue bricks and tiles as they were. Moreover, modern technology was employed to reinforce the structure and upgrade the infrastructure. While retaining the authentic style, the boutique homestay provides all sorts of conveniences of modern life to meet the needs of guests, thus protecting the old building while giving it a new life.

2. Attaching equal attention to cultural and industrial development

Firstly, permanent exhibitions were staged on the history and traditions of Langtou Village, including one dedicated to the peaceful and happy life in the village, one to the village's scholarly tradition, and one to the village's history. Secondly, camping sites, exhibitions, and cultural markets were developed. More than 30,000 square meters of public green space was created on the once idle scattered land to serve as a comprehensive outdoor park that brings together traditional culture, folk art, and modern trends, and a resort and leisure area with diversified scenes to appreciate and play in. Thirdly, resources such as the ancient village, agricultural parks, boutique home stays, and rural greenways are consolidated, and public infrastructure such as roads, leisure and recreation facilities, tourist toilets, and parking lots is improved in the hope of building Langtou Village into a tourist destination with unique cultural heritage and into a new engine for rural revitalization.

3. Attaching equal attention to brands and channels

Giving full play to the platform advantages of vip.com, Langtou Village has formed a new media team and built an omnichannel publicity matrix with multiple parties to jointly build up the cultural IP of Langtou Village. Firstly, characteristic cultural and tourism events were organized. In cooperation with the Guangzhou Academy of Fine Arts and the Guangzhou Sculpture Academy, it co-launched a series of exhibitions on fine arts, calligraphy, and sculpture, and more than 50 lectures by the master artists. It also jointly held the first singing competition in Tanbu with the town government, which attracted nearly 10 million exposures via various channels and improved Langtou's reputation and popularity. Secondly, it has opened public accounts on WeChat Channels and Douyin to reach a larger audience and has covered the village's activities, such as concerts, theme market fairs, art and cultural exhibitions, and light shows from various angles and on various levels, to enhance the village's visibility.

Results

Culture nourishes the soil and hard work writes the future. Langtou Village focuses on cultural revitalization in overall project planning to carry forward the Lingnan culture. Through cooperation with local governments and vip.com, it has dug deep into its cultural resources and fully integrated them

with modern trends to develop unique cultural IPs to enliven and pass the rural culture down. Since its launch, the project has created more than 200 jobs; the weekend visitor flow has increased from 200-300 per day to 7,000 per day and is still rising. The annual income of the village collective and the per capita annual income of the villagers are also expected to rise continuously.

Experience and Inspirations

1. Forge the soul of villages with cultural resources

Culture is the core and soul of traditional villages. Langtou Village, with its long tradition of valuing both farming and scholarship, is a living example of Chinese farming civilization. The rural revitalization project in Langtou Village focuses on the soul-forging role of culture, traces the development history of the village with a focus on its farming and scholarship tradition, places the cultural heritage in real-life scenes, and stimulates the village's inner drive for conservation and development.

2. Strengthen the foundation for rural revitalization with new models

Langtou Village innovatively implements the tripartite cooperation model of "government + enterprise + village collective". The local government took the initiative to follow up on the project's progress, secured more than 200 million yuan of financial funds from various levels, and improved basic support facilities. Vip.com, responsible for the overall planning, design, construction, and operation of the project, has invested more than 200 million yuan of charitable funds to give back to the villagers and support rural revitalization. The villagers actively participate in the co-governance and project

development. Langtou Village and Guangdong Vipshop Philanthropic Foundation established a joint venture to take charge of project operation and management, introduce new consumption scenes, and help the villagers develop skills needed for development.

3. Attract crowds to rural areas through tourism development

Focusing on the needs of tourists and market changes, the project team continues to improve the quality and expand the capacity of service, develop the cultural IPs of Tanbu, and build up Langtou's reputation as a characteristic tourist village. They use "Internet +" to promote the village and follow the hot trends of the cultural and tourism industries. Accordingly, more cultural, tourism, and sports activities with local characteristics have been held in Langtou Village and attracted crowds to the village, which in turn helped improve the visitor experience.

Plans

In the next step, Langtou Village will continue to leverage the guiding role of culture and the empowering role of philanthropic forces and draw a new picture of rural revitalization with cultural revitalization. Firstly, it will cooperate with provincial-, municipal- and district-level education bureaus and primary and secondary schools to host study tour activities. It will work with Sun Yat-sen University and other universities to build a study tour base. Secondly, it will continue to develop the second phase of the commercial district with distinct cultural characteristics of Lingnan, introduce catering, accommodation, transportation, travel, entertainment, sightseeing, shopping, and educational businesses, and strive to build it into a new cultural and tourism landmark that is both traditional and dynamic.

河南省信阳市光山县东岳村：
文化产业特派员制度创新助力乡村振兴

摘　要

　　2022年7月，河南省信阳市光山县东岳村与杭州余粮乡创文化旅游发展有限责任公司成功配对，打造"东岳美好·刚刚好"乡村建设品牌。在"文化产业特派员"余粮乡创团队各种"金点子"的加持下，东岳村瞄准文旅消费新热点，在乡村培育"年轻态、新玩法"的文旅新业态，拓展文化和旅游消费新项目。东岳乡村旅游品牌热度持续提升，逐步发展成为大别山知名旅游目的地，旅游市场"溢出效应"明显，有效带动乡村经济发展，扶贫成效显著，走出了一条制度创新引领的乡村振兴之路。

挑战与问题

东岳村文化底蕴丰厚,村内有花鼓戏、地灯戏、皮影戏、狮子舞、旱船舞、竹马舞等国家、省、市级非遗物质文化遗产12项;传统村落核心区方店组与檀树嘴、李庄、村文化中心有机融合,形成旅游景区,凸显生态观光、农业体验、民俗文化等特色旅游景观;毛尖茶、土鸡蛋、麻鸭蛋、蜂蜜、糍粑、印字馍等土特产享誉中原。但在旅游带动经济发展过程中,东岳村仍然存在以下问题。一是发展思路不清晰。东岳村没有形成产业发展共识,乡村旅游扶贫思路不明确,理念不清楚,引导不到位,产业联动发展机制没有形成。二是发展环境急需改善提升。东岳村旅游基础设施不完善,存在环卫设施不足、旅游标识不规范、旅游厕所不达标等问题。三是旅游产品缺乏竞争力。旅游产品低端化、同质化问题严重,效益不佳,开发方式粗放、急功近利、模式单一。

措施

1. 形成共识联动

光山县全力实施好"文化产业特派员"制度,坚持县委书记、县长"双挂帅"制度,四大家领导齐上阵,成立由县委书记任政委、县长任指挥长的光山县"文化产业特派员"项目建设指挥部,强化实践指导,推动工作落地见效。明确形成"一个项目团队由一名县处级领导牵头、一个县直单位负责、一个专班服务、一个平台公司参与"的工作机制,项目建设指挥部坚持周例会制度,研究解决相关问题,确保项目持续健康发展,初步探索出"制度创新、聚合协同、示范引领"的文化产业赋能乡村振兴的新路径。

2. 完善基础设施

东岳村余粮乡创团队将村庄整治与绿色生态家园建设紧密结合,同步推进环境整治和生态建设。一是建设杨湾大桥和停车场;二是打造美丽景观示范带,打造花丛绿化植被和彩灯夜景;三是发展农业种植、特色养殖、非遗传承和文化旅游等。东岳村因地制宜地对当地景观进行升级改造,建设生态友好型乡村。

3. 创新产品业态

东岳村余粮乡创团队从释放产业动力、推动文化变现、激发运营魅力三个层面着力,对东岳村在地资源进行产业梳理,规划升级当地特色产业。一是融合"农业+、文旅+"的概念,对当地优质产品进行包装、设计、销售渠道等多方面的优化升级与转化运营,设计出"有盐在先""不如吃茶去"等特色农文创产品,

在中国义乌文化和旅游产品交易博览会上展出,并在"余粮农集"小程序上架,销售辐射全国。二是创新打造出东岳村冷酷火锅、小余儿蓝莓园、无动力乐园等新潮旅游业态,为游客提供更多沉浸式新体验,让游客能够留下来、住下来。

成效

东岳村余粮乡创团队带领乡村走上振兴之路。截至 2024 年,带动贫困人口户数为 50 户,带动贫困人口为 100 余人,户均增收金额为 2000 元,真正实现了旅游扶贫。"文化产业特派员"余粮乡创团队通过盘活乡村文化资源,引导群众参与到乡村发展中,实现了资源共享、利益共赢。余粮乡创团队与东岳村合作打造的"共富工坊",通过开发伴手礼、孵化产业工坊等方式,让村民、村集体深度参与。在增加就业、带动相关产业发展的同时,也逐步培养出懂农村、爱农村的"守村人"。经过多年的发展,东岳村成功被评为中国首批传统村落、国家旅游试点村、中国美丽休闲乡村、河南省乡村旅游特色村、河南省文化产业特色乡村、河南省历史文化名村、河南省首批乡村康养旅游示范村。

经验与启示

1. 用好政策

2022 年 3 月,文化和旅游部等六部门联合发布《关于推动文化产业赋能乡村振兴的意见》,鼓励各地结合实际,探索实施"文化产业特派员"制度,首期试点工作落地河南。河南省文化和旅游厅携手清华大学文化创意发展研究院进行体系赋能和重点帮扶,光山县成功入选为首批制度试点县之一,东岳村成为首批试点村之一。

2. 定好制度

"文化产业特派员"由县政府机构授予正式身份,由河南省文化和旅游厅乡创赋能中心统筹管理与调度,与选派村在地政府紧密合作,开发乡村闲置资产和沉睡资源,共同引领乡村唤醒文化底蕴、形成发展动能、焕发内生活力。

3. 找好特色

光山县引入杭州余粮乡创文化旅游发展有限责任公司,在东岳村找准红色之"魂",通过设计东岳村的品牌 logo,改造村容村貌,设计村吉祥物,开发文创产品,打造伴手礼,带动各种现代发展要素进入旅游产业。

下一步计划

光山县将持续以乡村振兴扛旗为目标,充分发挥县域统筹规划、资源配置作用,突出特色,改革创新,为余粮乡创等已落地的文化产业特派项目继续提供高质量伴行服务,形成可复制、可推广的典型经验做法。一是利用节假日等机会在东岳村举办各类新潮活动,吸引各地游客;二是加大农文创产品开发与销售,不断延展产业链条、加快形成集群,促进乡村产业活力越来越足;三是汲取"文化产业特派员"在东岳村的成功经验,继续在其他试点村发力,依据不同乡村的不同特点,与"文化产业特派员"加强对接,详细沟通会商,每年推动不少于 10 个文化产业特派项目落地,帮助光山县更多的乡村打造属于自己的"金名片",创造共富价值,实现可持续发展。

Dongyue Village, Guangshan County, Xinyang City, Henan Province:

Promoting Rural Revitalization with the Cultural Industry Specialist System

Abstract

In July 2022, Dongyue Village of Guangshan County, Xinyang City, Henan Province, paired up with Hangzhou Yuliang Xiangchuang Culture and Tourism Development Co., Ltd. to jointly develop a country-building brand of "Beautiful Dongyue—Just Right". The Yuliang Xiangchuang team acted as cultural industry specialists and contributed many brilliant ideas. With their help, Dongyue Village targets on the latest hot spots of cultural and tourist consumption, cultivated a new cultural and tourism business that appeals to young consumers, and expanded new cultural and tourist consumption projects. As a result, the popularity of Dongyue's rural tourism brand continues to increase, and the village has gradually developed into a well-known tourist destination in the Dabie Mountains. The tourism industry has an obvious "spillover effect", effectively driving the development of the rural economy and achieving remarkable results in poverty alleviation. Dongyue Village has embarked on a road to rural revitalization driven by institutional innovation.

Challenges and Problems

Dongyue Village has a rich cultural heritage, including 12 national-, provincial- and municipal-level intangible cultural heritage items, such as the Flower Drum Opera, Floor Lantern Opera, Shadow Puppets, Lion Dance, Dry Boat Dance, and Bamboo Horse Dance. The Fangdian Group in the core area of the traditional village, Tanshuzui, Lizhuang, and the Village Culture Center form a scenic area, highlighting characteristic landscapes, such as eco-tourism, agritourism, and folk culture. Dongyue Village is also famous for its characteristic products, including Maojian tea, native eggs, duck eggs, honey, glutinous cakes, and character-printed buns. In the process of driving economic development through tourism, however, it still faces the following problems. Firstly, the development thought was not clear. No consensus has been reached on industrial development. It lacked specific guidelines, paths, and strong guidance on how to reduce poverty through tourism development. There was no mechanism for the coordinated development of industries. Secondly, the development environment was in urgent need of improvement. Tourist infrastructure was poor, with a shortage of sanitation facilities, non-standard tourist signs, and substandard tourist toilets. Thirdly, tourism products were not competitive. Most of the tourism products were low-end, homogeneous, and not profitable. The tourism development model was extensive and lacked diversity, rushing for quick money.

Measures

1. Forming a consensus on cross-sector collaboration

Guangshan County fully implements the system of cultural industry specialists, and engages the leaders of the Party committee, the People's Congress, the People's Government, and the People's Political Consultative Conference. Guangshan County has set up the "cultural industry specialist" project headquarters with the county Party secretary as the political commissar and the county chief as the chief commander to strengthen guidance for and push ahead with related work. A working mechanism is established, with one leading division-level official, one unit directly under the county government, one service task force, and one platform company for each project team. The headquarters meets every week to discuss and solve relevant problems and ensure the sustainable and healthy development of projects. Guangshan County has initially explored a new path of empowering rural revitalization through the cultural industry based on institutional innovation, synergy and coordination, and exemplary and leading roles of the government.

2. Improving infrastructure

The Yuliang Xiangchuang team closely combines village renovation with the building of a

green eco-homeland and simultaneously promotes environmental improvement and ecological conservation. Firstly, the Yangwan Bridge and the parking lot were built. Secondly, a landscape demonstration belt was built, with flowers, trees, and grass planted and a night scene of colorful lights. Thirdly, farming, characteristic breeding, intangible cultural heritage inheritance, and cultural and tourism businesses are developed. Dongyue Village has upgraded the local landscape according to local conditions, striving to build itself into an eco-friendly village.

3. Developing new products

The Yuliang Xiangchuang team combed through Dongyue's local resources and planned the upgrade of local characteristic industries to stimulate the momentum for local industrial development, capitalize on cultural heritage, and maximize the operational effect. Firstly, following "agriculture +" and "cultural and tourism +" approaches, they optimized and upgraded the packaging, design, and sale channels of local high-quality products, and have designed characteristic salt and tea products, among other agricultural and cultural and creative products, which were exhibited at the China Yiwu Cultural and Tourism Products Trade Fair, and launched on the mini-program "Yuliang Farm Market" and sold across the country. Secondly, they have developed trendy tourism businesses such as Cool Hot Pot, the U-pick blueberry farm, and the non-powered amusement park, attracting and retaining tourists with more immersive novel experiences.

Results

The Yuliang Xiangchuang team has led Dongyue Village onto the road of revitalization. Till 2024, it has benefited more than 100 poor people from 50 poor households, and increased their income by 2,000 yuan per household, truly realizing poverty alleviation through tourism. By leveraging local cultural resources, they guided the villagers to participate in rural development and share resources and benefits. They have also jointly launched the Common Prosperity Workshop with Dongyue Village, which deeply engages villagers and the village collective in the development of souvenirs and the incubation of more business workshops. In addition to promoting employment and the development of related industries, the workshop has gradually cultivated a batch of specialists who understand and love the countryside. After years of development, Dongyue Village has been rated among the first batch of traditional villages of China, the National Pilot Tourist Village, the Beautiful Leisure Village of China, the Rural Tourism Characteristic of Henan, the Village with Characteristic Cultural Industry of Henan, the Famous Historical and Cultural Village of Henan, and the first batch of Wellness Tourism Demonstration Villages of Henan.

Experience and Inspirations

1. Leverage policy support

In March 2022, the Ministry of Culture and

Tourism and other five ministries/commissions jointly issued the *Opinions on Further Empowering Rural Revitalization with the Cultural Industry*, encouraging localities to pilot the system of cultural industry specialists in light of actual conditions; the first phase of the pilot project was launched in Henan. The Culture and Tourism Department of Henan Province joined hands with the Institute for Culture Creativity of Tsinghua University to empower the system and provide key assistance. Guangshan County became one of the first pilot counties, and Dongyue Village was one of the first pilot villages.

2. Make sound institutional arrangements

The cultural industry specialists are officially designated by the county government, administered and dispatched by the Rural Makers Empowerment Center of the Culture and Tourism Department of Henan Province. They work closely with the local government of the host village to utilize idle assets and resources, tap into local cultural heritage, form development momentum, and rejuvenate internal vitality.

3. Capture the unique features

Hangzhou Yuliang Xiangchuang Cultural and Tourism Development Co., Ltd. helped Dongyue Village identify its positioning, designed the village brand logo, improved the village appearance, designed the village mascot, and developed cultural and creative products as souvenirs, thus infusing various modern development elements into the tourism industry.

Plans

Guangshan County will continue to promote rural revitalization, give full play to the role of the county government in coordinated planning and resource allocation, highlight characteristics, and advance reform and innovation. It will continue to provide high-quality services for the cultural industry specialist projects that have been implemented, including the Yuliang Xiangchuang team, and produce best practices that can be replicated and promoted. Firstly, it will hold various trendy activities in Dongyue Village on weekends and holidays to attract tourists from all over the country. Secondly, it will strengthen the development and sales of agricultural, cultural, and creative products, continuously extend the industrial chain, accelerate the formation of clusters, and continuously stimulate the vitality of rural industries. Thirdly, it will summarize the successful experience of the cultural industry specialist project in Dongyue Village, continue to promote it to other pilot villages, and strengthen communication and consultation with the cultural industry specialists over the different characteristics of different villages. The goal is to implement no less than ten cultural industry specialist projects a year, thus helping more villages in Guangshan County develop their characteristic industries, create value for common prosperity, and achieve sustainable development.

2024世界旅游联盟：旅游助力乡村振兴案例（中英文双语版）
WTA Best Practices of Rural Revitalization through Tourism 2024（Chinese-English Bilingual Edition）

陕西省汉中市留坝县：
交旅深融合 乡村新画卷

摘 要

陕西省汉中市留坝县在习近平总书记"四好农村路"重要论述的科学指引下，构建"快进+慢游"交通网络，推动交通+旅游+产业+乡村振兴全面深度融合发展，走出了一条"两山两化"转化之路。留坝县精心打造旅游环线，彰显山水特色、促进产业融合、强化"运游"衔接，以"交通先行、促旅发展、融合反哺"的特色发展模式，真正实现了建一条路、造一片景、富一方百姓，走出一条"公路美景变致富'钱'景、闲置资产变旅游资源、人员外流变人员回流、闲余劳力变民宿管家、土特产品变旅游商品"的交旅融合乡村振兴之路。

挑战与问题

留坝县位于陕西省汉中市北部，秦岭南麓腹地，总面积1970平方千米。全县辖7个镇、1个街道办事处、73个行政村、3个社区，总人口4.2万人，全县有近一半的村曾被认定为贫困村。留坝县一直面临"绿水青山"和"金山银山"不可兼得的困扰，如何践行"两山转化"是留坝县近年来持续探索的发展命题。

措施

1. 以路为景，打造留坝旅游环线

留坝县秉承"公路也是风景"的理念，以景引路，以路为景，依托丰富的文化旅游资源"借景、造景、融景、成景"，积极打造具有旅游功能和文化特色的精品示范线——留坝旅游环线。留坝旅游环线全长171千米，道路两旁水杉、梧桐和银杏等树木遮天蔽日，五彩斑斓，如一条彩链串联起张良庙紫柏山国家4A级旅游景区、栈道水世界国家4A级旅游景区、狮子沟牧场、紫柏山国际滑雪场等众多旅游景点，同时连接秦岭最美小镇火烧店镇、营盘运动小镇等历史文化名镇，实现了对外与干线路网无缝衔接，对内与重点景区紧密联系，形成了集"生态、景观、休闲、旅游"于一体的"畅、安、绿、舒、美"旅游千里景观廊道。

2. 交旅融合，创造路衍经济新模式

留坝县依托已建成的留坝旅游环线，进一步开发营盘自行车骑行、太子岭森林穿越、老街漫游、玉皇庙乡村徒步等近400千米的秦岭游线路；建成3条县域农村公路旅游主题线路和6条旅游公路支线，将全县16个景区景点、1个历史文化名镇、5个特色小镇、8个乡村旅游区以及景观节点、公路驿站和停车港等串点成线；沿途布局精品民宿19家，房车营地7处，农家乐100余家，实现交旅深度融合发展。

3. "交通+"，铺就和美乡村致富路

一是"交通+产业"。留坝县以旅游环线为依托，带动沿线特色产业的发展，先后建成代料食用菌栽培、土鸡和蜜蜂养殖，以及核桃、板栗、中药材种植等产业基地170余个，覆盖县、镇、村的三级农村物流网络和配送服务站打通了物流服务群众的"最后一公里"。二是"交通+体育"。留侯镇营盘村结合得天独厚的自然条件及便捷的交通，高起点建设营盘足球基地，打造足球特色小镇。建成以来先后承办省、市100多项赛事，接待国家女足等300多支球队集训，在足球训练基地的基础上陆续开发了紫柏山国际滑雪场、自行车漫道、登山步道，形成了集交通、住宿、餐饮、休闲观光于一体的体旅消费链。三是"交通+智慧"。留坝县积极试点智慧公路，建立智慧综合交通运输平台，在交通旅游环线全线安装智能监控系统18个、弯道预警系统12个、电子公交站牌9个，投用共享汽车7辆、共享单车480辆，实现对旅游信息、出行服务、公路养护、路况监测、灾害预警等服务数据的共享、融合和综合利用。

成效

2023年，留坝县实现生产总值增长6.5%，城乡常住居民人均可支配收入分别增长5.4%和7.8%。全县75个村（社区）集体经济经营性收入均达15万元以上，农户年人均增收6800元。全县接待游客588.61万人次，实现综合收入33.4亿元，吸纳1700余名群众在家门口就业，获得稳定收入8000余万元。昔日的国家贫困县发展成为国家级生态示范县、

全国休闲农业与乡村旅游示范县、全国首批"绿水青山就是金山银山"（两山论）实践创新基地、健康中国·康养旅游百强县。

经验与启示

1. 公路美景变致富"钱"景

留坝县以公路为载体，精心设计推出"观秋景、赏红叶"旅游环线快旅风景道、"最美山村公路"慢旅风景道，创立"红叶节""秦岭之夜"等一批乡村旅游品牌，打造公路景观节点、沿线露营基地、房车营地，让好路景变成好风景，好风景成为好"钱"景。

2. 闲置资产变旅游资源

留坝县科学合理开发利用闲置资产，在民宿"道班·宿"取得成功的基础上，又成功推广复制了"石门道班·宿""火烧店供销社三农书院""江口粮站红色文化服务中心"等一批项目。留坝县73个村3个社区的全部闲置资产实现了盘活利用，一块块腾退旧房和宅基地化身民宿集群，一段段废弃公路建设成交通驿站，一座座闲置粮站改造成历史文化博览馆，交通助推旅游、旅游反哺交通的"留坝模式"遍地开花。

3. 人员外流变人员回流

过去，留坝县青壮劳力都选择外出务工，大学生们更是走出大山后鲜少回乡就业；如今，交通物流的便利和乡村旅游的持续火热成为乡村振兴的流量引擎，有力促进了人才招引和回流。三农问题专家温铁军、隐居乡里创始人陈长春、杭州市民宿行业协会执行会长夏雨清等42名"新村民"落户留坝，大学毕业生回乡66人，乡贤能人回乡41人，企业家入乡25人，农民工返乡852人，实现人员从"走出去"到"走进来、留下来"的转变，乡村振兴更具生机和活力。

4. 闲余劳力变民宿管家

留坝县的交通旅游环线民宿提供了管家、主理人、农特产品销售、餐饮等多种就业岗位，农村闲余劳动力进入旅游服务行业。留坝县政府实施的"四个一百"工程（即打造一百个民宿，培训一百个管家，提升一百个农家乐，提供一百个就业岗位），新发展民宿172家，改造提升农家乐122家，培育民宿管家140人，带动创业1095人，培训"土专家""田秀才"800余人次，培育乡土人才2100余人。

5. 土特产品变旅游商品

留坝县在民宿、公路集市、旅游景点设置土特产品展示销售专区，深挖"土"，做足"特"，做大"产"。村集体对香菇、木耳、棒棒蜜、西洋参等传统农产品进行深加工和精包装，让土特产从山里田里走向四面八方。2023年，销售当地群众土特产品8000余万元，村集体收入增长1100余万元。

下一步计划

一是加快实施陕南交通旅游山水画卷项目，深度挖掘吃、住、行、游、购、娱等旅游元素，并与道路交通发展深度融合，在山水画卷沿线培育一批特色旅游小镇、美丽乡村、精品民宿等新业态，全力推动县域经济高质量发展。二是深入挖掘试点工作中的经验和做法，打造一批特色鲜明、示范性强、可供借鉴的典型案例和成功模式，为交通事业发展贡献"留坝经验"。

Liuba County, Hanzhong City, Shaanxi Province:

Deep Integration of Transportation and Tourism for New Rural Landscape

Abstract

Liuba County, located in Hanzhong City, Shaanxi Province, has followed the scientific guidance of General Secretary Xi Jinping's important remarks on "Four Good Rural Roads" to develop a "fast-in, slow-tour" transportation network. This approach has promoted comprehensive and deep integration of transportation, tourism, industry, and rural revitalization, creating a transformative path of "Two Mountains and Two Transformations". Liuba County has meticulously developed a tourist loop that highlights natural beauty, promotes industrial integration, and strengthens the connection between transportation and tourism. By prioritizing transportation to drive tourism development and integrating it to support overall development, Liuba County has successfully established a unique model where road building enhances the fame of a scenic area and enriches the local people. This approach has transformed scenic roads into "money-making" roads, turned idle assets into tourism resources, reversed population outflow, and transformed idle labor into homestay managers. It has also converted local specialties into tourist products, paving the way for rural revitalization through transportation and tourism integration.

Challenges and Problems

Liuba County is located in the northern part of Hanzhong City, Shaanxi Province, in the heart of the southern slopes of the Qinling Mountains, with a total area of 1,970 square kilometers. The county comprises 7 towns, 1 subdistrict, 73 administrative villages, and 3 communities, with a total population of 42,000. Nearly half of the villages in Liuba County were registered as impoverished. The county has long grappled with the dilemma of choosing between "protecting lucid waters and lush mountains" and "earning profits". The challenge of translating ecological assets into economic prosperity has been a key focus for Liuba County's development efforts in recent years.

Measures

1. Scenic roads and Liuba tourism loop

Liuba County adheres to the concept that "roads are also scenery", using scenery to guide road construction and creating roads as scenic attractions. Leveraging its rich cultural and tourism resources, the county has developed a boutique demonstration route with both tourism functions and cultural characteristics—the Liuba Tourism Loop. The 171-kilometer loop, lined with trees like dawn redwoods, Chinese parasol, and ginkgoes, connects various tourist attractions such as the Zhang Liang Temple and Zibai Mountain National 4A-Level Scenic Spot, the Stilted Houses Water World National 4A-Level Scenic Spot, the Shizigou Pasture, and Zibai Mountain International Ski Resort. This route links Liuba's most beautiful historical and cultural towns, like Huoshaodian Town and Yingpan Sports Town, achieving seamless connection with major road networks and close links with key scenic spots. As a result, a "smooth, safe, green, comfortable, and beautiful" tourist corridor is built, integrating "ecology, landscape, leisure, and tourism".

2. Transportation and tourism integration

Utilizing the Liuba Tourism Loop, the county has further developed nearly 400 kilometers of Qinling Mountains tourism routes, including those for Yingpan cycling, Taiziling forest trails, old street strolls, and rural hiking at Yuhuang Temple. Three rural road tourism theme lines and six tourism road branches have been established, connecting 16 scenic spots, one historical and cultural town, five featured towns, eight rural tourism areas, scenic nodes,

roadside stations, and parking lots into a network. Along the route, 19 boutique homestays, seven RV campsites, and over 100 farm stays have been developed so that deep integration of transportation and tourism is achieved.

3. "Transportation +" has paved the way for making the countryside prosperous and beautiful

Firstly, it is "Transportation + Industry". Liuba County has leveraged the tourism loop to boost the development of industries along the way, establishing over 170 industrial bases for mushroom cultivation, chicken farming, beekeeping, and the planting of walnuts, Chinese chestnuts, and Chinese medicinal herbs. The three-tier rural logistics network, covering county, town, and village levels, has ensured last-mile logistics services. Secondly, it is "Transportation + Sports". Yingpan Village in Liuhou Town, utilizing its natural advantages and convenient transportation, has built a football base, creating a football-themed town. Since its inception, the base has hosted over 100 provincial and city-level events and welcomed more than 300 teams for training, including the national women's football team. Additionally, the development of the Zibai Mountain International Ski Resort, cycling paths, and hiking trails has formed a comprehensive sports and tourism consumption chain integrating transportation, accommodation, catering, leisure, and sightseeing. Thirdly, it is "Transportation + Smart Solutions". Liuba County has piloted smart roads by establishing an integrated smart transportation platform. Along the tourism loop, 18 intelligent monitoring systems, 12 curve warning systems, and 9 electronic bus stops have been installed. The county also offers seven shared cars and 480 shared bicycles, enabling data sharing and integration of tourism information, travel services, road maintenance, road condition monitoring, and disaster warnings.

Results

In 2023, Liuba County's GDP grew by 6.5%, with urban and rural per capita disposable income rising by 5.4% and 7.8%, respectively. The operating income of the county's 75 villages (communities) exceeded 150,000 yuan each, and the annual per capita income of farmers increased by 6,800 yuan. The county received 5.89 million tourists, generating a total income of 3.34 billion yuan and creating stable jobs for over 1,700 locals, who earned nearly 80 million yuan. The once impoverished county has changed into the National Ecological Demonstration County, the National Demonstration County for Leisure Agriculture and Rural Tourism, and one of the first National Innovation Bases for Implementing the Guiding Thought that Lucid Waters and Lush Mountains are Invaluable Assets, and one of the Top Countries for Wellness Tourism of China.

Experiences and Inspirations

1. Turning scenic roads into wealth roads

Liuba County has designed and promoted tourist routes like the "Autumn Foliage Scenic Route" and the "Most Beautiful Village Road", creating a series of rural tourism brands such as the "Red Leaf

Festival" and "Qinling Night". The county has also developed scenic road nodes, camping sites, and RV camps, transforming scenic roads into lucrative tourist attractions.

2. Turning idle assets into tourism resources

Liuba County has scientifically and rationally developed and utilized idle assets. Based on the success of the "Daoban Su" homestay, the county has successfully replicated and promoted several projects, including "Shimen Daoban Su", "Huoshaodian Supply and Marketing Cooperative Rural Academy", and "Jiangkou Grain Station Red Culture Service Center". All idle assets in the county's 73 villages and three communities have been put to use. Old houses and vacant homesteads have been transformed into clusters of homestays, abandoned roads have been turned into transportation hubs, and the once idle grain stations have been converted into historical and cultural museums. The "Liuba Model", where transportation promotes tourism and tourism, in turn, supports transportation, is flourishing.

3. Population outflow giving way to inflow

In the past, young and able-bodied workers from Liuba County chose to work outside, and college students rarely returned to their hometowns for employment. Now, convenient transportation and logistics and the continued popularity of rural tourism have become a driving force for rural revitalization, significantly attracting and retaining talent. Experts on issues relating to agriculture, rural areas, and rural people like Wen Tiejun, founder of "Yinju Township" Chen Changchun, and Hangzhou B&B Industry Association executive chairman Xia Yuqing, are among the 42 "new villagers" who have settled in Liuba County. Additionally, 66 college graduates, 41 skilled workers, 25 entrepreneurs, and 852 migrant workers have returned home, changing the outflow of people into inflow, and giving new life and vitality to rural revitalization.

4. Idle people turning into homestay managers

Liuba County has created various job opportunities in homestays along the transportation and tourism route, including roles as managers, hosts, local product salespeople, and those for catering services, thus integrating the once idle rural labor into the tourism service industry. Through the government's "Four-Hundred" project (i.e., building 100 homestays, training 100 managers, upgrading 100 farm stays, and providing 100 jobs), 172 new homestays have been developed, 122 farm stays have been upgraded, 140 homestay managers have been trained, 1,095 people have been inspired to start businesses, over 800 "local experts" have been trained, and more than 2,100 local talents have been fostered.

5. Turning local specialty products into tourism goods

Liuba County has set up dedicated areas for displaying and selling local specialty products in homestays, roadside markets, and tourist attractions. By deeply exploring the uniqueness of these products, the county has enhanced their value and expanded production. The village collectives have undertaken

deep processing and high-end packaging of traditional agricultural products such as mushrooms, black fungus, honey sticks, and American ginseng, bringing these local specialties from the mountains and fields to markets far and wide. In 2023, local specialty products generated over 80 million yuan in sales, and the village collective income grew by more than 11 million yuan.

Plans

Firstly, it is to implement the Southern Shaanxi transportation landscape project. Liuba County will further integrate tourism elements such as catering, accommodation, transportation, travel, shopping, and entertainment with road development. The county will nurture new businesses, including featured tourism towns, beautiful villages, and boutique homestays, to drive high-quality economic development. Secondly, it is to draw on and disseminate successes and experiences. Liuba County will summarize its experiences and create exemplary cases to serve as models for others, contributing "Liuba's Experience" to the advancement of the transportation industry.

2024世界旅游联盟：旅游助力乡村振兴案例（中英文双语版）
WTA Best Practices of Rural Revitalization through Tourism 2024 (Chinese-English Bilingual Edition)

四川省乐山市夹江县石堰村：
"中国纸艺第一村"的乡村振兴之路

摘　要

四川省乐山市夹江县石堰村，是一个以手工竹纸制造为支柱产业的古村落，保留了传统的村落风貌和珍贵的手工造纸技艺资源。近年来，石堰村以文化产业为引擎，推动乡村振兴，深挖"竹纸制作技艺"这一非遗资源，聚焦"纸文化、纸产业、纸旅游"的融合发展，与四川美术学院团队紧密合作，全力构建"中国纸艺第一村"。经过三年精心打造，建成夹江县博物馆群落、石堰村村史馆、枷担桥文坊街集市、大千寓居群落和传统工艺工作站等重要文化设施，"中国纸艺第一村"绽放光芒。石堰村先后获得全国"一村一品"示范村、四川最美古村落、天府旅游名村等荣誉称号，并入选首批四川传统村落名录。

挑战与问题

石堰村占地面积 7.5 平方千米，位于浅山丘陵地带，土地以石骨子土为主，耕地面积有限，村民长期以来以造纸为业。然而，随着机制纸业的迅猛发展，手工纸行业面临巨大挑战。手工纸生产周期长、成本高、市场需求有限，加之品牌推广不足，导致越来越多的造纸工匠外出谋生。截至 2021 年，石堰村常住人口减少至 800 余人，其中老年人口占据多数，农村劳动力严重短缺。同时，人口外流也导致"竹纸制作技艺"的传承出现断层。如何振兴传统手工竹纸产业，吸引青壮年劳动力回流，成为石堰村突破乡村振兴瓶颈的关键。

措施

1. 提升基础设施建设

石堰村争取各类资金约 2000 万元，用于建设和完善石堰村内外旅游环线道路 11 千米，并进行整体黑化彩化；同时投入乡村振兴资金 600 余万元，对旅游环线、纸乡风景道沿线进行美化绿化和景观节点打造，统一农房风貌。石堰村大力实施"五清"行动、"厕所革命"和"亮化工程"，新改建农村厕所 357 个，清除黑臭水体，道路两旁安装路灯 170 余盏，全面清理各类垃圾和拆除露天垃圾池，建立生活垃圾收转运处置体系。石堰村整体环境得到大幅度提升，人居环境得到全面改善，"千年纸乡"的风貌焕然一新。

2. 盘活非遗传承资源

一是立足造纸文化，全面梳理全村自然人文资源，对全村 11 处保留完好的造纸作坊和遗址进行登记保护，并投入资金 45 万元进行改造升级。二是结合石堰村的民居特色，对 52 处百年老屋进行挂牌保护，鼓励村民自觉维护老宅，最大限度修复保留老宅古迹古朴自然的原始风貌。三是引入四川美术学院优秀团队智库，将"以人为本、以文为魂、以艺为基、以纸为业"作为行动理念，全力打造"中国纸艺第一村"。通过"一馆一街两片区"的项目布局，实现非遗"竹纸制作技艺"与文旅教的深度融合，形成石堰村独特的文化旅游产业。

3. 加强人才培养与回引

石堰村推行基层治理体系和治理能力现代化，形成"村级主导、乡贤带头、群众参与"的产业发展体系，全力打造川南片区独特的"文旅村落"。石堰村培育省级"纸旅游"研学基地和国家 3A 级旅游景区，首创"文家乐"特色民宿品牌。通过举办招商推介会、外出成功人士返乡恳谈会等活动，吸引在外成功人士回乡投资建设研学基地、民宿等旅游新业态。

成效

石堰村依托"纸文化"优势，提升"纸产业"集群化水平，实施"纸旅游"功能化改造。现在，村内共有手工纸作坊 12 家，年产量达 3 万刀，产值超 3000 万元；机制纸企业 2 家，年产量达 1.5 万吨，

总产值3亿元。全村"纸文化"研学旅游相关从事人员300余名，挂牌成立"文家乐"民宿12家，2023年接待游客超20万人次，实现旅游收入超7000万元，村集体经济收入达到30万元，村民人均可支配收入增加至3.36万元。

经验与启示

石堰村再现手工技艺的价值和精神信仰，重连工艺与生活的关系网络，推动传统村落的产业转型和升级，培育积极向上的乡村人文生态，建构集产业、生态、文化和人才于一体的现代新型乡村。

1. 高位谋划

石堰村招贤引智，邀请了中国美术学院、四川美术学院、乐山师范学院等高校的专家及行业精英参与项目设计，坚持"以景带村、以村实景、景村互动"的发展理念，深入挖掘乡村生态涵养与文化传承的复合功能，实现了从粗放式向集约化的转变。

2. 精细规划

石堰村与四川美术学院深化合作，合力打造乡村博物馆模式，完整呈现"纸文化"的价值，促进"纸产业"与"纸旅游"的持续发展。通过积极推动乡村旅游的功能化改造，实现"田园变公园、农房变客房、劳作变体验"转型升级，设计推出"书画纸乡""遗产揽胜""雅致生活""古法造纸体验""田园风光"5条乡村旅游线路，创造乡村振兴的新动力。

3. 品牌塑造

石堰村积极策划并举办一系列"纸文化"特色活动，承办各类文化交流会议，如四川美术学院"文化产业赋能乡村振兴"圆桌讨论会、国家社科基金项目汇报会等，并通过纪录片《竹纸之乡 纸薄情深》、原创电影《画不投机》等形式，在央视及各大媒体平台上推广石堰村"纸文化"，提升千年纸乡的知名度与影响力。

下一步计划

石堰村将紧扣中国纸乡发展定位，以发展"纸文化""纸产业""纸旅游"为抓手，走深走实文化产业赋能乡村振兴新路径。一是全域提升智能化服务，配套乡村智慧导览系统，将重要文旅点位接入旅游大数据平台，提供智能推送、票务预订、自主导览、应急保障等功能，实现乡村吃、住、行、游、购、娱等一站式服务。二是全方位培育专业化人才，充分调动乡贤人才积极性，"强教育、重激励"，"以老带新"，"产才联动"，持续开展非遗传承人的接力培育，优化老中青人员结构；加大回引优秀人才力度，重点培训一批有能力有干劲的乡村旅游能人，示范带动村民思维转变，充实乡村文旅服务人才库，实现新老村民共建、共享，振兴乡村。

Shiyan Village, Jiajiang County, Leshan City, Sichuan Province:

The Road to Rural Revitalization of "China's No. 1 Paper Art Village"

Abstract

Shiyan Village, Jiajiang County, Leshan City, Sichuan Province, is an ancient village with handmade bamboo paper manufacturing as its pillar industry. It retains the traditional village style and precious handmade papermaking skills. In recent years, Shiyan Village has taken cultural industries as an engine to promote rural revitalization, dug deep into the intangible cultural heritage resources of "bamboo papermaking skills", focused on the integrated development of "paper culture, paper industry, and paper tourism", and worked closely with the Sichuan Fine Arts Institute team to build "China's No. 1 Paper Art Village". After three years of devoted endeavor, important scenes, such as the Jiajiang County Museum Community, Shiyan Village History Museum, Jiadanqiao Wenfang Street Market, Daqian Residence Community and Traditional Craft Workstation have been built, and "China's No. 1 Paper Art Village" has shined. Shiyan Village has won many honors, such as the National "One Village, One Product" Demonstration Village, Sichuan's Most Beautiful Ancient Village and Tianfu Tourism Famous Village; it was selected into the first list of Sichuan Traditional Villages.

Challenges and Problems

Shiyan Village covers an area of 7.5 square kilometers and is located in a hilly area. The land is mainly stony and the arable land area is limited. Local villagers have long been engaged in papermaking. However, with the rapid development of the machine-made paper industry, the handmade paper industry faces huge challenges. The long production cycle, high cost and limited market demand of handmade paper, coupled with insufficient brand promotion, have led to more and more papermaking craftsmen going out to make a living. Till 2021, the permanent resident population of Shiyan Village was reduced to 800-plus, of whom the elderly accounted for the majority, and there was a serious shortage of rural labor. At the same time, the outflow of population has also led to a break in the inheritance of "bamboo papermaking skills". How to revitalize the traditional handmade bamboo paper industry and attract young and middle-aged labor to return has become the key for Shiyan Village to smash the bottleneck of rural revitalization.

Measures

1. Improve infrastructure construction

Shiyan Village has tried to win more than 20 million yuan of various funds to build and improve the 11-kilometer internal and external tourist ring roads of the village, and to blacken and colorize the entire road. Besides, rural revitalization funds of more than six million yuan were invested to beautify and green the tourist ring road and the paper village scenic road, and to create landscape nodes to unify the style of farmhouses. Shiyan Village has vigorously implemented the "Five-cleaning" action, "Toilet Revolution" and "Lighting Project", so that it has newly built and renovated 357 rural toilets, eliminated black and smelly water bodies, installed more than 170 street lights on both sides of the road,

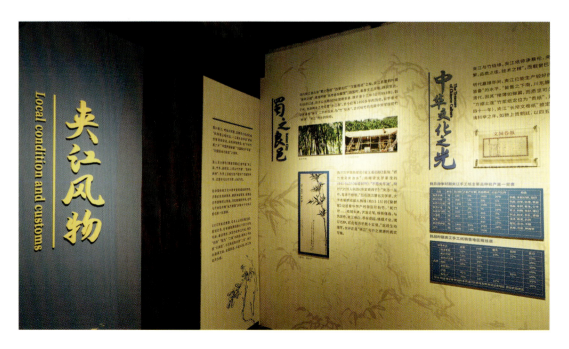

comprehensively cleaned up all kinds of garbage, demolished open-air garbage pools, and established a domestic garbage collection, transportation and disposal system. The overall infrastructure of Shiyan Village has been greatly optimized, the living environment has been comprehensively improved, and the style of the thousand-year-old paper village has been completely renewed.

2. Bring into use the resources of intangible cultural heritage

Firstly, based on the papermaking culture, Shiyan Village comprehensively sorts out the natural and cultural resources of the whole village, registers and protects the 11 well-preserved papermaking workshops and sites in the village, and invests 450,000 yuan for renovation and upgrading. Secondly, in view of the characteristics of the residential houses in Shiyan Village, the 52 century-old houses are listed for protection, villagers are encouraged to consciously maintain the old houses, so as to restore and preserve the original style of the old houses and monuments as far as possible. Thirdly, Shiyan Village leverages the think tank of the excellent team of Sichuan Fine Arts Institute. Upholding the people-oriented concept that takes culture as the soul, art as the basis, and paper as the industry, we go all out to build "China's No. 1 Paper Art Village". Through the project layout of "one museum, one street, and two zones", Shiyan Village has deeply integrated the intangible cultural heritage "bamboo papermaking skills" and cultural tourism education to build a unique cultural tourism industry in Shiyan Village.

3. Strengthen talent cultivation and attraction

Shiyan Village promotes the modernization of grassroots governance systems and governance capacity; puts in place an industrial development system that is dominated by the village collective, where the people of virtue and talent take the lead and the masses participate; and goes all out to create a unique cultural tourism village in south Sichuan. Shiyan Village has built a provincial "paper tourism" study tour base and a national 3A-level scenic spot, and created the "Wenjiale" characteristic homestay brand. By holding investment promotion meetings, symposiums of successful returnees and other activities, Shiyan Village attracts successful people from outside to return home to invest in the construction of study tour bases, homestays and other new tourism businesses.

Results

Shiyan Village on the strength of its "paper culture" has improved the "paper industry" clustering level and implemented functional transformation of "paper tourism". Currently, the village has 12 handmade paper workshops, with an annual output of 30,000 quires and an output value of over 30 million yuan; it also has two machine-made paper enterprises, with an annual output of 15,000 tons and a total output value of 300 million yuan. In the village, more than 300 people are engaged in "paper culture" study and tourism; and 12 "Wenjiale" homestays have been set up. In 2023, more than 200,000 tourists were received, tourism revenue exceeded 70 million yuan, the village collective economic income reached 300,000 yuan, and the per capita disposable income of villagers increased to 33,600 yuan.

Experiences and Inspirations

Shiyan Village reproduces the value and ethos of handicraft skills, reconnects craftsmanship and life, promotes industrial transformation and upgrading of traditional villages, cultivates a positive rural cultural ecology, and constructs a new modern village integrating industry, ecology, culture and talents.

1. High-level planning

Shiyan Village has recruited talents and invited experts from universities such as the China Academy of Art, Sichuan Fine Arts Institute, and Leshan Normal University, as well as industry elites, to participate in the project design. It adheres to the development concept of "leveraging the scenery to drive the village development, building up the village scene, and promoting interaction between the village and the scenery", deeply explores the compound functions of rural ecological conservation and cultural inheritance, and realizes the transformation from extensive to intensive growth.

2. Detailed planning

Shiyan Village and Sichuan Fine Arts Institute have deepened cooperation and worked together to create a rural museum model to fully present the value of "paper culture" and promote the sustainable development of the "paper industry" and "paper tourism". By actively promoting the functional transformation of rural tourism, the transformation and upgrading of "farmland into the park, farmhouse into the guest room, and farming as the wonderful experience" was realized. Five rural tourism routes respectively themed on "Painting and Calligraphy Paper Village", "Heritage Sightseeing", "Elegant Life", "Ancient Papermaking Experience" and "Rural Scenery", were designed and launched, becoming a new driving force for rural revitalization.

3. Brand building

Shiyan Village has actively planned and held a series of "paper culture" activities and hosted various cultural exchange meetings, such as the roundtable on "Cultural Industry Empowering Rural Revitalization" held by Sichuan Fine Arts Institute and the National Social Science Fund Project Report Meeting. Through the documentary *The Hometown of Bamboo Paper: Thin Paper, Deep Sentiment* and the original film *Things Around the Paintings Go the Wrong Way*, Shiyan Village's "paper culture" was promoted on CCTV and major media platforms to raise the profile and influence of the long-time paper town.

Plans

Shiyan Village will closely follow its development positioning as China's paper town, take the development of "paper culture", "paper industry" and "paper tourism" as the starting point, and make solid efforts to blaze a new path of rural revitalization through the empowerment of the cultural industry. Firstly, it will improve intelligent services in the whole region, put in place the rural supporting smart guide system, bring important cultural and tourism spots onto the tourism big data platform, perform intelligent sharing, ticket booking, self-guided tours, emergency support and other functions, and ensure the one-stop supply of services of catering, accommodation, transportation, travel, shopping and entertainment in the village. Secondly, it will cultivate professional talents in all aspects, fully mobilize the enthusiasm of local talents, "strengthen education, emphasize incentives", "bring the senior to guide green hands", "link production and talent", continue to carry out the relay cultivation of intangible cultural heritage inheritors, and optimize the structure of old, middle-aged and young personnel. Moreover, it will increase the efforts to attract outstanding talents, focus on training a group of capable and motivated rural tourism talents, set models to drive the change of villagers' thinking, enrich the talent pool of rural cultural and tourism services, and realize the co-construction and sharing by new and old villagers for the rural revitalization.

云南省德宏傣族景颇族自治州芒市出冬瓜村：
弘扬乡土文化 助力乡村振兴

摘　要

云南省德宏芒市三台山乡出冬瓜村以特色产业和德昂族非物质文化遗产为依托，传承和发扬德昂族酸茶制作、德昂族织锦、德昂族传统体育等非遗项目体验，实现了德昂族小众民族文化走进公众视野的转化，推动出冬瓜村从单一的第一产业向以第三产业为主导、一二三产业融合发展的产业模式转型，让出冬瓜村成为一张"以文塑旅、以旅彰文"的旅游名片，走出了一条以"文化赋能推动产业融合，助力乡村振兴"的特色发展之路。

挑战与问题

出冬瓜村位于全国唯一的德昂族乡,该村始建于明清时期,是德昂族传统民居古建筑群和德昂族古朴民风民俗保留得最完好的村落,对于德昂族文化的研究和传承具有很高的价值。出冬瓜村现有国家级非物质文化遗产"水鼓舞""达古达楞格莱标""浇花节""德昂族酸茶制作技艺"4个,以及德昂织锦、橄榄撒制作、德昂古歌等数个非物质文化遗产代表性项目。出冬瓜村在弘扬乡土文化,助力乡村振兴的道路上困难重重,面临着巨大挑战。一是资源开发不足,出冬瓜村有许多民族文化、景观景点还未得到进一步的挖掘与开发;二是旅游业态单一同质化,游客体验质量较差;三是旅游人才匮乏,影响旅游管理和运营质量的提升。

措施

1. 加强资源整合利用

一是村民以发展"庭院经济"为切入口,利用房前屋后零星地块和村内闲置土地种植果蔬花草、多肉植物,因地制宜建设小果园、小菜园、小花园,打造特色农家乐、咖啡馆、酸茶品鉴铺和网红观景打卡点等,既美化了村庄,也为村民创造了增收渠道。二是出冬瓜村打造德昂故事走廊、德昂非遗学院、水鼓广场、青昂阁、德昂人家、德昂小院、冬瓜农家乐等,发展农家乐、民宿、酸茶品鉴及非遗体验课程的多样化旅游业态。

2. 加大农文旅深度融合

一是推出以黄金百香果、牛油果、金钻凤梨等特色水果和羽叶金合欢(帕哈)、楤木(椿头)等森林蔬菜采摘为主的农文旅融合主题线路。二是打造一批春年糕、酸茶加工、织锦、水鼓制作、林下养鸡场捡鸡蛋等农文旅融合主题体验坊,让游客充分感受"悠悠乡愁"的韵味和古老神秘的德昂族文化魅力。

3. 聚焦人才队伍建设

一是加强对乡村旅游村干、旅游扶贫创业致富带头人的培训力度,安排他们外出参加文博会、云南省"村长"论坛等,提高旅游人才素质,提升旅游服务质量。二是积极吸引优秀大学生返乡参加工作,实现人才扎根农村基层,通过组织程序将回流的5名本乡优秀大学毕业生分配到村"两委"班子中,吸引20余名村民返乡创业。

成效

出冬瓜村以民族文化保护与开发并行、传承与创新并举为思路,让民族传统文化在助力乡村振兴中焕

发出新的活力,让越来越多的群众吃上香喷喷的"旅游饭"。出冬瓜村以村企合作为抓手,引进德宏华江旅游公司,按照"村集体以固定资产入股,企业具体负责项目软装和运营,以占股比例进行收益分红"的模式发展,每年为村集体创收30余万元。村集体对学成坚果加工厂投资了40万元,每年可获得2.4万元的分红;特色酸茶产业每年为村集体贡献3.4万元的租金收入;上上居特色民宿每年可带来2.5万元的租金收入;水鼓广场商铺每年也可带来2.1万元的租金收入。综合以上各项,全村每年的集体收入约为40万元,人均纯收入为1.41万元。出冬瓜村获评传统古村落、民族特色村寨示范、云南省最美乡愁旅游地和云南省金牌旅游村。

经验与启示

1. 坚持特色产业

出冬瓜村坚定发展特色产业,依托全乡4800余亩茶园,成立龙阳德昂茶专业合作社,推出采茶体验、酸茶制作、酸茶品鉴等旅游产品。酸茶制作坊的产品符合行业售卖标准,每公斤价格在600—1800元,该制作坊销售德昂酸茶的年收入可达20万—30万元。

2. 坚持生态优先

出冬瓜村践行"绿水青山就是金山银山"的发展理念,注重茶园、森林等生态系统的保护发展,统筹推进绿化建设、环境整治、院落美化,蓝天、白云、茶园、栈道、溶洞构成村庄美丽底色,出冬瓜村已成为"望得见山、看得见水、记得住乡愁"的幸福美丽新乡村。

3. 坚持文化传承

出冬瓜村着力打造德昂特色文化品牌,举办德昂族浇花节、德昂族体育运动会、德昂酸茶品鉴会等特色文化活动,建设德昂水鼓广场等公共文化空间,培养出冬瓜村水鼓舞队等特色文艺队伍,每年开展产业、文化方面的培训多达3000人次。

下一步计划

一是继续深挖民族文化资源,开展系列民族文化挖掘、保护与传承工作,集中对外开展酸茶制作、织锦、达古达楞格莱标传唱、水鼓舞蹈表演、传统体育项目等文化体验项目,将民族文化变活;二是持续完善旅游设施设备,积极申报国家A级旅游景区,为游客提供更好的旅游体验;三是实施乡村旅游人才培养战略,采取多样化人才培养形式,针对非物质文化遗产传承人、旅游扶贫创业致富带头人,加强培训力度,增加培训形式,丰富课程种类,不断壮大文化人才队伍,提高乡村旅游人才队伍素质,提升服务人员接待能力与水平;四是充分利用非物质文化遗产金字招牌,优化项目品牌包装。出冬瓜村将全力增强全乡文化凝聚力和软实力,加强文化与市场融合,提高旅游市场适应力和创新力,促进农文旅融合发展,全面推进乡村振兴。

Chudonggua Village, Mang City, Dehong Dai and Jingpo Autonomous Prefecture, Yunnan Province:

Carrying forward Local Culture to Boost Rural Revitalization

Abstract

Chudonggua Village, Santaishan Town, Mang City, Dehong Dai and Jingpo Autonomous Prefecture, Yunnan Province relies on its characteristic industries and the De'ang intangible cultural heritage to inherit and carry forward the De'ang sour tea making, De'ang brocade, De'ang traditional sports, and other intangible cultural heritage, making the De'ang ethnic minority culture attractive, and promoting the transformation of Chudonggua Village from a village dominated by agriculture to an industrial model dominated by the tertiary industry and characterized by the integrated development of the first, second, and third industries. Chudonggua Village has become a tourist business card that "relies on culture to shape tourism and leverages tourism to promote culture", and has embarked on a development path of "promoting industrial integration through cultural empowerment and rural revitalization".

Challenges and Problems

Chudonggua Village is located in the only De'ang township in China. The village was built in the Ming and Qing dynasties. It is the best-preserved village with the traditional ancient buildings and the simple folk customs of the De'ang people. Chudonggua Village is of great value for the study and inheritance of the De'ang culture. Chudonggua Village currently has four national intangible cultural heritages, namely "Water Drum Dance", "Dagudalenggelaibiao", "Flower Watering Festival" and "De'ang Sour Tea Making Skills" as well as several representative intangible cultural heritage projects such as De'ang brocade, Ganlansa making and De'ang ancient songs. Chudonggua Village faces many difficulties and challenges in promoting local culture and helping rural revitalization. Firstly, due to insufficient resource development, many ethnic cultures and scenic spots in Chudonggua Village have not been fully developed; secondly, the tourism industry is single and homogeneous, which leads to tourists' poor experience; thirdly, there is a shortage of tourism talents, which affects the improvement of tourism management and operation efficiency.

Measures

1. Strengthen resource integration and utilization

Firstly, villagers use the development of "courtyard economy" as an entry point, use scattered plots in front of and behind houses and idle land in the village to plant fruits, vegetables, flowers, and succulents, build small orchards, vegetable gardens, and flower gardens according to local conditions, and create characteristic farmhouses, coffee shops, sour tea tasting shops, and Internet celebrity viewing check-in spots, etc., which not only beautify the village but also create income-increasing channels for villagers. Secondly, Chudonggua Village has built the De'ang Story Corridor, De'ang Intangible Cultural Heritage College, Water Drum Square, Qing'ang Pavilion, De'ang Family, De'ang Courtyard, Winter Melon Farmhouse, etc., to create a diversified tourism industry of farmhouses, homestays, sour tea tasting and intangible cultural heritage experience courses.

2. Deepen the integration of agriculture, culture and tourism

Firstly, launch a theme route integrating agriculture, culture, and tourism, focusing on picking special fruits such as golden passion fruit, avocado, and golden diamond pineapple, and forest vegetables such as feather-leaved acacia (Paha) and Aralia (Chuntou). Secondly, create many theme experience workshops integrating agriculture, culture, and tourism, such as pounding rice cakes, sour tea processing, brocade, water drum making, picking eggs in forest chicken farms, etc., so that tourists can fully experience the charm of "long homesickness" and the charm of the ancient and mysterious De'ang culture.

3. Build talent teams

Firstly, Chudonggua Village strengthens the training of village officials in rural tourism and leaders of tourism poverty alleviation and entrepreneurship, and arranges them to participate in cultural and art fairs, Yunnan Province "Village Head" Forum, etc., to enhance the competence of tourism talents and the quality of tourism services. Secondly, Chudonggua Village attracts outstanding college students to return to work in their hometowns so that talents can settle down. Through due procedures, five outstanding university graduates were arranged to work with the village's "two committees", and more than 20 villagers returned to their hometowns to start businesses.

Results

Chudonggua Village takes the protection and development of ethnic culture in parallel and sticks to inheritance and innovation so that ethnic traditional culture can be revitalized in helping rural revitalization, more and more people can make a living and benefit from tourism development. Chudonggua Village takes village-enterprise cooperation as a starting point, brings in Dehong Huajiang Tourism Company, and develops by the model that "the village collective invests in fixed assets, the enterprise is responsible for the soft decoration and operation of the project, and the profit is distributed according to the proportion of shares", which generates about 300,000 yuan of income for the village collective each year. The village collective invested 400,000 yuan in Xuecheng Nut Processing Factory, and distributed 24,000 yuan in dividends each year; the characteristic sour tea industry collects a rent of 34,000 yuan per year; the Shangshangju characteristic homestay 25,000 yuan per year; the Shuigu Square shops 21,000 yuan per year. Based on the above, the annual collective income of the whole village is about 400,000 yuan, and the per capita net income is 14,100 yuan. Chudonggua Village was rated as a traditional ancient village, a characteristic demonstration village, the most beautiful tourist destination in Yunnan Province stimulating people's nostalgia, and a "gold medal" tourist village in Yunnan Province.

Experiences and Inspirations

1. Adhere to characteristic industries

Chudonggua Village firmly develops characteristic industries. Relying on the more than 4,800 *mu* of tea gardens in the township, it has established the

Longyang De'ang Tea Professional Cooperative and launched tourism products related to tea picking experience, sour tea making and tasting. The products of the sour tea workshop are sold by industry standards, with a price of 600-1,800 yuan per kilogram, and the annual income from the sales of De'ang sour tea reaches 200,000-300,000 yuan.

2. Adhere to ecological priority

Chudonggua Village practices the development concept of "lucid waters and lush mountains are invaluable assets", pays attention to the protection and development of tea gardens, forests, and other ecosystems, and coordinates the afforestation, environmental improvement, and courtyard beautification. The blue sky, white clouds, tea gardens, plank roads, and caves constitute the beautiful background of the village. Chudonggua Village has become a happy and beautiful new village where you can "see the mountains, see the water, and feel homesick".

3. Adhere to cultural inheritance

Chudonggua Village strives to create a unique cultural brand of De'ang; organizes unique cultural activities such as the De'ang Flower Watering Festival, the De'ang Sports Games, and the De'ang Sour Tea Tasting Meeting; builds public cultural spaces such as the "De'ang Water Drum Square"; cultivates unique art teams such as the Chudonggua Village Water Drum Dance Team; up to 3,000 people are trained in industry and culture every year.

Plans

Firstly, Chudonggua Village will continue to dig deep into ethnic cultural resources; carry out a series of ethnic cultural excavation, protection, and inheritance work; and focus on carrying out cultural experience projects such as sour tea making, brocade, Daguda Lenggelai Biao singing, water drum dance performances, and traditional sports to make ethnic culture alive. Secondly, Chudonggua Village will continue to improve tourism facilities and equipment, apply for the construction of national A-level scenic spots, and provide tourists with a better tourism experience. Thirdly, Chudonggua Village will implement the rural tourism talent training strategy, adopt diversified talent training forms, strengthen training, increase training forms, and enrich course types for inheritors of intangible cultural heritage and tourism poverty alleviation and entrepreneurship leaders, to continuously expand the cultural talent team, improve the competence of rural tourism talent team, and improve the reception capacity and level of service personnel. Fourthly, Chudonggua Village will fully leverage the prestigious label of intangible cultural heritage and intensify the branding of projects. Chudonggua Village will make every effort to enhance the cultural cohesion and soft strength of the township, strengthen the integration of culture and market, improve the adaptability and innovation of the tourism market, promote the integrated development of agriculture, culture, and tourism, and comprehensively promote rural revitalization.

飞猪旅行：
五力模型助力乡村振兴

摘　要

　　2023年，飞猪旅行与阿里巴巴公益合作发起的乡村旅游助力计划落户浙江省丽水市景宁畲族自治县，为景宁县创新性地定制了包括产品创新力、营销推广力、产业融合力、公共服务保障力、人才发展力的乡村旅游"五力模型"。飞猪以公益的方式，联动多方合作打造产品，线上线下整合营销，促进农文旅深度融合，提供完善的公共服务，推动人才发展。通过数字化引领，飞猪旅行与景宁县当地政府共同探索出一条乡村旅游转型升级的新路径，推动景宁乡村旅游向更高品质、更具竞争力的方向发展，为全球乡村旅游发展提供具有前瞻性和可操作性的参考范本。

挑战与问题

景宁县是全国唯一的畲族自治县,一直以来是浙江省的重点欠发达县之一,经济总量位居全省末位。景宁县坐拥云中大漈和中国畲乡之窗两大国家 4A 级旅游景区,以及千峡湖、炉西峡、望东垟等自然奇观,是体验原生态风光与独特畲族文化的理想之地。然而,在将这份自然与人文的宝藏转化为乡村振兴的驱动力方面,景宁县面临着重大挑战,主要问题如下。一是如何在保持原生态风貌的同时有效提升旅游服务质量和游客体验;二是旅游市场对于个性化、高品质旅游产品的需求日益增长,这对景宁县旅游产品的创新与营销提出了更高要求;三是如何有效融合旅游与其他产业,拓宽旅游产业链。

措施

1. 产品创新力

在阿里巴巴派驻景宁县乡村特派员的牵头下,飞猪旅行经过深度调研和市场分析,结合景宁县文旅资

源和时令特色,打造了以"畲韵撩人,秋醉景宁"为主题的旅游线路产品,并结合品质化供给,精心设计了度假酒景套餐,通过公益的方式上线"飞猪益起寻美"店铺,实现了旅游产品与市场需求的精准对接。

2. 营销推广力

飞猪利用其平台优势,采取线上线下整合营销策略。一是与头部主播合作,开展线上达人直播,极大地提升了景宁旅游的市场曝光度,双十一期间,为景宁当地如那云·天空之城等旅游产品带来了超过 400 万元的销售业绩;二是联合阿里公益开展"星光行动"活动,全网直播节目观看总量超 3000 万次,微博相关话题阅读量超 1 亿次,全平台热门话题 5 个;三是"理想乡村春耕季"直播活动走进浙江省景宁县,带大家领略如画的畲乡风光,深入景宁田间地头,体验独具特色的畲族民俗活动,感受绚丽多彩的畲族传统文化。"理想乡村春耕季"直播活动成功地将景宁的绝美风景、特色美食及文化底蕴呈现给了更多的观众,进一步提升了景宁的目的地影响力。

3. 产业融合力

阿里巴巴公益与景宁县政府共同发布"景宁产业公益创投计划",通过公益创投的方式,结合文旅项目,促进农文旅融合发展。飞猪旅行结合线上旅游直播,传播景宁县生态环境优势,多次为景宁县带货,让更多游客转化为景宁优质农特产品的消费用户。

4. 公共服务保障力

飞猪旅行以公益方式在丽水打造数字攻略,将景宁县作为核心推荐目的地,通过技术手段全景还原了

景宁县当地自然风光以及诸如畲乡之窗、云中大漈等地方特色景点。游客仅需通过扫码，即可实时获取数字攻略、行程规划、沉浸式的导览或实景交互体验、旅游商品预订及其他公共旅游服务。

5. 人才发展力

数字化营销为景宁县带来了线上流量和线下游客接待量的激增，飞猪旅行以公益方式精心设计了个性化培训课程，与景宁县文旅局共同组织了全县共计185名酒店从业者参与的专业服务培训活动。此次活动通过邀请高校、企业等多位行业专家围绕提升酒店服务能力进行了深入细致的讲解与指导，不仅为景宁县培养了一支高素质的旅游服务团队，也为旅游产品创新和服务质量的持续提升奠定了人才基础。

成效

通过"五力模型"的实施，景宁旅游在短期内实现了经济效益和社会影响力的双重提升。经济效益方面，不仅帮助那云·天空之城等当地旅游产品取得了显著成绩，全县头部度假酒店在"双11"期间的销售额也超过了400万元；服务品质方面，全县185名一线酒店从业者通过专业培训，显著提高了自身的服务接待水平，增强了游客满意度；社会影响力方面，飞猪平台联合头部主播和线下推广活动，让景宁旅游品牌声名鹊起，吸引了更多的游客关注。尤为重要的是，这一系列措施为景宁乡村旅游的可持续发展奠定了坚实基础，明确了"政府引导+企业参与+市场驱动"的乡村旅游发展模式。

经验与启示

1. 发挥飞猪产品推荐的优势

飞猪为景宁县量身定制了一系列主题旅游线路，详尽规划了游客的行程路线，并精心搭配了酒店与景区的组合推荐。例如那云温泉度假村→中国畲乡之窗（住宿推荐：云鹤水岸、朴宿、宿叶、山语间、听泉山庄、石上溪）→畲寨东弄田园综合体（住宿推荐：耕心舍）→千峡湖生态旅游度假区→畲寨仙草谷中医药生态旅游基地→云中大漈（住宿推荐：如隐小佐居、自在居、云曦山舍）→秋季乡村三大旅游节庆点（红色毛垟、秋收郑坑、古风雁溪）。这些综合规划与推荐能有效促进游客的旅行购买决策。

2. 发挥飞猪的OTA平台优势

飞猪不仅为景宁县提供全方位的线上推广策略，更是在节假日专门提供特色消费券和线上云游直播，极大提升了游客的旅行体验，再次促进游客购买决策。

下一步计划

飞猪旅行联合阿里巴巴公益将进一步深化文旅助力共富的公益项目实践，持续围绕"五力模型"进行拓展与升级。产品创新上，将更加注重利用数字技术提升旅游产品的个性化与互动性；营销策略上，探索更多元化的渠道和内容创新；产业融合方面，推动旅游农文旅与更多产业领域跨界合作，构建复合型旅游产品；公共服务上，融合AI，提升景宁县新质生产力在公共服务上的应用，实现更便捷、更智能的游客体验；人才建设上，建立健全人才培养与激励机制，激发创新思维与实践，为景宁旅游发展不断输送新鲜血液。

Fliggy Travel:
The Five-Force Model Helps Rural Revitalization

Abstract

In 2023, Fliggy Travel, in collaboration with Alibaba Public Welfare, launched a rural tourism support plan in Jingning She Autonomous County, Lishui City, Zhejiang Province. They put forward an innovative rural tourism "Five-Force Model" for Jingning County, encompassing product innovation, marketing promotion, industrial integration, public service guarantee, and talent development. By leveraging digital technology and promoting comprehensive development, Fliggy Travel aims to advance in-depth integration of agriculture, culture and tourism, provide well-rounded public services, push forward talent development, and elevate Jingning's rural tourism to a higher, more competitive level, with a view of offering a forward-looking operational reference model for global rural tourism development.

Challenges and Problems

Jingning, the only She Autonomous County in China, is one of the key underdeveloped counties in Zhejiang Province, ranking low in terms of economic output. With its rich natural and cultural resources, including two national 4A-level scenic spots (Daji the Clouds and Window of the She Village in China) and natural wonders like Qianxia Lake, Luxixia, and Wangdongyang, Jingning provides an ideal place for people to enjoy the original ecological scenery and unique She ethnic culture. However, Jingning County faces significant challenges in transforming these assets into drivers of rural revitalization. The main issues are as follows. Firstly, it is important to improve tourism services and tourist experiences while preserving the ecological landscape. Secondly, the growing demand for personalized, high-quality tourism products poses a higher demand for the innovation and marketing of Jingning County's tourism products. Thirdly, it is the challenge to integrate tourism with other industries to broaden the tourism industry chain.

Measures

1. Product innovation

Led by Alibaba's special commissioner stationed in Jingning County, Fliggy Travel conducted in-depth research and market analysis. Based on the local cultural tourism resources and seasonal characteristics, they created themed tourism route products such as "With the She style, Jingning Is Intoxicating in Fall", designed vacation wine and scenery packages, and launched the "Seeking Beauty with Fliggy" store. These initiatives ensured a precise connection between tourism products and market demand.

2. Marketing and promotion

Fliggy with its platform strengths adopted an online and offline integrated marketing strategy.

Key actions are as follows. Firstly, it cooperates with top anchors for online live broadcasts, enhancing Jingning tourism's market exposure. For example, during the Double Eleventh period, they sold tourism goods worth over 4 million yuan, including Nayun Sky City in Jingning. Secondly, it partners with Ali Public Welfare for the Starlight Action, achieving over 30 million live broadcast views and more than 100 million Weibo readings on related topics. It has altogether five topics. Thirdly, the "Ideal Village Spring Farming Season" live broadcast landed in Jingning County, taking views of local farming and showcasing the unique She ethnic activities, presenting Jingning's scenery, food, and cultural heritage to a broader audience, thus enhancing the influence of Jingning.

3. Industrial integration

Alibaba Charity and the Jingning County Government launched the "Jingning Industrial Philanthropy Venture Capital Plan" to promote the integrated development of agriculture, culture, and tourism. Fliggy Travel used online travel live broadcasts to highlight Jingning's ecological and environmental advantages and sell local premium agricultural products to more and more tourists.

4. Public service guarantee

Fliggy Travel has created a digital guide for Lishui, recommending Jingning as a core destination. It gives a panoramic presentation of local natural scenery in Jingning through technical methods, as well as local characteristic attractions such as the Window of She Township and Daji in Clouds. Tourists can access digital guides, tour planning, immersive guided tours, and travel product reservations by scanning a code, which is conducive to enhancing their travel experience.

5. Talent development

Digital marketing has brought a surge in online traffic and offline tourist reception to Jingning County. Fliggy Travel has customized its courses to be offered as public welfare and organized professional service training for 185 hotel practitioners in Jingning County through collaboration with the County Culture and Tourism Bureau. By inviting industry experts from universities and enterprises to give in-depth and detailed lectures and guidance on improving hotel service capabilities, a high-quality tourism service team is cultivated, laying a foundation for continuous improvement in tourism product innovation and service quality.

Results

The adoption of the "Five-Force Model" has brought about significant improvement in economic benefits and social influence of Jingning Tourism. In terms of economic benefits, it has significantly increased sales of local tourism products, such as Nayun Sky City; the leading resort hotel sales exceeded four million yuan during Double 11. In terms of service quality, the 185 first-line hotel practitioners across the county improved their service reception level and thus increased tourist satisfaction. Regarding social influence, Fliggy cooperates with leading anchors and conducts offline promotions, which has boosted Jingning's tourism brand and attracted more tourists' attention. More importantly, this series of measures has laid a solid foundation for the sustainable development of rural tourism in Jingning, clarifying the development model of rural tourism which is guided by the government, involves enterprises, and is driven by the market.

Experiences and Inspiration

1. Leveraging Fliggy's Product Recommendations

The themed tourism routes developed by Fliggy for Jingning County provided tourists with clear itineraries and recommended accommodations, enhancing their willingness to purchase things, such as Nayun Hot Spring Resort → Window of China She Township (accommodation recommendations: Yunhe Waterfront, Pusu, Suye, Shanyujian, Tingquan Mountain Villa, Shishangxi) → Dongnong Rural Complex of She Village (accommodation recommendation: Gengxin She) → Qianxia Lake Ecotourism Resort → Xiancao Valley Traditional Chinese Medicine Ecotourism Base of She Village → Daji in the Clouds (accommodation recommendations: Ruyin Xiaozuo Ju, Zizaiju, Yunxi Mountain Cottage) → Three major rural tourism spots in autumn (Red Maoyang, Autumn Harvest Zhengkeng, Yanxi of Ancient Charm)

2. Utilizing Fliggy's OTA Platform

Fliggy offers comprehensive online promotion strategies, and more importantly, special consumer coupons, and live broadcasts during holidays, which has significantly enhanced tourists' travel experiences and encouraged their spending.

Plans

Fliggy Travel and Alibaba Charity will further deepen the implementation of public welfare projects that push cultural tourism to promote common prosperity, and continue to expand and upgrade around the "Five-Force Model". In terms of product innovation, more attention will be paid to using digital technology to make tourism products personalized and interactive. In terms of marketing strategy, more diversified channels and content innovation will be explored; in terms of industrial integration, cross-border cooperation between tourism, agriculture, culture, and even more industrial fields will be promoted to build complex tourism products; in terms of public services, AI will be integrated to enhance the application of Jingning's new quality productive forces in public services, and deliver a more convenient and smarter tourist experience; in terms of talent development, a sound talent training and incentive mechanism will be established to stimulate innovative thinking and practice, and continuously provide fresh impetus for Jingning's tourism development.

宁夏回族自治区固原市原州区姚磨村：
"旅游+冷凉蔬菜"助力乡村振兴

摘　要

宁夏回族自治区固原市原州区彭堡镇姚磨村，聚焦区位优势和气候特点，把"旅游+冷凉蔬菜"作为调整乡村产业结构、转变乡村发展方式和增加农村居民收入的主导产业，通过扩规模、延链条、促融合，使蔬菜产业由小到大、从弱变强，从单一走向多元，从第一产业转向一二三产业相互融合发展，将菜地、菜园、大棚变成乡村旅游的景区景点。这一举措不仅让姚磨村村民们吃上了旅游饭，成为旅游从业者，也让姚磨村成为"农家柴火鸡 人间烟火味 招待八方客"的旅游目的地，以姚磨村为核心的24万亩冷凉蔬菜种植基地成为乡村旅游的"网红"打卡地。

挑战与问题

姚磨村发展乡村旅游主要面临以下问题。一是配套服务不完善。乡村民宿缺乏统一规划与等级划分，建筑结构、公共环境以及经营管理缺乏对应的标准，不能为游客提供舒适的住宿体验和充分的公共服务保障。二是缺乏资金和项目扶持。姚磨村文化旅游产品单一、旅游体验单调，乡村历史、民俗风情等人文资源挖掘不充分，没有得到很好的展示和传承。三是保护与开发之间的矛盾。乡村文化旅游项目的市场化运作，必须符合县域空间发展规划，按照乡村土地属性和建设用地指标要求，严格遵守生态保护和耕地保护红线，依法依规发展乡村旅游。

措施

1. 发展蔬菜产业，巩固乡村旅游基本盘

一是规模种植提高产量。姚磨村由传统的一家一户粗放种植转变为规模化、集约化种植，带动周边11个村种植冷凉蔬菜5.5万亩。二是优化品质提升口碑。姚磨村实行统一规划布局、统一育苗种植、统一田间管理、统一区域品牌、统一市场销售的"五统一"标准化种植模式，用优质蔬菜助力农户致富增收。三是多措并举拓宽销路。姚磨村紧盯市场需求，在广州江南果菜批发市场、西安西部欣桥农产品物流中心市场开设蔬菜外销窗口，与叮咚买菜、百果园等知名电商平台、大型连锁超市等建立合作关系，发展"订单农业"，蔬菜远销广州、郑州、西安等十几个大中城市，蔬菜外销率达到85%以上。

2. 融合乡村产业，构建乡村旅游新业态

一是积极探索"乡村产业+旅游"的有机融合模式，将当地特色柴火鸡、果蔬小火锅、文创产品等与旅游业紧密结合，提高乡村特色产品的加工转化率，形成全新的循环发展模式。二是顺应时代潮流、积极创新发展，开发了集观光、采摘、农耕体验、民宿于一体的乡村旅游项目，让越来越多的人感受到乡村旅游的美好与魅力。

3. 提升品牌效应，注入乡旅发展新动能

姚磨村充分发挥区位优势，大力强化科技农业、做优绿色农业、提升品牌农业、巩固质量农业，积极引导农民调整农业种植结构，以"南果北种"为主要内容，推动特色种植与生态观光相结合的融合发展。通过"文旅+合作社+销售"的种植经营模式，培育特色农业种植产业，持续打造休闲农业旅游品牌，以特色产业发展助力乡村振兴。

成效

姚磨村乡村旅游发展带动了"美丽乡村"建设，实现了山更青、水更绿、生活更美好。一是产业规模越来越大。姚磨村先后建设1座700平方米的点播中

心；20000平方米的育苗中心，年育苗能力1.2亿株以上，育苗自给率90%以上；有机无公害蔬菜大棚20栋，高标准果蔬拱棚24栋，高标准日光温室70栋；预冷库15000平方米，制冰车间500平方米，年预冷各类蔬菜15万吨；泡沫箱厂2600平方米，加工泡沫箱200万个；蔬菜分栋加工包装车间2400平方米，根茎类鲜切标准化生产线1条，叶菜类鲜切智能化生产线3条，外销各类蔬菜13万吨，蔬菜外销至成都、西安、南京、广州、厦门等20多个大中城市。注册的"六盘清水河"冷凉蔬菜商标荣获第十届宁夏著名商标品牌。二是农民收入越来越多。除种植户每亩增收8500元左右，农民还可以通过土地流转获得"租金"，或在基地务工获得"薪金"。村民人均可支配收入从2016年的9500元增加到2023年的23000元。姚磨村先后获得全国"一村一品"示范村、全国乡村旅游重点村等荣誉称号。

行旅游长廊2千米，做好冬至河水库的生态治理修复，开发水上游乐项目。二是结合农业基地建设，种植草莓、火龙果、百香果、葡萄等特色水果，打造亲子科普温室观光园、亲子拓展区、农耕文化记忆长廊，提供有机蔬菜种植采摘体验，不断吸引游客。

3. 突出打造特色

姚磨村积极顺应游客倾向亲近自然、热衷假日短途旅游的休闲趋向及消费心理，突出乡村文化旅游体验感。结合原有的水产养殖、蔬菜基地，建成水产养殖观赏区、垂钓中心、水上娱乐中心、优质果蔬观光采摘区、冷凉蔬菜示范区、特色农产品体验区及各类花开展示区等休闲旅游点，打造集垂钓、观光、休闲、采摘、民宿等功能于一体的乡村特色旅游品牌，吸引固原市区及周边县区游客前来观光体验。

经验与启示

1. 优化发展环境

姚磨村不断完善党建引领基层治理制度体系，推进平安乡村、法治乡村建设。开展乡级文明家庭、星级文明户、美丽庭院评选活动，培育文明乡风、良好家风、淳朴民风，倡导文明健康的社会风尚，为文化旅游业发展提供良好的社会环境。

2. 深入挖掘资源

一是绿化美化入村主干道路5千米，打造绿色步

下一步计划

一是持续培育蒋口村以"村史馆—武家堡子—双河湾遗址—杏花人家"为主要内容的休闲观光旅游线路，充分挖掘隔城子遗址历史文化底蕴，力争将姚磨村、蒋口村、别庄村打造成集休闲、文化、产业、旅游于一体的特色文化旅游村，以点带面，在各村培育打造乡村旅游点。二是在村情民俗上靶向发力，让濒临消失的传统建筑、农耕器具、民间技艺、民俗礼仪、风土人情等以活态化方式进行传承创新，让优秀传统农耕文化中蕴含的思想观念、人文精神、道德规范得以广泛传播，让游客"望得见山、看得见水、记得住乡愁"。

Yaomo Village, Yuanzhou District, Guyuan City, Ningxia Hui Autonomous Region:

"Tourism + Cool-Climate Vegetables" Boost Rural Revitalization

Abstract

Yaomo Village in Pengbao Town, Yuanzhou District, Guyuan City, Ningxia Hui Autonomous Region, leverages its geographical advantages and climate characteristics, adopting "tourism + cool-climate vegetables" as the leading industry to adjust the rural industrial structure, transform rural development mode, and increase rural residents' income. By expanding the scale, extending the industrial chain, and promoting integration, the village has built up the vegetable industry which embraces diversified businesses rather than a single business. Integrating primary, secondary, and tertiary industries, the village has turned vegetable plots, gardens, and greenhouses into tourist attractions, which enables Yaomo villagers to benefit from tourism and become tourism practitioners. The Yaomo Village has become a popular tourist destination known for its "farmhouse wood-fired chicken, rustic charm, and hospitality for guests from all directions" and the 240,000 *mu* cool-climate vegetable planting base centering around Yaomo Village has become a photogenic for rural tourism.

Challenges and Problems

Yaomo Village faces the following challenges in developing rural tourism. Firstly, supporting services were inadequate. The rural homestays lacked unified planning and classification, with building structures, public environments, and management lacking corresponding standards, which led to insufficient comfort and public service guarantees. Secondly, there was a lack of funding and project support. The cultural tourism products in Yaomo Village were limited, and the tourists' experience was monotonous. The village's history, folk customs, and other cultural resources were underexplored and not well showcased or inherited. Thirdly, there was the contradiction between protection and development. The market-based operation of rural cultural tourism projects must align with the county and district spatial development plans, adhere to rural land use requirements, and strictly follow ecological and arable land protection guidelines, to develop rural tourism by laws and regulations.

Measures

1. Develop the vegetable industry to consolidate the foundation of rural tourism

Firstly, the village carries out large-scale planting to increase yield. The Yaomo Village has shifted from traditional small-scale household farming to large-scale, intensive farming, driving the cultivation of 55,000 *mu* of cool-climate vegetables across 11 surrounding villages. Secondly, quality improvement of the agricultural products enhances the village's reputation. The "five-unified" standardized planting model (unified planning layout, unified seedling cultivation and planting, unified field management, unified regional branding, and unified marketing) is adopted to help farmers increase income by planting high-quality vegetables. Thirdly, various measures expand sales channels. Focusing on market demand, the village has set vegetable export windows at Guangzhou Jiangnan Fruit and Vegetable Wholesale Market and Xi'an Western Xinqiao Agricultural Products Logistics Center Market, and partnered with well-known e-commerce platforms like Dingdong (Cayman) Limited and Pagoda as well as large chain supermarkets to develop "contract farming", with vegetables sold to over ten major cities including Guangzhou, Zhengzhou, and Xi'an. The export rate of vegetables exceeds 85%.

2. Integrate rural industries to build new businesses of rural tourism

Firstly, the village has vigorously explored

the organic integration model of "rural industry + tourism", combining local specialties like wood-fired chicken, fruit and vegetable hotpots, and cultural and creative products with the tourism industry, to increase the processing and conversion rate of rural specialty products and develop a brand new circular development model. Secondly, the village endeavors to adapt to modern trends and seek innovative development, developing rural tourism projects that integrate sightseeing, picking, farming experiences, and homestays, to attract more people to enjoy the beauty and charm of rural tourism.

3. Enhance brand effects and inject new development momentum into rural tourism

Yaomo Village fully leverages its geographical advantages, strongly promotes technological agriculture, improves green agriculture, enhances brand agriculture, and consolidates quality agriculture. Great efforts are made to guide farmers to adjust agricultural planting structures and promote the integrated development of specialty planting and ecological tourism with the "southern fruit planting and northern farming" approach. Through the "cultural tourism + cooperatives + sales" planting and operation model, characteristic agricultural planting industries are fostered and leisure agricultural tourism brands are built by incessant efforts to contribute to rural revitalization through specialty industry development.

Results

The development of rural tourism in Yaomo Village has driven the construction of a "beautiful countryside", which helps to beautify the environment and contributes to people's well-being. Firstly, the scale of the industry is growing. Yaomo Village has successively built a 700-square-meter seeding center; a 20,000-square-meter seedling center with an annual seedling capacity of over 120 million plants, achieving a self-sufficiency rate of over 90%;

20 organic, pollution-free vegetable greenhouses; 24 high-standard fruit and vegetable arch sheds; and 70 high-standard sunlight greenhouses. The village also has a 15,000-square-meter pre-cooling storage facility, a 500-square-meter ice-making workshop with an annual pre-cooling capacity of 150,000 tons of various vegetables; a 2,600-square-meter foam box factory with a processing capacity of 2 million foam boxes; a 2,400-square-meter vegetable sorting, processing, and packaging workshop; one standardized production line for root vegetable fresh-cut products; and three intelligent production lines for leaf vegetable fresh-cut products. The village sells 130,000 tons of various vegetables to over 20 major cities including Chengdu, Xi'an, Nanjing, Guangzhou, and Xiamen. The registered "Liupan Qing Shuihe" cool-climate vegetable trademark has won the Ningxia 10th Famous Trademark Award. Secondly, farmers' income is increasing. In addition to an increase of about 8,500 yuan per *mu* for growers, farmers can also earn "rent" through land transfers and "wages" by working on the farms. The per capita disposable income of villagers has risen from 9,500 yuan in 2016 to 23,000 yuan in 2023. Yaomo Village has been awarded titles such as the National Demonstration Village for the "One Village, One Product" Initiative and the National Key Village for Rural Tourism Development.

Experiences and Inspirations

1. Optimize the development environment

Yaomo Village continuously improves the grassroots governance system led by Party building, advancing the construction of a peaceful and law-abiding village. It conducts township-level evaluations for exemplary families, star-rated outstanding households, and beautiful courtyards, cultivating rural civilization, good family virtues, and simple folkways, advocating for civility and a healthy social atmosphere, and providing a sound social

environment for the development of the cultural tourism industry.

2. Deeply explore resources

Firstly, the village endeavors to green and beautify the 5-kilometer main road into the village, creating a 2-kilometer green walking tourism corridor. Comprehensive ecological restoration of the Dongzhi River Reservoir has been carried out, and waterborne recreational projects have been developed. Secondly, in conjunction with the construction of agricultural bases, strawberries, dragon fruits, passion fruits, grapes, and other specialty fruits have been planted, with the parent-child science greenhouse sightseeing park, parent-child outdoor activity area, and farming culture memory corridor set to offer tourists organic vegetable planting and picking experiences.

3. Highlight distinctive features

Yaomo Village actively responds to the trend of tourists preferring to embrace nature and engage in short holiday trips, emphasizing the experiential aspect of rural cultural tourism. Based on the existing aquaculture and vegetable bases, the village has established aquaculture viewing areas, fishing centers, water entertainment centers, high-quality fruit and vegetable sightseeing and picking areas, cool-climate vegetable demonstration areas, specialty agricultural product experience areas, and various flower display areas, creating a rural tourism brand that integrates fishing, sightseeing, leisure, picking, and homestays to attract visitors from Guyuan City and surrounding counties for sightseeing and related experiences.

Plans

Firstly, Yaomo Village will continue to develop the Jiangkou Village leisure sightseeing route featuring the "Village History Museum — Wujiabaozi — Shuanghewan Ruins — Apricot Blossom Home", fully exploring the historical and cultural significance of the Gechengzi Ruins, and endeavoring to build Yaomo Village, Jiangkou Village, and Biezhuang Village into a unique cultural tourism village integrating leisure, culture, industry, and tourism. Over time, Yaomo Village will foster scenic spots in all the villages. Secondly, Yaomo Village will focus on village customs and traditions, and make targeted efforts to preserve and innovate the traditional buildings, farming tools, folk crafts, customs, and rituals that are on the verge of disappearing, ensuring that the thoughts, humanist spirits, and moral rules embedded in excellent traditional farming culture are widely disseminated and tourists can "see the mountains, see the water, and feel homesick".

河北省邢台市内丘县杏峪村：
精品民宿集群赋能乡村振兴

摘 要

　　河北省邢台市"内丘县杏峪村乡村振兴一二三产业融合项目"，由内丘鹊起文化旅游发展有限公司实施建设，得到了内丘县乡村振兴局的鼎力支持。项目中心位于太行山脉东麓的锦绣堂前，紧邻明长城隘口，不仅服务于杏峪村的村民，也惠及周边村庄的居民。项目借助当地深厚的人文历史和独特的自然资源，以民宿集群为引擎，融入精品旅游步道、生态停车场、景观提升建设等，引领全域一二三产业融合发展。杏峪村已发展成为太行山脉康养第一村和乡村振兴新样板。

挑战与问题

杏峪村由柴炭窑、西沟、北沟、大庄四个自然村庄组成。杏峪村自然生态环境优越，历史文化厚重，旅游资源丰富。2022年，"内丘县杏峪村乡村振兴一二三产融合项目"开始实施，总投资6000多万元。杏峪村在发展过程中，主要面临以下挑战。一是杏峪村的植被盖度和植被绿度均值位于全省第一，发展旅游不能触碰生态红线，因此发展生态旅游成为首选；二是发展旅游产业会逐渐弱化原有的特色农林产品种植加工产业，需要积极做好生态康养农林转型发展；三是精品民宿和农家民宿等第三产业的发展需找准特色定位。

措施

1. 打造精品民宿集群

杏峪村精品民宿集群项目受到内丘县乡村振兴局的大力扶持。乡村振兴局斥资2600多万元，委托东方农道（北京）工程设计有限公司设计施工，并在杏峪村西沟自然庄完成"润石居宿集"建设。该项目打造了具有太行山脉原生态、特色化、融合性的高端康养品牌"宿集"，总建筑面积3714.80平方米，占地面积8768.67平方米，包括8栋44间民宿，另建有接待中心、火塘景观、沿河景观、生态停车场、高端餐厅等配套设施。该项目旨在构建乡村振兴一二三产融合产业发展的典范，探索太行山区人与自然和谐共生的发展模式。

2. 促进产业融合和升级

首先，"宿集"建设带动了当地特色农业、林果种植和加工产业的发展，以及山区特色文创艺术品加工业，如核桃油加工、野生葡萄酒酿造、特色蔬菜种植、野生木耳和黄精的培植和加工等。其次，精品民宿带动了农家民宿全域兴起，以及餐饮服务业和商业的繁荣。

3. 突出森林康养特色

杏峪村自然资源优越，植被覆盖率达98%以上；

其嶂石岩地貌特征称绝，鹤栖丹崖，山川锦绣，是太行山少有的避暑、康养绝佳之地。杏峪村作为太行山脉中植物覆盖率较高的区域之一，借助精品民宿，建设精品旅游步道、生态停车场、景观提升、给排水和供配电等配套设施，打造太行山康养第一村。

成效

杏峪村"宿集"建设带动了农家民宿的兴旺。截至2024年4月，杏峪村拥有正常运营且入住人数超30人的民宿3家，年收入50多万元，家庭式民宿18户，户均收入超10万元。2023年，杏峪村实现年接待游客量25万人次以上，带动就业岗位1000多个，村集体收入达50万元，村民人均收入超过1.5万元。

经验与启示

1. 品牌民宿激活客源市场

杏峪村凭借其深厚的历史文化和绮丽的山川地貌，曾吸引大量全国各地热衷旅游探险的游客前来游览，但苦于餐饮住宿的困扰，旅游业一直未能实现突破性进展。"宿集"建设致力于打造优美山涧、锦绣奇石、和合宜居的"涧石居宿集"，在设计和运营上充分融合自然环境和人文历史，有效带动杏峪村客源市场的发展。

2. 文旅赋能助力产业兴旺

"宿集"项目建设发掘乡村价值，拓展农业新业态，发展特色乡村旅游，奠定农村一二三产业融合发展的基础，让杏峪村走上了可持续发展的产业振兴之路，实现农民不断增收、生活富足的目标。

3. 森林康养激活环保理念

杏峪村坚持"生态为本、产业为基、百姓为根"的思路，以文化根脉促旅游，以"绿水青山"作康养，倾力打造锦绣堂文旅驿站和森林康养小镇。

下一步计划

一是高水平加快历史文化体验和生态康养体验等特色体验项目建设，加快推进"绸缪束薪"锦绣堂洞房的《诗经》场景体验，以及寒山松林和康养登山运动体验项目发展，并着力开发体验式健康休闲产品、特色山货和特色食品。二是高起点打造新场景、新业态。统筹推进夜间经济、文创经济、研学经济、假日经济，培育露营、研学、康养、避暑等新业态，引领区域经济产业全面转型升级。三是推行先进管理模式，加强从业人员培训，提升服务水平。

Xingyu Village, Neiqiu County, Xingtai City, Hebei Province:

Boutique Homestay Clusters Empower Rural Revitalization

Abstract

The rural revitalization project in Xingyu Village, Neiqiu County, Xingtai City, Hebei Province, is an initiative that integrates primary, secondary, and tertiary industries. It is being implemented by Neiqiu Queqi Cultural Tourism Development Co., Ltd., with strong support from the Neiqiu County Rural Revitalization Bureau. The project is centered at Xingyu Village, located at the eastern foothills of the Taihang Mountains, near the Jinxiutang pass of the Great Wall. The project benefits the surrounding villages and residents by leveraging the area's rich cultural history and unique natural resources. By focusing on the development of boutique homestay clusters, the project incorporates premium tourist trails, eco-friendly parking lots, and landscape enhancements to promote the integrated development of primary, secondary, and tertiary industries throughout the region. Xingyu Village has become a leading model for rural revitalization and the premier health and wellness destination in the Taihang Mountains.

Challenges and Problems

Xingyu Village consists of four natural villages: Chaitanyao, Xigou, Beigou, and Dazhuang. The village boasts excellent natural ecology, rich history and culture, and abundant tourism resources. The "Xingyu Village Rural Revitalization Integration Project", launched in 2022, whose total investment exceeds 60 million yuan, faces several challenges. Firstly, located in the Taihang Mountains, the village has the highest average vegetation coverage and greenness in the province. Ecological tourism has become the preferred development path since it is essential to avoid crossing ecological red lines. Secondly, the development of the tourism industry could gradually weaken the traditional agricultural and forestry product processing industries, so it is essential to do a good job in transitioning to eco-friendly health and wellness businesses. Thirdly, the development of the boutique and farmhouse homestays needs to be carefully positioned to maintain their unique characteristics.

Measures

1. Build a boutique homestay cluster

The Xingyu Village Boutique Homestay Cluster project, supported by the Neiqiu County Rural Revitalization Bureau, has invested over 26 million yuan. The project was designed and constructed by Oriental Nongdao (Beijing) Engineering Design Co., Ltd., with the construction of the "Jianshi Homestay Cluster" completed in the Xigou natural village. This project aims to create a high-end health and wellness brand with a distinctive Taihang Mountains character, featuring a blend of natural and cultural elements. It covers a total building area of 3,714.80 square meters on a land area of 8,768.67 square meters, including eight buildings with 44 guest rooms, along with a reception center, fire pit landscape, riverside scenery, eco-friendly parking lots, and high-end restaurants. This initiative serves as a model for the integrated development of primary, secondary, and tertiary industries in rural areas, exploring the development mode of harmonious coexistence between man and nature in the Taihang Mountains area.

2. Promote industrial integration and upgrading

Firstly, the project has brought about the development of local specialty agriculture, fruit planting and processing, and unique mountain arts and crafts processing, such as walnut oil production, wild grape wine brewing, specialty vegetable

cultivation, and the cultivation and processing of wild mushrooms and Polygonatum. The boutique homestays have stimulated the growth of farmhouse homestays across the region, contributing to the prosperity of the catering and retail sectors.

3. Highlight the forest health and wellness characteristics

Xingyu Village is blessed with excellent natural resources, with a vegetation coverage rate of over 98%. The village's unique Zhangshiyan landscape as seen in the Hexi Danya, picturesque mountains, and rivers, makes it an ideal destination for summer retreats and health and wellness tourism. Leveraging its status as the greenest area in the Taihang Mountains, Xingyu Village is enhancing its offerings with boutique homestays, premium tourist trails, eco-friendly parking lots, landscape improvements, and infrastructure upgrades, aiming to establish itself as the premier health and wellness village in the Taihang Mountains.

Results

The construction of the "homestay cluster" in Xingyu Village has spurred the growth of farmhouse homestays. Up to April 2024, three homestays have

been operating successfully, each with more than 30 guests, generating an annual revenue of over 500,000 yuan. Additionally, there are 18 family-run homestays, each earning over 100,000 yuan annually. In 2023, the village received more than 250,000 visitors, creating over 1,000 jobs and contributing 500,000 yuan to the village collective income, with per capita income exceeding 15,000 yuan.

Experiences and Inspirations

1. Brand homestays contribute to the tourist market

Xingyu Village's rich historical and cultural heritage coupled with its stunning mountain scenery has attracted many adventure-loving tourists from across the country. However, the lack of adequate dining and accommodation facilities hindered tourism growth. The construction of the "homestay cluster" intends to create a beautiful mountain retreat with unique stone formations and a harmonious living environment. By integrating natural surroundings with cultural history in its design and operations, the project has successfully stimulated the growth of the tourist market in Xingyu Village.

2. Cultural and tourism development fuels industrial prosperity

The construction of the "homestay cluster" project has tapped into the value of the countryside, expanded new agricultural businesses, and fostered the development of characteristic rural tourism. This has laid the foundation for the integrated development of primary, secondary, and tertiary industries in rural areas, paving a sustainable path to industrial revitalization that continually increases farmers' incomes and enhances their quality of life.

3. Forest health and wellness business promotes environmental awareness

Xingyu Village adheres to the philosophy of "ecology first, industry as the foundation, and the people at the core". By leveraging its cultural roots to promote tourism and its "lush mountains and lucid waters" for health and wellness, the village is committed to creating a vibrant cultural and tourism hub, with a focus on laid on the forest health and wellness town.

Plans

Firstly, it is to accelerate the development of unique experiential projects such as those related to historical and cultural experiences and ecological wellness. This includes the rapid advancement of "Chou Mou Shu Xin" Jinxiutang's bridal chamber experience featuring scenes from *The Book of Songs*, as well as the development of the Han Mountain Pine Forest Wellness and Mountaineering Experience Project. Additionally, the village shall focus on developing experiential health and leisure products, as well as specialty mountain goods and distinctive foodstuffs. Secondly, it is to create new scenes and business models at a high starting point. This involves coordinating the development of the night economy, cultural and creative economy, study tour economy, and holiday economy while cultivating new businesses such as camping, study tours, wellness, and summer resorts, to lead the comprehensive transformation and upgrading of the regional economic industries. Thirdly, it is to implement advanced management models, strengthen the training of practitioners, and improve services level.

2024世界旅游联盟：旅游助力乡村振兴案例（中英文双语版）
WTA Best Practices of Rural Revitalization through Tourism 2024 (Chinese-English Bilingual Edition)

广西壮族自治区来宾市金秀瑶族自治县：
瑶医药产业赋能乡村振兴

摘 要

广西壮族自治区来宾市金秀瑶族自治县瑶医药文化历史悠久，药用植物资源丰富，是全国第二大药物基因库和广西中草药品种最齐全的县。金秀县利用其作为自治县的独特优势，立足优势特色资源，按照"山上种药、山中康养、山下制药"的一二三产业融合发展理念，以"强龙头、补链条、聚集群、抓创新、创品牌、拓市场"为思路，稳步推进中草药材生产发展，加强瑶医应用研究和推广，加快瑶医药和康养产业发展，打造集瑶医药种植基地、研发、康养于一体的大健康全产业链，走出金秀县乡村振兴的特色之路。

挑战与问题

金秀瑶族自治县地处广西中部偏东的大瑶山主体山脉上,是世界瑶族支系较多的县份和瑶族主要聚居县之一,瑶医药文化历史悠久,素有"世界瑶都"之称。金秀县的环境和气候得天独厚,动植物资源丰富,县境内森林覆盖率达 87.91% 以上,年平均气温 17℃,适宜的自然条件造就了丰富的瑶医药资源。当地 1528 种原生植物中,药用类植物多达 1351 种,其中包括"五虎、九牛、十八钻、七十二风"等 104 种经典"老班瑶药"(祖上传下的瑶药)。金秀县的当务之急是大力推动瑶医药产业集聚发展,助力金秀"瑶都"变"药都",药材变"药财",进一步巩固拓展脱贫攻坚成果,全面推进乡村振兴。

措施

1. 传承赋能,打造县、乡、村三级瑶医药服务网络

1959 年金秀县成立了医药研究所,2017 年金秀瑶族自治县瑶医医院创建二级甲等民族医院,瑶医医院和瑶医药研究所发挥平台优势,挖掘整理并传承创新瑶医药文化,迄今共申请瑶医药专利 70 多个,收集整理民间偏方、秘方 5000 多条,采集瑶药材标本 1000 多份,编写《广西大瑶山金秀瑶医瑶药效方集(第一集)》,推动民族医药的保护、挖掘、传承和利用。金秀县制定《金秀瑶族自治县瑶医药发展条例》,将瑶医诊疗项目、瑶药饮片、瑶药成药和医疗机构制剂按照民族医药标准体系建设要求纳入基本医疗保险基金支付范围 2024 年,金秀县 10 个乡(镇)卫生院及 70 多家村卫生室均开展中(瑶)药健康服务,形成了以县瑶医医院为龙头,以乡镇卫生院为中枢,以村卫生室为网底的县、乡、村三级中(瑶)医药服务网络。

2. 政策赋能,扩大瑶医药种植规模

金秀县编制了《金秀瑶族自治县林下中草药产业发展方案》,以"产业奖补 + 基地建设"为重要抓手,逐步扩大中草药种植规模。一方面,金秀县出台《金秀瑶族自治县发展中草药产业奖励办法》等,着力发展砂仁、天冬、百部、黄精、广金钱草、重楼、鸡血

藤、两面针和钩藤等品种的种植，对主要的瑶医药品种进行以奖代补，鼓励企业和专业合作社参与，并带动农户发展中草药种植。另一方面，金秀县投入资金2100万元重点打造金秀香草岭瑶药标准化种植基地和金秀瑶药产业技术实训基地，农户将土地租给基地种植，基地免费发放种苗给农户种植并保价回收。

3. 平台赋能，促进瑶医药发展创新

金秀县紧盯瑶医药产业发展，搭建招商引资平台。一是建设民族医药健康产业园，设立瑶医药科技孵化基地，引进27家瑶药生产企业，对入驻孵化基地的企业实行免租两年的优惠政策，瑶医药产业规模化雏形显现。二是投入资金1.5亿元，建设瑶医药研究所、创业创新服务平台及科技企业孵化器，推动产业集群发展，打造瑶医药特色示范园。三是努力培育瑶药植物创新药，开发瑶医药康养产品和女性健康产品，完成瑶医药康养服务标准和服务体系的编写。金秀县的22个瑶医药特色技法（疗法）获得国字号版权证书，全县共有国药准字号产品8项、食字号产品11项、妆字号产品15项、消字号产品30项。

4. 品牌赋能，拓宽瑶医药销售渠道

金秀积极探索瑶药销售路径，同时实施"引进来"与"走出去"相结合的策略。一方面借力医药公司品牌，在北京、上海、东莞、福州、烟台、南宁等地开办瑶医药康养连锁店13家，与大参林医药集团股份有限公司、浙江云落瑶健康管理有限公司等4家企业签订合作协议，打造瑶族康养品牌店和开发产品，宣传和销售金秀的特色医药产品。另一方面，培育龙头药企品牌，在广西德坤瑶药业有限公司建设瑶医药精深加工生产线，着力培育"德坤瑶宝""圣塘山""瑶都"等品牌，将其打造为特色鲜明、面向粤港澳、辐射东盟的中药材加工龙头企业，助推金秀瑶药走出国门、销往海外。目前公司产品出口东南亚、北美洲、澳大利亚等11个国家和地区，积极开拓民族医药海外市场。

5. 生态赋能，推动瑶医药康养提级

生态旅游成为金秀县近十年来发展最快的主导产业，金秀县入选首批"国家全域旅游示范区"和"全国森林康养基地建设试点县"。金秀县将辖内7个国家4A级旅游景区、1个国家3A级旅游景区、7家职工疗休养基地整合打造，探索出一条"旅游＋瑶医药特色康养"的新赛道。金秀县探索创新康养模式，依托大瑶山丰富的药膳原料，研发了瑶药养生酒、瑶药养脑提神药膳汤等系列产品共四十多种，推出"盘王宴""簸箕宴"等有药膳功能的瑶族特色美食，不断改良本地特色美食的药膳功能，突出药膳的健康养生主题。各星级酒店、特色民宿的药膳菜谱从无到有、从有到"新"，琳琅满目的药膳让游客"沉浸式"地体验到了金秀康养旅游的魅力。

成效

目前，金秀县瑶医药产业链综合产值达11.6亿元，全县从事瑶医药康养旅游产业的群众达3.2万人，市场主体共有500多家。2023年，全县瑶药材种植累计超18万亩，产量2.42万吨，产值6.52亿元，全县累计获自治区级中（瑶）药材种植示范基地4个。瑶医药产业园总建筑面积5万多平方米，入驻企业27家，生产瑶浴粉、药枕等80多种产品，申请专利24项，注册商标225个，桐木镇因此荣获国家农业产业强镇、自治区瑶医药科技创新小镇等称号，逐步发展成为瑶医药产业集聚区。2023年，金秀旅游量达655.46万人次，同比增长56.57%，旅游总收入58.71亿元，同比增长57.7%。

经验与启示

1. 坚持抓好"土特"文章

金秀县结合本土传统瑶医药优势产业，深入挖掘传承和发展瑶医药特色产业，推动瑶医药一二三产业融合发展。这种以民族医药特色为依托的乡村振兴产业发展模式，既能够因地制宜开展健康帮扶，又有利于更好发挥区域资源禀赋，达到民族医药助力县域高质量发展的预期效果。

2. 坚持建设生态文明

因地制宜发展瑶医药产业集群和大健康旅游发展，是贯彻落习近平总书记提出的"广西生态优势金不换"精神，牢牢把握国家推进美丽中国建设，加快发展方式绿色转型的创新措施。做大做强瑶医药新兴产业，努力推进产学研深度融合，有利于推动绿色发展迈上新步伐，在推动民族地区高质量发展上闯出新路子。

3. 坚持创新发展和人才振兴

金秀县通过建设瑶医药产业技术研究院、开展瑶医药产业技术培训等方式，深入开展瑶医药科技研究，提高瑶医药产业的技术水平和人才素质，为广西乃至全国民族医药产业的持续、健康发展注入新的活力。

下一步计划

一是培育壮大瑶医瑶药产业，鼓励医药生产企业向瑶药材种植和产地初加工、精深加工领域延伸，拓展产业链，引导区域内外医药龙头企业采取"公司＋合作社＋基地＋农户"的模式开展原生态、仿生态中药材种植，实现中药材种植标准化、规模化和产业化发展。二是创新发展康养旅游产业，利用金秀县特有的自然资源和瑶医药资源，因地制宜开发森林康养、乡村康养等特色疗养休闲度假产品，创新和丰富康养旅游。三是融合打造健康运动名片，大力举办自行车挑战赛、登山赛、半程马拉松赛、越野赛，通过"运动＋瑶医药＋旅游"，促进金秀县运动康养产业的发展。

2024 世界旅游联盟：旅游助力乡村振兴案例（中英文双语版）
WTA Best Practices of Rural Revitalization through Tourism 2024 (Chinese-English Bilingual Edition)

Jinxiu Yao Autonomous County, Laibin City, Guangxi Zhuang Autonomous Region:

Empowering Rural Revitalization with the Yao Medicine Industry

Abstract

Jinxiu Yao Autonomous County in Laibin City, Guangxi Zhuang Autonomous Region, is rich in Yao medicinal culture and plant resources, boasting the second-largest medicinal gene bank in China and the most diverse array of traditional Chinese herbal medicines in Guangxi Province. The county leverages its unique status as an autonomous county to capitalize on its abundant resources. Following the integrated development concept of "growing medicine on the mountains, keeping health in the hills, and producing medicine at the foothills", Jinxiu County has focused on strengthening leading enterprises, enhancing industry chains, and fostering innovation. By steadily promoting the development of the production of Chinese medicinal herbs, advancing Yao medicine research and application, and accelerating the development of the Yao medicine and wellness industries, Jinxiu County is establishing a comprehensive health industry chain. This approach has paved a distinctive path for rural revitalization in Jinxiu County.

Challenges and Problems

Jinxiu Yao Autonomous County is located in the central-eastern part of Guangxi Province, within the main mountain range of the Dayaoshan mountains. It is home to the largest number of Yao ethnic groups and one of the main areas where Yao people reside, earning the title "World Capital of the Yao People". With a rich history in Yao medicine and an abundance of plant resources, the county's forest coverage exceeds 87.91%, and the average annual temperature is 17°C. These favorable conditions have nurtured a wealth of medicinal resources, with 1,351 out of 1,528 native plant species being medicinal, including 104 classic herbs like the "5 Hu, 9 Niu, 18 Zuan, and 72 Feng" of the Yao tradition. The immediate priority for Jinxiu County is to promote the concentrated development of the Yao medicine industry, transforming itself from a "Capital of the Yao" to a "Capital of Medicine", turning medicinal herbs into "medicinal wealth" to consolidate and expand the county's poverty alleviation successes and fully advance rural revitalization.

Measures

1. Heritage empowerment: establishing a three-tier Yao medicine service network at the county, township, and village levels

In 1959, Jinxiu County established a medical research institute. In 2017, Jinxiu Yao Autonomous County founded the Yao Medicine Hospital, a second-tier ethnic hospital. Both the Yao Medicine Hospital and the Yao Medicine Research Institute leverage their platforms to dig into, comb through, and carry forward Yao medicine culture. To date, they have applied for over 70 Yao medicine patents, collected more than 5,000 folk remedies and secret recipes, and gathered over 1,000 Yao medicinal herb specimens. They also compiled the first volume of the *Guangxi Dayaoshan Jinxiu Yao Medicine Efficacious Formulas*, advancing the protection, exploration, inheritance, and utilization of ethnic medicine. Jinxiu County enacted legislation through the People's Congress, adopting the *Jinxiu Yao Autonomous County Yao Medicine Development Regulations*, which integrates Yao medicine treatment projects, Yao medicinal slices, Yao medicine preparations, and medical institution preparations into the basic medical insurance payment system as per the ethnic medicine standard system. Currently, all 10 township health centers and over 70 village clinics in Jinxiu County offer traditional Chinese (Yao) medicine health services, forming a three-tier traditional Chinese (Yao) medicine service network led by the county Yao Medicine Hospital, with township health centers as the hub and village clinics as the network base.

2. Policy empowerment: expanding the scale of Yao medicine cultivation

Jinxiu County has formulated the *Jinxiu Yao Autonomous County Under-the-Forest Herbal*

Medicine Industry Development Plan, "using industrial development incentives" and "base construction" as key strategies to gradually expand the scale of herbal medicine cultivation. On the one hand, the county issued the *Jinxiu Yao Autonomous County Herbal Medicine Industry Development Incentive Measures*, focusing on the cultivation of such species as fructus amomi, radix asparagi, sessile stemona root, manyflower solomonseal rhizome, desmodii styracifolii herb, Yunnan manyleaf paris rhizome, suberect spatholobus stem, shinyleaf pricklyash root, and gambir plant. The county offers awards instead of subsidies for key Yao medicine species, encouraging enterprises and professional cooperatives to participate and motivating farmers to engage in herbal medicine cultivation. On the other hand, 21 million yuan has been invested to establish the Standardized Cultivation Base for Yao Medicine at Xiangcaoling in Jinxiu County and the Yao Medicine Industry Technical Training Base. Farmers can lease their land to the base for cultivation, with the base providing free seedlings to farmers and guaranteeing herb purchase at an insured price.

3. Platform empowerment: promoting innovation in Yao medicine development

Jinxiu County focuses on Yao medicine industry development and has established an investment attraction platform. Firstly, an ethnic medicine health industry park has been constructed with a Yao medicine technology incubation base. The park has attracted 27 Yao medicine production enterprises, offering a two-year rent-free policy for businesses settling in the incubation base, marking the beginning of large-scale Yao medicine industry development. Secondly, 150 million yuan has been invested to build a Yao Medicine Research Institute, an entrepreneurship and innovation service platform, and a technology enterprise incubator, promoting the development of industry clusters and creating a distinctive Yao medicine demonstration park. Thirdly, efforts are underway to cultivate three brands in Yao medicinal plant innovation drugs, Yao medicine

wellness, and women's health products. The county has completed the compilation of the Yao medicine wellness service standards and service system, with 22 Yao medicine distinctive techniques (therapies) receiving national copyright certificates. The county has a total of eight products with national medicine approval, 11 with food certification, 15 with cosmetic certification, and 30 with disinfection product certification.

4. Brand empowerment: expanding Yao medicine sales channels

Jinxiu County actively explores Yao medicine sales channels, adopting a dual strategy of "bringing in and going out". On the one hand, leveraging the brands of pharmaceutical companies, Jinxiu County has opened 13 Yao medicine wellness chain stores in Beijing, Shanghai, Dongguan, Fuzhou, Yantai, and Nanning. The county has signed cooperation agreements with four companies, including the Dashenlin Pharmaceutical Group Co., Ltd., and Zhejiang Yunluo Yao Health Management Co., Ltd., to create Yao wellness brand stores and develop products, promoting and selling Jinxiu's specialty medicine products. On the other hand, the county is fostering leading pharmaceutical brands. Guangxi Dekun Yao Pharmaceutical Co., Ltd. is building an intensive processing production line for Yao medicine, focusing on cultivating brands like "Dekun Yaobao", "Shengtangshan", and "Yaodu", aiming to develop them into leading enterprises in the Chinese herbal medicine processing industry with distinctive features, serving the Guangdong-Hong Kong-Macao region and reaching ASEAN. This will help Jinxiu Yao medicine reach overseas markets. Currently, the company's products are exported to an expanding ethnic medicine market in 11 countries and regions, including those in Southeast Asia, North America, and Australia.

5. Ecological empowerment: upgrading Yao medicine wellness tourism

Ecotourism has become the fastest-growing leading industry in Jinxiu County over the past decade. Jinxiu has been selected as one of the first "National All-for-One Tourism Demonstration Zones" and "National Pilot County for Forest Wellness Base Construction". Jinxiu County has integrated its seven national 4A-level scenic spots, one national 3A-level scenic spot, and seven staff wellness resorts to explore a new "tourism + Yao medicine wellness" track. Jinxiu County is innovating wellness models and developing over 40 Yao medicinal products, such as Yao medicinal health wine and Yao medicinal brain-refreshing soups, by relying on the rich herbal resources of Greater Yao Mountain. The county

has also launched Yao ethnic specialty dishes with medicinal functions, such as the "Panwang Banquet" and "Boji Banquet", continuously improving the medicinal functions of local specialty dishes to highlight the health and wellness theme of medicinal cuisine. The medicinal cuisine menus of star hotels and characteristic homestays have evolved and are updated, offering a wide variety of medicinal dishes that provide tourists with an immersive taste of Jinxiu's wellness tourism charm.

Results

Currently, the total output value of the Yao medicine industry chain in the county has reached 1.16 billion yuan. Over 32,000 people in the county are engaged in the Yao medicine wellness tourism industry, and there are more than 500 market entities. In 2023, the total Yao medicine cultivation area in the county exceeded 180,000 *mu*, with a production volume of 24,200 tons and an output value of 652 million yuan. The county has four autonomous region-level traditional Chinese (Yao) medicine planting demonstration bases. The total construction area of the Yao Medicine Industrial Park exceeds 50,000 square meters, housing 27 enterprises producing over 80 products, including Yao medicinal bath powder and medicinal pillows. The park has applied for 24 patents and registered 225 trademarks. On this account, Tongmu Town has been honored with titles such as the National Competitive Town for Agricultural Industry and the Yao Medicine Technology Innovation Town in the Autonomous Region, gradually developing into a Yao medicine industry cluster area. In 2023, the wellness tourism sector in Jinxiu County attracted 6.5546 million visitors, a year-on-year increase of 56.57%, generating a total tourism revenue of 5.871 billion yuan, a year-on-year increase of 57.7%.

Experiences and Inspirations

1. Emphasizing "local and specialty" development

The county leverages its strengths in the traditional Yao medicine industry, digging into, inheriting, and developing the unique Yao medicine industry, to promote the integration of primary, secondary, and tertiary industries for Yao medicine development. Leveraging the unique characteristics of ethnic medicine to boost rural revitalization is a development model that proceeds from regional characteristics. It not only allows for localized health assistance but also helps better utilize regional

resources, achieving the expected results of high-quality county development with the help of ethnic medicine.

2. Adhering to ecological civilization construction

Developing Yao medicine industry clusters and large-scale health tourism in line with local conditions reflects the essence of President Xi Jinping's remarks that Guangxi should value its ecological advantages. It seizes the opportunity presented by national efforts to build a beautiful China and accelerate the green transformation of development models. The endeavor to expand and strengthen the emerging Yao medicine industry and promote the deep integration of production, learning, and research is conducive to pushing green development to a new level and exploring new paths for high-quality development in ethnic regions.

3. Prioritizing innovation and revitalization by relying on talent

Jinxiu County has, through the establishment of a Yao Medicine Industry Technology Research Institute and the implementation of Yao medicine industry technology training, deepened its scientific research in Yao medicine, and enhanced the technological level and personnel competence of the Yao medicine industry, injecting new vitality into the sustainable and sound development of the ethnic medicine industry in Guangxi Province and nationwide.

Plans

Firstly, it is to cultivate and expand the Yao medicine industry. Jinxiu County encourages pharmaceutical companies to extend into Yao medicinal herb cultivation, primary processing, and deep processing fields; and expand the industrial chain by guiding leading pharmaceutical companies within and outside the region to adopt the "company + cooperative + base + farmer" model for herbal medicine cultivation, achieving standardized, large-scale, and industrialized development of herbal medicine cultivation. Secondly, it is to innovate and develop the wellness tourism industry. Jinxiu County utilizes its unique natural resources and Yao medicine resources to develop specialized wellness and leisure vacation products related to forest wellness and rural wellness based on local conditions. In this way, Jinxiu County innovates and diversifies wellness tourism offerings. Thirdly, it is to build a healthy sports brand with an inclusive approach. Jinxiu County promotes the development of Jinxiu's sports wellness industry by organizing cycling challenges, mountain climbing competitions, half marathons, and cross-country races; and develops "sports + Yao medicine + tourism" to enhance Jinxiu County's wellness tourism brand.

2024世界旅游联盟：旅游助力乡村振兴案例（中英文双语版）
WTA Best Practices of Rural Revitalization through Tourism 2024（Chinese-English Bilingual Edition）

江苏省盐城市大丰区恒北村：
梨旅融合趟出乡村振兴致富路

摘　要

江苏省盐城市大丰区恒北村是全国最大的早酥梨生产基地，全村连片种植万亩梨园。近年来，恒北村围绕"梨园风光、生态宜居、乡村旅游"的发展定位，以农文旅融合为主抓手，一手抓"水果梨"，一手抓"文化梨"，形成以"梨"为媒，以"旅"为介，走出了一条一二三产业融合的绿色发展、富民强村之路。先后获得全国文明村、国家级生态村、全国乡村旅游重点村、全国"一村一品"示范村、全国休闲农业与乡村旅游示范点、江苏省新农村建设示范村等荣誉。

挑战与问题

恒北村的发展之路并非一帆风顺。一是先天条件不优。恒北村地处平原地区，不依山、不傍水，既缺少自然山水资源，也没有多样性生物资源，同时历史遗迹资源也相对匮乏，旅游产业基础薄弱。二是产业链条不强。尽管恒北村以万亩梨园著称，2022年就已成为全国最大的早酥梨生产基地之一，然而在发展旅游业之前，村民和村集体收入主要依靠梨果种植，产业形态传统单一，经济收入增长不明显。三是旅游人才缺乏。村庄老龄化和空心化严重，许多农民选择离乡外出打工，旅游发展的主体缺失，特别是缺乏文化创意、非遗传承专业人才和会组织、善经营的综合性人才。

措施

1. 依托"梨"风景，打造恒北魅力新空间

恒北村一是以生态果园为背景，按照"绿色、生态、宜居、宜旅"设计理念，建设连体别墅、农民公寓300多户，配套建成道路、绿化、亮化、排污等公共设施，构建青瓦白墙、小桥流水、绿树环绕、鸟语花香的美丽村庄。二是依托万亩梨园风光，先后建成了梨园风光主题公园、恒北果品苑等乡村旅游景点，集聚开发果林飘香、美满河畔、生态长廊等乡村田园特色观景地。三是配套建设恒北本场人酒店、原乡温泉度假酒店、精品民宿等食宿设施，打造"春赏花，夏沐绿，秋摘果，冬泡泉"的乡村休闲旅游目的地。

2. 聚焦"梨"主题，激发乡村旅游新活力

一是连续举办十一届恒北梨花文化节，承办江苏省乡村旅游节，组织举办非遗文创集市、江苏省非遗精品展、江苏现代农业（梨）产业技术体系中晚熟梨品鉴评价暨技术研讨会等活动，提升恒北特色乡村旅游影响力。二是利用梨产业优势，保护性注册了涵盖45个系列的175个"恒北"品牌商标，前延后伸开发七级延伸产品。三是创意开发"真的梨不开你"系列恒北文创产品100多种，创办恒北梨文创店，推进延伸"梨"主题乡村旅游产业链。

3. 丰富"梨"内涵，拓展乡村旅游新业态

一是深入挖掘梨文化，建成中国梨博物馆。二是引入非遗、摄影、国学、手工制作等，建成6000平方米的非遗文化园，开设国家级非遗瓷刻、省级非遗麦秆剪贴等一批非遗工作室以及现代园林艺术静水斋、梨缘手工坊等一批文艺工坊，丰富恒北文化内涵。三是做好"旅游+康养"文章，整合村内及周边康养度假资源，打造"以静养生泡温泉+以动养生体验农耕"的融合产品，开启"生态村+中医疗养+温泉度假"新模式，建立盐城市职工劳模疗休养基地。四是发展"旅游+会展"业态，设立恒北培训基地，开设恒北现场教学点，推出长三角乡村振兴示范培训班，创造乡村旅游新的经济增长点。

成效

恒北村结合江苏省第三批特色田园乡村创建和整村推进人居环境改善项目，进行高标准设计，建设新型农村社区典范。整村实现党建引领、产业发展、人居环境、基础设施、公共服务全面提升；同时，对老村庄实施农户改厕、垃圾分类、道路提升、绿化美化、桥梁改造、水系疏浚、污水管网等提升工程，配套完善道路、绿化、亮化等基础设施和村民公园、健身步道、灯光球场等公共服务设施，获评中国美丽乡村、全国示范性老年友好型社区、首批国家森林村庄等荣

誉称号。2023年，全村共接待游客50万人次，旅游收入1500万元；旅游带动本地就业达150人；农民人均纯收入达到3.91万元，其中果品收入2.85万元；村集体收入400万元。

经验与启示

1. 发挥产业优势、做大做强

恒北村坚持生态农业与乡村旅游有机结合，在做优做精育苗基地、果品加工等早酥梨特色产业的基础上，做足"梨"文章，开发全梨宴、本场菜等地标美食，推出农业观光、农事体验、康养度假、亲子游乐、会务培训等业态，积极推行"乡村旅居+梨园康养"模式。

2. 放大品牌效应、凝聚力量

恒北村围绕"名人、名村、名品"三大亮点，通过书记代言、直播带货、品牌活动等形式开展宣传，坚持举办恒北梨花文化节，放大"真的梨不开你"品牌效应，积极争取央视、"学习强国"等国家级主流平台的关注和报道，利用微博、微信、抖音等热点平台推广引流，不断提升恒北果品产业和乡村旅游知名度。

3. 鼓励全民参与、共建共享

积极带动村民参与，鼓励村民开办农家乐、民宿、餐饮等，完善落实激励政策，通过村里引导、村民主导，对符合条件的村民进行奖补；为村民自建民宿开

展线上宣传和线下指导，带领村民发家致富。加强引导，鼓励村民自发宣传，营造旅游氛围。

4. 坚持以文塑旅、以旅彰文

梳理本地历史沿革、产业变迁和人文精神，挖掘本场人文化、语言、饮食等文化习俗，形成恒北地方文化。做优做精恒北系列文创产品，将厚重的文化底蕴和秀美的梨园景观转化为看得见、摸得着、拿得走、用得上的文创、农创产品，以实现农文旅融合的可持续发展。

下一步计划

一是增强农旅融合。积极对接争取梨产业深加工项目，开发延伸梨产品，做大做强早酥梨特色产业；每年举办恒北梨花文化节乡村旅游品牌活动，促进农业旅游业有机融合。二是深化文旅融合。加快建设非遗舞台，围绕国家级非遗项目"大丰瓷刻"，组织非遗秀等非遗主题演出，打造恒北特色非遗文化街区；进一步延伸开发恒北梨文创产品，发展非遗特色产品、地方农副产品和文创产品。三是提升旅游服务水平。建立基层旅游服务人员管理和培训机制，发挥乡村旅游发展的"领头羊"作用，建设一支素质高、能力强的乡村旅游人才队伍。

Hengbei Village, Dafeng District, Yancheng City, Jiangsu Province:
Integrating Pear Cultivation and Tourism to Blaze a Path to Rural Revitalization and Prosperity

Abstract

Hengbei Village, located in the Dafeng District of Yancheng City, Jiangsu Province, is the largest Zaosu pear production base in China, with 10,000 acres of pear orchards planted throughout the village. In recent years, Hengbei Village has focused on developing a strategy centering around "pear orchard landscape, making the environment eco-friendly and livable, and rural tourism". By integrating agriculture, culture, and tourism, the village has pursued a dual approach: focusing on both the "fruit pear" and the "cultural pear". This strategy uses "pears" as a medium and "tourism" as a vehicle to achieve a green development path that integrates primary, secondary, and tertiary industries, ultimately bringing about rural prosperity and building up the village. Hengbei Village has won numerous accolades, including the National Civilized Village, the Nation-Level Eco-friendly Village, the National Key Village for Rural Tourism Development, the National Demonstration Village for the "One Village, One Product" Initiative, the National Demonstration Point for Leisure Agriculture and Rural Tourism, and Demonstration Village for New Countryside Construction in Jiangsu Province.

Challenges and Problems

The development of Hengbei Village has not been a smooth journey. Firstly, the village's natural conditions are not favorable. Situated in a plain area, Hengbei Village lacks mountainous terrain, water resources, and diverse biological resources, and has limited historical sites, which makes it challenging to develop the tourism industry. Secondly, the industrial chain is weak. Despite Hengbei Village's reputation for its extensive pear orchards and being one of the largest Zaosu pear production bases in China by 2022, before developing the tourism industry, the villagers and the village collective primarily relied on pear cultivation for earning income. This single, traditional industry had limited economic growth. Thirdly, there is a lack of tourism talent. The village faces serious aging and depopulation issues as farmers leave to work elsewhere, which leads to a lack of key personnel for tourism development, particularly those with expertise in cultural creativity, intangible cultural heritage (ICH) preservation, and comprehensive skills in organization and management.

Measures

1. Leveraging pear scenery to create a new attractive Hengbei space

Firstly, taking its ecological orchard as a backdrop, Hengbei Village designed and built over 300 connected villas and farmers' apartments and built roads as well as greening, lighting, and sewage facilities based on the concept of "being green, eco-friendly, and good for living and tourism". As a result, Hengbei Village has been transformed into a beautiful village with black-tiled white walls, small bridges, flowing water, green trees, and birds singing among the flowers. Secondly, Hengbei Village on the strength of its expansive pear orchards, developed rural tourism attractions like the Pear Orchard Scenery Themed Park and Hengbei Fruit Garden, which feature fragrant orchards, picturesque riverbanks, and ecological corridors. Thirdly, supporting facilities such as the Hengbei Benchangren Hotel, Yuanxiang Hot Spring Resort Hotel, and boutique homestays were also constructed to create a rural leisure tourism destination where visitors can enjoy flowers in spring, greenery in summer, fruit-picking in autumn, and hot springs in winter.

2. Focusing on the pear theme to stimulate rural tourism

Firstly, Hengbei Village has hosted the Hengbei Pear Blossom Cultural Festival for 11 consecutive years and organized the Jiangsu Provincial Rural Tourism Festival, as well as activities like the ICH Cultural and Creative Market, Jiangsu Provincial Selected ICH Exhibition, and Evaluation and Technical Seminar on Late maturing Pear Tasting in Jiangsu Modern Agriculture (Pear) Industry Technology System to enhance the village's rural tourism appeal. Secondly, Hengbei Village registered 175 "Hengbei" brand trademarks covering 45 series of products, developing a seven-level extended product line. Thirdly, over 100 types of Hengbei cultural and creative products under the theme "We Cannot Be Without Pears" were developed, and a Hengbei Pear Cultural and Creative Store was established to further the pear-themed rural tourism industry chain.

3. Enriching the pear concept to expand new rural tourism forms

Firstly, the village conducted an in-depth exploration of pear culture and built the China

Pear Museum. Secondly, the village integrated ICH, photography, traditional Chinese studies, and handicrafts, establishing a 6,000-square-meter ICH Cultural Park that houses various ICH studios, such as those for national-level porcelain carving and provincial-level wheat straw cutting, along with modern artistic workshops like Jingshuizhai and Pear Handicrafts Workshop, to enrich Hengbei's cultural heritage. Thirdly, the village promoted "tourism + wellness" by combining local and surrounding wellness and vacation resources to create integrated products like "hot springs + farming experiences", thereby establishing a new model of "ecological village + rehabilitation supported by traditional Chinese medicine + hot spring vacation". Hengbei Village was recognized as a sanatorium for the exemplary workers in Yancheng City. Additionally, the village developed "tourism + conference and exhibition" by setting up the Hengbei Training Base and offering rural revitalization demonstration courses for the Yangtze River Delta, which has created a new economic growth point for rural tourism.

Results

Hengbei Village, as part of Jiangsu Province's

third batch of characteristic pastoral village construction and the whole-village environment improvement project, built itself into a high-standard model for new rural communities. The village implemented comprehensive improvement in party leadership, industrial development, living environment, infrastructure, and public services. Meanwhile, the old village underwent enhancements in sanitation, garbage sorting, road upgrades, landscaping, bridge renovation, water system dredging, and sewage networks. The village also improved the roads, greenery, and lighting, and developed public service facilities including the village park, fitness trails, and lighted sports courts, earning titles such as China's Beautiful Village, the National Model Age-Friendly Community, and one of the National First Batch of Forest Villages. In 2023, Hengbei Village received 500,000 tourists, earning a tourism income of 15 million yuan; tourism created 150 jobs for locals; the farmers' per capita net income reached 39,100 yuan, including 28,500 yuan from fruit sales; and the village collective income amounted to four million yuan.

Experiences and Inspirations

1. Leverage industrial strengths to expand the business

By combining ecological agriculture with rural tourism, Hengbei Village has focused on improving its seedling base and fruit processing industries while going all out to develop its pear-related initiatives. The village has created local culinary specialties like the all-pear feast and Hengbei cuisine and promoted agricultural sightseeing, farming experience, wellness vacations, parent-child activities, and conference training through implementing the "rural residence + the pear orchard as the sanatorium" model.

2. Amplify brand effects to pool strength

Hengbei Village, seeking to enhance its fame through high-profile personnel and quality products,

has promoted itself via various channels, including endorsements by village leaders, live streaming, and brand activities, while consistently hosting the Hengbei Pear Blossom Cultural Festival. The "We Cannot Be Without Pears" brand has been further popularized through the coverage by national mainstream platforms like CCTV and the "Xuexi Qiangguo" app, as well as on social media platforms like Weibo, WeChat, and Douyin, continuously boosting the reputation of the village's fruit industry and rural tourism

3. Encourage broad participation and co-development

Hengbei Village has actively involved villagers by encouraging them to run farm stays, homestays, and restaurants, with supporting incentive policies in place. The village provides grants and subsidies to those who meet relevant conditions; and offers online promotion and offline guidance for those building their homestays, helping villagers prosper. Additionally, villagers are encouraged to promote tourism independently, which helps to create a strong tourism atmosphere.

4. Integrate culture with tourism

Hengbei Village has combed through local history, industrial transformation, and cultural spirit, highlighting the village's unique culture, language, cuisine, and customs, which has given rise to Hengbei's local culture. The village has refined its series of Hengbei cultural products, transforming the rich cultural heritage and beautiful pear orchard landscapes into tangible, marketable cultural and agricultural products to facilitate the sustainable integrated development of agriculture, culture, and tourism.

Plans

Firstly, it is to enhance the integration of agriculture and tourism. Hengbei Village plans to secure deep-processing projects for the pear industry and further develop pear-related products to strengthen its unique Zaosu pear industry. The village will continue hosting the annual Hengbei Pear Blossom Cultural Festival to promote the organic integration of agriculture and tourism. Secondly, it is to deepen integration between culture and tourism. Hengbei Village aims to accelerate the construction of an ICH stage by focusing on national ICH projects like "Dafeng Porcelain Carving" and organizing themed performances to create a distinctive ICH cultural block. The village will further develop Hengbei pear cultural and creative products and expand ICH-featured products, local agricultural products, and cultural products. Thirdly, it is to improve tourism services. Hengbei Village will establish a management and training mechanism for grassroots tourism service personnel, enhancing the village's role as a leader in rural tourism development and building a competent rural tourism workforce.

2024 世界旅游联盟：旅游助力乡村振兴案例（中英文双语版）
WTA Best Practices of Rural Revitalization through Tourism 2024（Chinese-English Bilingual Edition）

贵州省遵义市正安县：
吉他文化旅游赋能乡村振兴

摘　要

贵州省遵义市正安县坚持高位推动、健全机制、优化服务、市场主体、全民参与和守牢底线，自2013年引进第一家吉他企业后，正安县仅用3年时间便荣获"中国吉他制造之乡"的称号，在第8年创建了国家级文化产业示范园区，第9年荣获"中国吉他之都"的称号，创造了西部欠发达地区新型工业经济发展的奇迹，探索出山区文化产业高质量发展的新路径。正安县的吉他产业实现了从无到有的飞跃，一拳打开新世界，摘掉了正安县千百年来的绝对贫困的帽子，随着吉他产业从无到有、从有到优、从优到强，正安吉他文化旅游产业也实现了创造性转化和创新性发展，正安县探索出了一条独特的、差异化的可持续发展之路。

挑战与问题

正安县位于贵州省东北部,面积2595平方千米,总人口66万人。一座座大山曾经见证了县里农民的极度贫困。正安县虽然有着"尹珍故里""中国小说之乡""中国白茶之乡"等光辉称号,却依然面临着经济增速慢、工业底子薄、贫困面大的现实境遇。

措施

1. 立足企业"招得来"

一是实施三级联动。省市县三级将吉他产业写入"十四五"发展规划,编制《遵义市正安吉他文化产业园创建国家级文化产业示范园区工作方案》《贵州正安吉他文化旅游产业总体规划》,正安吉他文化产业的总体思路、空间布局、重点任务和保障措施清晰。二是在离县城中心5千米区域,打造了核心区近4平方千米的正安吉他文化产业园,先后投入资金28.5亿元,建成80万平方米的标准厂房、近10.44千米的园区道路,为企业"拎包入住"创造条件;同时,建立健全园区生态环境保护网格化管理机制,加强污水处理厂和污水管网管理,实施水土保持和绿化工作,守牢生态环境底线。三是出台一系列招商入驻优惠政策,吸引吉他企业及关联项目落地。四是积极动员先期入驻企业深入长三角、珠三角地区,积极开展以商招商、精准招商。

2. 立足企业"留得下"

一是园区运营管理方式摒弃"房东型",坚持"服务型"。正安县采用一站式、保姆型服务,优化规划布局,齐全服务功能,打造出全球现有吉他乐器生产基地最好的产业生态、最好的发展土壤、最好的发展平台。二是加大金融支持力度,先后实施创业贷、惠农贷、产业贷等政策,帮助企业缓解资金难题。三是聚焦企业所需的原材料加工、配件、包装、维修、物流等环节,进一步延链、补链、强链。

3. 立足企业"做得强"

一是设立品牌创新奖励基金,鼓励企业建立研发中心、培育自主品牌,支持开办地标直播基地,推动吉他工厂转变为"吉他工匠",全力打造"正安智造"的吉他。二是培育跨境电商等吉他出口企业,多次组织企业参加国际乐器展和进博会、广交会等外贸推广展会,帮助企业打通吉他外贸关键环节,推动正安吉他进军国际市场。三是发挥带动效应,建设吉他文化创业综合孵化中心,包括"吉他文化+新型业态孵化基地"、吉他跨境电商与直播孵化基地、吉他文化创新创意孵化基地等载体,拉动全县文化类小微企业发展,带动了白茶、辣椒、方竹笋等农特产品销售。

4. 立足企业"走得稳"

一是加强岗位收集,每年在正安吉他文化产业园组织招工招聘大会,为群众提供就业岗位。二是实施"百千万"工程(百名吉他演奏教师、千名吉他弹奏骨干、万名吉他弹奏爱好者),全面开展吉他文化"五进"(进学校、进机关、进企业、进社区、进乡村)活动,累计对五万余人进行了吉他弹唱培训,占全县常住人口的五分之一,百姓成为吉他文化产业发展主力军。三是围绕打造"吉他之都·音乐之城",把吉他元素深度融入城镇建设中,建成全世界最大的吉他雕塑,打造与吉他相关的主题广场、风情街、博物馆,培育研学实践基地,倾力推动吉他旅游。

成效

作为西部欠发达地区的正安县先行先试,敢闯敢为,做强吉他产业,实现大产业、大文化、大扶贫、大开放、大带动。正安县是被财政部纳入的中央财政支持普惠金融发展示范区。吉他产业成为正兴县乡村文化振兴的火车头,正安吉他登上中欧班列销往全球各地,其中70%的产品销往海外40多个国家和地区。吉他销售和会演展出带动了农特产品的推广,使"黔货出山";吉他园区里90%以上的工人为返乡农民工和留守妇女,为解决农村空巢老人和留守儿童等社会问题探索了有效路径。正安县以吉他为特色的全域旅游模式,吸引了全民参与,完善了旅游、购物、娱乐等多种旅游业态。以正安吉他文化产业园、自然景区、传统村落等为支点,融入吉他大师工作坊、吉他音乐实习基地、乡村音乐创作基地等元素,从商业创意的角度进行全面开发,形成"吉他乡村音乐""吉他山水音乐""吉他民谣""吉他夏令营"等业态。通过创意开发吉他旅游衍生商品,正安县打造了具有地方特色的文化旅游品牌,为乡村振兴提供了有力支持。

经验与启示

1. 党的领导是根本

正安吉他文化旅游产业赋能乡村振兴取得显著成效,各级党委的高度重视和园区完善的党建工作机制起到了至关重要的作用。只有坚持党的领导,把党的"触角"延伸到一线,发挥党员作用,调动各方力量,动员广大群众参与,才能形成合力,取得更大成效。

2. 融合互促是核心

坚持吉他工业、吉他文化、吉他旅游"三位一体"融合发展,正安吉他产业生存能力才更强、生命活力才更旺,赋能乡村振兴才更有力。

3. 市场主体是关键

只有发挥市场主体作用,优化产业生态,为企业纾困解难,让企业心无旁骛谋发展,才能提升企业核心竞争力,稳住经济发展增长极。

4. 全民共享是动力

正安吉他文化产业坚持以人为本,把人民群众对美好生活的向往作为工作的出发点和落脚点,把企业建在家门口,让群众在就业增收的同时,享受家庭团聚和精神文化等多项福祉,从而得到群众的大力支持,产业生命力也更加持久。

下一步计划

一是创新工作体制机制,创新文化旅游产业用地模式,努力将正安建设成为文化产业赋能乡村振兴的标杆和示范区,将正安吉他文化产业园打造成"乡村振兴"示范园。二是以吉他产业赋能,促进文旅深度融合,推动文化和旅游项目建设运营,做强乡村特色文化和旅游产业。三是以吉他文化铸魂,加强文化和旅游人才队伍建设。四是整合文化惠民活动资源,全面提升公共文化和旅游设施效能。

Zheng'an County, Zunyi City, Guizhou Province:

Guitar Cultural Tourism Injects Impetus into Rural Revitalization

Abstract

After the first guitar enterprise was introduced in 2013, it takes Zheng'an County of Zunyi City, Guizhou Province, three years to gain the reputation of "Town of Guitar Manufacturing in China", eight years to develop the national cultural industry demonstration park, and nine years to be recognized as the "Capital of Guitar in China". By providing high-level support, improving mechanisms and services, engaging market entities and the people, and securing the bottom line, Zheng'an County has created a miracle of the new industrial economy and opened a new path of high-quality development of the cultural sector in less developed western regions of China. Zheng'an County's guitar industry has been built from the ground up, eliminating absolute poverty that had existed for thousands of years. With its guitar industry starting from scratch and growing better and stronger, Zheng'an County has also achieved the transformation and innovative development of the guitar cultural tourism industry, blazing a unique and differentiated path of sustainable development of the guitar industry.

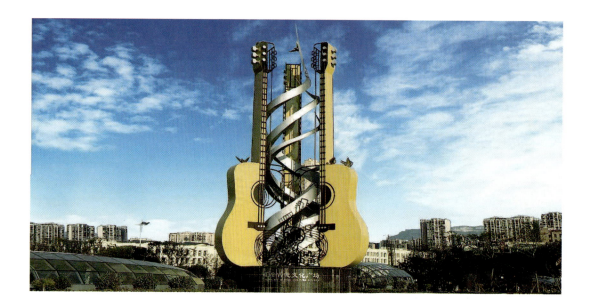

Challenges and Problems

Located in the northeast of Guizhou Province, Zheng'an County has a land area of 2,595 square kilometers and a population of 660,000. The vast mountains once witnessed the utter poverty of farmers living in the county. Known as the "Hometown of Yin Zhen (a famous scholar in the eastern Han Dynasty)", "Hometown of Chinese Novels", and "Hometown of Chinese White Tea", Zheng'an County was faced with the challenges of slow economic growth, a weak industrial foundation, and large-scale poverty.

Measures

1. Bring in businesses

Firstly, governments at the provincial, city, and county levels have collaborated with each other, all including the guitar industry into the development plans for the 14th Five-Year Plan period, and released the *Work Plan for Establishing a National Cultural Industry Demonstration Park in Zheng'an Guitar Culture Industry Park, Zunyi City* and the *Master Plan for the Guitar Cultural Tourism Industry in Zheng'an County*, specifying the general approach, spatial layout, key tasks, and safeguards of the county's guitar cultural industry. Secondly, the Zheng'an Guitar Cultural Industrial Park, which is 5 kilometers away from the county seat, has a core area of nearly 4 square kilometers. Funds of 2.85 billion yuan have been invested to build a standard workshop of 800,000 square meters and park roads of nearly 10.44 kilometers, enabling businesses to move in and start operations immediately. At the same time, the county has put in place the grid management mechanism of eco-environmental protection in the park, strengthened the management of sewage treatment plants and sewage systems, carried out soil and water conservation and greening efforts, and secured the bottom line of eco-environmental protection. Thirdly, adopt a series of preferential policies to attract guitar businesses and related projects. Fourthly, mobilize businesses that moved in early to help attract other businesses in the Yangtze

River Delta and the Pearl River Delta regions.

2. Retain businesses

Firstly, in terms of the operational and management modes, the park positions itself as a "service provider" rather than a "landlord". Zheng'an County provides a full range of one-stop, considerate services and refines the planning and layout to foster an enabling industry ecosystem and development platform among the world's guitar production bases. Secondly, increase financial support. Policies such as entrepreneurial loans, loans for farmers, and industrial loans have been implemented to help businesses address funding issues. Thirdly, further extend, supplement, and strengthen the industry chain, with a focus on raw material processing, accessories, packaging, maintenance, logistics, and other aspects necessary to the businesses.

3. Enable businesses to grow stronger

Firstly, a brand innovation fund was set up to encourage businesses to establish Research and Development centers, foster independent brands, support the establishment of live streaming bases, and promote the transformation of guitar workshops into "guitar craftsmen" in a push for intelligent manufacturing of guitars in Zheng'an. Secondly, cultivate guitar export-oriented businesses such as cross-border e-commerce enterprises, organize businesses to participate in international musical instrument exhibitions and international trade promotional events such as the China International Import Expo and the Canton Fair, help businesses connect the key links of international trade in guitars, and bring guitars made in Zheng'an to the global markets. Thirdly, give full play to the driving role. A comprehensive guitar cultural entrepreneurship and incubation center was built, including the guitar culture + incubation base for new business forms, guitar cross-border e-commerce and live streaming incubation base, and the guitar culture innovation and creativity incubation base, thus propelling the development of small and micro cultural enterprises in the county and driving the sales of agricultural specialities such as white tea, pepper, and square bamboo shoots.

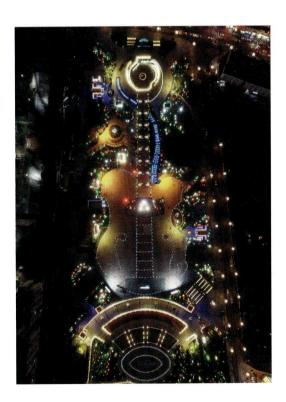

4. Help businesses achieve steady development

Firstly, increase efforts in gathering job vacancies, and organize job fairs in the Zheng'an International Guitar Industrial Park every year. Secondly, carry out the campaign aimed at training 100 guitar teachers, 1,000 guitar players, and 10,000 guitar enthusiasts, and bring the guitar culture into schools, public institutions, enterprises, communities, and villages. Training has been provided for more than 50,000 guitar players and singers, accounting for one-fifth of the county's permanent population. The people have been the mainstay in the development of the guitar culture industry. Thirdly, for the purpose of building a "Capital of Guitar, City of Music", guitar elements are integrated into urban construction. The county has built the largest guitar sculpture in the world, a theme square, distinctive street, museum, and a practice bas to promote guitar-themed tourism.

Results

Zheng'an, a less developed county in West China, takes the lead in piloting with and developing the guitar industry, achieving the coordinated development of industry, culture, poverty alleviation, and opening up and exerting a great driving role. Zheng'an County has been designated by the Ministry of Finance as the central government-subsidized inclusive finance demonstration zone. The guitar industry has become a key driver of rural cultural revitalization. Guitars made in Zheng'an are carried to all over the world on the China-Europe freight train, 70% of which are sold to more than 40 overseas countries and regions. Guitar shows and exhibitions drive the agricultural specialties of Guizhou out of the mountains. More than 90% of the workers in the guitar park are returning migrant workers and left-behind women, offering effective ways to solve social problems such as empty nesters and left-behind children. Zheng'an County with guitar as the characteristics of the global tourism model, attracting the participation of the whole people, improving the tourism, shopping, entertainment and other forms of tourism. The guitar master workshop, guitar practice base, and country music creation base in the Zheng'an Guitar Cultural Industrial Park, natural scenic areas, and traditional villages are designed with commercial creativity. New business forms such

as "country music on guitar", "landscape music on guitar", "folk music on guitar", and "guitar summer camp" have taken shape, and guitar-related derivative products for tourism have been developed to boost cultural tourism with Zheng'an characteristics and support rural revitalization.

Experiences and Inspirations

1. Party leadership is the bedrock

The guitar cultural tourism industry of Zheng'an County has given a strong boost to rural revitalization, thanks to the great importance from Party committees at all levels and the sound Party building mechanisms in the park. Only by upholding the Party's leadership, extending the Party's reach to the frontline, giving full play to the role of Party members, pooling resources, and engaging the people can we form synergy and accomplish greater things.

2. Integration and interplay are the core

Pursuing the integrated development of the guitar industry, guitar culture, and guitar-themed tourism injects strong vitality into the county's guitar industry and rural revitalization.

3. Market entities are the key

It is necessary to give full play to the role of market entities, improve the industry ecology, help businesses solve difficulties, and enable them to focus on development. Only in this way can their core competitiveness be enhanced and new economic growth drivers can be fostered.

4. Development shared by the people is the driving force

Putting the people first, the guitar cultural industry of Zheng'an County aims to meet the

people's aspirations for a better life. It provides jobs for the people living nearby, allowing them to get more incomes without having to leave their hometown and also enriching their cultural life. With the people's support, the industry is flourishing with stronger vitality.

Plans

Firstly, adopt innovative working systems and mechanisms, explore new land use models for the cultural tourism industry, strive to build Zheng'an County into a benchmark and demonstration zone in empowering rural revitalization through the development of the cultural industry, and turn Zheng'an Guitar Cultural Industrial Park into a demonstration park for rural revitalization. Secondly, exploit the momentum of the guitar industry to promote the integration of culture and tourism, advance the construction and operation of cultural and tourism projects, and strengthen the rural cultural and tourism industries with local features. Thirdly, foster the guitar culture and enhance the building of cultural and tourism talent teams. Fourthly, integrate the resources of public-benefit cultural activities and deliver better public cultural and tourism facilities.

2024 世界旅游联盟：旅游助力乡村振兴案例（中英文双语版）
WTA Best Practices of Rural Revitalization through Tourism 2024（Chinese-English Bilingual Edition）

吉林省梅河口市小杨满族朝鲜族乡古城村：
坚持以绿色发展走农旅融合之路

摘 要

吉林省梅河口市小杨满族朝鲜族乡古城村，从深入挖掘朝鲜族农耕文化、发挥资源优势入手，注重彰显特色，大力发展乡村旅游。2018年至2022年间，乡政府累计整合资金500余万元建设古城朝鲜族民俗风情村，打造古城朝鲜族民俗博物馆、古城民俗风情村精品民宿、餐厅等产业项目。2023年，小杨乡整合资金千万元进一步打造古城农旅田园综合体项目。古城村以美丽乡村建设为抓手，走出一条独具特色的乡村振兴之路。

挑战与问题

吉林省梅河口市小杨满族朝鲜族乡古城村，辖区面积4.6平方千米，辖2个自然屯，6个村民小组，216户756人。古城村位于通往著名旅游景点鸡冠山和磨盘湖的必经之路上，交通优势明显。古城村坚持以绿色发展为引领，结合其传统建筑、格局和村貌，走农旅融合发展之路。古城村近些年在发展过程中存在一些挑战和问题：一是相关基础配套设施不足，古城民俗村体量相对较小，承载能力有限，还需要进一步打造升级；二是人才短缺，大量年轻劳动力外流，缺乏有能力、有干劲的人才来推动各项建设工作的开展；三是目前古城村的历史故事存在片面化的情况，没有载体，村民传承与开发民俗文化的观念意识薄弱。

措施

1. 着眼大局，科学谋划

一是城乡携手，助推乡村旅游。小杨乡积极与企事业单位、中小学校和旅发集团深度对接，打好"梅河热+景区热+民宿热"的组合拳，努力构建"景城联动、城乡互动"的良好格局；二是聚焦重点，打造精品线路。古城村依托磨盘湖、鸡冠山等自然优势资源，持续加强古城朝鲜族民俗村和古城博物馆等优质旅游点位，形成点带动线、线带动面的集聚联动效应，进一步提高乡村旅游融合带动发展的积极作用。三是农旅融合，赋能乡村振兴。小杨乡构建全新农旅产品销售平台，为小杨乡牛肉、蔬菜等特色产品提供销售平台，扩展农特色产品销售渠道，为小杨百姓增产增收。

2. 抢抓机遇，提升品质

一是完善基础设施，提升游客体验感。古城村以农旅一期续建项目为抓手，完成8000米农田作业道、7000米水渠、边沟及路面基础建设，以及增设农田观光栈道、改造民宿、安装空气能热泵及相关配套设施等。二是加强招商引资，培育产品新体系。古城村持续盘活闲置民房，吸引社会资本进入，以古城村供销社为载体，发挥产品集聚效应，形成小杨乡特色品牌，提升了古城民俗村的自我发展能力和市场竞争力。三是优化管理模式，提升服务能力。古城村建立游客、村民、市场反馈机制，定期邀请专业人员对民宿工作人员进行精细化指导，提升接待能力和服务水平，同时重视专业人才储备，留住"自家人"、吸引"外来客"，激励各类人才在农村广阔天地大有作为。

3. 加强宣传，激活市场

一是以古城村为重点，线上线下同步宣传。积极与融媒体、小杨乡本土网红定期开展网络宣传，推介本土农特产品、乡村旅游精品路线，提升农旅融合影响力。二是丰富文化活动，提高古城知名度。积极举办"丰收节""辣白菜节""民俗文化节"等系列文化活动，主动承接婚礼、宴席等市场业务，发挥古城民俗博物馆和"红石榴"广场的实践教学优势，与市教育局对接，利用寒暑假及休息日组织学生现场研学，让古城村成为全市中小学生的"民俗文化补给站"。

成效

古城村已经成为集餐饮住宿、休闲康养、农业观光、农耕体验、文化展示为一体的朝鲜族特色乡村，为周边村屯农民提供就业岗位100多个，带动贫困户18户，切实将资源优势转化为富民资本，为农民创造就业、实现增收。古城乡村旅游集精品水稻种植、特色产品加工、旅游商贸服务于一体，2023年累计

接待游客及研学人员 4 万余人，2 月实现收入 15 万余元。古城村先后获得中国美丽休闲乡村、吉林省民族团结进步示范单位和省级朝鲜族民俗文化传承教育基地等荣誉。

经验与启示

1. 提高思想认识，打开格局，铸牢古城旅游平台

古城村在旅游发展的过程中，要突破狭隘的地域观念与单一的发展模式，积极借鉴各地区先进的旅游发展理念与经验，以及与古城村同体量同规模村庄的优秀案例，结合古城村自身的特色与优势，从基础设施建设、服务质量提升、文化内涵挖掘等多个方面进行全面发力。

2. 深挖文化资源，打开思路，努力讲好古城故事

古城村皇粮御米碑作为历史见证，标志着此地曾为清朝皇室种植御用稻米，是梅河口"皇粮御米之乡"美誉的起源。古城村深入挖掘其所蕴含的丰富文化资源，摒弃传统思维局限，以创新开放的思路，运用多样化的手段与方式，如多媒体展示、艺术创作等，生动而深入地讲述古城的故事，凭借其独特的魅力赢得了广泛的关注和喜爱。

3. 强化招商引资，打开胸怀，优化古城运营模式

古城村要强化招商引资，引入优质的项目、资金和人才，为古城村的建设与提升提供坚实的支撑。同时，不断优化古城村运营模式，提升管理水平与服务质量，营造良好的发展环境，以适应不断变化的市场需求和发展形势。

下一步计划

古城村要继续以少数民族文化为载体，以乡村旅游为抓手，继续优化现有业态，引入更多新兴业态。古城村将继续以"朝鲜族村庄 + 生态田园 + 主题民宿 + 特色产业"的模式，打造产业融合创新示范区、农业科普教育研学基地、周末休闲乡村游、户外扩展训练基地、田园风光写生摄影基地的古城农旅田园综合体。

Gucheng Village, Xiaoyang Manchu and Korean Ethnic Township, Meihekou City, Jilin Province:

Pursue Green Development by Integrating Agriculture and Tourism

Abstract

Gucheng Village, Xiaoyang Manchu and Korean Ethnic Township, Meihekou City, Jilin Province has boosted rural tourism with local features by exploring the depths of the Korean farming culture and exploiting its advantages in resources. From 2018 to 2022, the township spent more than 5 million yuan in building the Gucheng Korean Folk Village, where the projects such as the Gucheng Korean Folk Museum, characterful homestays, and restaurants were carried out. In 2023, the township invested more than 10 million yuan in the agritourism project in Gucheng Village. For the purpose of building of a beautiful countryside, Gucheng Village has blazed a unique path to rural revitalization.

Challenges and Problems

Covering an area of 4.6 square kilometers, Gucheng Village has jurisdiction over two natural villages, six villagers groups, 216 households, and a population of 756. It is conveniently situated on the only tourist route leading to Jiguan Mountain and Mopan Lake. In pursuing green development, Gucheng Village has embarked on the path of integrated development of agriculture and tourism by combining its traditional architecture, pattern, and landscape. The following are the challenges and problems faced by Gucheng Village in recent years. Firstly, the infrastructure is inadequate. The Gucheng Korean Folk Village is relatively small with limited carrying capacity, so it needs to be further expanded and upgraded. Secondly, human resources are in short supply. Many young people are working out of town, leaving few capable and highly driven people to keep things going. Thirdly, stories about Gucheng Village are still fragmented without effective means of transmission, and villagers lacks awareness regarding the preservation and development of folk culture.

Measures

1. Bear in mind the big picture and draw up scientific plans

Firstly, pool urban and rural strengths to boost rural tourism. Xiaoyang Manchu and Korean Ethnic Township closely collaborates with enterprises and public institutions, primary and secondary schools, and tourism development groups to increase the popularity of Meihekou City, scenic areas, and homestays in a coordinated way, so as to form synergy between the city and scenic areas and between urban and rural areas. Secondly, focus on key areas to build high-quality tourist routes. Relying on its natural resources such as Mopan Lake and Jiguan Mountain, Gucheng Village has continuously strengthened premium tourist attractions such as the Gucheng Korean Folk Village and Gucheng Korean Folk Museum to create cascading effects, and enhanced the positive role of agritourism in promoting local development. Thirdly, integrate agriculture and tourism to empower rural revitalization. The township has built a new sales platform for agricultural and tourism products such as beef, vegetables, and other specialty products, expanding the sales channels of agricultural specialties and raising the incomes of local people.

2. Seize opportunities and improve the service quality

Firstly, improve infrastructure and enhance tourist experiences. Gucheng Village has expanded the Phase I agritourism project, including competing the construction of 8,000-meter farm roads, 7,000-meter canals, side ditches, and pavement infrastructure, the renovation of farmland sightseeing plank roads and homestays, and the installation of air source heat pumps and supporting facilities. Secondly, redouble efforts in attracting investment and fostering a new

product mix. Gucheng Village has put idle houses to good use and engaged private capital in its development. It has leveraged the platform of the Gucheng Village Supply and Marketing Cooperative to create the effects of agglomeration for products, build its own brand, and sustain the development of the Gucheng Korean Folk Village. Thirdly, improve the management models and service capabilities. Gucheng Village has an effective feedback mechanism for tourists, villagers, and the market, and regularly invites specialists to provide guidance and training for the staff of homestays in an effort to improve their reception capacity and service quality. Meanwhile, it pays high attention to the building of a talent pool, works to retain local human sources and attract out-of-town visitors, and encourages highly skilled people in different fields to accomplish things in rural areas.

3. Strengthen publicity and build hype

Firstly, carrying out online and offline promotional campaigns centered around Gucheng Village. The measures include working with integrated media and local influencers to promote agricultural specialties and rural tourism routes, thus strengthening the influence of agritourism. Secondly, organize a diverse range of cultural activities to increase the visibility of Gucheng Village. For example, the village holds a series of cultural activities such as the Harvest Festival, the Spicy Cabbage Festival, and the Folk Culture Festival, actively engages in commercial businesses such as weddings and banquets, and works with the Meihekou Municipal Education Bureau to organize students to visit the Gucheng Korean Folk Museum and the Red Pomegranate Cultural Square during winter and summer vacations and weekends, making the village a favored folk culture educational base for primary and secondary school students in the city.

Results

Today's Gucheng Village is a distinctive Korean ethnic village integrating such functions as catering and accommodation, leisure and wellness, agricultural sightseeing, farming experience, and cultural showcase. It has provided more than 100 jobs for farmers in surrounding villages and supported 18 poor households in getting out of poverty, effectively translating its resource strengths into capital to create jobs for farmers and raise their incomes. Rural tourism in Gucheng Village encompasses high-standard rice planting, specialty product processing,

and tourism and business services. In 2023, it received a total of more than 40,000 visitors, and posted tourism revenue of over 150,000 yuan in February alone. Gucheng Village has been selected the Beautiful Leisure Village of China, the Model in National Unity and Progress in Jilin Province, and the Korean Folk Culture Preservation and Education Base at the provincial-level.

Experiences and Inspirations

1. Take new perspectives, bear in mind the full picture, and consolidate the tourism platform

In the process of tourism development, Gucheng Village takes a broad perspective, adopts diversified development models, draws on the concepts and experience of other places and best practices of villages of a similar size, and capitalizes on its own characteristics and advantages to improve the infrastructure, service quality, and dive into local culture in an all-round manner.

2. Dig deep into cultural resources, keep an open mind, and tell its story well

The Monument of Imperial Rice in Gucheng Village commemorates the ancestors who planted rice for the royal family of the Qing Dynasty. This is why Meihekou City is hailed as the "town of imperial rice". Gucheng Village dives deep into its rich cultural resources and tells its story with innovative and open concepts and in diversified means and ways, such as multimedia presentation and artistic creations, gaining extensive attention and popularity with its unique charm.

3. Redouble efforts in investment attraction, open its arms wide, and improve its operational models

Great efforts are made to attract investment and bring in high-quality projects, funds, and talent to provide strong support for its development. At the same time, the village constantly refines its operational models, improves its management and service quality, and betters the development environment to meet the ever-changing market demand and development conditions.

Plans

Gucheng Village will continue to boost rural tourism highlighting ethnic minority cultures, improve the existing business forms, and introduce new business forms. The village will further improve the model of "Korean ethnic village + pastoral leisure complexes + theme homestays + featured industries" and develop agritourism complexes including the industrial integration innovation demonstration zone, agricultural sci-tech education and research base, weekend rural tourism, outbound training base, and pastoral sketch and photography base.

湖北省宜昌市长阳土家族自治县郑家榜村：

农文旅融合催生山乡巨变

摘　要

　　湖北省宜昌市长阳土家族自治县郑家榜村依托特有的山水资源，引进长阳中武当文化旅游开发有限公司，于村内投资并建成了国家 4A 级旅游景区——清江方山，积极探索景村共建发展道路，引源活水催生山乡巨变。郑家榜村全村群众团结一心，坚持生态立村、旅游兴村、产业富村、文化活村、队伍强村的五村工作思路，集全村之力，支持企业开发高品质旅游景区。该村与企业积极探索并实施了三权分置、三管一体的制度模式，有效推动了景村共建的构想落地，使村民搭上致富快车，乡村走上振兴道路。

挑战与问题

郑家榜村占地面积为41.21平方千米，下辖10个村民小组，共包含765户家庭，总人口数为2204。该村的森林覆盖率接近90%。郑家榜村地处长阳土家族自治县龙舟坪西部，是一个典型的山区农村，山多地少，交通极为不便，2008年底为全镇综合排名倒数第一，是县委和县政府高度关注的贫困地区。那时郑家榜村基础设施建设严重滞后，老百姓的思想观念封闭落后，村内缺乏具有引领作用的龙头产业，导致群众普遍感到发展前景不明朗，缺乏明确的奋斗目标和动力。出现问题的根源主要有以下三个方面：一是群众的思想观念封闭落后，只知道自己生活在穷山恶水的地方，没有意识到所拥有的资源优势；二是中国城市化建设步伐越来越快，大量的劳动力和各种技术人才被城市吸引，村内无人能治、无人来建；三是金融企业在农村只存不贷，村级核心产业无法形成。

措施

1. 提出发展思路

郑家榜村召回有才能的村民回村担任主要领导，进行全村大走访、大调查。村集体结合群众实际情况和村情，提出山上林下养山鸡、河下泉水喂大鲵、依溪沿路农家乐、建村造田坡改梯的发展思路，以及生态立村、旅游兴村、产业富村、文化活村、队伍强村的工作思路。

2. 借助政策东风

2010年，在全省开展的城乡互联、结对共建的活动中，郑家榜成为省直机关工委驻点联系村；2013年，郑家榜村成功招引长阳中武当文化旅游开发有限公司建设清江方山景区。随着清江方山景区的开发与建设，郑家榜村进一步积极借力和借势，拉开乡村发展大幕。

3. 探索景村共建

郑家榜村提出景村共建的战略设想，将景区、村、村民结合在一起，探索景村共建制度设计，成立村级龙兴文旅发展有限公司，最终形成景区、村集体、村民三者共同利益联结机制，有效化解矛盾，营造优良发展环境。郑家榜村挖掘土家"抬格子"吃蒸肉的习俗，景区、村集体、村民共同创办七届孝山冬祭万人年猪宴，形成省内冬季旅游名片，提升景区知名度和美誉度，带动景村共同发展。

成效

郑家榜村积极探索景村共建，实现景区安置就业一批，依托产业链延伸积极扶持一批，壮大村集体经济吸纳一批，实现了旅游企业、村集体和村民三者均丰收的可喜局面。截至 2022 年，郑家榜村从 2008 年底全镇 26 个村（社区）综合排名倒数第一跃升为全镇前三强，人均纯收入从不足 5000 元跃升到 17400 元，全村银行存款从 130 万元跃升到近 2000 万元，村集体收入从零提升到近 100 万元。

郑家榜村先后获得了全国民族团结进步示范村、全国文明村、全国少数民族特色村寨、全国乡村旅游重点村、全国旅游扶贫模范村、全国绿色低碳示范案例等多项殊荣，为全省山区乡村振兴提供了有益经验。

经验与启示

1. 特色产业是乡村振兴的决胜之招

产业振兴是乡村振兴的重中之重，选准选并培育形成主导产业，是郑家榜村实现良好发展的重要筹码。山区乡村各地条件差异较大，必须依托自身资源优势，在科学论证的基础上因地制宜地打造具有较大市场潜力的主导产业，为实现乡村振兴奠定坚实物质基础。

2. 人才是乡村振兴的活力源泉

郑家榜村通过近年来的产业建设与环境营造，不仅留住了村内人，引回了乡贤，还招来了外地商，实现常住人口持续增长。各种能工巧匠、文化艺人、非遗传承人等都有了才能展示的舞台、价值实现的机会。人人皆可为、人人皆能为的人才培育与人才队伍建设，是凝聚乡村人气、朝气与烟火气的关键举措。

3. 利益联结机制是乡村振兴的根本动力

利益共享才能合作共赢，共同奋斗方可共同富裕。通过构建景区企业、村级组织和村民之间的利益共享机制，充分激发了多元主体功能，全面提升了各类主体的参与感、获得感。共建共享、共同缔造是郑家榜村得以实现良好发展的关键所在。

下一步计划

一是加快数字乡村建设，培育更多的智慧民宿，加快从销售产品向提供体验转变，努力提升游客的舒适感。二是进一步完善利益分配机制，进一步稳定景村共建的利益分配，强化联农带农措施，保障脱贫群众拥有自我发展能力，确保全村均衡发展、共同致富。三是积极营造投资环境，争取景区加大投入，提升景区市场竞争力，加快推进景村合作共同开发客源市场，打开旅游消费能力，推动村集体经济收入尽快突破 100 万元，引领全村产业发展，带动更多的农户增收，实现高质量乡村振兴。

2024 世界旅游联盟：旅游助力乡村振兴案例（中英文双语版）
WTA Best Practices of Rural Revitalization through Tourism 2024（Chinese-English Bilingual Edition）

Zhengjiabang Village, Changyang Tujia Autonomous County, Yichang City, Hubei Province:

Agriculture, Culture and Tourism Integration Effecting Profound Changes in the Mountainous Village

Abstract

Zhengjiabang Village of Changyang Tujia Autonomous County, Yichang City, Hubei Province, boasts unique mountains and water resources and has introduced Changyang Zhongwudang Culture and Tourism Development Co., Ltd. to invest and develop the national 4A-level scenic spot—Qingjiang Fangshan in the village. It actively explores the development path featuring cooperation between the scenic area and the village and introduces external resources to effect profound changes in the mountainous village. The villagers work with one mind and adhere to the five-sphere approach covering ecological conservation, tourism, rural industries, culture, and team building. The village and the enterprise actively explored and implemented the institutional model of separation of three rights and three-in-one regulation, effectively promoting the implementation of the idea of joint construction between the scenic spot and the village, increase the people's income, and embark on the road to rural revitalization.

Challenges and Problems

Zhengjiabang Village covers an area of 41.21 square kilometers, home to a population of 2,204 who are divided into 10 villager groups of 765 households, and with a forest coverage rate of nearly 90%. Located in the west of Longzhouping, Changyang Tujia Autonomous County, it is a typical mountainous village, with many mountains and little cultivated land, and inconvenient transportation. It ranked at the bottom of the county at the end of 2008 and was a poor area that the Party committee and the government of the county were highly concerned about. Back then, the infrastructure in the village was outdated, there was no industry leader, and the people were conservative and saw no way out. There are mainly three root causes. Firstly, the villagers only knew that they lived in harsh conditions, not aware of the advantageous resources they had. Secondly, the quickening pace of urbanization lured away a large number of labor and skilled talents, resulting in a shortage of talent for village governance and development. Thirdly, financial enterprises took only deposits but did not lend money, making it impossible to cultivate village-level core industries.

Measures

1. Clarifying the development approach

Zhengjiabang Village asked some of the capable migrant workers to return and serve as leading officials and conducted village-wide interviews and surveys. Based on the actual situation of the villagers and the village, the village collective suggested raising pheasants in the mountains and forests, raising giant salamanders with spring water, opening farm stays on the riverside, and turning mountain slopes into terraced fields and proposing the five-sphere development approach covering ecological conservation, tourism, rural industries, culture, and team building.

2. Taking advantage of policy support

In 2010, Zhengjiabang Village became a contact village for the working committee of the organs directly under the provincial government as Hubei launched an urban-rural paired-up assistant program. In 2013, it introduced Changyang Zhongwudang Culture and Tourism Development Co., Ltd. to develop the Qingjiang Fangshan in the village, which has lent more momentum to rural development in Zhengjiabang.

3. Exploring the collaborative and integrated development of the scenic spot and the village

Zhengjiabang Village worked with the scenic spot and villagers to jointly design a system for the collaborative and integrated development of the scenic spot and the village, established Longxing Culture and Tourism Development Co., Ltd., and finally formed an interest connection mechanism between the scenic spot, the village collective and villagers, effectively resolving contradictions and creating a good environment for development. Carrying forward the Tujia people's custom of eating Steamed Pork to celebrate the New Year, the village collective mobilized the scenic spot and the villagers to jointly host seven editions of Xiaoshan Winter Festival Pork Banquet, which has become a popular winter tourism product in Hubei, building up the popularity and reputation of the scenic spot, and driving the common development of the scenic spot and the village.

Results

Zhengjiabang Village actively explores the collaborative development of the scenic spot and the village. Some of the locals have found jobs in the scenic spot, some in the extended industrial chain, and some in the village collective economy, resulting in a win-win for the tourism enterprise, the village collective, and the villagers. By the end of 2022,the village has jumped from the bottom of the 26 villages (communities) in the town at the end of 2008 to the top three in the town; its per capita net income soared from less than 5,000 yuan to 17,400 yuan; the bank deposits of the whole village increased from 1.3 million yuan to nearly 20 million yuan, and the village collective's income grew from zero to nearly 1 million yuan.

Zhengjiabang Village has been awarded the National Demonstration Village for Ethnic Unity and Progress, the National Civilized Village, the National Village with Characteristics of Ethnic Minorities, the National Key Village for the Development of Rural Tourism, the National Model Village for Poverty Alleviation through Tourism, and the National Best Practice of Green and Low-Carbon Demonstration, providing a useful experience for the revitalization of other mountainous villages in Hubei.

Experience and Inspirations

1. The development of characteristic industries is the key to rural revitalization

Industrial revitalization is the top priority of rural revitalization, and choosing the right industry

and cultivating it into the leading industry is an important guarantee for the village's development. Each mountainous village has its unique conditions, so they must proceed from their advantageous resources, develop leading industries with great market potential based on scientific demonstration and local conditions, and thus lay a solid material foundation for rural revitalization.

2. Talent is the source of vitality for rural revitalization

Through industrial development and environmental improvement in recent years, Zhengjiabang Village has not only retained the people and lured back the migrant workers, but also attracted external investors, with an ever-growing permanent resident population. It provides all the craftsmen, artists, and intangible cultural heritage inheritors a stage and opportunities to shine and realize their value. Talent cultivation and team-building efforts for everyone to shine are key to stimulating population growth, vitality, and everyday activity in the village.

3. The interest linkage mechanism is the fundamental driving force for rural revitalization

Only by sharing interests can we achieve win-win cooperation, and only by working together can we achieve common prosperity. Through the benefit-sharing mechanism between the tourism enterprise, village-level organizations, and villagers, the stakeholders are fully motivated, and their sense of participation and gain has been comprehensively enhanced. Join contribution and shared benefits are the key to Zhengjiabang's success.

cultivate more smart homestays, accelerate to develop more experiential tourism products, and strive to improve the visitor experience. Secondly, further improve the benefit distribution mechanism, stabilize the distribution of benefits for the joint contribution of the scenic area and the village, step up to engage farmers, help them develop employment skills, and ensure the balanced development and common prosperity of the whole village. Thirdly, actively create an investment environment, strive to increase investment in the scenic spot to enhance its market competitiveness, accelerate the cooperation between the scenic spot and the village to jointly attract more visitors, and boost the tourism consumption capacity. Zhengjiabang Village will also work hard to increase the village collective income to over 1 million yuan as soon as possible, to lead the development of local industries, increase the income of more farmers, and achieve high-quality rural revitalization.

Plans

Firstly, speed up the digitization of the village,

2024 世界旅游联盟：旅游助力乡村振兴案例（中英文双语版）
WTA Best Practices of Rural Revitalization through Tourism 2024（Chinese-English Bilingual Edition）

黑龙江省牡丹江市穆棱市孤榆树村：
"抗联路"里走出的"致富路"

摘 要

黑龙江省牡丹江市穆棱市下城子镇孤榆树村依托自然资源和区位优势，不断加强基础设施建设，全面整治村庄环境，持续提升村民素质，深入挖掘红色记忆，融入红色文化，以党建引领激活乡村振兴发展"红色引擎"。2017年，孤榆树村投资1.2亿元打造"孤榆树东北抗联密营教育基地"，使其成为集教学、研学、培训、体验、拓展于一体，兼具"吃、住、行、游、娱、购"的抗联文化教育基地和红色旅游景区。孤榆树村以发展农村经济为支撑，以红色旅游为动能，从抗联路里走出了一条独特的乡村振兴致富路。

挑战与问题

孤榆树村距下城子镇中心10千米，辖区行政区域面积28平方千米，辖3个自然村，现有耕地18057亩，全村共346户，户籍人口1143人，常住人口506人。近年来，随着孤榆树村红色旅游业的快速发展，存在的问题也逐步显现。一是游客在孤榆树东北抗联密营教育基地的旅游活动多以参观为主，消费动力不足，且淡旺季游客流量落差大。二是孤榆树村是一个典型的山区村落，山多地少，土质较为贫瘠，村民多以种植大豆、玉米为主，农作物生长缓慢，村民收入较低。三是由于农村经济条件的制约，村内青壮年为改善生活纷纷外出务工，导致村内常住人口减少，且老龄化严重，村落逐步失去活力，"空心村"问题愈发突出。

措施

1. 打造红色演出，塑造红色教育品牌

孤榆树村以红色旅游为载体，村民们围绕党性教育、爱国主义教育和国防教育打造了歌舞剧、红歌等文艺节目，文艺演出项目的开发留住了游客、留住了乡愁，增加了村民收入，提高了村民参与红色旅游发展建设的积极性。

2. 促进商旅结合，赋能乡村产业发展

孤榆树村紧抓"孤榆树东北抗联密营教育基地"建设的有利契机，成立了穆棱市孤榆树文化推广有限公司和穆棱市孤榆树旅游服务有限公司，大力推进"公司＋合作社"发展模式，有效整合了村内的鱼池、凉亭、房屋等资源，将其纳入教育基地的整体建设规划之中。与此同时，公司积极促进教育基地与海月湾等周边景区的串联，让红色旅游在市场中发展壮大。

3. 创新经营模式，拓宽村民致富渠道

孤榆树村积极推进"公司＋农户"的统筹发展模式。一是大力盘活各家各户闲置农房，通过旧屋改造落实民宿项目，每所民宿配置一个菜园，吸引游客从城市走到乡村，了解当地红色文化、欣赏自然景观、体验农村生产生活。二是鼓励群众积极投身到旅游服务中来，带动村民利用农闲时间开展家庭餐厅、超市商店、抗联煎饼铺、摔碗酒等经营项目拓宽收入来源。

三是因地制宜谋划和发展自然旅游观光、徒步休闲旅游、采摘园、农家乐等项目，促进村民和村集体的同步增收。

4. 发展冰雪经济，激发乡村振兴活力

2022年，孤榆树村以全国红色美丽村庄建设试点为根基，大力发展冰雪经济，成立了穆棱市极地圈冰雪文化推广有限公司，打造孤榆树雪上乐园，填补了孤榆树村冬季旅游空缺。雪上乐园项目吸引一系列餐饮企业和雪上娱乐项目设施的入驻，进一步盘活了孤榆树村的自然资源和人力资源，实现了农户、村集体和市场主体的"三赢"。

成效

孤榆树村紧抓东北抗联密营教育基地和雪上乐园建设的有利契机，从一个偏僻贫穷的落后村转变成为远远闻名的红色文化旅游村，从房屋低矮、交通不便的传统农村变成了环境优美、设施齐全的美丽新村。孤榆树村通过"公司+农户"和"公司+合作社"的统筹发展模式，有效带动村集体增收50万元，为当地村民提供就业岗位40余个，年人均增收12000元，促进了村民和村集体的同步增收。2023年，孤榆树旅游产业收入达356万元，当地村民年均收入达2.78万元。孤榆树村先后获得国家3A级旅游景区、中国美丽休闲乡村、全国乡村旅游重点村等荣誉称号。

经验与启示

1. 发展红色旅游

红色旅游是保护文化遗产的契机，是弘扬中国革命红色文化的一种新的体现形式。通过发展红色旅游既可以缓解资金不足，带动偏远地区发展，还可以保护珍贵的红色遗产，形成良好的生态循环，有效发挥"红色吸引人、精神感染人、绿色留住人"的红色旅游资源优势。

2. 打造红色品牌

在对红色遗产进行保护开发的基础上，结合实际情况，不断开拓创新，打造出独具特色的红色旅游品牌项目，贴近实际、贴近生活、贴近群众，将革命传统教育与旅游开发有机结合，寓游于教。

3. 创新红色教育

红色旅游具有不可比拟的教育宣传功能，对青少年成长具有重要意义。以旅游为手段，学习和旅游相呼应，营造出自我启发的教育氛围，达到"游中学、学中游"的效果，达到润心无声的境界。

下一步计划

孤榆树村将继续践行习近平总书记的重要指示，把红色资源利用好、把红色传统发扬好、把红色基因传承好。一是将孤榆树东北抗联密营教育基地与镇域内的海月湾、保安采摘园景点串线，整体打包营销，探索市场化发展的新路径。二是继续完善孤榆树东北抗联密营基地配套服务设施，建设培训中心、服务中心，挖掘利用周边遗址遗迹群，开发更多体验式、参与性、互动性项目，并实现公司化运营。三是加大基地与省内外培训机构合作，探索形式多样、丰富多彩的载体活动，寻求更大的发展空间和平台，使更多的党员干部和高校师生来重走"抗联路"，重思抗联魂，接受东北抗联历史文化的洗礼，感受老一辈无产阶级革命家的崇高情怀和魅力风范，激活内心深处的红色基因，让红色基因代代相传。

Guyushu Village, Muling City, Mudanjiang City, Heilongjiang Province:

Leveraging the Heritage of the Northeast Anti-Japanese United Army for Rural Prosperity

Abstract

Based on its natural resources and prime location, Guyushu Village of Xiachengzi Town, Muling City, Mudanjiang City, Heilongjiang Province, has continuously increased investment in infrastructure construction, and comprehensively improved the village environment and the overall quality of villagers. It has dug deeply into local revolutionary history, integrated the CPC heritage, and advanced Party building to drive rural revitalization. Guyushu Village has invested 120 million yuan to build the Northeast Anti-Japanese United Army Secret Campgrounds Educational Base and turn them into CPC heritage-themed educational bases and tourist attractions offering extensive services such as education, study tours, training, experiential and outbound activities, with catering, accommodation, transportation, travel, entertainment, and shopping facilities. Guyushu Village has embarked on a unique road of rural revitalization by developing red tourism to drive rural economic development.

Challenges and Problems

Guyushu Village is 10 kilometers away from the center of Xiachengzi Town, with an administrative area of 28 square kilometers covering three natural villages with 18,057 *mu* of cultivated land. It has 346 registered households and a registered population of 1,143, including 506 permanent residents. In recent years, the rapid development of red tourism has increasingly exposed the problems facing Guyushu Village. Firstly, tourist spending at the Northeast Anti-Japanese United Army Secret Campgrounds Educational Base is low, and the tourist flow varies greatly in the off and peak seasons. Secondly, Guyushu Village is a typical mountainous village, with many mountains and little cultivated land, and the soil is not fertile. The main crops are the slow-growing soybeans and corn, and the villagers' income is low. Thirdly, since the economy is poor, the young and middle-aged have left the village to improve their livelihoods, resulting in a decrease in the permanent population who are aging quickly. The village has gradually lost its vitality and become increasingly "hollow".

Measures

1. Producing red performances and building the brand of red heritage education

For red tourism, villagers have produced song and dance dramas, CPC heritage-themed songs, and other artistic programs for advocating the Party spirit, patriotism, and national defense education. These performances have retained tourists and increased the income of villagers, incentivizing them to participate in the development of red tourism.

2. Promoting business-tourism integration to empower the development of rural industries

While building the Northeast Anti-Japanese United Army Secret Campgrounds Educational Base, Guyushu Village established Muling Guyushu Culture Promotion Co., Ltd. and Guyushu Tourism Service Co., Ltd., vigorously promoted the "company + cooperative" development model, and included such resources as fish ponds, pavilions, and houses into the educational bases. At the same time, the two companies actively promote the connectivity between the base and surrounding scenic spots, such as Haiyue Bay, to expand the market for red tourism.

3. Introducing a new business model and diversifying the income source for villagers

Guyushu Village actively promotes the coordinated development model of "company + farmer". Firstly, it vigorously utilizes idle farmhouses and transforms old houses into homestays, with a vegetable garden for each homestay, to attract urban dwellers to come and appreciate local CPC heritage and natural landscape, and experience rural production and life. Secondly, villagers are encouraged to actively participate in tourist services, to open family restaurants, grocery stores, pancake shops, wine shops, and other businesses in their spare

time, and thus to broaden their source of income. Thirdly, it has planned and developed sightseeing tours, hiking and leisure tours, U-pick gardens, and farmhouses according to local conditions, increasing the income of villagers and the village collective.

4. Developing the winter economy and stimulating the vitality for rural revitalization

In 2022, Guyushu Village became a pilot village for the national action to build beautiful villages with CPC heritage and started to vigorously develop the winter economy. It founded Muling Polar Circle Winter Culture Promotion Co., Ltd. and opened a snow park, the first winter tourist attraction in the village. The snow park has attracted many catering enterprises and snow entertainment businesses to move in, further tapping into the village's natural resources and human resources and achieving a win-win situation for farmers, the village collective, and market entities.

Results

Seizing development opportunities that came along with the Northeast Anti-Japanese United Army Secret Campgrounds Educational Base and the snow park, Guyushu Village, once a remote, poor, backward, and inaccessible village with low, old houses, has become a well-known destination for red tourism and a beautiful, well-equipped village. Through the coordinated development model of "company + farmer" and "company + cooperative", the income of the village collective has increased by 500,000 yuan, and more than 40 jobs have been created for local villagers, increasing their per capita income by 12,000 yuan a year, allowing them to benefit from tourism development as the village collective has. In 2023, the tourism industry generated 3.56 million yuan in revenue, and the annual income of local villagers reached 27,800 yuan. Guyushu Village has won such honorary titles as the National 3A-level scenic spot, the Beautiful Leisure Village of China, and the National Key Village for the Development of Rural Tourism.

Experience and Inspirations

1. Develop red tourism

Red tourism offers an opportunity to protect cultural heritage and is a new way to carry forward the CPC revolutionary culture. The development of red tourism can not only alleviate the fund shortage and promote the development of remote areas, but also protect the CPC heritage, form a benign cycle, and effectively leverage tourism resources related to

the CPC heritage to attract tourists, impart the Party spirit, and improve the ecological environment.

2. Build brands of red tourism

Based on the protection and development of the CPC heritage, it is necessary to seek innovation based on the actual situation and develop unique red tourism brands that are close to reality, close to life, and close to the general public. It is also necessary to combine revolutionary tradition education and tourism development and make sure that the two are mutually reinforcing.

3. Introduce new forms of CPC heritage education

Red tourism has an incomparable advantage in education and publicity and plays an important role in the growth of youngsters. In the form of a tour, they combine learning and tourism and create a self-enlightening atmosphere so that students can learn while sightseeing and take in the CPC heritage before they know it.

Plans

Guyushu Village will continue to follow the instructions of President Xi Jinping to make good use of, carry forward, and inherit the CPC heritage. Firstly, it will connect the Northeast Anti-Japanese

United Army Secret Campgrounds Educational Base with Haiyue Bay and Bao'an U-Pick Garden in the town, market them as a package, and explore new paths of market-oriented development. Secondly, it will continue to improve the supporting service facilities at the base, build training centers and service centers, tap into the surrounding ruins and relics, develop more experiential, participatory, and interactive projects, and establish companies to run them. Thirdly, it will step up cooperation between the base and training institutions inside and outside Heilongjiang, to jointly launch various and colorful activities at the base, and expand their development space and platforms. For example, they can attract more Party members and college faculty and students to visit the Northeast Anti-Japanese United Army Secret Campgrounds Educational Base and appreciate their revolutionary spirit, history, and culture. By inspiring tourists to learn from the noble and charismatic older generation of proletarian revolutionaries, Guyushu Village will pass the CPC heritage from generation to generation.

河南省洛阳市栾川县陶湾镇：
伊源康养谷沟域旅游助力乡村振兴

摘　要

　　河南省洛阳市栾川县陶湾镇近年来凭借栾川县乡村旅游发展大势和自身得天独厚的自然资源，大力发展伊源康养谷沟域旅游，通过明确旅游发展方向和目标，构建科学合理的产业布局，在多层次组织带动下，形成政府、旅游企业和农户合作共赢的良好局面。陶湾镇多渠道积极争取发展资金，在全链条产业发展的推动下，乡村旅游逐渐形成了从农产品种植、加工到旅游接待、休闲娱乐的完整产业链。如今，伊源康养谷已成为远近闻名的乡村旅游目的地，实现了农业、文化、旅游等多个领域的融合发展，吸引大量游客前来观光、休闲和度假。陶湾镇的乡村旅游正以其独特的魅力和活力，为乡村振兴贡献着重要力量。

挑战与问题

陶湾镇距栾川县城19千米，辖19个行政村（社区）。伊源康养谷沟域内有4个行政村，原来均为贫困村，有1576户5627人。陶湾镇自然资源丰富，风景秀丽，但长期以来面临以下三个问题。一是产业单一，以传统的观光农业和农家乐为主，产品缺乏创新和特色，同质化严重，游客的参与度和满意度不高。二是基础设施不完善，乡村道路狭窄，影响出行便利性和可达性，住宿设施条件较差，旅游服务设施如停车场、洗手间等不足。三是缺乏人才，从事乡村旅游的从业人员普遍缺乏专业知识和技能，服务水平较低，难以满足游客的多样化需求。这些问题不仅制约了陶湾镇乡村旅游的进一步发展，也影响了乡村振兴的整体进程。

措施

1. 高规格规划引领

2016年，陶湾镇编制了《陶湾镇乡村旅游规划》和《栾川县陶湾镇协心村乡村旅游规划》，将乡村旅游确定为主导产业，提出"康养小镇"概念。2017年，陶湾镇提出沟域整体发展，打造以健康养生、运动休闲、田园观光为主题的深山区开放式"康养小镇"，并开设"栾川陶湾康养小镇"微信公众号。2022年，陶湾镇明确打造沟域核心IP"伊水之源，鲜养陶湾"，知名度和美誉度不断提高。

2. 各方面资金保障

陶湾镇近年来累计投入资金超25亿元，其中政策性资金4亿元，招商引资12亿元，本地乡贤投资9亿元。一是政策性资金夯实基础设施，建设高标准"四好农村路"示范路、停车场、公厕、自行车骑游步道、池水沟堰坝、景观墙、道路两侧绿化等，并实施房屋改造，建设民宿聚落四合院。二是招商引资做大优势产业，吸引洛阳未央园房地产开发有限公司投资3亿余元，建设雅谷鹿鸣旅游地产。吸引洛阳丽都酒店投资1000余万元，建成精品民宿栖鸾山居。以统筹整合资金500万元为杠杆，撬动吸引社会投资1200万元，共计1700余万元，建设集餐饮、住宿、娱乐于一体的云天荷居。三是积极动员在外乡贤党员常石宝等返乡，投资3000余万元建设占地30余亩的精品民宿静水山居，引导乡贤在自家新建或改建农家宾馆，发展布草清洗、土特产品加工等配套延伸产业。

3. 全链条产业发展

一是农业景观化。通过土地流转，将原来种植的传统农作物全部改为景观作物，建设鲜桃采摘园1000余亩，茯苓、百合等6个特色产业园200余亩，高山牡丹观赏基地50亩，形成了三季有花、两季有果、处处是景的景观产业带。二是工业绿色化。立足康养旅游定位，协心村土特产品加工厂实施绿色生产，春夏加工百合粉、土豆粉、橡子凉粉、鸡尾酒等，秋冬加工网红烧烤炉、采暖炉等。三是旅游业规模化。陶湾镇伊源康养谷现有民宿10余家，农家乐173家，涵盖高中低三种档次，可满足不同人群的需求，同时建设有集线上线下产品展览销售于一体的豫见村味馆和土特产展销长廊，提供餐饮、旅游商品展卖服务。

成效

陶湾镇乡村旅游的成功发展，不仅带动了当地经济的繁荣，也促进了农村环境的改善和农民收入的增加。随着基础设施的不断完善和公共服务设施的日益健全，村民们的居住环境和生产条件得到了极大的改善。道路硬化、水电设施升级、网络覆盖扩大等工程的实施，让村民们享受到了更加便捷、舒适的生活和生产环境。

乡村旅游的蓬勃发展，带动贫困群众增收致富。现陶湾镇伊源康养谷内发展有173家农家宾馆和10余家精品民宿，床位3600余张，其中由脱贫人口经营的农家宾馆就达70余家。现共有旅游从业人员1500余人，其中脱贫户、低保户、残疾户等困难群众从业人员480人。陶湾镇年游客量超60万人次，旅游综合收入达2.4亿元。沟域内村落实现全面脱贫，贫困发生率下降为0，人均收入大幅提高。依托政府到户增收、铁路扶贫、小额信贷等政策的扶持，村民胡留献实现了由脱贫户到农家宾馆老板身份的转变，从原来需要依靠政府救助生存到现在实现年收入约15万元，不仅提高了自家的收入水平，也给周边村民提供了工作岗位，实现了就地就业、就地致富。

经验与启示

1. "三变"改革与资源整合

陶湾伊源康养谷通过"三变"改革，即资源变资产、资金变股金、农民变股东，有效整合了农村资源，将闲置的土地、房屋等资源转化为旅游资产，提高了资源利用效率。农民成为乡村旅游的参与者和受益者，增强了农民的发展动力和获得感。

2. 集中连片与差异化发展

陶湾镇将沟域内四个村集中连片发展，抱团取暖，实现规模效益。为了避免同质化，每个村在坚持乡村旅游主导产业的基础上，差异化发展，如协心村突出龙头村的带动和整体服务功能，红庙村突出康养旅游，西沟村突出研学亲子，唐家庄村突出运动探险。

3. 产业融合与全链条发展

陶湾镇注重农业、文化等产业的融合发展，形成了集休闲旅游、生态农业、文化体验、森林康养等多种功能于一体的综合示范村。通过发展农家乐、生态酒店、沙地摩托、休闲垂钓等旅游项目，促进了乡村

基础设施的提升和乡村旅游产品的丰富化。

下一步计划

下一步，陶湾镇将立足"品质"，提升"魅力"，拓展伊源康养谷发展模式，塑造康养小镇旅游品牌。一是持续盘活闲置资源。陶湾镇目前还有待开发小沟域5条，建设用地1500余亩，闲置民居1800余座。要通过招商引资、乡贤创业等多种模式，尽快盘活闲置资源，实现变废为宝。二是拓展发展区域。将伊源康养谷发展模式向三合村、肖坊塔村、前锋村等陶湾镇西部各村拓展，开发红叶谷、樱花谷等旅游资源，实现更大范围的区域发展。三是丰富旅游产品。结合伊源康养谷的自然风光和人文特色，开发更多具有地方特色的旅游产品，如农耕体验、民俗文化表演等，满足游客多样化的需求。同时，加强从业人员培训，提高服务意识和专业素养，确保为游客提供优质的服务。四是加强品牌建设。通过加强品牌宣传和推广，提升陶湾镇乡村旅游的品牌知名度和美誉度，吸引更多游客前来参观旅游。积极与其他地区的乡村旅游项目开展交流合作，分享成功经验和做法，共同推动乡村旅游的发展。

Taowan Town, Luanchuan County, Luoyang City, Henan Province:
Promoting Rural Revitalization with All-Area-Advancing Tourism of Yiyuan Wellness Valley

Abstract

In recent years, Taowan Town of Luanchuan County, Luoyang City, Henan Province, has vigorously developed all-area-advancing tourism in the Yiyuan Wellness Valley by following the general trend of rural tourism development in the county and utilizing its unique natural resources. It has established clear development directions and goals, as well as a scientific, rational layout of the tourism industry. Driven by multi-level organizations, it has made a good head start with win-win cooperation between the government, tourism enterprises, and farmers. Taowan Town also actively seeks development funds through multiple channels. Driven by the whole-chain industrial development, rural tourism has gradually formed a complete industrial chain covering the planting and processing of agricultural products, tourist reception, leisure, and entertainment. Today, Yiyuan Wellness Valley has become a well-known destination, realized the integrated development of agriculture, culture, and tourism, and attracted a large number of tourists for sightseeing, leisure, and holidaymaking. The rural tourism industry of Taowan Town is contributing to the rural revitalization with its unique charm and vitality.

Challenges and Problems

Taowan Town is 19 kilometers away from the seat of Luanchuan County, with jurisdiction over 19 administrative villages and communities. There are 4 administrative villages in Iyuan Kangyanggu Valley, all of which used to be poor villages, with a population of 5,627 in 1,576 households. Taowan Town is richly endowed with natural resources and boasts beautiful scenery, but it has long faced the following three problems. Firstly, it relied excessively on traditional sightseeing agriculture and farm stays and lacked original and characteristic tourism products, which were too homogenous. The participation and satisfaction degree of tourists was low. Secondly, the infrastructure was poor. The rural roads were so narrow that it was difficult to travel to and access the villages, the accommodation conditions were bad, and there was a shortage of service facilities, such as parking lots and toilets. Thirdly, there was a lack of workforce. Those engaged in rural tourism generally lacked professional knowledge and skills, resulting in poor services that could not meet the diverse needs of tourists. These problems not only restrict the further development of rural tourism but also affect the whole rural revitalization process.

Measures

1. High-standard and top-level design

In 2016, the *Rural Tourism Development Plan of Taowan Town* and the *Rural Tourism Development Plan of Xiexin Village* were compiled, establishing rural tourism as the dominant industry and putting forward the concept of "wellness town". In 2017, Taowan Town called for the coordinated development of the valley area and proposed to build an open "wellness town" in the deep mountain featuring health preservation, sports and leisure facilities and services, and pastoral landscape. A corresponding public account was opened on WeChat. In 2022, it proposed to build the core IP of the valley as "A wellness resort at the source of the Yihe River". Since then, its popularity and reputation have continued to rise.

2. Diverse financing channels

In recent years, Taowan Town has invested more than 2.5 billion yuan, including 400 million yuan in policy funds, 1.2 billion yuan from external investors, and 900 million yuan from local investors. Firstly, it spent the policy funds improving the infrastructure, including building high-standard demonstration rural roads that meet four criteria, parking lots, public toilets, biking trails, pond weirs, landscape walls, and roadside greening. Rural houses were also renovated, and homestay courtyards were built. Secondly, it attracted investment to expand advantageous industries. For example, Luoyang Weiyangyuan Real Estate Development Co., Ltd. has invested more than 300 million yuan to develop the tourism real estate project Yagu Luming; Luoyang Lidu International Hotel has invested more than 10 million yuan to build a boutique homestay. Taowan Town consolidated 5 million yuan and used it as a lever to attract 12 million yuan of social investment, totaling more than 17 million yuan, which is used to develop a complex for catering, accommodation, and entertainment businesses. Thirdly, it actively mobilizes capable migrant workers to return and start their businesses. One of them is Chang Shibao, a Party member, who has invested more than 30 million yuan to build a boutique homestay covering an area of more than 30 *mu*. It also guides the villagers to build or reconstruct farm stays and extend the tourism industry to linen cleaning and local product processing.

3. Whole-chain development

Firstly, building agricultural landscapes. Through the transfer of land use rights, all the traditional crops originally planted have been replaced by landscape crops, and more than 1,000 *mu* of U-pick peach gardens have been built, in addition to more than 200 *mu* of six characteristic industrial parks for poria and lily planting, and 50 *mu* of alpine peony plantations. A landscape industrial belt is hence formed, with flowers blooming in three seasons, fruits harvesting in two seasons, and scenery everywhere. Secondly, developing green industries. Positioned for wellness tourism, Xiexin Village promotes green processing of local products, including lily powder, potato powder, acorn jelly, and cocktails in spring and summer, and barbecue grills and heating stoves in fall and winter. Thirdly, expanding the scale of the tourism industry. There are more than 10 homestays and 173 farm stays in Yiyuan Wellness Valley, which can meet the

diverse needs of different groups of people. There is also a product exhibition and sales hall and corridor to provide catering services and exhibit and sell tourist commodities online and offline.

Results

The rural tourism boom in Taowan Town has not only stimulated local economic development but also improved the rural environment and increased villagers' income. With the continuous improvement in infrastructure and public service facilities, the living environment and production conditions of the villagers have also been greatly improved. The hardened roads, upgraded hydropower facilities and expanded network coverage have made it easier and more comfortable for the villagers to live and work.

The rural tourism boom has increased the income of the people. At present, there are 173 farm stays and more than 10 boutique homestays with more than 3,600 beds in Yiyuan Wellness Valley, of which more than 70 are operated by people who have recently been lifted out of poverty. The tourism industry hires a workforce of more than 1,500, including 480 from households that have recently emerged from poverty, live on subsistence allowance, and have at least a person with a disability. Taowan Town receives more than 600,000 tourists and generates a comprehensive tourism income of 240 million yuan a year. The villages in the area have all been lifted out of poverty, with the incidence of poverty dropping to zero, and the per capita income rising significantly. Thanks to the government's policy support, the opening of a new railway, and microcredit, the villager Hu Liuxian has not only lifted himself out of poverty but become the owner of a rural hotel and earns about 150,000 yuan a year, no longer in need of government assistance. He has not only improved his own life but also created jobs for other villagers and increased their income too.

Experience and Inspirations

1. Reform and resource consolidation

By turning resources into assets, capital into shares, and farmers into shareholders, Yiyuan Wellness Valley has effectively consolidated rural resources, transformed idle land, houses, and other resources into tourism assets, and improved the efficiency of resource utilization. Farmers have contributed to and benefited from tourism development, which has enhanced their motivation and sense of gain.

2. Centralized and differentiated development

Taowan Town plans and promotes the development of the four villages in the valley area as a whole to achieve economies of scale. Meanwhile, to avoid homogenization, each village has differentiated itself while adhering to the dominant status of rural tourism: Xiexin Village highlights its driving role as the lead village and its overall services, Hongmiao Village highlights wellness tourism, Xigou Village highlights study tours and parent-child tours, and Tangjiazhuang Village highlights sports and adventure activities.

3. Industrial integration and whole-chain development

Taowan Town values the integrated development of agriculture, culture, and other industries, and has developed comprehensive demonstration villages that offer leisure tours, eco-agriculture, cultural experiences, and wellness tours in the forest. It has also developed such tourism projects as farm stays, eco-hotels, sandmobiles, and leisure angling to improve rural infrastructure and diversify rural tourism products.

Plans

In the next step, Taowan Town will maintain its quality and enhance its charm. It will expand the development model of Yiyuan Wellness Valley, and build a strong tourism brand of wellness towns. Firstly, it will continue to utilize idle resources. At present, Taowan Town still has five small valleys to develop, with more than 1,500 *mu* of construction land and more than 1,800 idle houses. It is necessary to turn the idle resources into assets as soon as possible by attracting external investors and locals to start a business. Secondly, it will expand the development area. It will promote the development model of Yiyuan Wellness Valley to Sanhe Village, Xiaoqita Village, and Qianfeng Village in the western part of the town, and develop the Red Leaf Valley and the Cherry Blossom Valley to promote regional development on a larger scale. Thirdly, it will diversify the portfolio of tourism products. Based on the natural scenery and cultural characteristics of Yiyuan Wellness Valley, it will develop more tourism products with local characteristics, such as farming experience and folk cultural performances, to meet the diverse needs of tourists. At the same time, it will strengthen the training of practitioners, and raise their service awareness and job competency to deliver high-quality services to tourists. Fourthly, it will strengthen brand building. Taowan Town will increase efforts to promote brands of rural tourism, enhance their visibility and reputation, and attract more tourists. It will actively carry out exchanges and cooperation with rural tourism projects in other areas, share best practices, and jointly promote the development of rural tourism.

山东省烟台市蓬莱区东方海岸果谷：
海岸苹果品牌化助力乡村振兴

摘　要

　　山东省烟台市蓬莱区东方海岸果谷，依托其独特的海洋气候与资源优势，致力于打造未来农业与海岸苹果品牌化的中国模式。东方海岸果谷以"蓬莱仙海"为背景，通过实施"果业产业化、产业园区化、园区景区化、农旅一体化"战略，不仅推动了1.9万亩果树的产业化种植，更将苹果文化与乡村旅游深度融合，形成了五大功能区。此举不仅强化了烟台苹果作为国家地理标志的品牌效应，还有效拉动了区域海洋经济和乡村旅游的发展，为村民增收开辟新途径，也为全国提供了现代特色农业与乡村振兴的示范样板。

挑战与问题

蓬莱东方海岸果谷地理位置优越，交通便捷，被纳入黄渤海新区规划建设范围，但在推进乡村振兴示范区的建设中，仍面临诸多挑战。一是如何打破传统的单一产业模式，寻找多元化的经济发展路径，拓宽村民的收入来源并增加村集体经济的创收。二是刘家沟镇拥有丰富的海洋文化资源和"世界七大葡萄酒海岸之一"的地域优势，如何充分利用这些资源，深化品牌营销，使"海岸苹果"地域品牌更加响亮。三是如何在保护区域生态环境和人文景观的前提下，完善果谷环线的基础配套设施，确保可持续发展，实现农文旅高质量融合。

措施

1. 推进全域环境升级，展现乡村振兴新风貌

一是开展东方海岸果谷环线环境整治。以美丽乡村分类推进、农村基础设施网建设、乡村建设行动、村庄清洁行动为抓手，先后投入资金6800万元，建设项目31个，完成15.87千米道路整修，持续改善农村基础设施条件。二是全面提升沿乌沟河环境。开展乌沟河绿化美化、拦河坝整修、水生植物栽种等项目工程，完善河侧漫步道防护栏杆、过水管等附属设施，完成沿线1.44万平方米的养殖场拆迁回收工作。三是提升沿线村庄环境和打造示范村。对乌沟河示范带沿线安香寺、李茂庄等8个村庄开展农村环境综合整治，弥补公共设施短板。

2. 深化产业融合战略，拓展全方位增收体系

一是借助蓬莱环渤海湾苹果产业发展核心区优势与乡村特色文化基底，串联旅游要素，推出系列精品旅游线路和系列纪念品伴手礼。二是全力开展项目招引，中粮白兰地超级工厂、奥蓝之海文旅综合体等投资近8亿元的项目先后落户，为地区经济注入新活力。三是建设苹果科技示范基地、苹果商品化处理中心、果蔬采后智能装备制造等项目，实现一二三产业高度融合发展。

3. 打造精准品牌战略，深挖与弘扬苹果文化

以国家4A级旅游景区的标准，积极推进苹果与生态旅游、民俗节庆、文化创意相结合，放大苹果文化、旅游价值和品牌效益。一是进一步挖掘园艺学校历史，提升百年果园的展示功能；二是策划举办百年果树开花节、采摘节等一系列活动，在国际、国家级媒体层面广泛宣传推广，提高知名度和影响力。三是积极打造电商平台，通过线上线下的营销方式助推"蓬

莱苹果"品牌价值的提升，将"蓬莱苹果"推向更广阔的市场。

成效

东方海岸果谷已稳固确立"蓬莱海岸苹果"的地域品牌特色，推动了第一二三产业的深度融合。果谷围绕全区涉农产业，开展项目招引，现已拥有苹果深加工企业 5 家、葡萄酒生产企业和特色酒庄 3 家，以及昊林果蔬、沃森农业、中粮龙脊园等在内的海岸优质示范园。此外，还建有嘉桐苹果酒技术研发中心和奥蓝之海文旅综合体，形成多元化产业生态。目前，果谷内有新型农业经营主体 166 个，其中包括省级以上龙头企业 1 个、农民合作社 117 个和家庭农场 48 个。通过引进和培育苹果深加工、葡萄酒生产及多个特色项目，果谷已形成了一个多元化、高效益的产业布局。这不仅为当地创造了大量的就业机会，还有效地拓宽了村庄和村民的收入来源，使村集体收入得到了显著提升。2023 年，乌沟张家村、吕家沟村获评省级美丽乡村示范村，刘家沟镇获评省级乡村振兴示范镇。

经验和启示

1. 文化赋能，打造地域品牌

东方海岸果谷规划建设不仅是空间业态的更新，也承续了蓬莱古海上丝绸之路的基因密码，把文化基因植入产业发展全过程，依托乌沟河沿岸特色农业、海洋文化资源高度集中的区域，全力打造"东方海岸果谷"农业和植业和苹果产业高质量发展示范区域，树立地域品牌。

2. 三产融合，推动产业升级

东方海岸果谷通过优化资源配置，突出区域特色，以苹果苗木种植、有机苹果生产等一产为基础，以仓储保鲜、果蔬加工等二产为支撑，以苹果文化鉴赏及生态旅游、信息物流和科技创新服务等三产为补充，

实现三产高度融合。

3. 创新驱动，实现多元化发展

东方海岸果谷依托烟台国家农业科技园区高水平打造苹果科研区，应用信息技术、生物技术、新材料技术、新能源技术等，通过"农业科研 + 农业数字化研究 + 教育培训 + 技术孵化"的模式，区别于传统的种植和销售模式，积极探索乡村体验、田园采摘、运动休闲、葡萄酒风情观光、伴手礼展销等全新市场策略。

下一步计划

一是提升产业链条发展能级。加快建设东方海岸果谷文化服务中心，打造承载苹果文化传播、旅游接待服务、党群服务、田园休闲等职能于一体的产业发展空间，形成与沃族酒庄、嘉桐酒庄，以及毗邻村庄联动发展的良好局面。二是加快完善旅游功能要素。设计乡村体验漫步、苹果文化展示及栽培技术培训、休闲采摘、葡萄酒风情观光等四条主题旅游路线；持续擦亮"东方海岸果谷"品牌，丰富伴手礼系列产品。三是激活闲置低效资源动能。加快推动园艺场破产拍卖程序，摸清家底，理顺产权关系，对果汁厂、冷库、鑫园工贸等闲置资产和 1522 余亩国有农业用地进行整体开发打造。四是加快推进苹果交易平台招商引资。搭建立足蓬莱，辐射山东乃至全国的苹果销售平台，推行订单农业，促进苹果销售和品牌打造，带动群众增收。

Oriental Coast Fruit Valley in Penglai District, Yantai City, Shandong Province:

Coastal Apple Branding Helps Rural Revitalization

Abstract

Oriental Coast Fruit Valley in Penglai District, Yantai City, Shandong Province, leverages its unique maritime climate and resource advantages to create a Chinese model for future agriculture and coastal apple branding. With the backdrop of "Penglai Fairy Sea", the Fruit Valley implements strategies for industrializing fruit production, creating industrial parks, transforming parks into scenic areas, and integrating agriculture with tourism. This has not only industrialized the cultivation of 19,000 *mu* of apple orchards but also deeply integrated apple culture with rural tourism, forming five functional zones. This initiative strengthens the brand effect of Yantai apples as a national geographic indicator, effectively drives the development of the regional marine economy and rural tourism, opens new paths for villagers to increase their income, and provides a model of modern specialized agriculture and rural revitalization for the entire country.

Challenges and Problems

Despite its advantageous location and convenient transportation, being included in the planning and construction scope of the Yellow Sea and Bohai Sea New Area, Oriental Coast Fruit Valley faces several challenges in promoting the construction of a rural revitalization demonstration area. Firstly, it concerns breaking the traditional single-industry model, finding diversified economic development paths to broaden villagers' income sources, and increasing the income of the village collective. Secondly, it is about fully utilizing Liujiagou Town's rich marine cultural resources and its status as one of the "World's Seven Major Wine Coasts" to deepen brand marketing and make the "Coastal Apple" regional brand more prominent. Thirdly, it is about improving the basic supporting facilities of the Fruit Valley loop to ensure sustainable development and achieve high-quality integration of agriculture, culture, and tourism under the premise of protecting the regional ecological environment and cultural landscape.

Measures

1. Promoting comprehensive environmental upgrading to demonstrate the new look of rural revitalization

Firstly, it is to conduct environmental improvement along the Oriental Coast Fruit Valley loop. Focusing on beautiful countryside construction by classification, rural infrastructure network construction, rural environment improvement, and village cleaning action, Oriental Coast Fruit Valley has successively invested 68 million yuan in 31 projects, completing the renovation of 15.87 kilometers of roads and continuously improving rural infrastructure. Secondly, it is to comprehensively improve the environment along the Wugou River by undertaking greening and beautification projects, dam repairs, aquatic plant planting; improving auxiliary facilities such as river-side walkways, protective railings, and water pipes; and demolishing and reclaiming 14,400 square meters of breeding farms along the route. Thirdly, it is to improve the environment of villages and build demonstration villages. Oriental Coast Fruit Valley has conducted environment comprehensive rectification of eight villages including the Anxiang Temple and Li Maozhuang in the Wugou River demonstration belt, addressing public facility defects.

2. Deepening the industrial integration strategy to expand the system for increasing income in an all-round way

Firstly, it is to utilize the Penglai Bohai Bay Rim apple industry core area advantages and the rural characteristic cultural basis to link up tourism elements and launch a series of boutique tourism routes and commemorative gifts. Secondly, it is to go all out to bring in projects. The Brandy Super Factory of China Oil and Foodstuffs Corporation and the Aolan Ocean Cultural Tourism Complex involving an investment of nearly 800 million yuan have settled down, injecting new vitality into the regional economy. Thirdly, it is to establish an apple technology demonstration base, an apple commercialization processing center, and a post-picking fruit and vegetable intelligent equipment manufacturing project, to achieve high integration of primary, secondary, and tertiary industries.

3. Developing the targeted branding strategy, and deeply exploring and promoting the Apple culture

Following the standards of a national 4A-level scenic spot, we promote the integration of apples with ecological tourism, folk festivals, and cultural creativity to amplify the cultural, tourism, and brand value of apples. Firstly, it is to further explore the history of the horticultural school, and enhance the century-old orchard display function. Secondly, it is to plan and organize a series of activities such as the Century-old Apple Tree Blooming Festival and the Apple Picking Festival, and conduct extensive publicity through international and national media to increase the fame and influence. Thirdly, it is to develop an e-commerce platform to boost the "Penglai Apple" brand value through online and offline marketing, expand the market reach and enhance the brand value.

Results

The Oriental Coast Fruit Valley has successfully established the regional characteristics of "Penglai Coastal Apples", promoting deep integration of the primary, secondary, and tertiary industries. The Fruit Valley focuses on agricultural-related industries to bring in projects. It has five apple deep-processing enterprises, three wine production companies, and specialty wineries, such as Haolin Fruits and Vegetables, Watson Agriculture, and COFCO Longji Garden among other demonstration parks. Additionally, the Jia Tong Apple Wine Technology Research and Development Center and

the Aulan Ocean Cultural Tourism Complex have been established, contributing to the formation of a diversified industrial ecosystem. Now, the Valley has 166 new agricultural business entities, including one provincial-level leading enterprise, 117 farmer cooperatives, and 48 family farms. Through the introduction and cultivation of apple deep-processing, wine production, and multiple characteristic projects, the Fruit Valley embraces a layout of diversified and high-efficiency industries. This has created numerous jobs, significantly broadened the income sources for villages and villagers, and notably increased the village collective's income. In 2023, Wugou Zhangjia Village and Lujia Gou Village were newly recognized as provincial-level demonstration villages, and Liujiagou Town was rated as a provincial-level rural revitalization demonstration town.

Experiences and Inspirations

1. Cultural empowerment to create regional brands

The planning and construction of Oriental Coast Fruit Valley is not only about updating spatial formats but also inheriting the genetic code of Penglai's ancient maritime Silk Road. By embedding cultural genes into the entire process of industrial development, relying on the highly concentrated characteristic agriculture and marine cultural resources along the Wugou River, the area goes all out to build a high-quality development demonstration area for agricultural planting and the apple industry, establishing a regional brand.

2. Three-Industry integration to promote industrial upgrading

By optimizing resource allocation and highlighting regional characteristics, Oriental Coast Fruit Valley promotes high integration of primary industries (apple seedling planting, organic apple production), secondary industries (storage and preservation, fruit and vegetable processing), and tertiary industries (apple culture appreciation, ecological tourism, information logistics, and technological innovation services).

3. Innovation-driven diversified development

Leveraging the high-level construction of Yantai National Agricultural Science and Technology Park's apple research area, the Fruit Valley applies information technology, biotechnology, new material technology, and new energy technology. By combining "agricultural research + agricultural digitalization research + education and training + technology incubation", the Fruit Valley explores new market strategies such as offering rural experiences,

picking at the orchard, recreational sports, wine-themed sightseeing, and souvenir exhibitions, moving beyond traditional planting and sales models.

Plans

Firstly, it is to enhance the industrial chain development capacity. Oriental Coast Fruit Valley will speed up efforts in the construction of the Oriental Coast Fruit Valley Cultural Service Center to create a space that integrates apple culture dissemination, tourism reception services, party and masses services, and rural leisure functions, forming a good situation of common development among the adjacent villages and wineries including Wozu Winery and Jiatong Winery. Secondly, it is to accelerate efforts for improving tourism functional elements. Oriental Coast Fruit Valley will design four themed tourism routes, including the rural experience walk, apple culture display, apple cultivation technology training, leisure picking, and wine-themed sightseeing. Oriental Coast Fruit Valley will continue to enhance the "Oriental Coast Fruit Valley" brand and enrich the series of souvenir products. Thirdly, it is to bring into use the otherwise idle and inefficient resources. Oriental Coast Fruit Valley will speed up the bankruptcy auction process of the horticultural farm, make clear the ownership of the assets, and straighten out property relations. Oriental Coast Fruit Valley will comprehensively develop such assets as the juice factory, cold storage, and Xinyuan Industry and Trade which once stayed idled in addition to the 1,522 *mu* of state-owned agricultural land. Fourthly, it is to speed up efforts to attract businesses to the Apple trading platform. Oriental Coast Fruit Valley will establish an apple sales platform based in Penglai, radiating to Shandong and nationwide, to promote order-based agriculture, boost apple sales and brand building, and increase villagers' income.

陕西省榆林市佳县赤牛坬村：
农文旅融合助力乡村振兴

摘　要

陕西省榆林市佳县赤牛坬村充分挖掘黄河流域优秀农耕文化底蕴，融合"农文旅"，贯通"产加销"，让"老物件"讲述文化，让"老窑洞"留住乡愁，让"老农民"走上舞台。全村老百姓捧起了"文化碗"，吃上了"旅游饭"，走上了"致富路"。

挑战与问题

赤牛坬村位于佳县县城南30千米的黄河西岸，全村共352户1008人，总面积6平方千米。这里是一个偏僻落后、鲜为人知的小村庄，村民主要以种地、种枣、打工为生，每年人均纯收入仅有三五千元。赤牛坬景区在基础设施、公共服务、产业发展、生态保护和管理运营等方面面临着一些挑战和问题。在产业发展方面，核心景区空间有限，景点之间串联不足，配套娱乐休闲和服务设施落后，缺乏当地特色的农旅结合，导致游客滞留时间短，经济带动效应不足。在基础设施和公共服务方面，污水处理、环境卫生、景区供电线路和夜间灯光设施等有待提升，景区整体绿化覆盖率低，标志标牌缺乏规范化和明确性导向，住宿和餐饮设施不达标。这些问题都制约了赤牛坬景区的长期可持续发展。

措施

1. 提升旅游设施

赤牛坬民俗文化村景区一是对原有餐厅进行了全方位的提升改建；二是对特色化民宿窑洞和院落进行提升改造；三是对酒瓶博物馆进行重新设计和选址建设，运用现代设计手法和声光电技术，增设了文创、多媒体等多种互动形式，增强博物馆的吸引力；四是进一步完善牛岭山寨窑洞群落、十二生肖馆、姻缘桥等旅游吸引项目，全面提升了旅游观赏价值。

2. 优化民宿庭院

赤牛坬村满足不同游客需求体验，打造25间民宿庭院。民宿根据陕北各县区不同文化特色进行修建，游客在赤牛坬村能感受到陕北各县区文化魅力，真正实现"一步一景观、一院一特色"。民宿运营过程中开展庭院的评星定级工作，建立奖补机制，形成"比学赶超"的良好氛围。

3. 实现文旅融合

一是让"老物件"讲述文化，景区搜集整理了传统生产生活用品，修复保护后建成民俗博物馆，展示陕北的黄土文化和农民原生态的生活方式；二是让"老窑洞"留住乡愁，依托原有山形地貌，对核心区域的上千孔老窑洞建筑群进行翻修改造，建成具有陕北特色的"窑洞群落"；三是让"老农民"走上舞台，打造国内首部农民自编自导自演的大型原生态实景演

出"高高山上一头牛"。这些举措不仅丰富了景区的文化内涵，也为游客提供了更具有吸引力的旅游体验。

成效

赤牛坬景区累计接待游客上百万人次，其中境外游客近1.2万人次，实现年均旅游综合收入近千万元，带动200余名群众就业。2022年，赤牛坬景区游客达28万人次，旅游综合收入5200万元，村民人均增收15000元左右；2023年，赤牛坬游客达35万人次，旅游综合收入6720万元，同比增加33.5%。赤牛坬村先后获得中国乡村旅游模范村、中国美丽休闲乡村、全国文明村镇、全国乡村旅游重点村、中国美丽宜居村、中国美丽乡村创建示范村、国家3A级旅游景区、中国传统村落等国家级荣誉称号。

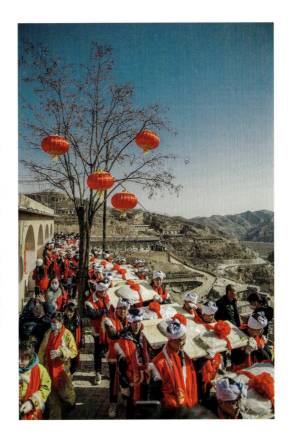

经验与启示

1. 注重人才培养

赤牛坬村通过听课积分、积分分红等激励机制，鼓励村民积极参与景区建设和管理，提高自身素质和技能水平。这种做法不仅有利于村民个人发展，也为村庄的长远发展奠定了坚实基础。

2. 注重综合利用

赤牛坬村将农民、农具、窑洞等元素融入景区规划中，打造出独具特色的乡村文化景观，不仅提升了村庄的知名度和美誉度，也为村民带来了实实在在的收益。同时，景区注重三产联动发展，将旅游、销售、农耕产业有机结合，形成完整的产业链，为村庄经济发展注入了新的活力。

3. 注重协同发展

赤牛坬村通过吸引周边村庄的劳动力参与景区建设和管理，实现劳动力资源的优化配置，同时也促进了周边村庄的经济发展。这种模式有利于打破地域限制，实现区域间的协同发展。

下一步计划

一是着力打造亮点工程。全面推进景区高岇庄园建设项目，积极争取陕北民俗博物洞立项建设，加快景区道路完善，串联景点，进一步扩展景区空间。二是全面提升服务水平。开展服务人员日常培训，全面提升服务水平，通过以奖代补的形式激发群众创办民宿的热情，让游客能够吃得放心、住得安心、玩得开心。三是着力打造沉浸式体验。借助"高高山上一头牛"实景舞台剧，进一步开发和探索各类小型的互动型舞台剧，增加游客的参与度，让他们深度体验和感受陕北民俗文化。四是探索产业融合发展。不断衍生和延伸产业链条，通过旅游产业带动红枣、小杂粮产业以及养殖业的发展，探索黄米馍馍、枣糕以及手工挂面等特色产业，全面实现村内无闲人、人人有事做，达到一人一技、一家一业的良好效果。

2024 世界旅游联盟：旅游助力乡村振兴案例（中英文双语版）
WTA Best Practices of Rural Revitalization through Tourism 2024 (Chinese–English Bilingual Edition)

Chiniuwa Village, Jia County, Yulin City, Shaanxi Province:

Integration of Agriculture, Culture and Tourism Promotes Rural Revitalization

Abstract

Chiniuwa Village in Jia County, Yulin City, Sichuan Province, fully tapped into the excellent farming culture of the Yellow River Basin, integrated "agriculture, culture and tourism", and linked up "production, processing and sales", to make old objects tell about culture, old caves stimulate people's nostalgia, and old farmers take the stage. The villagers make a living by engaging in culture-related business, benefit from tourism, and become increasingly rich.

Challenges and Problems

Chiniuwa Village is located on the west bank of the Yellow River, 30 kilometers south of the Jia County seat. The village has 352 households and 1,008 people, covering a total area of 6 square kilometers. This is a remote, backward, and little-known small village. Villagers mainly make a living by tilling, jujube farming, and doing odd jobs, with a per capita net income of only three to five thousand yuan per year. The Chiniuwa Scenic Area faces challenges and problems related to infrastructure, public services, industrial development, ecological protection, and management and operation. Concerning industrial development, there are such problems as the limited space of core scenic areas, inadequate connection between scenic spots, and backward supporting entertainment and leisure service facilities. Moreover, there is a lack of agricultural tourism of local characteristics, which leads to the phenomenon that the tourists tend to have a short stay here and therefore tourism has a poor effect in driving economic development. In terms of infrastructure and public services, sewage treatment, environmental sanitation, scenic area power supply lines, and night lighting facilities need to be improved, the overall green coverage rate of the scenic area is low, a clear guide is yet to be put in place to make the signage standard and clear-cut, and accommodation and catering facilities fail to meet standards. These problems have restricted the long-term sustainable development of the Chiniuwa Scenic Area.

Measures

1. Improve tourism facilities

Firstly, the Chiniuwa Folk Culture Village Scenic Area carried out an all-round upgrading and reconstruction of the original restaurant. Secondly, it upgraded and reconstructed the characteristic cave-style homestays and courtyards. Thirdly, it redesigned and built the wine bottle museum at the chosen spot, and enhanced the attraction of the museum by using modern design techniques and sound and light technology and adopting various interactive forms based on cultural creativity and multimedia. Fourthly, the Niuling Cave Dwelling Community, the Zodiac Museum, the Marriage Bridge and other tourist attraction projects have been further improved to comprehensively enhance the sightseeing experience for tourists.

2. Optimize the homestay courtyards

Chiniuwa Village, to meet the needs for

diversifying experiences of tourists, has built 25 homestay courtyards. The homestays are built according to the different cultural characteristics of the counties and districts in northern Shaanxi Province. Tourists can feel the cultural charm of the counties and districts in northern Shaanxi Province at Chiniuwa Village since the "one step, one landscape, one courtyard, one feature" effect is truly realized. During the operation of homestays, the star rating and grading of courtyards is carried out, and a reward and subsidy mechanism is established to form a good atmosphere of learning from each other and catching up.

3. Integrate culture and tourism

Firstly, Chiniuwa Village lets the "old objects" talk about the culture. The scenic spot has collected and sorted out traditional production and living supplies and built a folk museum based on the restored and preserved supplies to showcase the loess culture of northern Shaanxi and the authentic lifestyle of farmers. Secondly, the scenic spot makes the old caves stimulate people's nostalgia. Relying on the original mountainous landform, the thousands of old cave buildings in the core area were renovated and rebuilt to put in place a cave community with the characteristics of northern Shaanxi. Thirdly, Chiniuwa Village made old farmers take the stage to create the first ever large-scale real-life performance in China written, directed and performed by farmers, "A Cow on the High Mountain". These measures not only enrich the cultural connotations of the scenic spot but also provide tourists with a more interesting experience.

Results

The Chiniuwa Scenic Area has received more than one million tourists, including nearly 12,000 foreign tourists, and has earned an average annual tourism comprehensive income of nearly 10 million yuan, creating more than 200 jobs. In 2022, the tourists to the Chiniuwa Scenic Area numbered 280,000, bringing in a comprehensive tourism income of 52 million yuan, and enabling the per capita income of villagers to increase by about 15,000 yuan. In 2023, the tourists to Chiniuwa numbered 350,000, bringing in a comprehensive tourism income of 67.2 million yuan, an increase of 33.5% year-on-year. Chiniuwa Village has successively won national honorary titles such as China Model Village for Rural Tourism, the Beautiful Leisure Village of China, the National Exemplary Village, the National Key Village for Rural Tourism, China Beautiful and Livable Village, China Demonstration Beautiful Village, the national 3A-level scenic spot, and China Traditional Village .

Experiences and Inspirations

1. Attach importance to talent cultivation

Through incentive mechanisms such as lecture points and bonus points, Chiniuwa Village encourages villagers to actively participate in the construction and management of the scenic area and improve their competence and skills. This approach is not only conducive to the personal development of villagers but also lays a solid foundation for the long-term development of the village.

2. Put a premium on comprehensive utilization

Chiniuwa Village incorporates elements such as farmers, farming tools, and cave dwellings into the planning of the scenic area, creating a unique rural cultural landscape, which not only enhances the popularity and reputation of the village but also brings substantial benefits to the villagers. At the same time, the scenic area focuses on the coordinated development of the three industries, organically combining tourism, sales, and farming industries to form a complete industrial chain, injecting new vitality into the economic development of the village.

3. Focus on coordinated development

By attracting labor from surrounding villages to participate in the construction and management of the scenic area, Chiniuwa Village has achieved the optimal allocation of labor resources, while promoting the economic development of surrounding villages. This model is conducive to breaking regional restrictions and achieving coordinated development among regions.

Plans

Firstly, we will focus on creating highlight projects. We will comprehensively promote the construction project of Gaohu Manor in the scenic area, actively strive for the construction approval of the Shaanxi Folk Museum Cave, speed up the

improvement of the roads in the scenic area, and link up scenic spots, to further expand the scenic zone. Secondly, we will comprehensively improve the service level. We will carry out regular training among service personnel, comprehensively improve the service level, and stimulate the enthusiasm of the masses to establish homestays by granting them awards instead of subsidies, so that tourists can enjoy satisfactory accommodations and have fun. Thirdly, we will focus on delivering an immersive experience. With the help of the "A Cow on a High Mountain" real-life stage play, we will further develop and explore various small interactive stage plays to increase the participation of tourists and enable them to have an in-depth experience and feel of the folk culture of Northern Shaanxi. Fourthly, we will explore the integrated development of industries. We will continue to extend the industrial chain; drive the development of red dates, small grains, and aquaculture through the tourism industry; explore ways to develop special industries of yellow rice steamed buns, date cakes, and handmade noodles; fully realize that there are no idle people in the village or everyone has something to do; and achieve the result that everyone has certain skills and every household runs some business.

2024世界旅游联盟：旅游助力乡村振兴案例（中英文双语版）
WTA Best Practices of Rural Revitalization through Tourism 2024（Chinese-English Bilingual Edition）

云南省楚雄彝族自治州楚雄市紫溪彝村：
农文康旅融合助力乡村振兴

摘　要

云南省楚雄彝族自治州楚雄市紫溪彝村拓展乡村旅游发展思路，坚持以农业为根、文化为魂、生态为基、旅游为路，大力实施"农文康旅融合"发展战略，持续丰富乡村旅游业态产品，打造了观光采摘、农家体验、民族风情、民族节庆、特色餐饮、休闲度假、康体养生等系列旅游产品，极大地促进了紫溪彝村一二三产业融合发展，推动紫溪彝村走上乡村振兴之路。

挑战与问题

紫溪彝村隶属云南省楚雄彝族自治州楚雄市紫溪镇紫溪社区，距楚雄市区13千米，位于国家级森林公园、国家4A级旅游景区紫溪山的北侧，是进入紫溪山景区的必经之地。全村现有89户396人，包括汉、彝、苗、白4个民族，少数民族比例达93%。作为彝族移民聚居村，紫溪彝村展现了浓厚的彝族民族风情，包括彝族美食、服饰、歌舞、节庆等，同时也是彝族传统文化保存较为完整的彝族村寨。紫溪彝村最高海拔1870米，森林覆盖率达83%，野生菌类品种繁多，冬无严寒、夏无酷暑、阳光充足。优越的区位条件、绚烂的少数民族文化和丰富的生态资源，为紫溪彝村开展农业休闲、文化体验、康体养生等旅游活动提供了良好条件。紫溪彝村历经两次整体搬迁，虽然整体村落基础设施得到提升，但产业基础依旧薄弱，乡村旅游业态产品较为单一，以农家乐为主要形式，缺乏多元化的旅游体验。这种状况导致旅游核心吸引力不强，带动群众增收效果不显著。实施哪种乡村旅游发展模式，带动更多群众就近就地增收致富，成为紫溪彝村可持续发展面临的首要问题。

措施

1. 统筹规划，形成发展合力

紫溪彝村依托区位优势，充分考虑以城带乡，城乡互动共赢，突出现代民居、彝族特色、文化旅游三个重点，编制了"科学规划布局美、生态宜居村庄美、产业富民生活美、文明和谐乡风美"的村庄发展总体规划，合理布局建设村庄居住区、休闲旅游区、旅游商业服务区、特色种植区、特色养殖区和山林生态观光区等功能区域，并按旅游区标准配套公共服务等基础设施。

2. 整合资源，推动融合发展

紫溪彝村于2013年3月全面启动"美丽乡村"项目建设，该项目结合易地搬迁新建和原址提升改造措施，通过整合各方面资金，建成了自然环境优美的紫溪彝村。遵循"统一规划、集中投入、形成合力、渠道不乱、性质不变、各司其职、各记其功"的原则，整合美丽乡村、民族特色旅游村寨、农村环境综合整治、水利建设、生态园林绿化、特色产业培育、特色村庄发展等25个项目，共计筹集资金1.15亿元。紫溪彝村在完善配套基础设施的同时，还建成了游客接待中心、彝族特色商业风情街、彝族趣味运动场、自驾游营地、乡村旅游乐园、农家乐等旅游服务项目，实现乡村旅游与美丽乡村建设的融合发展。

3. 培植产业，夯实发展基础

一是以农家乐为切入点，积极发展乡村旅游。依托优美的环境和彝族文化资源，大力发展以"吃农家饭、住农家院、享农家乐"为主题的乡村旅游品牌，制定了《紫溪彝村特色农家乐评定标准》，通过以奖代补的方式，积极扶持农家乐的发展。二是积极推进"合作社+农户+基地"的综合开发模式，与旅行社合作成立乡村旅游专业合作社，全力打造楚雄州现代乡村生态旅游基地，定期在紫溪彝村举办传统民俗活动，如元旦、春节、周年庆、火把节、中秋节等节庆活动，并推出"过彝族年、吃彝家年饭"等长期性品牌经营促销活动，带动彝村片区乡村旅游发展。三是强化招商引资，确定5家投资企业，推动片区产业发展。

4. 创新机制，构建工作格局

一是政府主导，政府负责项目建设的规划设计、质量监理、安全监管、资金监管、统筹协调、组织动员和保障工作。二是以农民为主体，与施工相关的各项重要决策都由村民小组干部组织村民讨论商议，力求议深议透，以统一思想认识，建设质量好不好、满意不满意，由村民代表和户主说了算，真正把知情权、决策权、管理权交给农民群众。三是干部帮扶，省、州、市、镇、村共派出38名党员干部，成立项目管理、资金监管、民主督导、绩效考核4个工作小组，指导和组织村、农户参与工程建设。

成效

通过统一规划和资源整合，紫溪彝村生产生活设施条件极大改善，整村风貌既保留了彝族建筑特色、民居特点及彝族文化元素，又融入了现代规划理念，将传统与现代完美结合，展现了城乡和谐、人与自然

思路，深入挖掘紫溪风光、农家田园等资源，依托"紫溪冬桃、紫溪樱桃、紫溪红梨"，扶持扶贫群众大力发展采摘农业、观光农业，积极培育田园风光、民俗度假等乡村旅游产品，带动乡村旅游热度持续攀升。

2. 突出民族特色，注重"乡村旅游+文化"

坚持"民族文化搭台、旅游经济唱戏"的原则，以民族歌舞、民族餐饮、民族节庆为核心业务形式，打造"彝族松毛长街宴""火把节农货市场"和"彝族演艺表演"等乡村旅游民族文化项目，成功通过民族文化的挖掘利用，有效提升旅游知名度、吸引力。

3. 突出生态宜居，实施"乡村旅游+康养"

聚焦"特色、产业、生态、易达、宜居、智慧、成网"要素，依托紫溪山森林公园丰富的森林生态资源，建设森林健康步道、森林半山酒店和康复疗养中心，精心打造森林疗愈、健康运动、养生养老等高端康养产品。

和谐之美，凸显了创新的艺术魅力和深厚的人文底蕴，营造出一种"人在村中行，如在画中游"的优美环境氛围。通过发展乡村旅游促进乡村特色产业发展，村集体经济收入实现了从零到目前的700余万元的显著增长，村民人均纯收入也大幅提升至1.87万元，这一数字相比1994年的近500元，增长了近30倍。广大村民通过乡村旅游发展实现了增收致富，发展观念得到极大提升，爱护环境、保护环境、提升环境质量的理念深入人心，全村绿化美化亮化和自然环境保护持续推进，生态质量持续提高，获评国家3A级旅游景区、中国美丽休闲乡村、中国少数民族特色村寨、全国生态文明村、全国文明村等。

下一步计划

一是突出彝族特色风情。具体措施包括设计具有彝族特色的招牌，采用彝汉双语店名，以及配置彝家传统的大火塘、火盆，彝族特色餐桌、餐椅、餐具等，切实让农家乐凸显彝族文化特色元素。二是突出彝族特色风味。通过深入挖掘本地彝族菜系，组织厨艺培训，创新研发出具有彝村特色的菜品。做足"羊"文化，推出羊八碗、全羊宴、烤全羊等"羊"系列特色菜肴；打造"彝王鸡宴"；挖掘推广彝家罐罐茶；做优彝家传统坨坨肉、盖碗肉、血肠旺等，打造彝家饮食亮点。三是突出彝族特色歌舞。组建文艺队创作彝族特色歌舞，把社会主义核心价值观、民族团结等融入舞蹈、彝剧、酒歌中，充分展示彝族文化、彝族歌舞和彝家儿女精神风貌，传承和弘扬彝族大三弦舞、葫芦笙舞、羊皮鼓舞和左脚舞等民族歌舞。四是办好彝族特色节日。创新举办紫溪彝村火把节、彝村羊汤锅美食节、"畅享圆月·醉爱紫溪"中秋节、"发现最美彝村"国庆节、吉祥彝族年等系列节庆活动。

经验与启示

1. 突出绿色发展，坚持"乡村旅游+农业"

按照"农旅融合、以农促旅、以旅强农"的发展

Zixi Yi Village, Chuxiong City, Chuxiong Yi Autonomous Prefecture, Yunnan Province:

Integration of Agriculture, Culture, Health and Tourism Promotes Rural Revitalization

Abstract

Zixi Yi Village in Chuxiong City, Chuxiong Yi Autonomous Prefecture, Yunnan Province has expanded its rural tourism development ideas; insisted on taking agriculture as its root, culture as its soul, ecology as its basis, and tourism development as its path; vigorously implemented the integrated development of agriculture, culture, healthcare and tourism; and continuously enriched rural tourism products, developing a series of tourism products related to sightseeing and picking, farming experience, ethnic customs, ethnic festivals, special catering, leisure and vacation, and healthcare. These efforts have greatly promoted the integrated development of the primary, secondary, and tertiary industries in Zixi Yi Village, and pushed Zixi Yi Village onto the road of rural revitalization.

Challenges and Problems

Zixi Yi Village belongs to Zixi Community, Zixi Town, Chuxiong City, Chuxiong Yi Autonomous Prefecture, Yunnan Province. About 13 kilometers away from downtown Chuxiong, it is located on the north side of Zixi Mountain, a national forest park and a national 4A-level scenic spot. It is a must-go place to enter the Zixi Mountain Scenic Area. The village currently has 89 households of 396 people, including four ethnic groups: Han, Yi, Miao, and Bai. Here the people of ethnic minorities account for 93% of all the residents. The strong Yi ethnic customs and features are seen in the food, clothing, singing and dancing, and festivals. It is a typical Yi immigrant village and a Yi village with a well-kept Yi traditional culture. At the highest point, Zixi Yi Village is 1,870 meters above sea level, with a forest coverage rate of 83%. There are many varieties of wild mushrooms; it has neither severe cold in winter nor scorching heat in summer, but plenty of sunshine. The superior location, splendid ethnic culture, and rich ecological resources provide favorable conditions for Zixi Yi Village to build the bases for agricultural leisure, cultural experience, healthcare, and other tourism activities. Zixi Yi Village has undergone two overall relocations. Although the overall village infrastructure has been improved, the industrial foundation is still weak. The village has less than rich rural tourism products which are mainly farm stays. The core attraction of tourism is less than strong, and the effect of increasing the income of the masses is not obvious. Which rural tourism development model to adopt to enable more people to increase their income and get rich nearby has become the primary issue facing the sustainable development of Zixi Yi Village.

Measures

1. Conduct overall planning to form a synergy for development

Relying on its advantageous location, Zixi Yi Village fully considers the city leading the countryside and the win-win interaction between urban and rural areas. Based on the three key points of highlighting modern residential buildings, Yi characteristics, and cultural tourism, it has compiled a village development master plan for "a beautiful layout, eco-friendly development, affluent living of villagers and nice ethos". It rationally arranges the residential areas, leisure and tourism areas, tourism and commercial service areas, characteristic planting areas, characteristic breeding areas, mountain forest sightseeing areas, and other functional areas, and provides supporting public services and other infrastructure according to the standards of tourist areas.

2. Integrate resources to promote coordinated development

In March 2013, Zixi Yi Village fully launched the "Beautiful Village" project construction. Combining relocation and new construction with the upgrading and renovation at the original site,

it integrated various funds and built the beautiful Zixi Yi Village. Following the principle of "unified planning, centralized investment, building a synergy, no confusion in channels, unchanged nature, each doing its job, and each crediting its own merits", it integrated 25 projects related to beautiful villages, ethnic tourism villages, rural environmental comprehensive improvement, water conservancy, ecological gardening, characteristic industries, and characteristic villages; and collected funding of 115 million yuan. Along with the improvement of the supporting infrastructure, the tourist reception centers, Yi-style commercial streets, Yi-style fun sports fields, self-driving camps, rural tourism parks, farm stays, and other tourism service projects have been built to achieve coordinated development of rural tourism and beautiful village construction.

3. Cultivate industries and consolidate the foundation for industrial development

Firstly, Zixi Yi Village takes farm stays as the starting point and actively develops rural tourism. Relying on the beautiful environment and Yi cultural resources, Zixi Yi Village vigorously develops rural tourism brands with the theme of "eating farmhouse meals, living in farm stays, and having fun at farm stays", formulates the *Zixi Yi Village Characteristic Farmhouse Assessment Standards*, and supports the development of farm stays with awards instead of subsidies. Secondly, Zixi Yi Village actively promotes the comprehensive development model of "cooperatives + farmers + bases", cooperates with travel agencies to establish rural tourism professional cooperatives, and strives to build a modern rural ecological tourism base in Chuxiong Prefecture. Zixi Yi Village regularly holds traditional folk activities, like the festive activities on New Year's Day, Spring Festival, anniversaries, Torch Festival, Mid-Autumn Festival, and other festivals and launch "Yi People's Year, Yi New Year dinner" and other long-term brand management and promotion activities to drive the development of rural tourism in the village as well as the surrounding area. Thirdly, Zixi Yi Village strengthens investment promotion and identifies five investment companies to promote industrial development in the area.

4. Innovate mechanisms and build an appropriate work pattern

Firstly, the government plays the leading role. The government is responsible for the planning and design, quality supervision, safety supervision, financial supervision, overall coordination, organization and mobilization, and support work for project construction. Secondly, farmers are

the mainstay. All important decisions related to construction are discussed at meetings organized by villagers' group officials; they endeavor to discuss things thoroughly to unify their thinking. Whether the construction is satisfactory or not is decided by village representatives and household heads, thus the rights to understanding, decision-making, and management are truly in the control of farmers. Thirdly, officials help. A total of 38 Party members and officials from the province, prefecture, city, town, and village have been sent to set up four working groups for project management, financial supervision, democratic supervision, and performance appraisal to guide and organize villages and farmers to participate in project construction.

Results

Through unified planning and resource integration, the production and living facilities of Zixi Yi Village have been greatly improved. The whole village has retained the architectural features, residential characteristics, and cultural elements of the Yi people, and incorporated modern planning concepts, combining tradition with modernity, showcasing harmony between urban and rural areas, harmony between man and nature, and the beauty of innovation and humanity, creating an atmosphere of "walking in the village is like traveling in a painting". By developing rural tourism to promote rural characteristic industries, the village collective economic income has grown from nothing to more than 7 million yuan now, and the per capita net income has reached 18,700 yuan, nearly 30 times the level of nearly 500 yuan in 1994. The majority of villagers have increased income and wealth

through the development of rural tourism, and their development concepts have been greatly improved. The concept of caring for, protecting, and improving the environment has been deeply rooted in the hearts of the people. The greening, beautification, and lighting of the village and the protection of the natural environment have been continuously promoted, and the ecological quality has been continuously improved. It has been recognized as the national 3A scenic spot, the Beautiful Leisure Village of China, China's Ethnic Minority Characteristic Village, the National Village with Advanced Ecological Civilization, and the National Exemplary Village.

Experiences and Inspirations

1. Highlight green development and adhere to "rural tourism + agriculture"

Under the development idea of "integration of agriculture and tourism, promoting tourism with agriculture, and strengthening agriculture with tourism", we will deeply explore the resources of Zixi scenery and farmland, rely on "the winter peach, cherry, and red pear of Zixi", support the poor people to vigorously develop picking agriculture and sightseeing agriculture, actively cultivate

rural tourism products such as rural scenery and folk vacation, and drive the continued rise in the popularity of rural tourism.

2. Highlight ethnic characteristics and focus on "rural tourism + culture"

Adhere to the principle of "ethnic culture as the stage and tourism economy as the show", take ethnic songs and dances, ethnic catering, and ethnic festivals as the core business forms, create rural tourism ethnic cultural projects such as "Yi Songmao Long Street Banquet", "Torch Festival Agricultural Products Market", and "Yi Performing Arts Performance", and successfully explore and utilize ethnic culture to effectively enhance tourism popularity and attractiveness.

3. Highlight ecological and livable features and implement "rural tourism + health care"

Focusing on the elements of "characteristics, industry, ecology, accessibility, livability, intelligence, and networking", we rely on the rich forest ecological resources of Zixi Mountain Forest Park to build forest health trails, forest mid-mountain hotels, and rehabilitation centers, and to deliver high-end health care products such as forest therapy, healthy sports, and health care for the elderly.

Plans

Firstly, it is to highlight the characteristics of the Yi ethnic group. Specific measures include designing Yi-style signs, adopting shop names in both Yi and Chinese languages, and setting Yi-style large fire pits and fire basins, Yi-style dining tables, chairs, and tableware, the farm stays can truly highlight the cultural characteristics of the Yi ethnic group. Secondly, it is to highlight the flavors of the Yi ethnic group. We deeply explore the local Yi cuisine, carry out cooking training, create Yi village-style cuisine, and make full use of the "sheep" culture to create a "mutton" series of dishes like the eight bowls of mutton dishes, the all-mutton banquet, and the whole roasted sheep. We will create the "Yi King Chicken Banquet"; seek to expand the Yi family pot tea business; make the traditional Yi family Tuotuo meat, covered bowl meat, and blood sausage, etc., to create highlights of Yi family food. Thirdly, it is to highlight the Yi ethnic group's singing and dancing. We organize an art team to create Yi ethnic songs and dances; integrate the core socialist values and national unity into dances, Yi operas, and drinking songs; fully display the Yi culture, Yi ethnic songs and dances, and the outlook of Yi people; and carry forward the Yi ethnic group's dance to the big erhu plectrum, gourd pipe dance, sheepskin drum dance, and left-foot dance. Fourthly, it is to do a good job in holding festive activities of the Yi ethnic group. We will hold innovative festive activities on the Zixi Yi Village Torch Festival, the Yi Village Lamb Soup Pot Food Festival, the "Enjoy the Full Moon and Love Intoxicating Zixi" Mid-Autumn Festival, the "Discover the Most Beautiful Yi Village" National Day, and the auspicious Yi New Year.

内蒙古自治区锡林郭勒盟多伦县温塘河村：

挖掘滦河文化 谱写振兴篇章

摘 要

温塘河村锁定"滦河文化"，通过"旅游+"，整合区域资源，开展"农文旅"产业联动，形成融合发展结构，促进乡村振兴综合产业优化升级。温塘河村的"蝶变"是我国北方乡村，尤其是内蒙古自治区东部农村发展变化的一个缩影。温塘河村依托区域内"山水林田湖草沙"等资源，克服重重困难实现蜕变的发展模式，为众多资源类型相近的村庄助力居民群众增收、实现乡村振兴提供了可借鉴可复制的经验。

挑战与问题

内蒙古自治区锡林郭勒盟多伦县滦源镇温塘河村地处浑善达克沙地南端，村内远古火山运动遗迹众多，被誉为"火山博物馆村"。全村地貌属于典型的低山丘陵地区，因当地无霜期只有94天，土地产值极低，各类基础设施落后，村民经济收入来源主要靠饲养牛羊家畜维持。温塘河村发展面临诸多问题：一是大量养殖废弃物让整个村庄环境卫生堪忧，到处是粪便污泥，蚊蝇成群、臭味扑鼻，过度放牧等问题导致村庄周边生态系统脆弱。二是部分村民虽然开始探索发展文旅产业，但目前处于零散、非组织化的"散兵游勇"发展模式，管理无序，出现了恶性竞争。三是村庄的农业土地分布零散且收成不佳，难以留住年轻人，他们大多选择外出务工，导致村庄变得荒凉。

措施

1. 挖掘梳理村内资源

温塘河村邀请国内知名地质学家、中国工程院院士等专业人士进村考察，发掘村庄丰富的自然、人文和生物资源。一是国内最年轻火山碎屑流地质奇观；二是挖掘普查出村内8平方千米的新旧石器时代古人生产生活遗迹区；三是温塘古泉水被确定为世界范围内罕见的高偏硅酸、弱碱性火山矿泉水；四是统计出村内矿产资源主要有玛瑙石、萤石、水晶石、红绿鸡肝石、模树石等；五是发现温水泉眼18处、野生动物30多种、野生鱼类13种和药用植物36种。

2. 盘活村庄土地和房产

一是村党支部带头，号召种植大户将村民分散耕地通过自愿有偿的方式进行集中流转，同时对集中连片的耕地进行标准化农田改造。二是率先启动了全村范围的"人畜分离＋舍饲圈养"的人畜分离工程，解决村庄庭院养殖品质不高和破坏生态的困境，同时村庄大部分庭院闲置下来了，发展文化旅游产业有了空间。

3. 创新设置文旅项目

温塘河村"吃非遗、住非遗、乘非遗、游非遗、购非遗、玩非遗"，48项非物质文化遗产已经融入旅游六要素的方方面面，非遗作坊、非遗工厂、非遗餐厅、非遗体验等项目让流传了千百年的非遗文化融入现代文旅生活。同时设置地质文化研学游、远古"滦河文化"探秘游、温塘古泉康养游、农耕文化体验游、农家生活体味游、乡村古道穿越游等主题旅游项目。

4. 创新发展模式

一是2023年温塘河村与第三方合作，通过村企合作的模式建设了锡林郭勒盟南五旗县规模最大的助农土特产中转仓项目，集中研发、销售当地各类农副产品，增加村集体收入的同时，解决就业90多人，带动周边配套服务就业50多人。二是温塘河村配套建设69户集中连片的草原火山·长寿民宿小镇，开发环村150千米乡村深度穿越游线路和乡村大集等"接地气"项目。

成效

温塘河村的"农文旅"改革经过几年努力,已经让昔日脏乱差的小山村发生了较大变化,社会、经济、环境等各个方面都取得了良好效益。温塘河村与国内300多家旅行社合作,每天进村游客高峰时达到4000多人,全年可实现旅游销售额3800多万元。截至2023年底,滦源镇温塘河村村民人均纯收入从过去的几千元增长到19200元;2024年村集体收入预计突破100万元;村内各类文旅项目落地资金突破7000万元。温塘河村先后获得中国美丽休闲乡村、内蒙古自治区乡村旅游重点村、内蒙古自治区乡村振兴试点村等多项荣誉称号。

经验与启示

1. 摸清家底

温塘河村党支部带头,摸清自身自然、人文、生物资源家底,理清发展"农文旅"产业思路,帮助村民解放劳动力,安顿好农牧业发展空间,轻松投入到文化旅游产业中。

2. 规范管理

温塘河村打破村民"单打独斗"发展"农文旅"产业的模式,由"散兵游勇"到"统一管理",通过"党支部+企业+农户"的发展模式,实现乡村产业的产业化、规模化和标准化。

3. 丰富业态

深挖当地"农文旅"资源,打造独有的旅游业态产品。目前,温塘河村的"农文旅"产业涵盖休闲观光、地质科普研学、乡村非遗美食体验、夜间民俗非遗项目观光、家庭亲子采摘、农事操作体验、传统民宿体验、儿童乡村娱乐、星空露营、团建接待、中老年康养体验等,旅游业态渗透到社会的方方面面。

4. 文化塑魂

温塘河村依托距今1万多年的远古"滦河文化",深挖当地丰富的地质、非遗、生物、文化资源,植入到"农文旅"产业的各项业态中,为其注入文化灵魂。

下一步计划

一是凸显乡土特征。温塘河村将紧紧围绕"滦河文化"的宏观定位,突出"温塘古泉康养村庄"的核心竞争力,打造我国北方高原休闲康养村庄。二是创新研发高质量农副产品。充分挖掘村内牛羊、野生蘑菇、系列野菜、野果、道地药材等丰富资源,并通过线上、线下多渠道加大营销推广力度。三是进一步完善配套服务规模和质量。提高各领域接待能力,对投入到"农文旅"产业当中的村民进行常态化规范培训,提升其服务意识和能力。四是"走出去"推广温塘河村"农文旅"业态,多形式展示温塘河村远古遗存、非遗项目及衍生产品,扩大温塘河村的综合影响力。

Wentanghe Village, Duolun County, Xilin Gol League, Inner Mongolia Autonomous Region:

Uncovering Luan River Culture and Writing a Chapter of Revitalization

Abstract

Wentanghe Village has focused on "Luan River Culture" and adopted a "tourism+" approach to integrate regional resources, promoting the "agriculture, culture, and tourism" linkage. This has resulted in a structure of integrated development that optimizes and upgrades the village's industries, driving rural revitalization. The transformation of Wentanghe Village is a microcosm of the changes taking place in rural areas of north China, particularly in the eastern part of the Inner Mongolia Autonomous Region. By leveraging its resources, such as mountains, rivers, forests, fields, lakes, grasslands, and sands, the village has overcome numerous challenges to embrace a development model that provides valuable, replicable experience for similar villages in the region, helping residents increase their income and achieve rural revitalization.

Challenges and Problems

Wentanghe Village is located at the southern end of the Hunshandake Sandland in Luanyuan Town, Duolun County, Xilin Gol League, Inner Mongolia Autonomous Region. Known as the "Volcano Museum Village", it has numerous ancient volcanic remnants. The village's terrain is characterized by typical low mountains and hills. However, the frost-free period lasts only 94 days, which leads to very low agricultural productivity. The infrastructure is underdeveloped, and the villagers' main source of income is livestock farming. The village faces several challenges. Firstly, the large amount of waste from livestock farming has led to severe environmental problems, with manure and sludge contaminating the village, attracting swarms of flies, and giving off a foul odor. Overgrazing has further weakened the surrounding ecosystem. Secondly, some villagers have started exploring ways to engage in the cultural tourism industry, but their efforts are fragmented, leading to unhealthy competition and disorganized management. Thirdly, the village's scattered agricultural land, with low yields, struggles to retain young people, who go for work elsewhere, leaving the village desolate.

Measures

1. Sorting through the resources of the village

Wentanghe Village invited renowned geologists and academicians from the Chinese Academy of Engineering to conduct a field investigation which led to the finding of the village's rich natural, cultural, and biological resources, including the youngest volcanic pyroclastic flow geological wonder in China; an 8-square-kilometer area with Neolithic and Paleolithic relics; Wentang's ancient spring, one of the rare volcanic mineral springs with a high concentration of metasilicic acid and mild alkalinity in the world; various mineral resources such as agate, fluorite, crystal, jasper, and dendrite; 18 hot spring eyes, over 30 species of wild animals, 13 species of wild fish, and 36 herbal plants.

2. Utilizing the land and property

The Village Party Branch led the efforts to encourage large-scale farming households to voluntarily and compensatorily gather the villagers' scattered agricultural land, which was then standardized for farming. They also initiated a "human-animal separation" project to solve the problems of poor-quality livestock farming and ecological degradation, freeing up space for cultural tourism development.

3. Setting innovative cultural tourism projects

The village integrated 48 items of intangible cultural heritage with a history of thousands of years into all aspects of tourism, offering experiences with intangible cultural heritage workshops, factories, restaurants, and activities. Additionally, the village developed thematic tourism projects such as geological study tours, ancient "Luan River Culture" exploration tours, Wentang's ancient spring

health tours, farming culture experiences, farm life experience tours, and rural old ways through tours.

4. Adopting innovative development models

In 2023, Wentanghe Village collaborated with a third party to build the largest agricultural specialty transit warehouse in Five banners in South Xilin Gol League. This project centralizes the development and sale of local agricultural and sideline products, increasing the village collective income, creating over 90 jobs, and enabling over 50 people to work for supporting services. The village also developed a cluster of 69 prairie-volcano-themed longevity homestays and established a 150-kilometer deep cross-country village tour route and a village market, adding local charm.

Results

After several years of reform in agriculture, culture, and tourism, Wentanghe Village has undergone a significant transformation. The village's once dirty and disorderly environment has improved, yielding positive social, economic, and environmental benefits. The village now collaborates with over 300 domestic travel agencies, attracting more than 4,000 tourists a day during peak days and generating an annual tourism revenue of over 38 million yuan. By the end of 2023, the per capita income of the villagers increased from a few thousand yuan to 19,200 yuan; in 2024, the village collective income is expected to exceed 1 million yuan; the village has attracted over 70 million yuan in investment for various cultural tourism projects. Wentanghe Village has been recognized as the Beautiful Leisure Village of China, the Key Rural Tourism Village in Inner Mongolia Autonomous Region, and the Pilot Village for Rural Revitalization in Inner Mongolia Autonomous Region etc.

Experiences and Inspirations

1. A clear idea about the resources

The Village Party Branch led the efforts to gain a clear idea about the village's natural, cultural, and biological resources, which helped to clarify the development strategy for the agriculture, culture, and tourism industries. This enabled villagers to free up labor and space for cultural tourism while maintaining agricultural husbandry development.

2. Standardize management

The village shifted from fragmented individual efforts to unified management of agriculture, culture, and tourism, transitioning from "scattered development" to a "party branch + enterprise + farmer" development model, and achieving industrialization, and standardization of rural industries developing on a scale.

3. Diversified industries

By deeply exploring local agriculture, culture, and tourism resources, the village has developed unique tourism products that now encompass leisure

sightseeing, geological research tours, rural intangible cultural heritage (cuisine) experiences, night-time folk heritage (sightseeing) projects, family-friendly (picking) activities, farming experiences, traditional homestays, rural amusement parks for children, stargazing, team-building exercises, and health programs for the middle-aged and elderly, developing tourism across various aspects of society.

4. Cultural enrichment

Wentanghe Village leveraged its 10,000-year-old ancient "Luan River Culture", integrating its rich geological, intangible cultural heritage, and biological resources into the agriculture, culture, and tourism industries, thereby infusing them with cultural significance.

Plans

Firstly, it is to highlight local features. The village plans to focus on its "Luan River Culture" and emphasize the core competitiveness of "Wentang's Ancient Spring Health Village", aiming to become a premier highland leisure and health village in northern China. Secondly, it is to innovatively develop high-quality agricultural and sideline products. The village will tap into its abundant resources, including cattle, sheep, wild mushrooms, various wild vegetables, wild fruits, and medicinal herbs, and expand online and offline marketing efforts. Thirdly, it is to enhance service quality and scale. The village will improve its service capacity in all areas, providing regular training for villagers involved in agriculture, culture, and tourism industries to enhance their service awareness and capabilities. Fourthly, it is to promote the Wentanghe Village's agricultural, cultural, and tourism model. The village plans to showcase its ancient relics, intangible cultural heritage projects, and derived products in diverse forms, expanding its overall influence.